ハヤテのごとく! 19
Hayate the combat butler

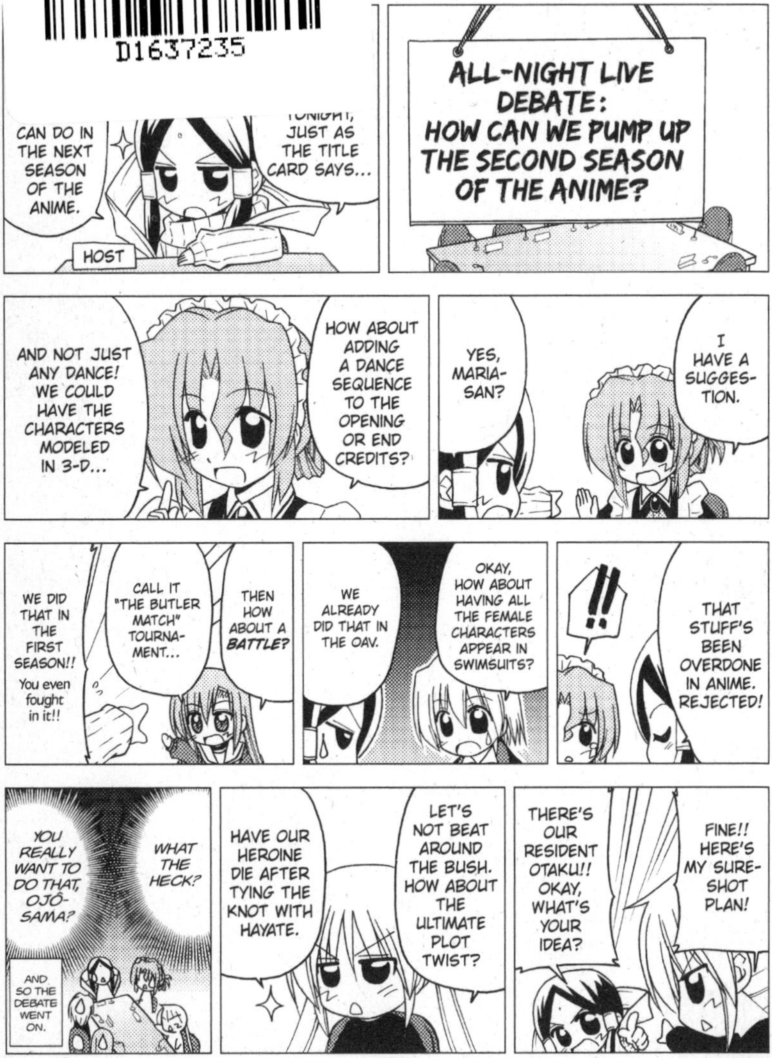
ALL-NIGHT LIVE DEBATE: HOW CAN WE PUMP UP THE SECOND SEASON OF THE ANIME?
TONIGHT, JUST AS THE TITLE CARD SAYS…
CAN DO IN THE NEXT SEASON OF THE ANIME.
HOST
I HAVE A SUGGES-TION.
YES, MARIA-SAN?
HOW ABOUT ADDING A DANCE SEQUENCE TO THE OPENING OR END CREDITS?
AND NOT JUST ANY DANCE! WE COULD HAVE THE CHARACTERS MODELED IN 3-D…
!!
THAT STUFF'S BEEN OVERDONE IN ANIME. REJECTED!
OKAY, HOW ABOUT HAVING ALL THE FEMALE CHARACTERS APPEAR IN SWIMSUITS?
WE ALREADY DID THAT IN THE OAV.
THEN HOW ABOUT A *BATTLE?*
CALL IT "THE BUTLER MATCH" TOURNA-MENT…
WE DID THAT IN THE FIRST SEASON!! You even fought in it!!
FINE!! HERE'S MY SURE-SHOT PLAN!
THERE'S OUR RESIDENT OTAKU!! OKAY, WHAT'S YOUR IDEA?
LET'S NOT BEAT AROUND THE BUSH. HOW ABOUT THE ULTIMATE PLOT TWIST?
HAVE OUR HEROINE DIE AFTER TYING THE KNOT WITH HAYATE.
WHAT THE HECK?
YOU REALLY WANT TO DO THAT, OJÔ-SAMA?
AND SO THE DEBATE WENT ON.

No matter what, please watch the anime! ☆

HAYATE THE COMBAT BUTLER
VOL. 19
Shonen Sunday Edition

STORY AND ART BY
KENJIRO HATA

© 2005 Kenjiro HATA/Shogakukan
All rights reserved.
Original Japanese edition "HAYATE NO GOTOKU!" published by SHOGAKUKAN Inc.

English Adaptation/Mark Giambruno
Translation/Yuki Yoshioka and Cindy H. Yamauchi
Touch-up Art & Lettering/Hudson Yards
Design/Yukiko Whitley
Editor/Shaenon K. Garrity

Printed in Canada

Published by VIZ Media, LLC
P.O. Box 77010
San Francisco, CA 94107

10 9 8 7 6 5 4 3 2 1
First printing, February 2012

viz media
www.viz.com

SHONEN SUNDAY
WWW.SHONENSUNDAY.COM

Hayate the Combat Butler

19

KENJIRO HATA

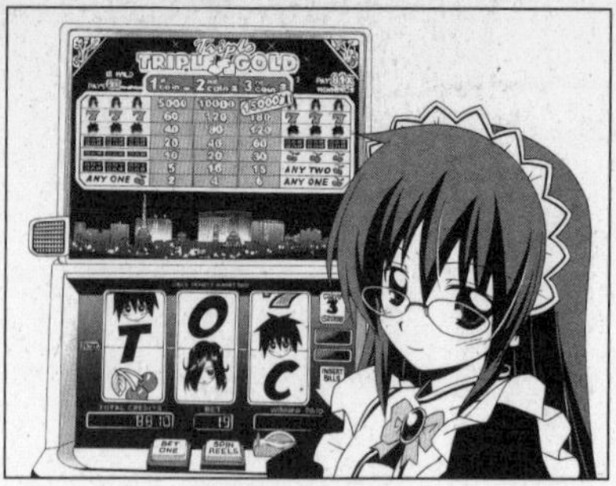
TRIPLE GOLD
ANY ONE
ANY TWO
ANY ONE
T
O
C

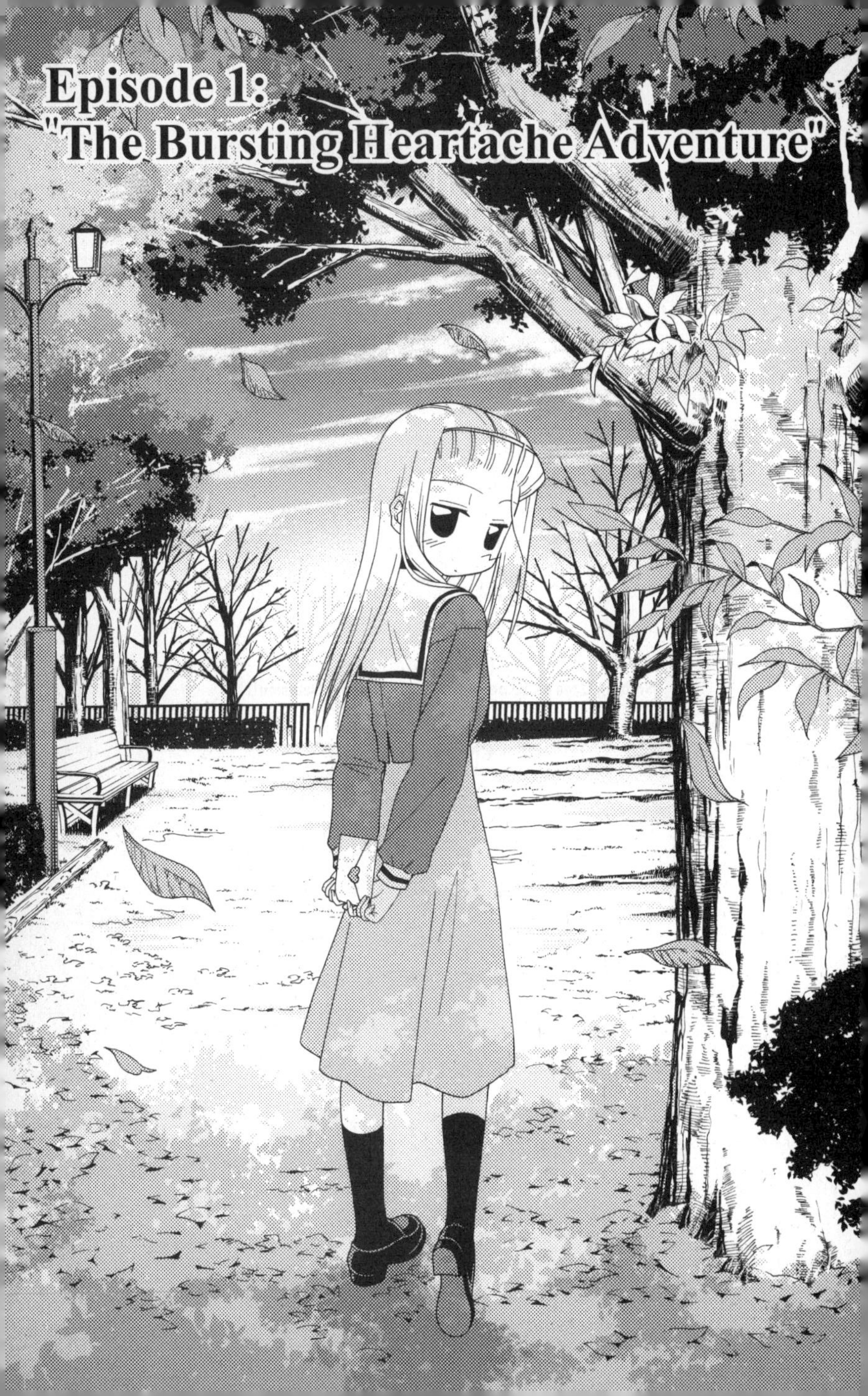
Episode 1:
"The Bursting Heartache Adventure"

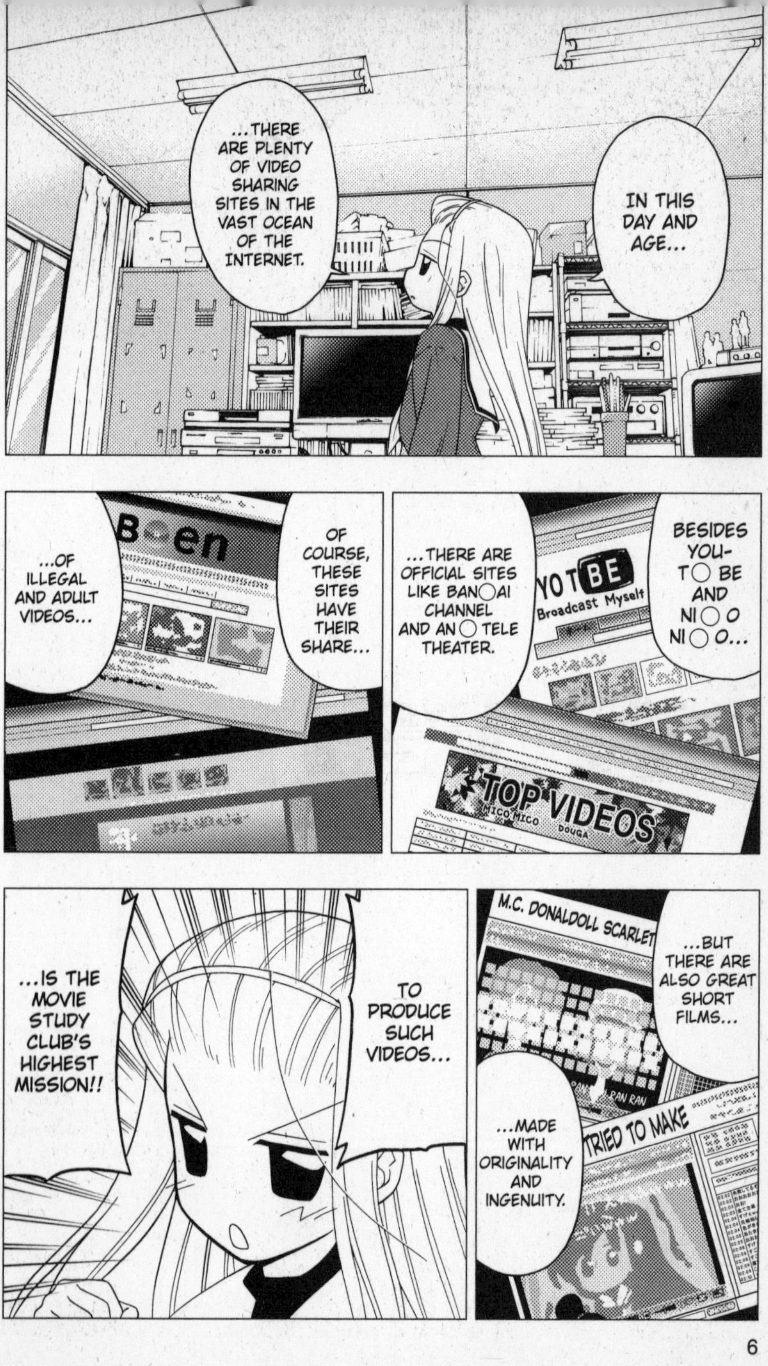
IN THIS DAY AND AGE...
...THERE ARE PLENTY OF VIDEO SHARING SITES IN THE VAST OCEAN OF THE INTERNET.
BESIDES YOU-T◯BE AND NI◯◯O NI◯◯O...
...THERE ARE OFFICIAL SITES LIKE BAN◯AI CHANNEL AND AN◯TELE THEATER.
YO T BE
Broadcast Myself
TOP VIDEOS
MICO MICO DOUGA
OF COURSE, THESE SITES HAVE THEIR SHARE...
...OF ILLEGAL AND ADULT VIDEOS...
M.C. DONALDOLL SCARLET
...BUT THERE ARE ALSO GREAT SHORT FILMS...
...MADE WITH ORIGINALITY AND INGENUITY.
TRIED TO MAKE
TO PRODUCE SUCH VIDEOS...
...IS THE MOVIE STUDY CLUB'S HIGHEST MISSION!!

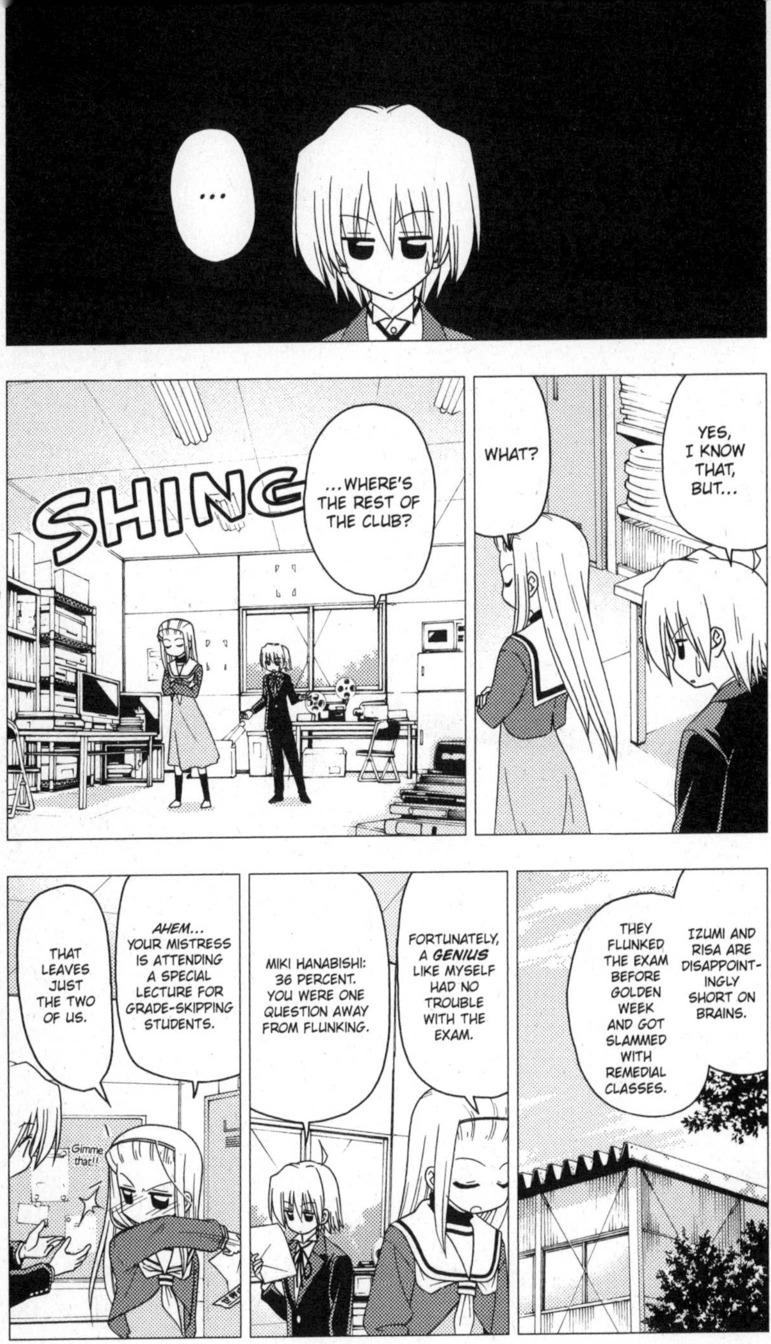
...
YES, I KNOW THAT, BUT...
WHAT?
...WHERE'S THE REST OF THE CLUB?
SHING
IZUMI AND RISA ARE DISAPPOINT-INGLY SHORT ON BRAINS.
THEY FLUNKED THE EXAM BEFORE GOLDEN WEEK AND GOT SLAMMED WITH REMEDIAL CLASSES.
FORTUNATELY, A *GENIUS* LIKE MYSELF HAD NO TROUBLE WITH THE EXAM.
MIKI HANABISHI: 36 PERCENT. YOU WERE ONE QUESTION AWAY FROM FLUNKING.
AHEM... YOUR MISTRESS IS ATTENDING A SPECIAL LECTURE FOR GRADE-SKIPPING STUDENTS.
THAT LEAVES JUST THE TWO OF US.
Gimme that!!

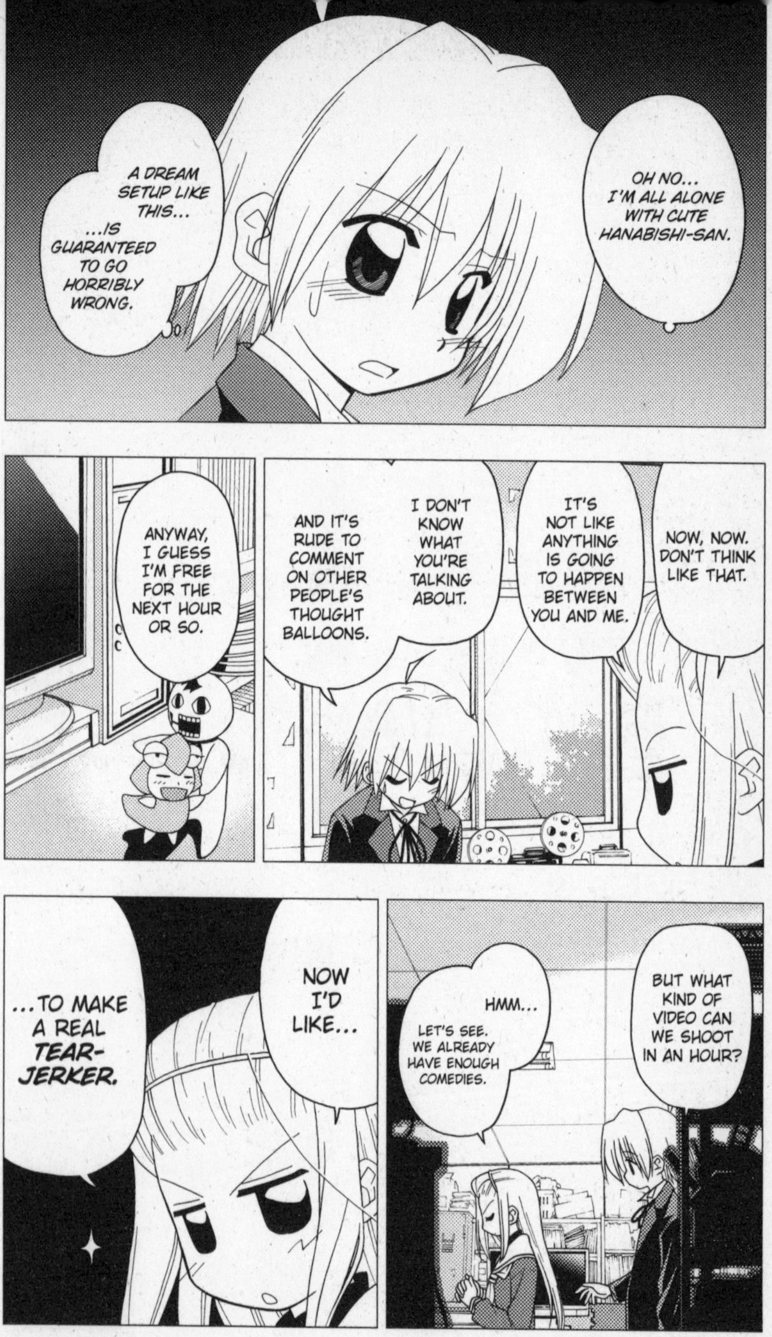
OH NO... I'M ALL ALONE WITH CUTE HANABISHI-SAN.
A DREAM SETUP LIKE THIS... ...IS GUARANTEED TO GO HORRIBLY WRONG.
NOW, NOW. DON'T THINK LIKE THAT.
IT'S NOT LIKE ANYTHING IS GOING TO HAPPEN BETWEEN YOU AND ME.
I DON'T KNOW WHAT YOU'RE TALKING ABOUT.
AND IT'S RUDE TO COMMENT ON OTHER PEOPLE'S THOUGHT BALLOONS.
ANYWAY, I GUESS I'M FREE FOR THE NEXT HOUR OR SO.
BUT WHAT KIND OF VIDEO CAN WE SHOOT IN AN HOUR?
HMM...
LET'S SEE. WE ALREADY HAVE ENOUGH COMEDIES.
NOW I'D LIKE...
...TO MAKE A REAL *TEAR-JERKER.*

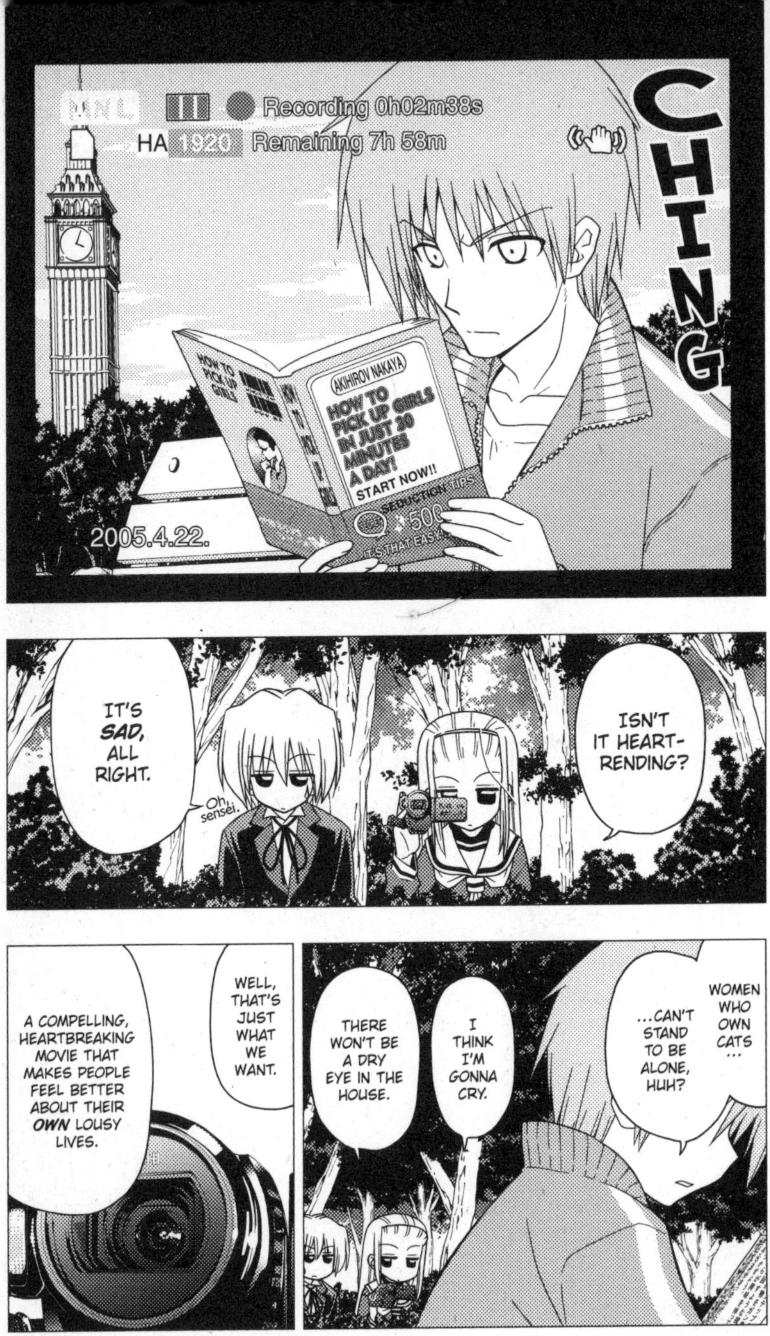
Recording 0h02m38s
HA 1920 Remaining 7h 58m
HOW TO PICK UP GIRLS
AKIHIROV NAKAYA
HOW TO PICK UP GIRLS IN JUST 30 MINUTES A DAY!
START NOW!!
SEDUCTION TIPS
500
IT'S THAT EASY.
2005.4.22.
CHING
ISN'T IT HEART-RENDING?
Oh, sensei.
IT'S SAD, ALL RIGHT.
WOMEN WHO OWN CATS...
...CAN'T STAND TO BE ALONE, HUH?
I THINK I'M GONNA CRY.
THERE WON'T BE A DRY EYE IN THE HOUSE.
WELL, THAT'S JUST WHAT WE WANT.
A COMPELLING, HEARTBREAKING MOVIE THAT MAKES PEOPLE FEEL BETTER ABOUT THEIR OWN LOUSY LIVES.

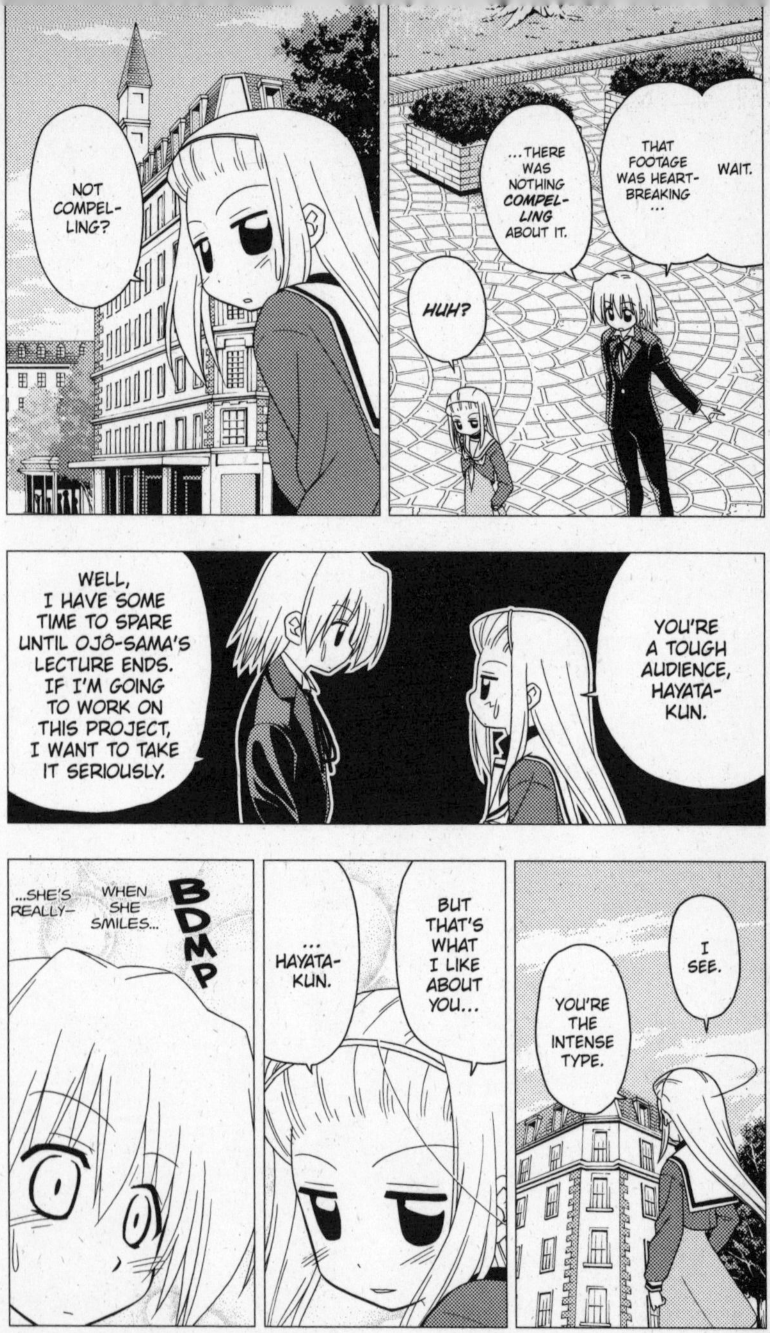
WAIT.
THAT FOOTAGE WAS HEART-BREAKING ...
...THERE WAS NOTHING COMPELLING ABOUT IT.
HUH?
NOT COMPEL-LING?
YOU'RE A TOUGH AUDIENCE, HAYATA-KUN.
WELL, I HAVE SOME TIME TO SPARE UNTIL OJÔ-SAMA'S LECTURE ENDS. IF I'M GOING TO WORK ON THIS PROJECT, I WANT TO TAKE IT SERIOUSLY.
I SEE.
YOU'RE THE INTENSE TYPE.
BUT THAT'S WHAT I LIKE ABOUT YOU...
... HAYATA-KUN.
BDMP
WHEN SHE SMILES...
...SHE'S REALLY-

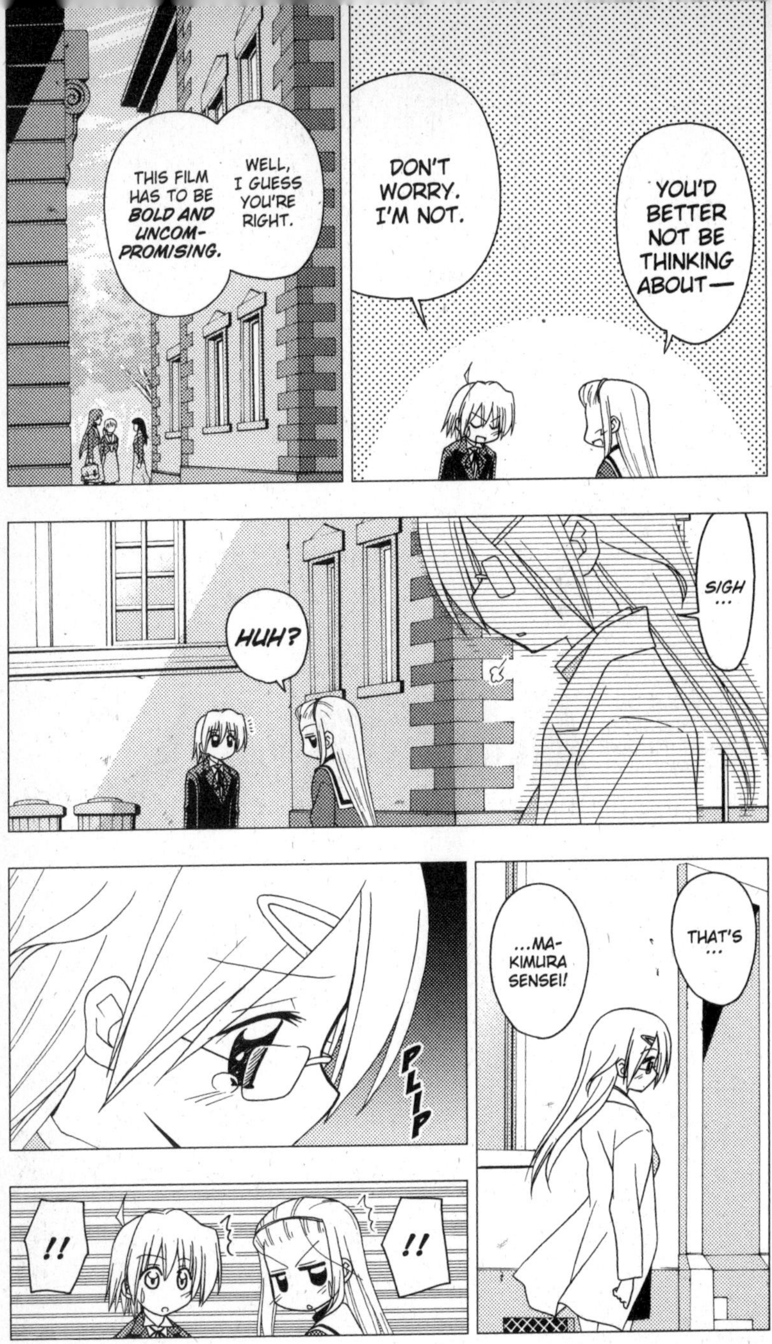
YOU'D BETTER NOT BE THINKING ABOUT—
DON'T WORRY. I'M NOT.
WELL, I GUESS YOU'RE RIGHT.
THIS FILM HAS TO BE *BOLD AND UNCOM-PROMISING.*
SIGH...
HUH?
THAT'S...
...MA-KIMURA SENSEI!
PLIP
!!
!!

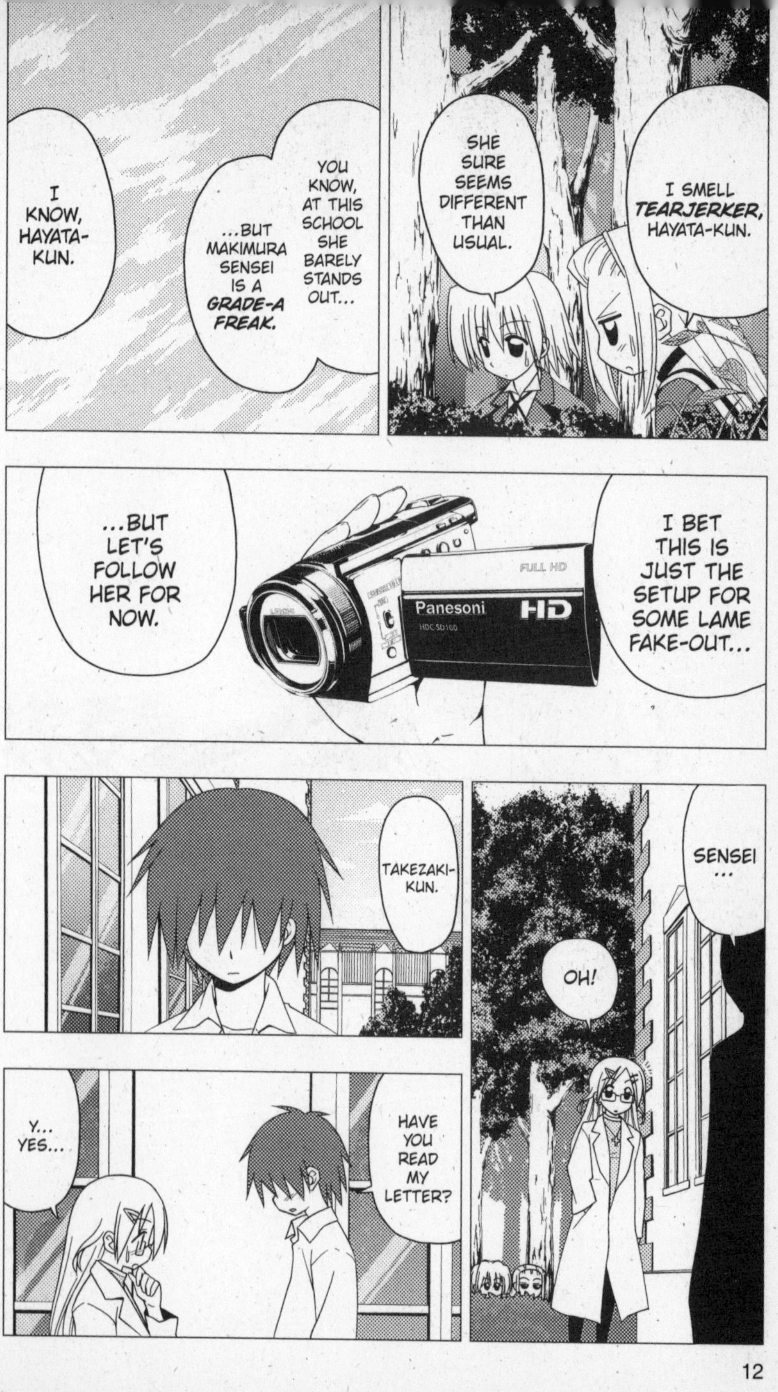
I SMELL TEARJERKER, HAYATA-KUN.
SHE SURE SEEMS DIFFERENT THAN USUAL.
YOU KNOW, AT THIS SCHOOL SHE BARELY STANDS OUT...
...BUT MAKIMURA SENSEI IS A GRADE-A FREAK.
I KNOW, HAYATA-KUN.
I BET THIS IS JUST THE SETUP FOR SOME LAME FAKE-OUT...
FULL HD
Panesoni
HD
HDC SD100
...BUT LET'S FOLLOW HER FOR NOW.
SENSEI...
OH!
TAKEZAKI-KUN.
HAVE YOU READ MY LETTER?
Y... YES...

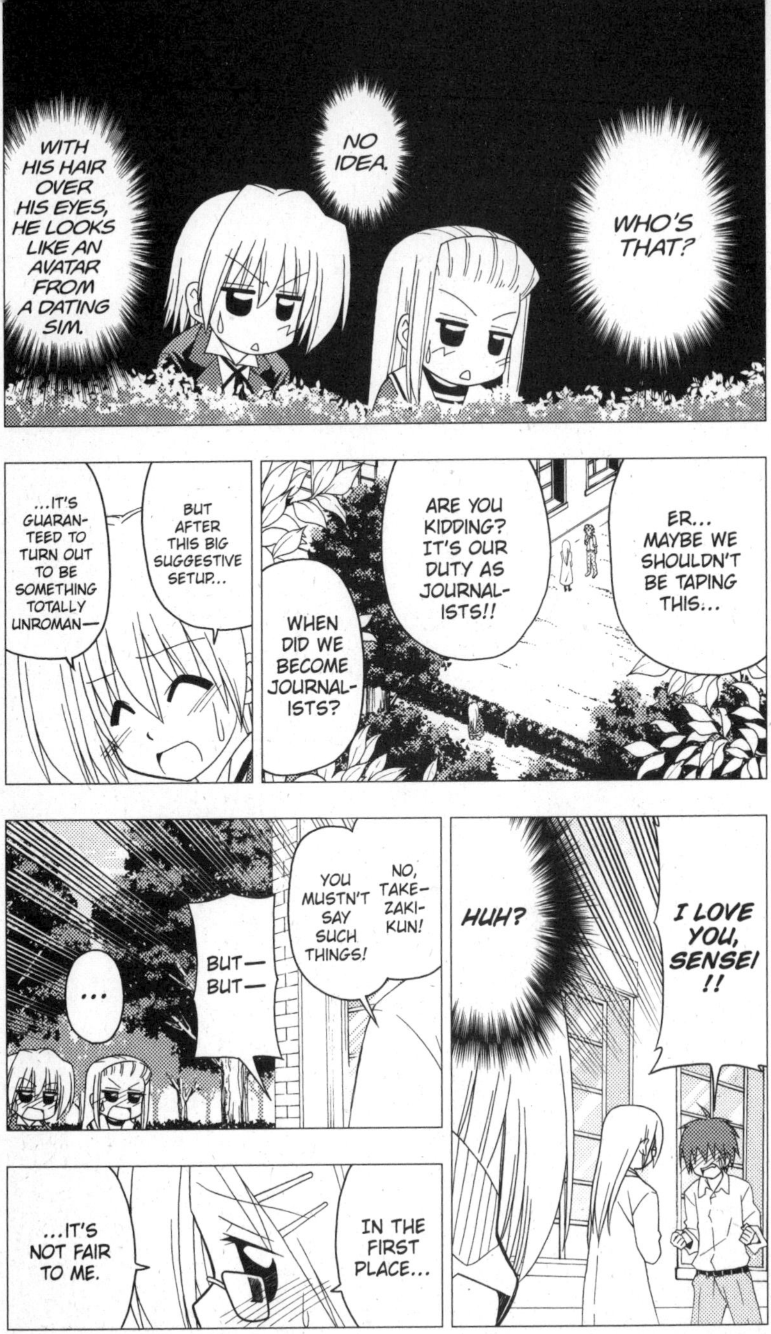
WHO'S THAT?
NO IDEA.
WITH HIS HAIR OVER HIS EYES, HE LOOKS LIKE AN AVATAR FROM A DATING SIM.
ER... MAYBE WE SHOULDN'T BE TAPING THIS...
ARE YOU KIDDING? IT'S OUR DUTY AS JOURNAL-ISTS!!
WHEN DID WE BECOME JOURNAL-ISTS?
BUT AFTER THIS BIG SUGGESTIVE SETUP...
...IT'S GUARAN-TEED TO TURN OUT TO BE SOMETHING TOTALLY UNROMAN—
I LOVE YOU, SENSEI!!
HUH?
NO, TAKE-ZAKI-KUN!
YOU MUSTN'T SAY SUCH THINGS!
BUT— BUT—
...
IN THE FIRST PLACE...
...IT'S NOT FAIR TO ME.

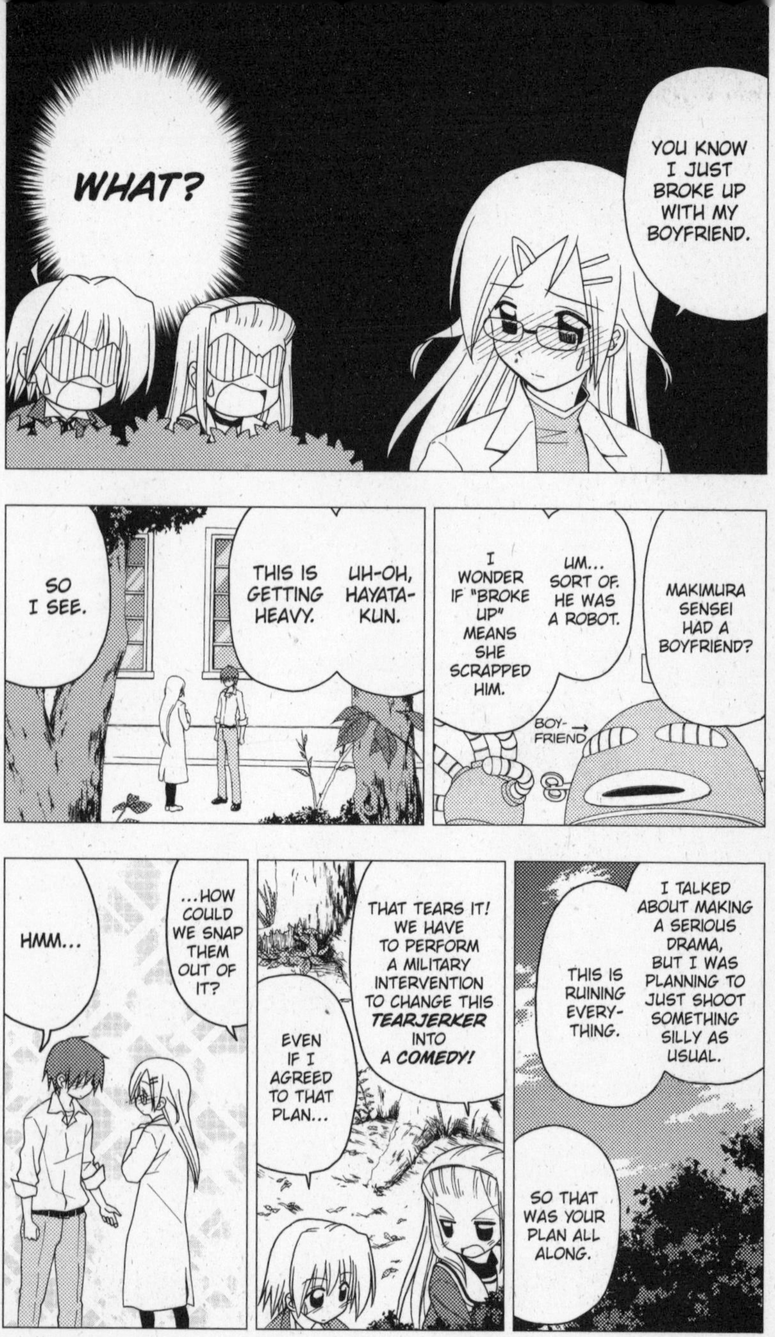
YOU KNOW I JUST BROKE UP WITH MY BOYFRIEND.
WHAT?
MAKIMURA SENSEI HAD A BOYFRIEND?
UM... SORT OF. HE WAS A ROBOT.
I WONDER IF "BROKE UP" MEANS SHE SCRAPPED HIM.
BOY-FRIEND
UH-OH, HAYATA-KUN.
THIS IS GETTING HEAVY.
SO I SEE.
I TALKED ABOUT MAKING A SERIOUS DRAMA, BUT I WAS PLANNING TO JUST SHOOT SOMETHING SILLY AS USUAL.
THIS IS RUINING EVERY-THING.
SO THAT WAS YOUR PLAN ALL ALONG.
THAT TEARS IT! WE HAVE TO PERFORM A MILITARY INTERVENTION TO CHANGE THIS TEARJERKER INTO A COMEDY!
EVEN IF I AGREED TO THAT PLAN...
...HOW COULD WE SNAP THEM OUT OF IT?
HMM...

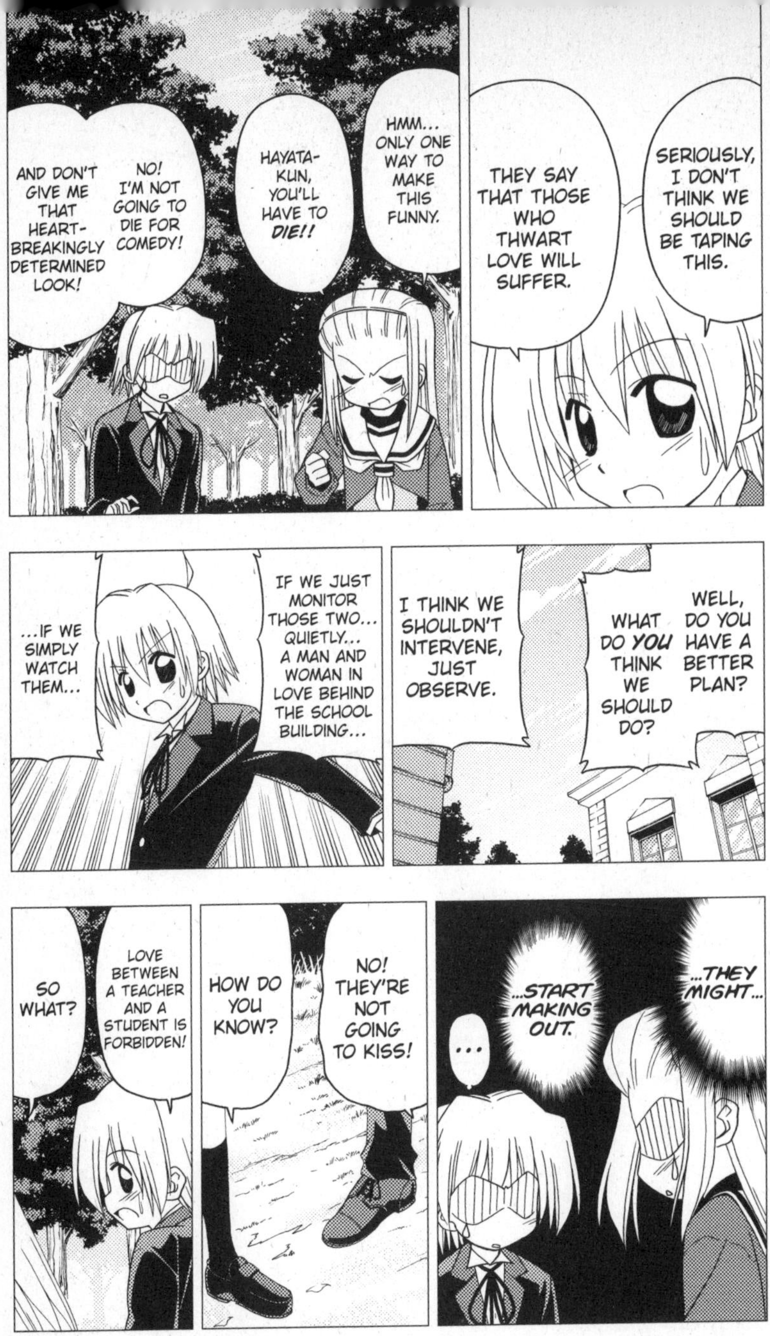
SERIOUSLY, I DON'T THINK WE SHOULD BE TAPING THIS.
THEY SAY THAT THOSE WHO THWART LOVE WILL SUFFER.
HMM... ONLY ONE WAY TO MAKE THIS FUNNY.
HAYATA-KUN, YOU'LL HAVE TO *DIE!!*
NO! I'M NOT GOING TO DIE FOR COMEDY!
AND DON'T GIVE ME THAT HEART-BREAKINGLY DETERMINED LOOK!
WELL, DO YOU HAVE A BETTER PLAN?
WHAT DO *YOU* THINK WE SHOULD DO?
I THINK WE SHOULDN'T INTERVENE, JUST OBSERVE.
IF WE JUST MONITOR THOSE TWO... QUIETLY... A MAN AND WOMAN IN LOVE BEHIND THE SCHOOL BUILDING...
...IF WE SIMPLY WATCH THEM...
...THEY MIGHT...
...START MAKING OUT.
...
NO! THEY'RE NOT GOING TO KISS!
HOW DO YOU KNOW?
LOVE BETWEEN A TEACHER AND A STUDENT IS FORBIDDEN!
SO WHAT?

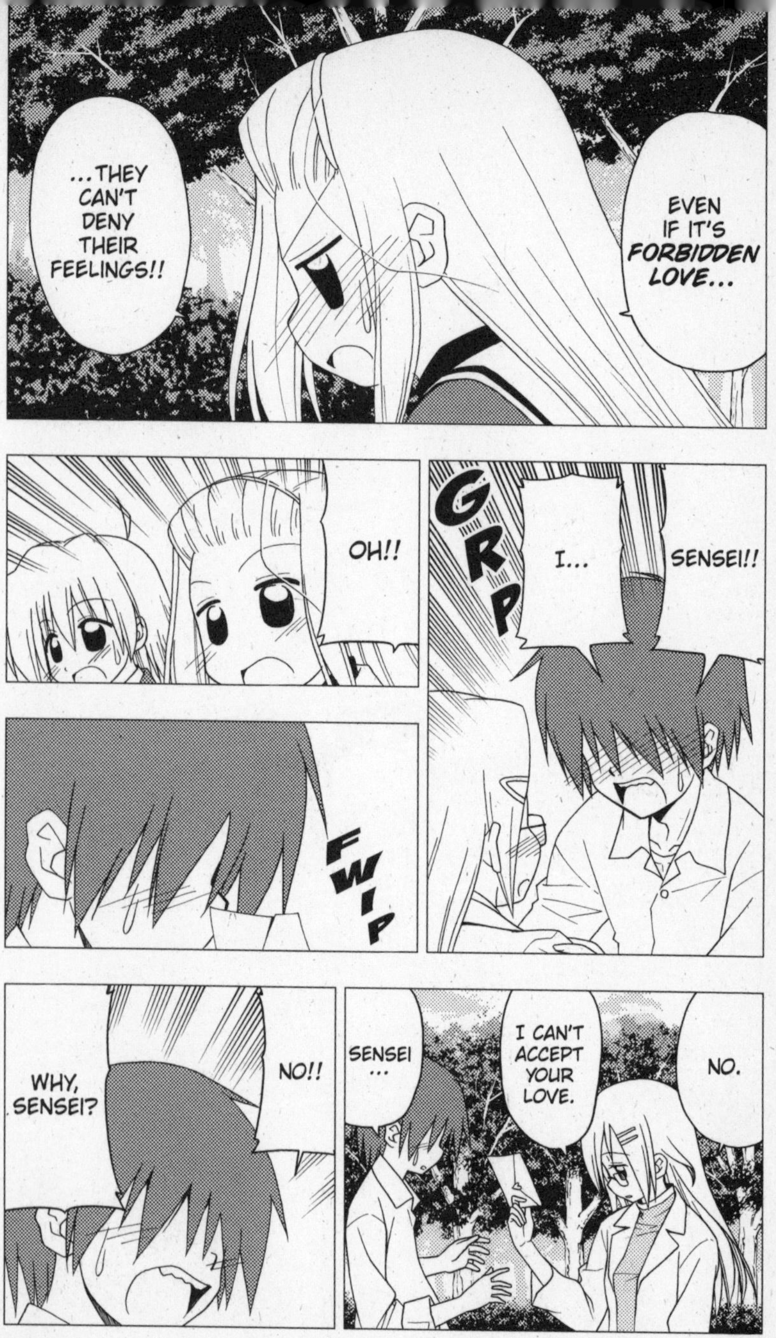
EVEN IF IT'S FORBIDDEN LOVE...
...THEY CAN'T DENY THEIR FEELINGS!!
SENSEI!!
I...
GRP
OH!!
FWIP
NO.
I CAN'T ACCEPT YOUR LOVE.
SENSEI...
NO!!
WHY, SENSEI?

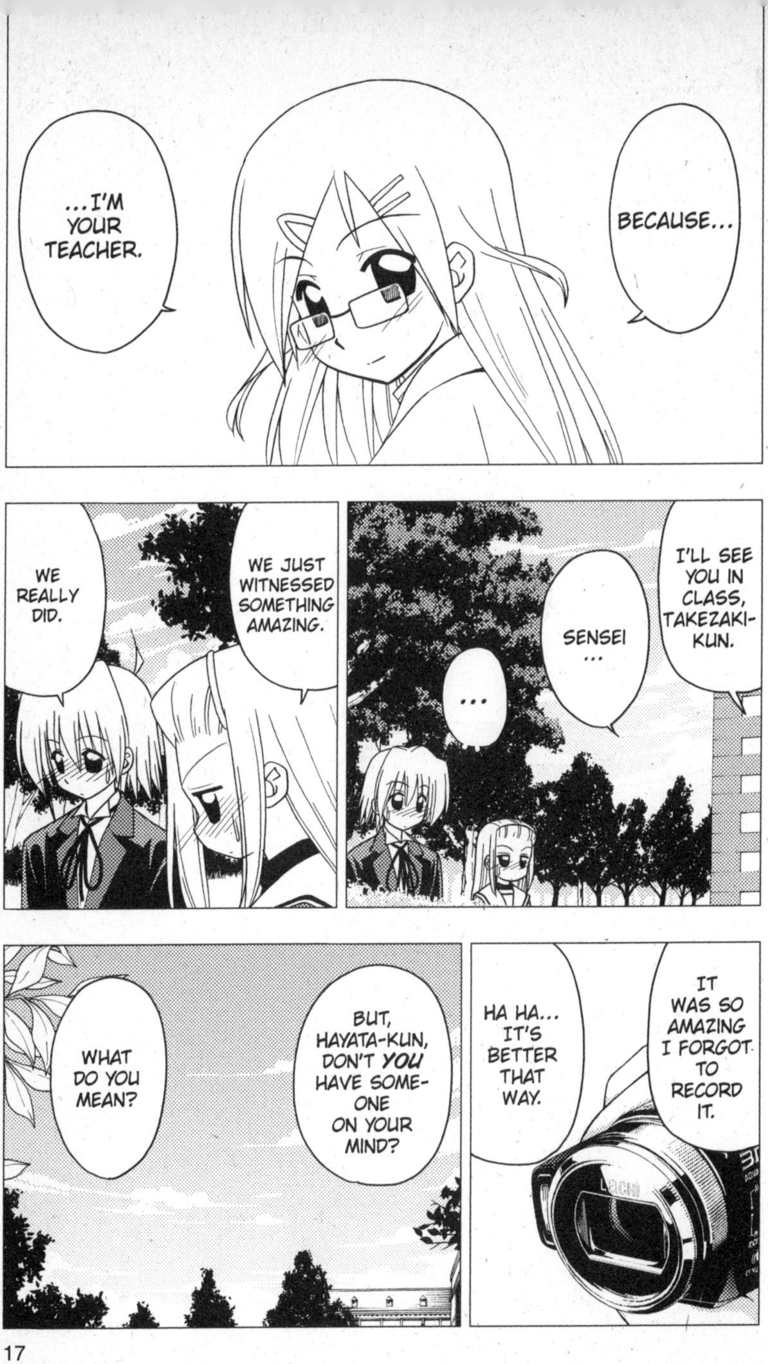
BECAUSE...
...I'M YOUR TEACHER.
I'LL SEE YOU IN CLASS, TAKEZAKI-KUN.
SENSEI...
...
WE JUST WITNESSED SOMETHING AMAZING.
WE REALLY DID.
IT WAS SO AMAZING I FORGOT TO RECORD IT.
HA HA... IT'S BETTER THAT WAY.
BUT, HAYATA-KUN, DON'T *YOU* HAVE SOME-ONE ON YOUR MIND?
WHAT DO YOU MEAN?

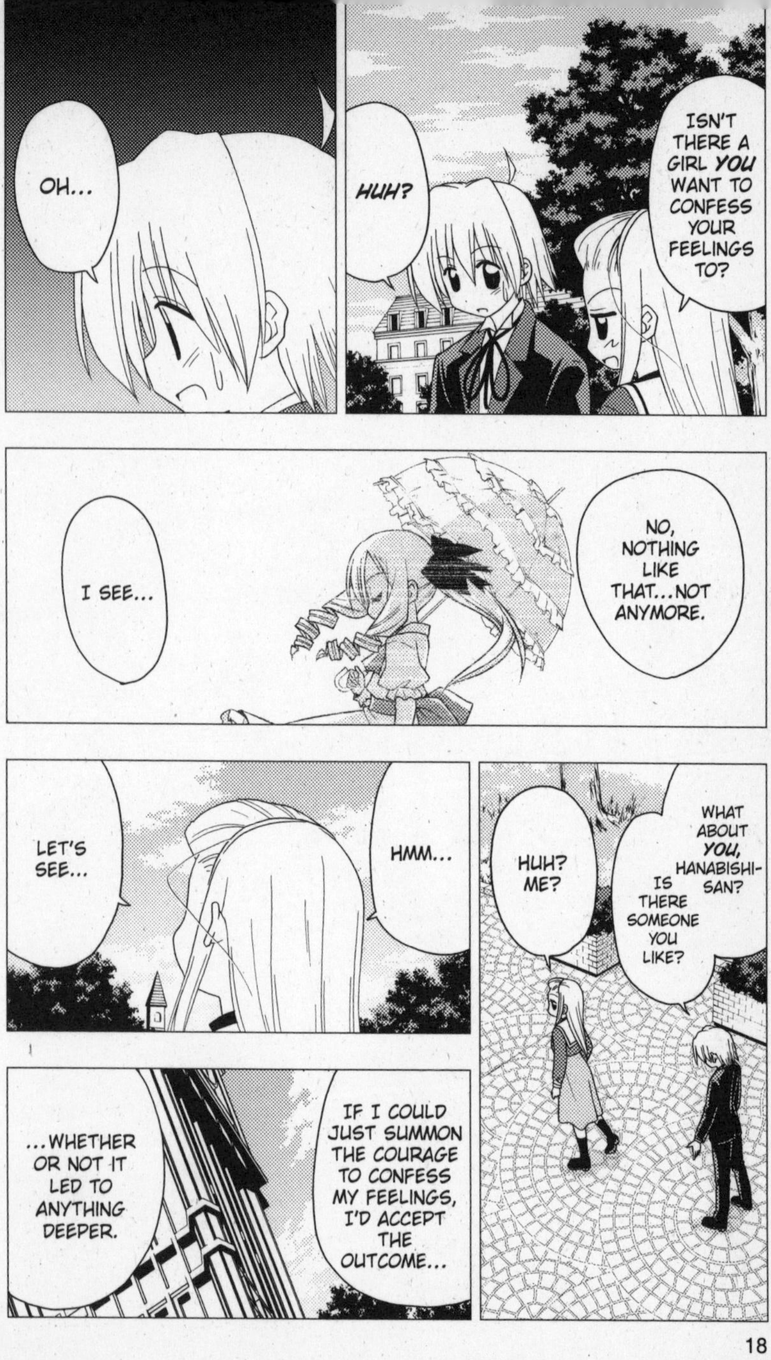
ISN'T THERE A GIRL *YOU* WANT TO CONFESS YOUR FEELINGS TO?
HUH?
OH...
NO, NOTHING LIKE THAT...NOT ANYMORE.
I SEE...
WHAT ABOUT *YOU,* HANABISHI-SAN?
IS THERE SOMEONE YOU LIKE?
HUH? ME?
HMM...
LET'S SEE...
IF I COULD JUST SUMMON THE COURAGE TO CONFESS MY FEELINGS, I'D ACCEPT THE OUTCOME...
...WHETHER OR NOT IT LED TO ANYTHING DEEPER.

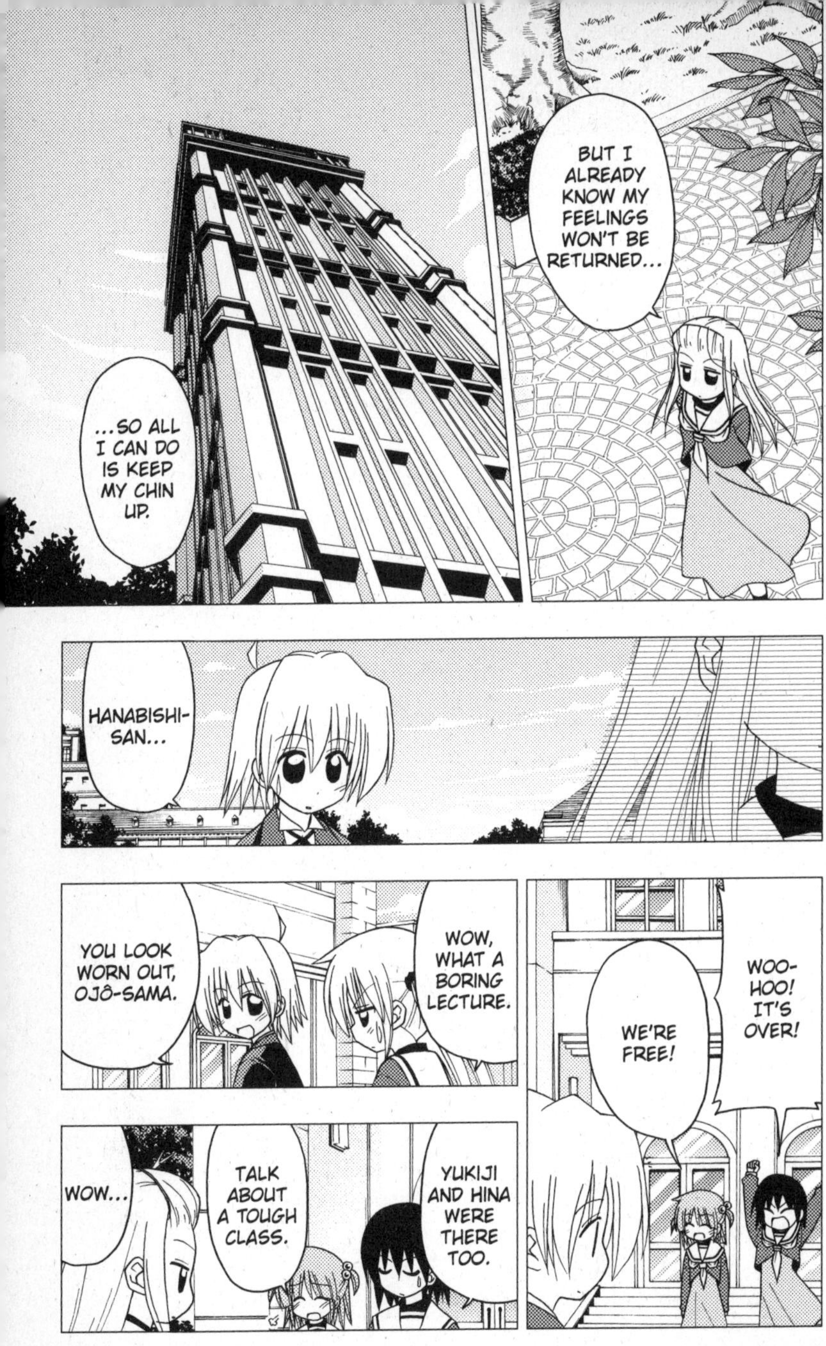

BUT I ALREADY KNOW MY FEELINGS WON'T BE RETURNED...
...SO ALL I CAN DO IS KEEP MY CHIN UP.
HANABISHI-SAN...
WOO-HOO! IT'S OVER!
WE'RE FREE!
WOW, WHAT A BORING LECTURE.
YOU LOOK WORN OUT, OJÔ-SAMA.
YUKIJI AND HINA WERE THERE TOO.
TALK ABOUT A TOUGH CLASS.
WOW...

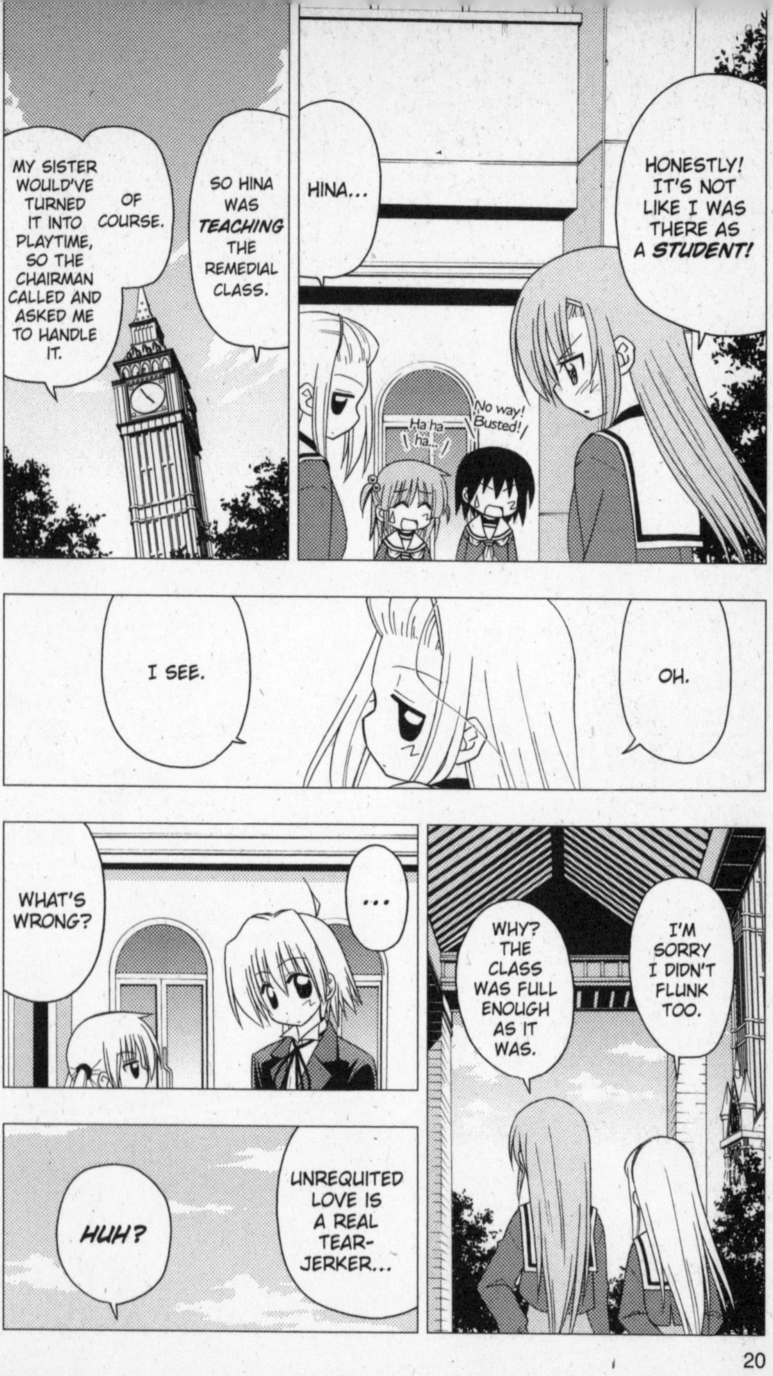
HONESTLY! IT'S NOT LIKE I WAS THERE AS A *STUDENT!*
HINA...
No way! Busted!
Ha ha ha...
SO HINA WAS *TEACHING* THE REMEDIAL CLASS.
OF COURSE.
MY SISTER WOULD'VE TURNED IT INTO PLAYTIME, SO THE CHAIRMAN CALLED AND ASKED ME TO HANDLE IT.
OH.
I SEE.
I'M SORRY I DIDN'T FLUNK TOO.
WHY? THE CLASS WAS FULL ENOUGH AS IT WAS.
...
WHAT'S WRONG?
UNREQUITED LOVE IS A REAL TEAR-JERKER...
HUH?

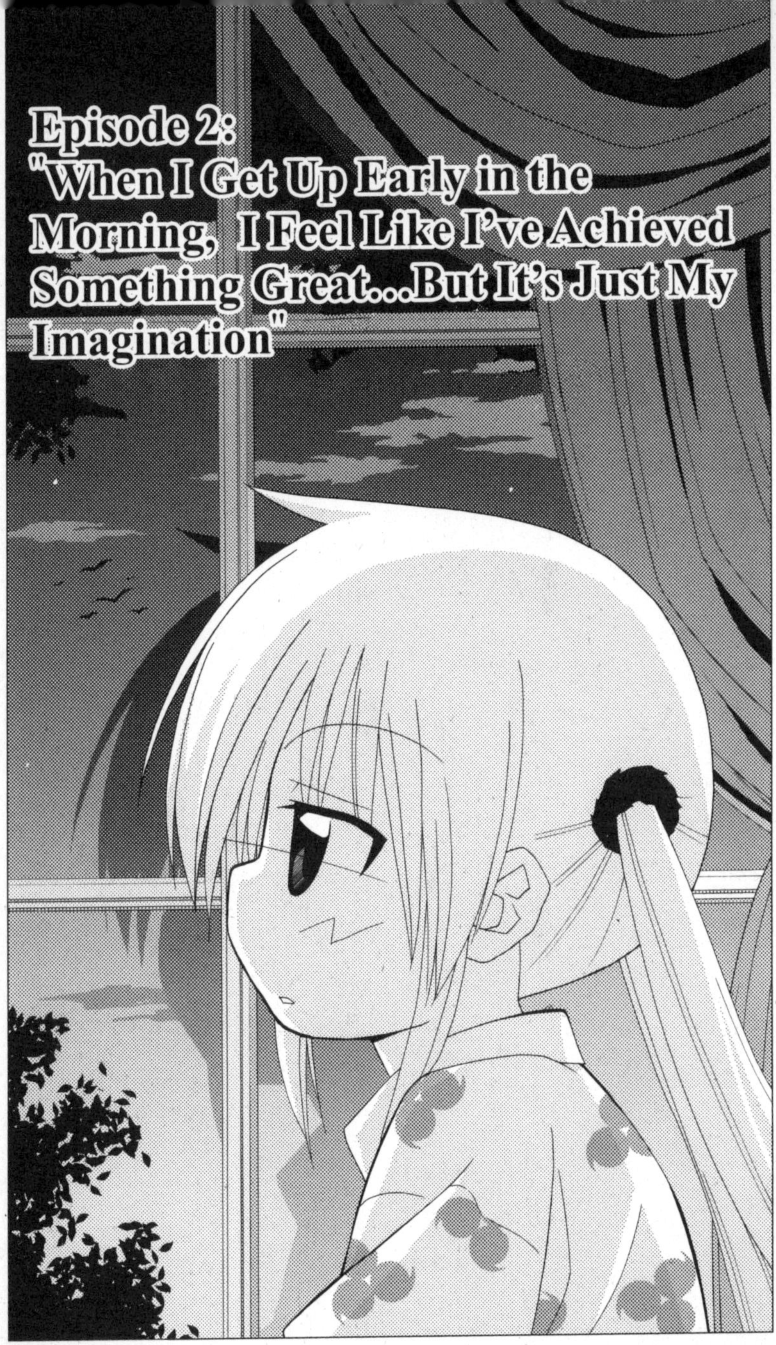
Episode 2:
"When I Get Up Early in the Morning, I Feel Like I've Achieved Something Great...But It's Just My Imagination"

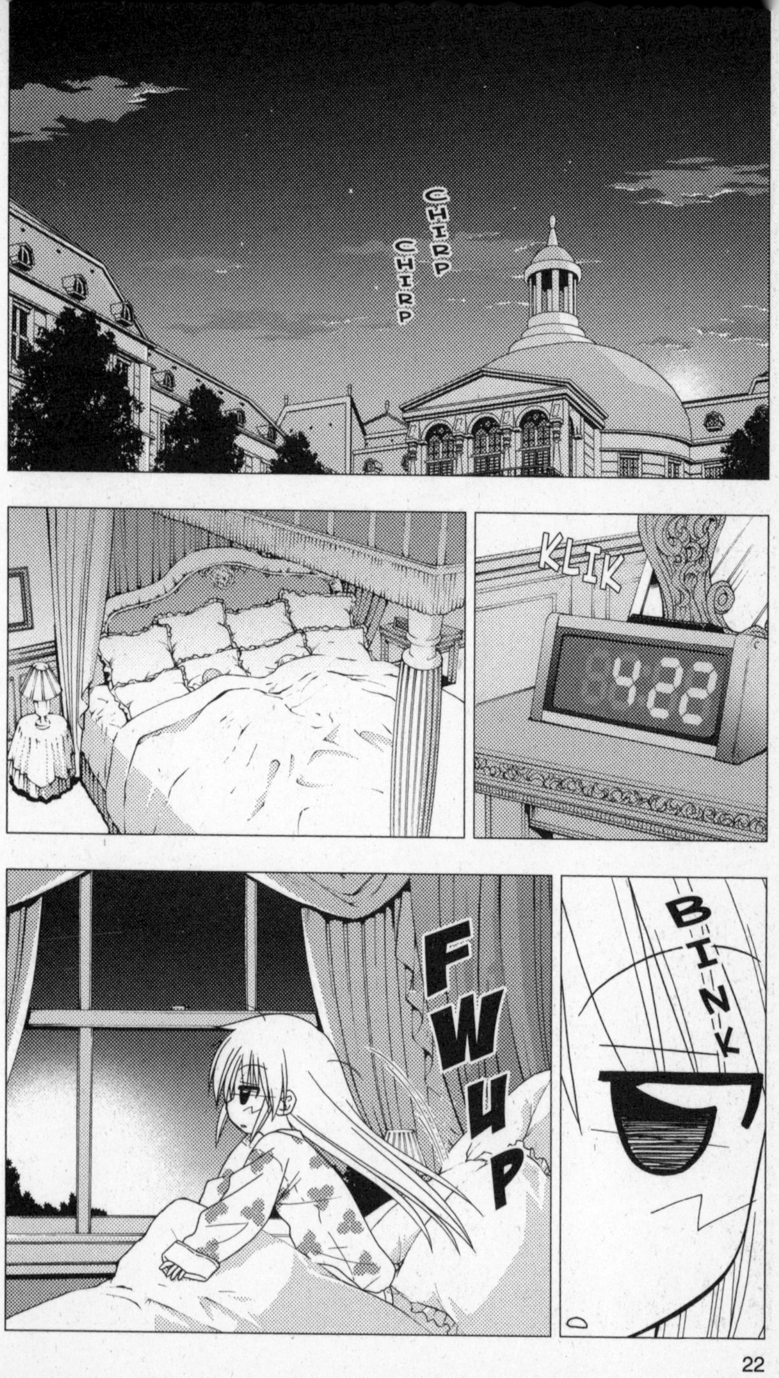
CHIRP
CHIRP
KLIK
422
BINK
FWUP

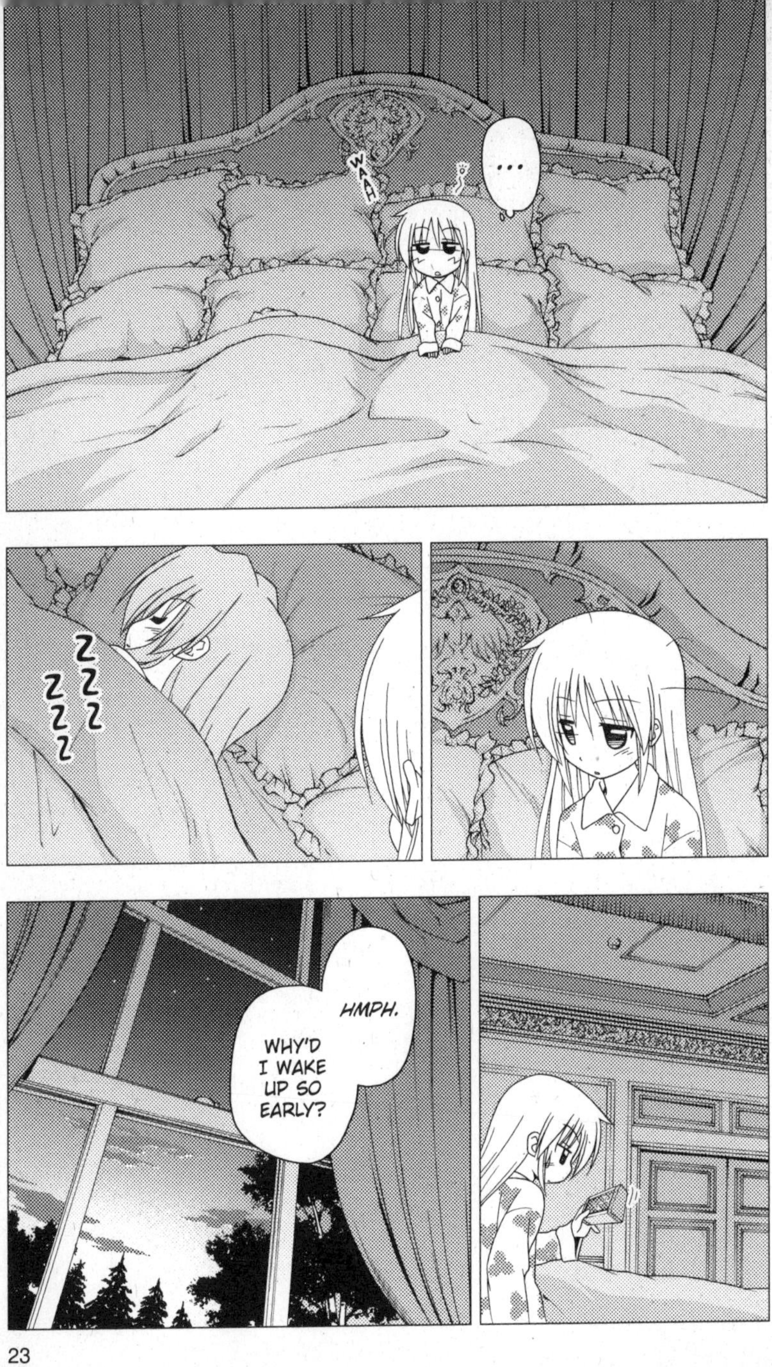
WAAH
...
ZZZ
ZZZ
HMPH.
WHY'D I WAKE UP SO EARLY?

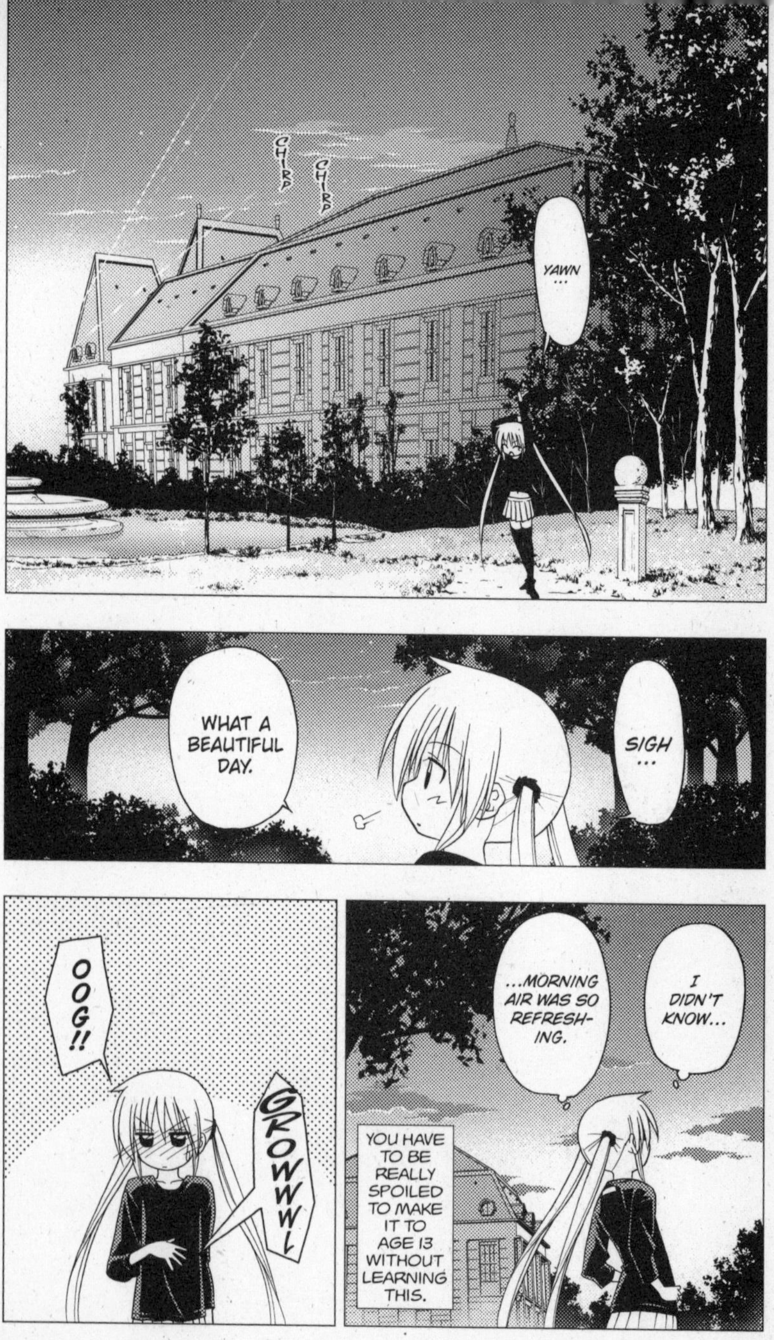
CHIRP
CHIRP
YAWN...
SIGH...
WHAT A BEAUTIFUL DAY.
I DIDN'T KNOW...
...MORNING AIR WAS SO REFRESHING.
YOU HAVE TO BE REALLY SPOILED TO MAKE IT TO AGE 13 WITHOUT LEARNING THIS.
GROWWWL
OOG!!

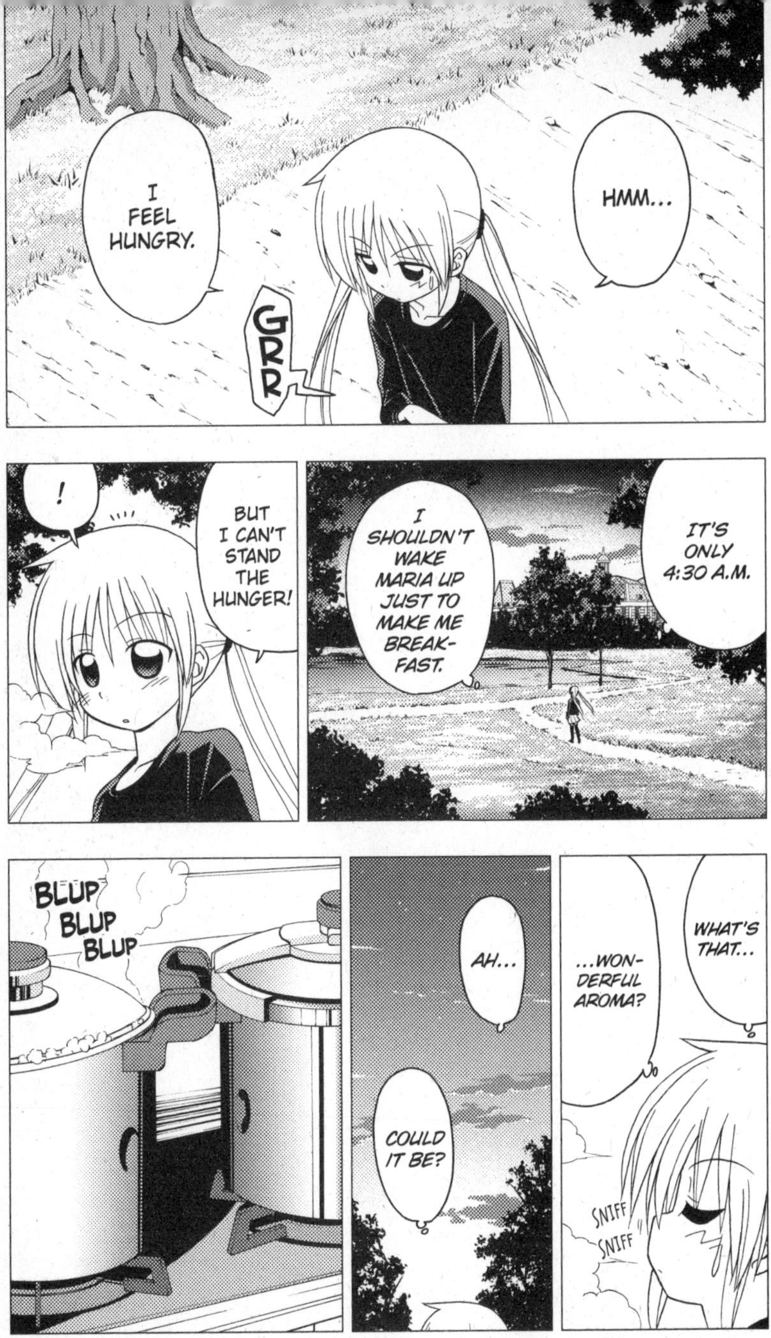
HMM...
I FEEL HUNGRY.
GRR
IT'S ONLY 4:30 A.M.
I SHOULDN'T WAKE MARIA UP JUST TO MAKE ME BREAK-FAST.
BUT I CAN'T STAND THE HUNGER!
!
WHAT'S THAT...
...WON-DERFUL AROMA?
SNIFF SNIFF
AH...
COULD IT BE?
BLUP BLUP BLUP

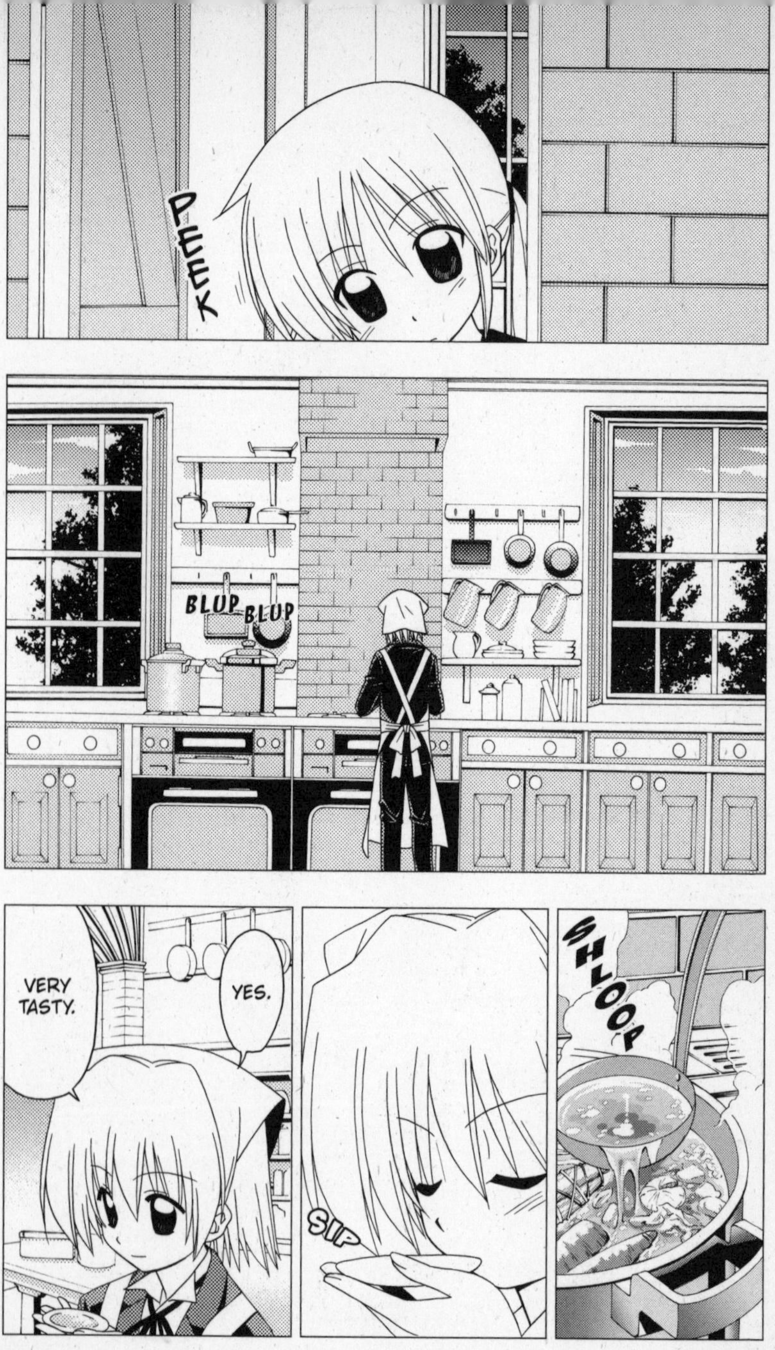
PEEK
BLUP BLUP
SHLOOP
SIP
YES.
VERY TASTY.

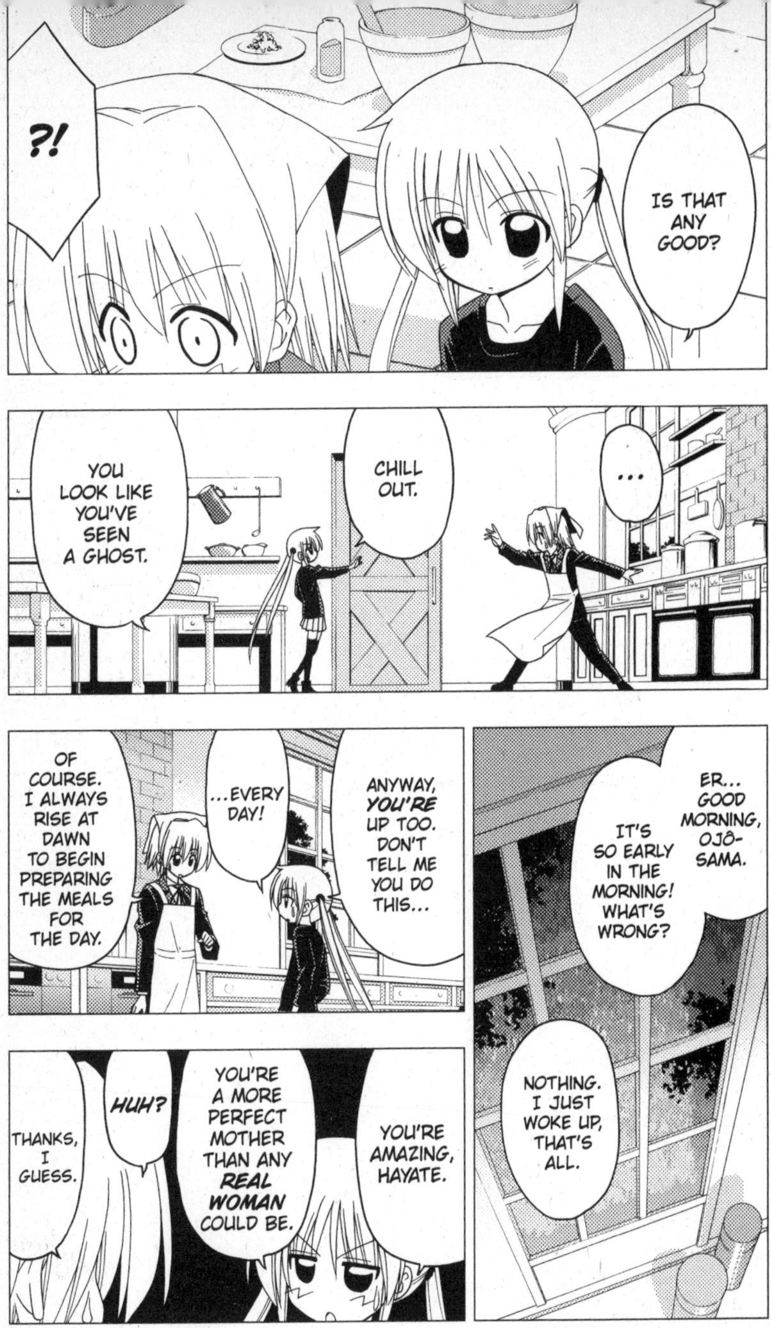
IS THAT ANY GOOD?
?!
...
CHILL OUT.
YOU LOOK LIKE YOU'VE SEEN A GHOST.
ER... GOOD MORNING, OJÔ-SAMA.
IT'S SO EARLY IN THE MORNING! WHAT'S WRONG?
NOTHING. I JUST WOKE UP, THAT'S ALL.
ANYWAY, YOU'RE UP TOO. DON'T TELL ME YOU DO THIS...
...EVERY DAY!
OF COURSE. I ALWAYS RISE AT DAWN TO BEGIN PREPARING THE MEALS FOR THE DAY.
YOU'RE AMAZING, HAYATE.
YOU'RE A MORE PERFECT MOTHER THAN ANY REAL WOMAN COULD BE.
HUH?
THANKS, I GUESS.

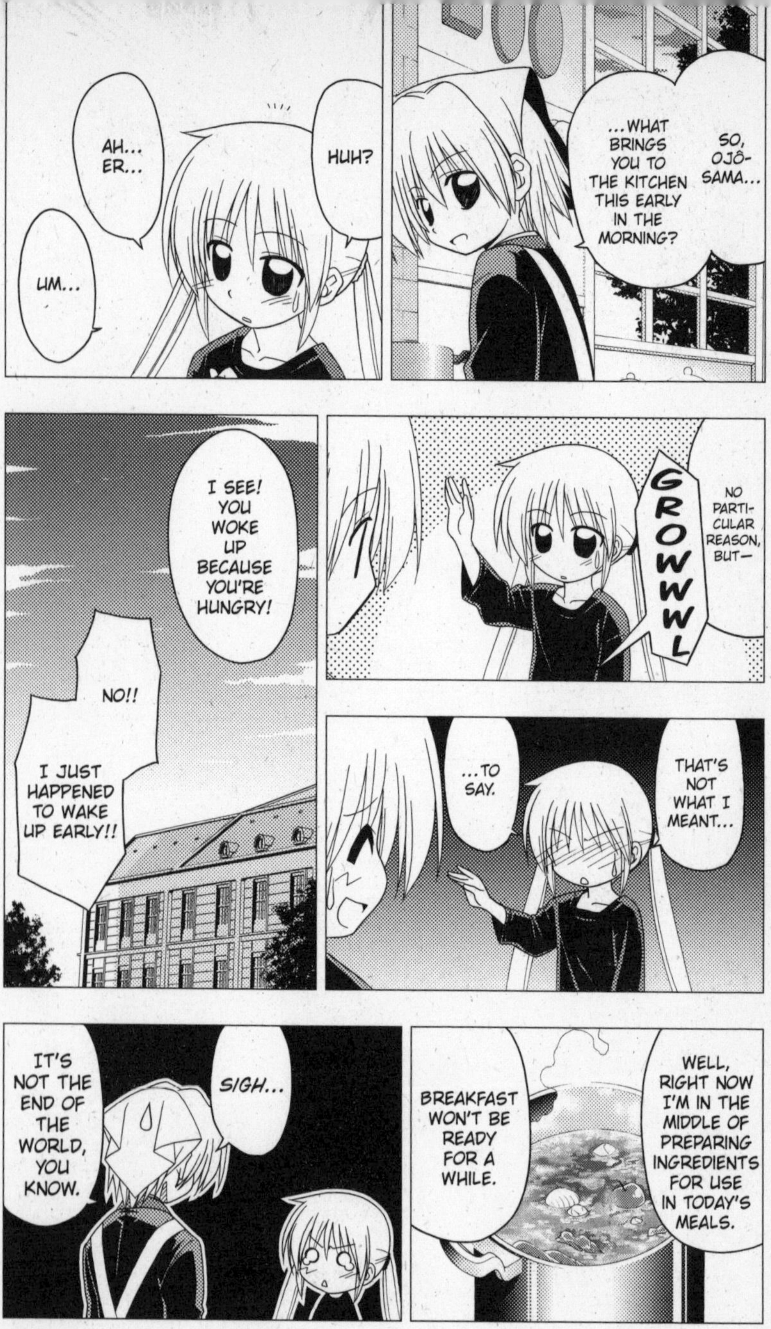
SO, OJÔ-SAMA...
...WHAT BRINGS YOU TO THE KITCHEN THIS EARLY IN THE MORNING?
HUH?
AH... ER...
UM...
NO PARTICULAR REASON, BUT—
GROWWWL
THAT'S NOT WHAT I MEANT...
...TO SAY.
I SEE! YOU WOKE UP BECAUSE YOU'RE HUNGRY!
NO!!
I JUST HAPPENED TO WAKE UP EARLY!!
WELL, RIGHT NOW I'M IN THE MIDDLE OF PREPARING INGREDIENTS FOR USE IN TODAY'S MEALS.
BREAKFAST WON'T BE READY FOR A WHILE.
SIGH...
IT'S NOT THE END OF THE WORLD, YOU KNOW.

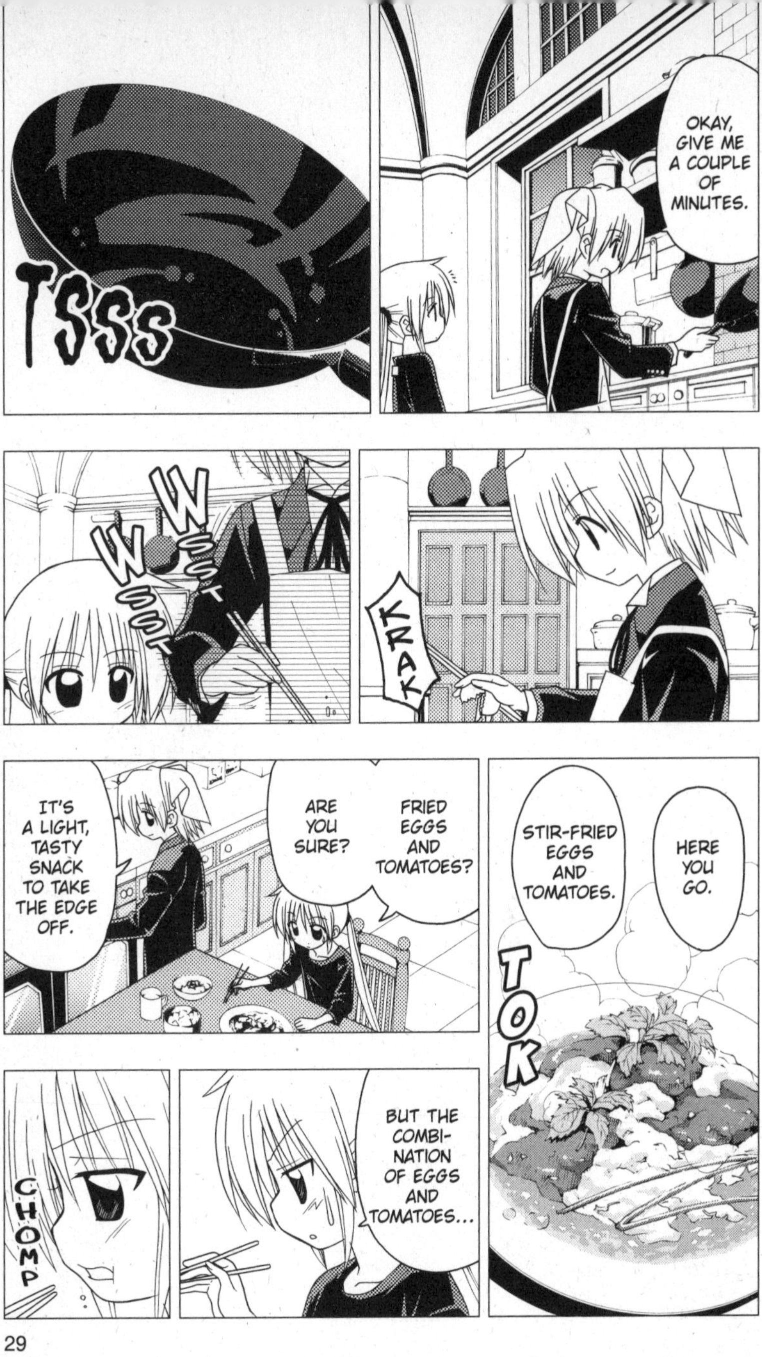
OKAY, GIVE ME A COUPLE OF MINUTES.
TSSS
KRAK
WSSST
WSSST
HERE YOU GO.
STIR-FRIED EGGS AND TOMATOES.
TOK
FRIED EGGS AND TOMATOES?
ARE YOU SURE?
IT'S A LIGHT, TASTY SNACK TO TAKE THE EDGE OFF.
BUT THE COMBINATION OF EGGS AND TOMATOES...
CHOMP

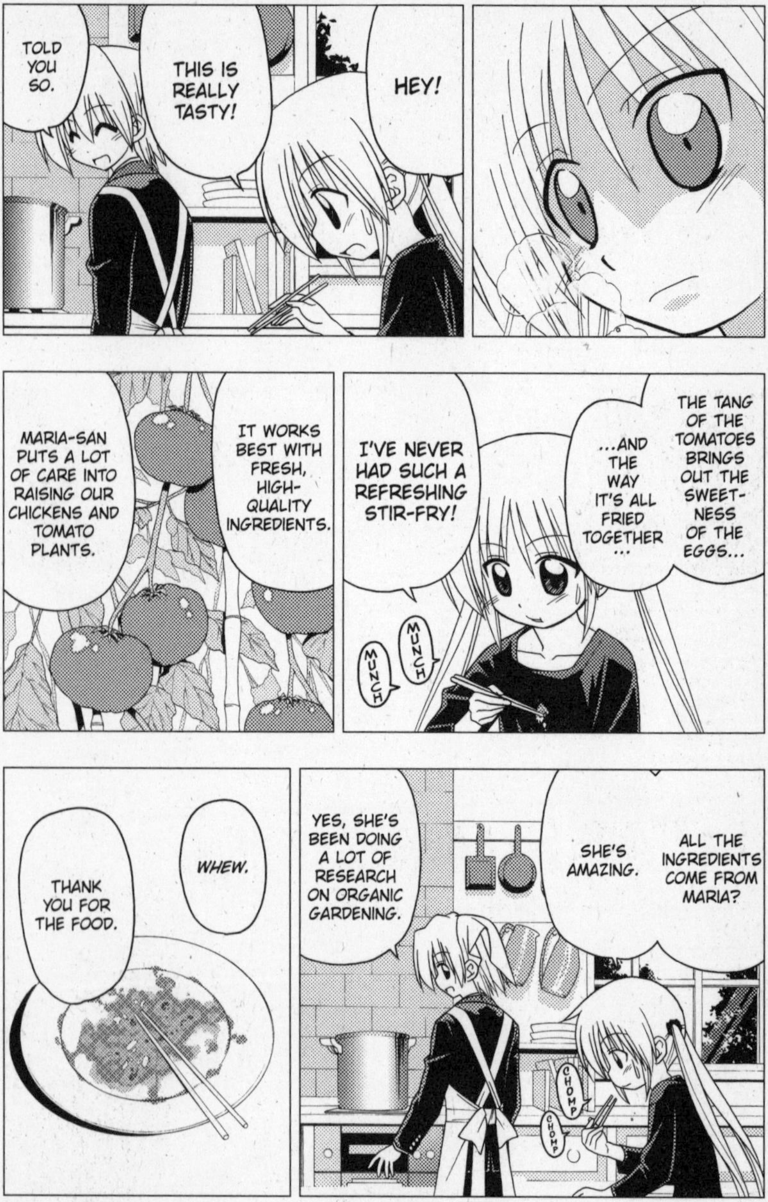
HEY!
THIS IS REALLY TASTY!
TOLD YOU SO.
THE TANG OF THE TOMATOES BRINGS OUT THE SWEET-NESS OF THE EGGS...
...AND THE WAY IT'S ALL FRIED TOGETHER...
I'VE NEVER HAD SUCH A REFRESHING STIR-FRY!
MUNCH
MUNCH
IT WORKS BEST WITH FRESH, HIGH-QUALITY INGREDIENTS.
MARIA-SAN PUTS A LOT OF CARE INTO RAISING OUR CHICKENS AND TOMATO PLANTS.
ALL THE INGREDIENTS COME FROM MARIA?
SHE'S AMAZING.
YES, SHE'S BEEN DOING A LOT OF RESEARCH ON ORGANIC GARDENING.
CHOMP
CHOMP
WHEW.
THANK YOU FOR THE FOOD.

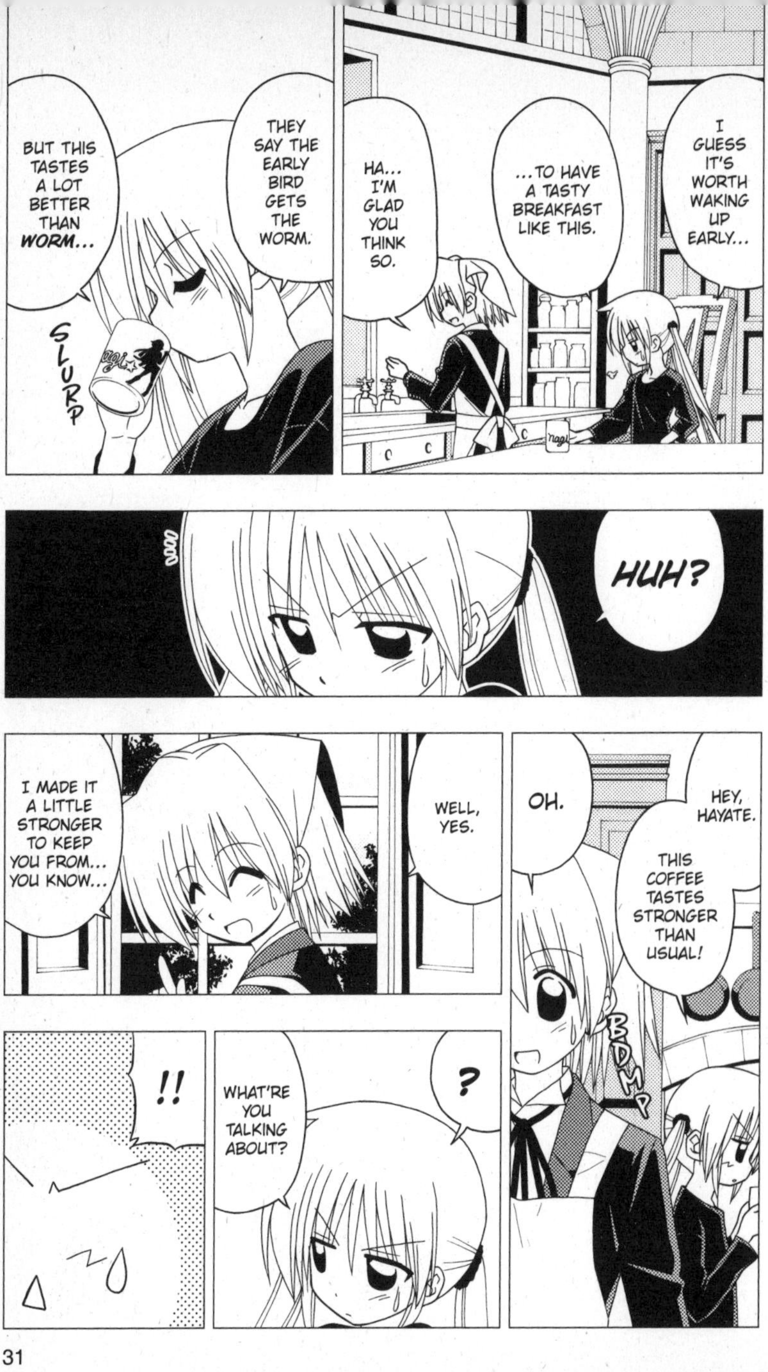
I GUESS IT'S WORTH WAKING UP EARLY...
...TO HAVE A TASTY BREAKFAST LIKE THIS.
HA... I'M GLAD YOU THINK SO.
THEY SAY THE EARLY BIRD GETS THE WORM.
BUT THIS TASTES A LOT BETTER THAN ***WORM***...
SLURP
HUH?
HEY, HAYATE.
THIS COFFEE TASTES STRONGER THAN USUAL!
OH.
BDMP
WELL, YES.
I MADE IT A LITTLE STRONGER TO KEEP YOU FROM... YOU KNOW...
?
WHAT'RE YOU TALKING ABOUT?
!!

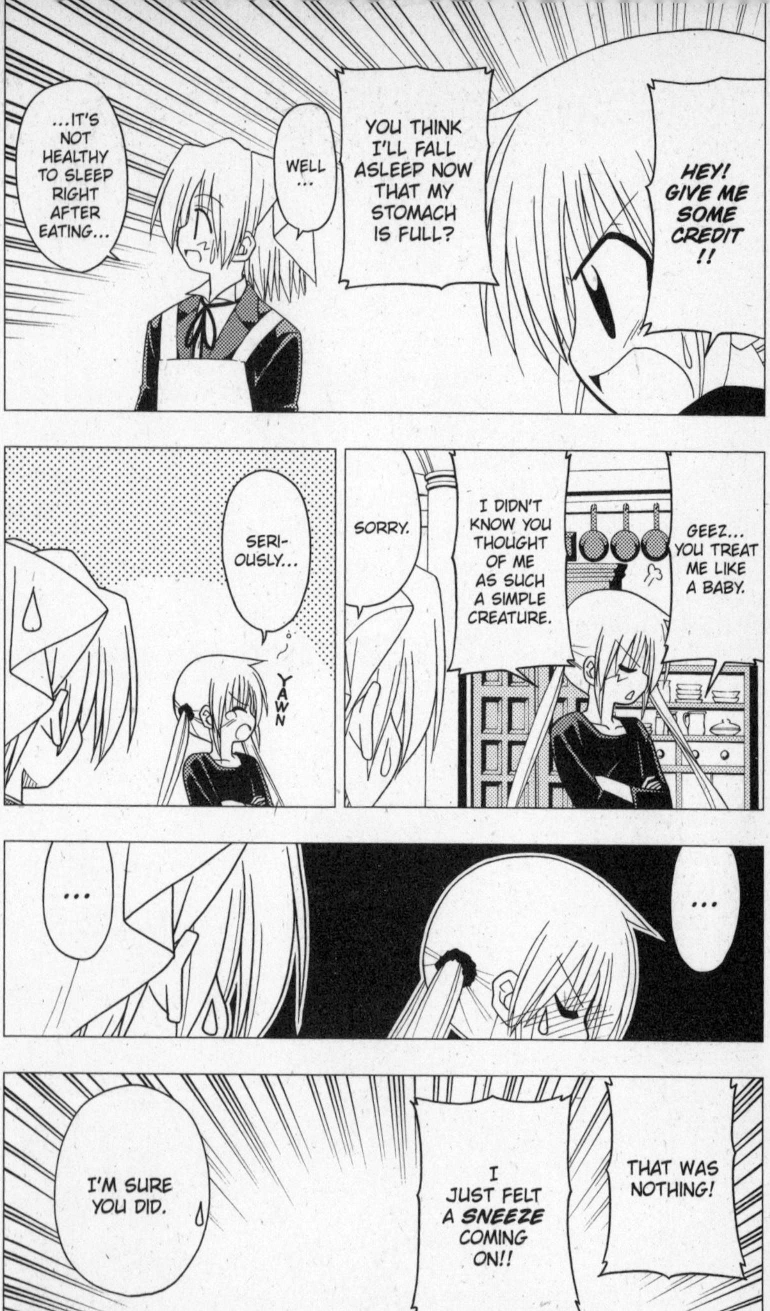

HEY! GIVE ME SOME CREDIT!!
YOU THINK I'LL FALL ASLEEP NOW THAT MY STOMACH IS FULL?
WELL ...
...IT'S NOT HEALTHY TO SLEEP RIGHT AFTER EATING...
GEEZ... YOU TREAT ME LIKE A BABY.
I DIDN'T KNOW YOU THOUGHT OF ME AS SUCH A SIMPLE CREATURE.
SORRY.
SERI-OUSLY...
YAWN
...
...
THAT WAS NOTHING!
I JUST FELT A *SNEEZE* COMING ON!!
I'M SURE YOU DID.

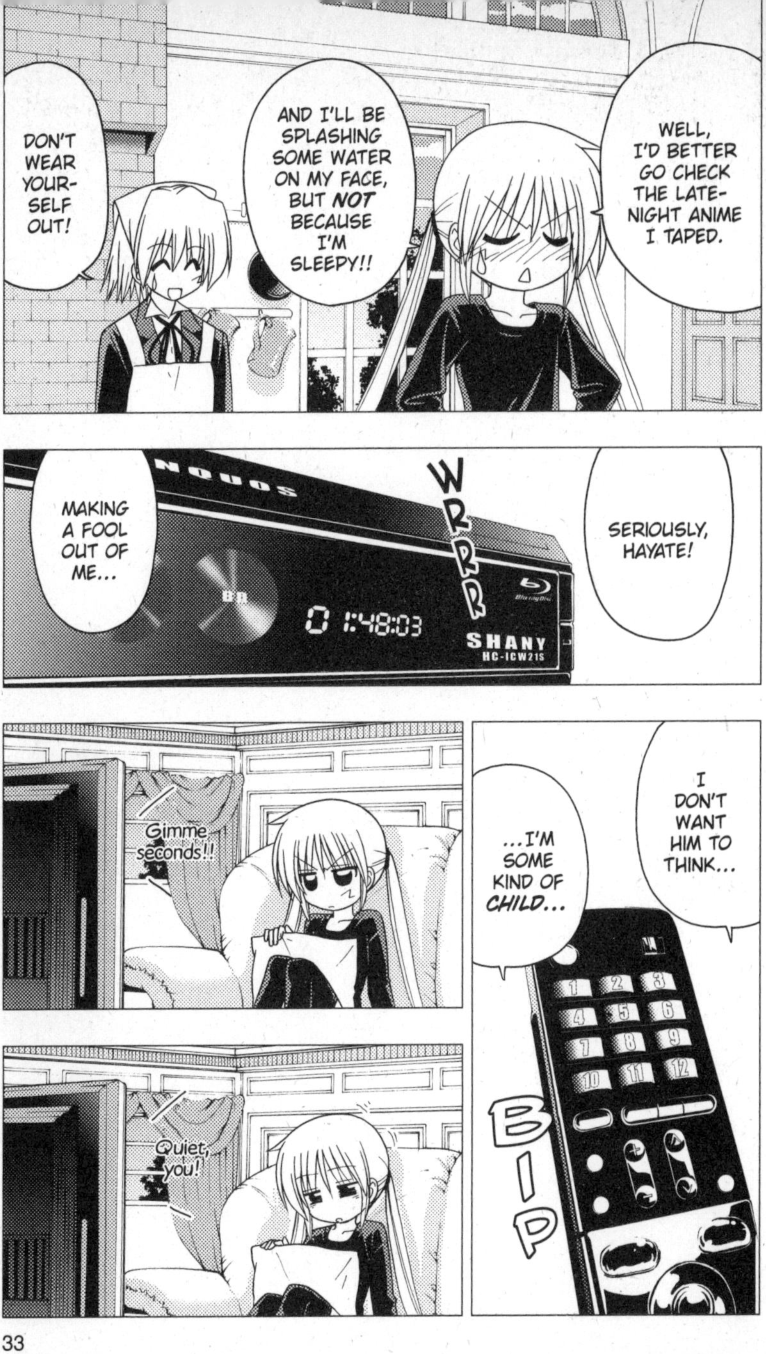
WELL, I'D BETTER GO CHECK THE LATE-NIGHT ANIME I TAPED.
AND I'LL BE SPLASHING SOME WATER ON MY FACE, BUT *NOT* BECAUSE I'M SLEEPY!!
DON'T WEAR YOURSELF OUT!
SERIOUSLY, HAYATE!
WRRR
SHANY
HC-ICW21S
01:48:03
MAKING A FOOL OUT OF ME...
I DON'T WANT HIM TO THINK...
...I'M SOME KIND OF *CHILD*...
BIP
Gimme seconds!!
Quiet, you!

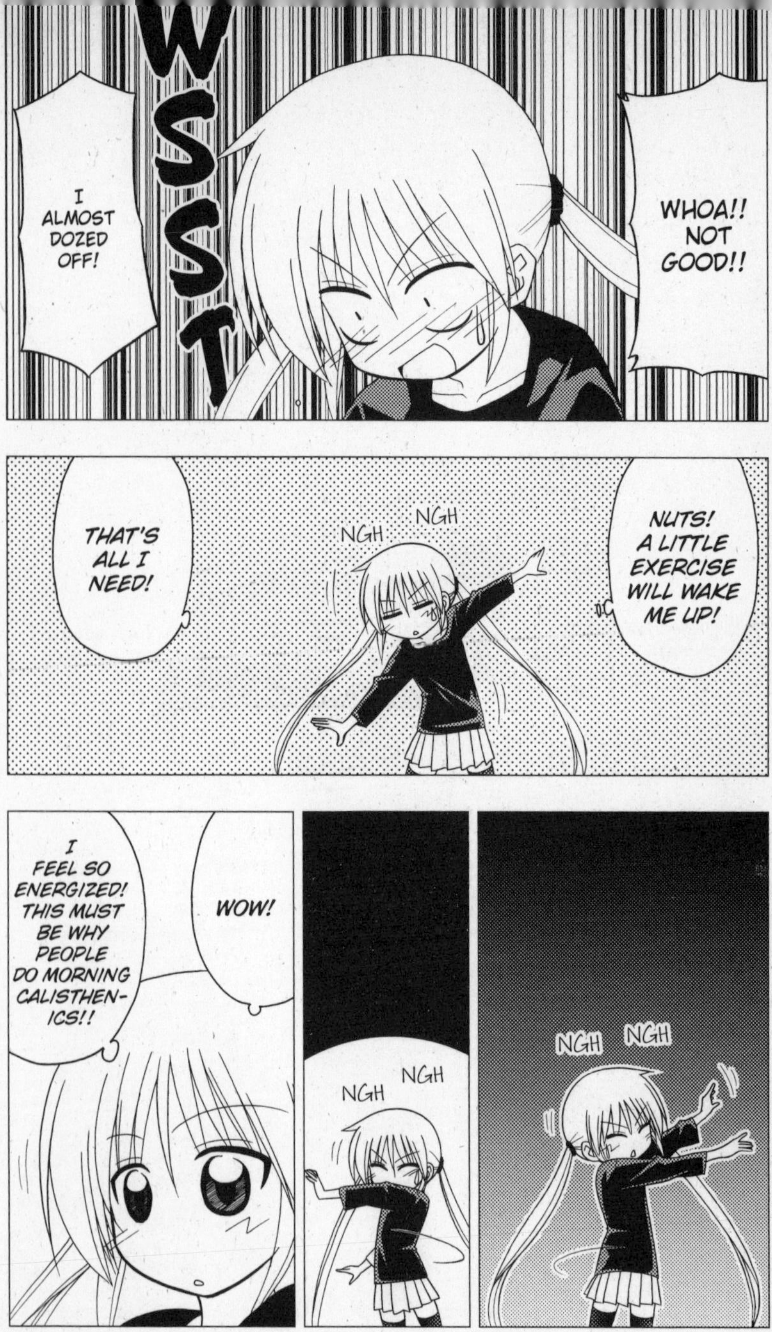
WHOA!! NOT GOOD!!
WSST
I ALMOST DOZED OFF!
NUTS! A LITTLE EXERCISE WILL WAKE ME UP!
NGH NGH
THAT'S ALL I NEED!
NGH NGH
NGH NGH
WOW!
I FEEL SO ENERGIZED! THIS MUST BE WHY PEOPLE DO MORNING CALISTHEN-ICS!!

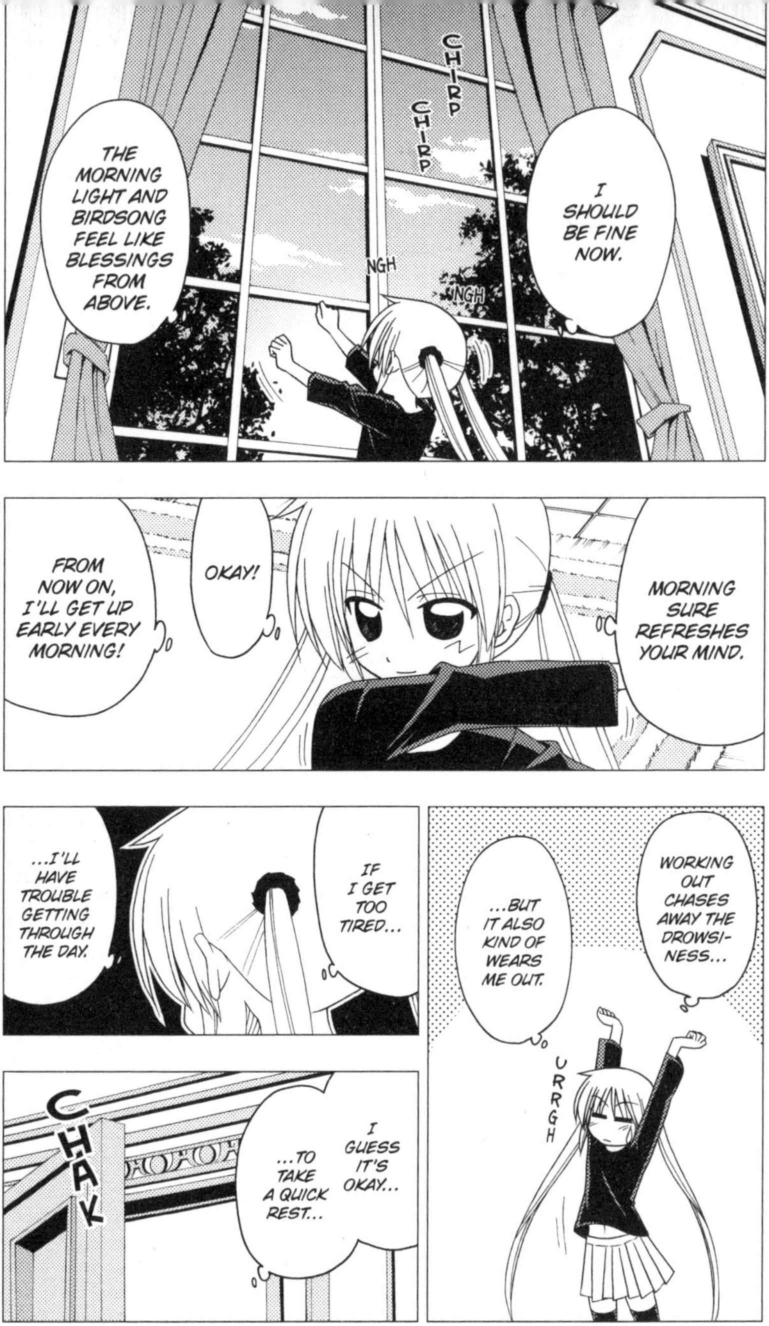
CHIRP
CHIRP
I SHOULD BE FINE NOW.
THE MORNING LIGHT AND BIRDSONG FEEL LIKE BLESSINGS FROM ABOVE.
NGH
NGH
MORNING SURE REFRESHES YOUR MIND.
OKAY!
FROM NOW ON, I'LL GET UP EARLY EVERY MORNING!
WORKING OUT CHASES AWAY THE DROWSI-NESS...
...BUT IT ALSO KIND OF WEARS ME OUT.
URRGH
IF I GET TOO TIRED...
...I'LL HAVE TROUBLE GETTING THROUGH THE DAY.
I GUESS IT'S OKAY...
...TO TAKE A QUICK REST...
CHAK

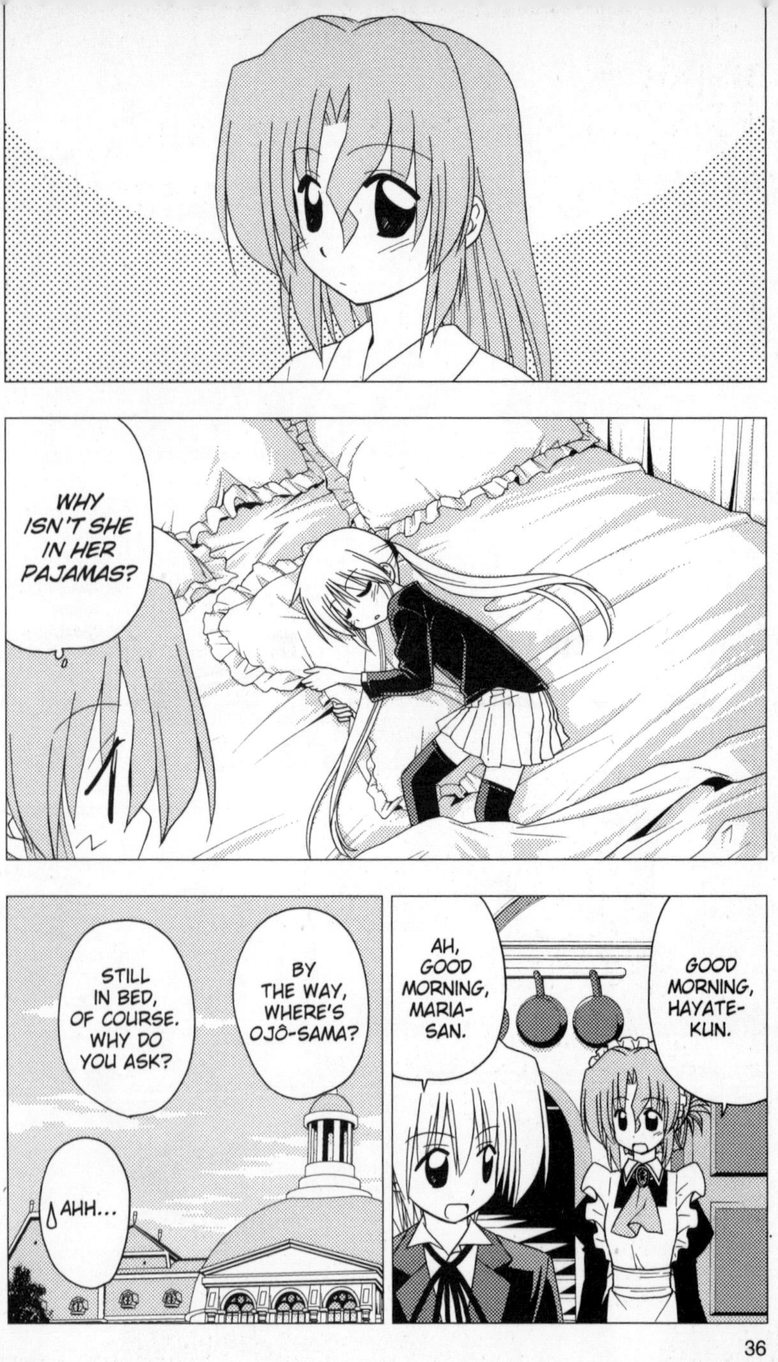
WHY ISN'T SHE IN HER PAJAMAS?
GOOD MORNING, HAYATE-KUN.
AH, GOOD MORNING, MARIA-SAN.
BY THE WAY, WHERE'S OJÔ-SAMA?
STILL IN BED, OF COURSE. WHY DO YOU ASK?
AHH...

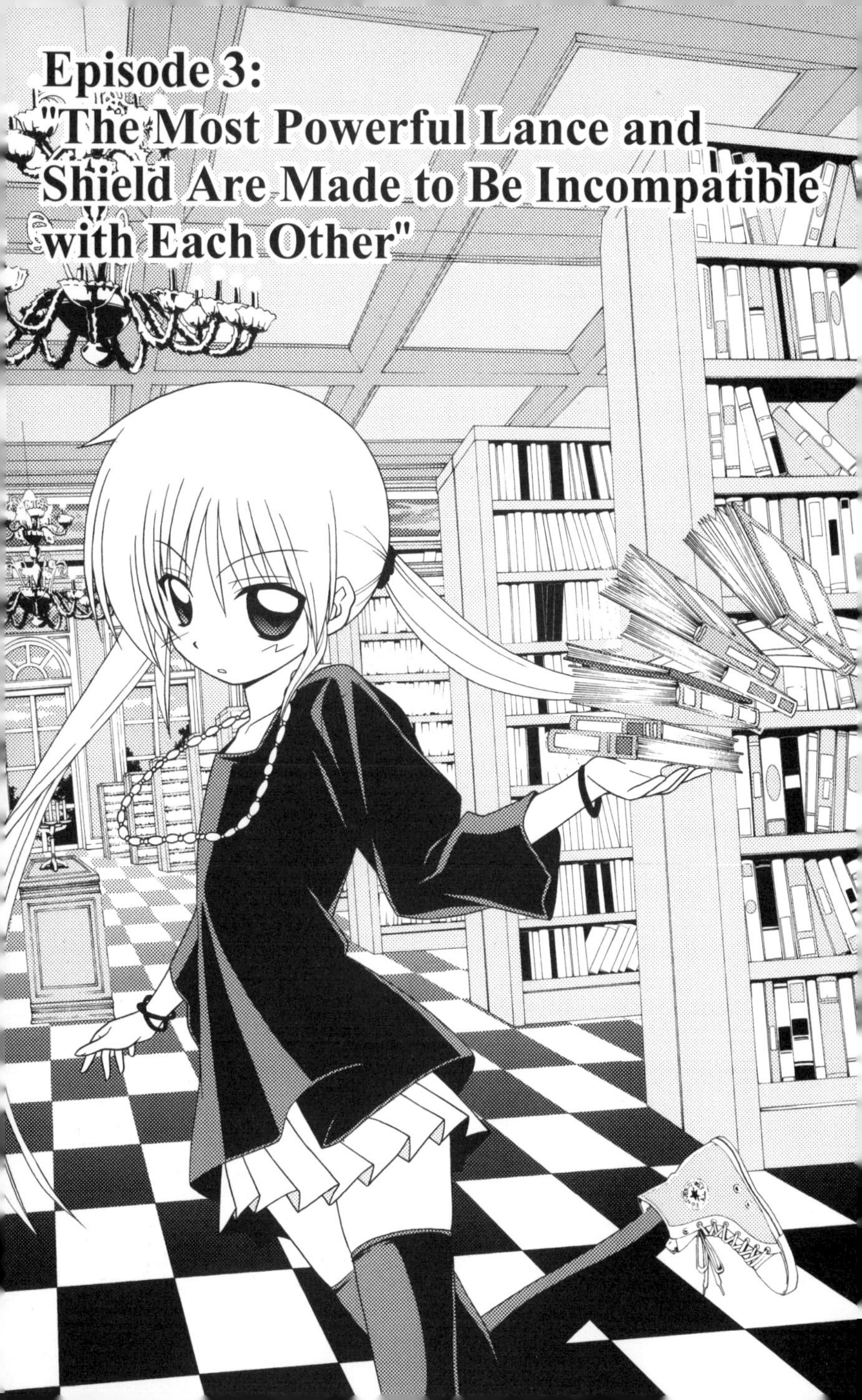
Episode 3:
"The Most Powerful Lance and Shield Are Made to Be Incompatible with Each Other"

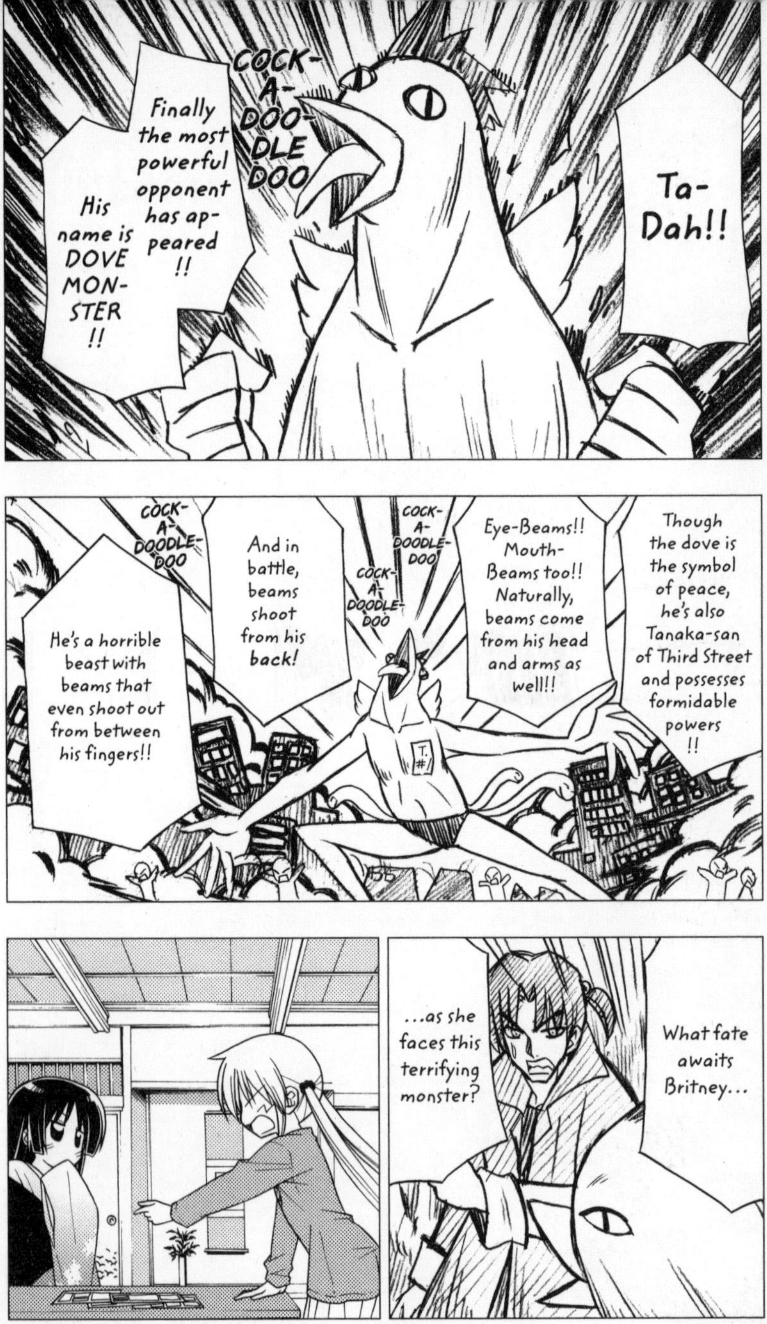
Ta-Dah!!
COCK-A-DOO-DLE DOO
Finally the most powerful opponent has appeared!!
His name is DOVE MONSTER!!
Though the dove is the symbol of peace, he's also Tanaka-san of Third Street and possesses formidable powers!!
Eye-Beams!! Mouth-Beams too!! Naturally, beams come from his head and arms as well!!
COCK-A-DOODLE-DOO
COCK-A-DOODLE-DOO
And in battle, beams shoot from his back!
COCK-A-DOODLE-DOO
He's a horrible beast with beams that even shoot out from between his fingers!!
What fate awaits Britney...
...as she faces this terrifying monster?

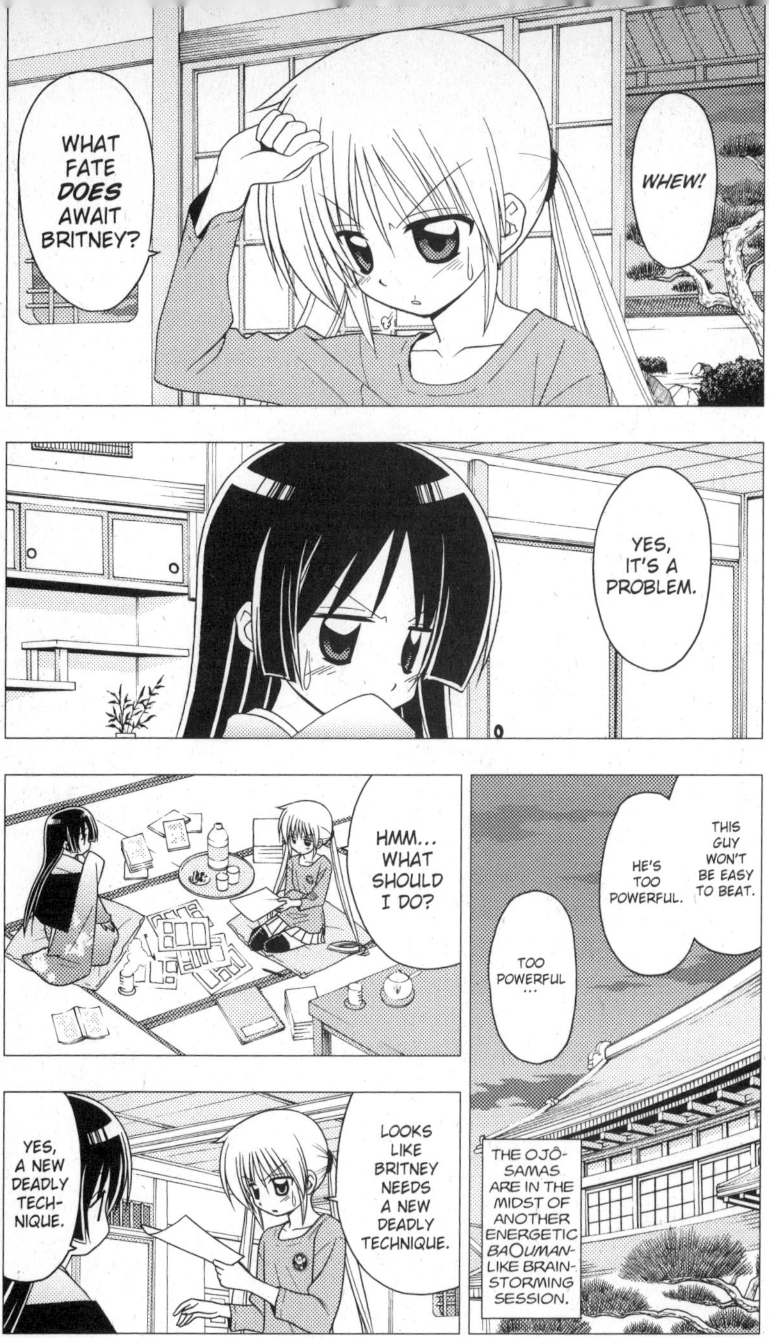
WHEW!
WHAT FATE DOES AWAIT BRITNEY?
YES, IT'S A PROBLEM.
THIS GUY WON'T BE EASY TO BEAT.
HE'S TOO POWERFUL.
TOO POWERFUL...
THE OJÔ-SAMAS ARE IN THE MIDST OF ANOTHER ENERGETIC BAQUMAN-LIKE BRAIN-STORMING SESSION.
HMM... WHAT SHOULD I DO?
LOOKS LIKE BRITNEY NEEDS A NEW DEADLY TECHNIQUE.
YES, A NEW DEADLY TECHNIQUE.

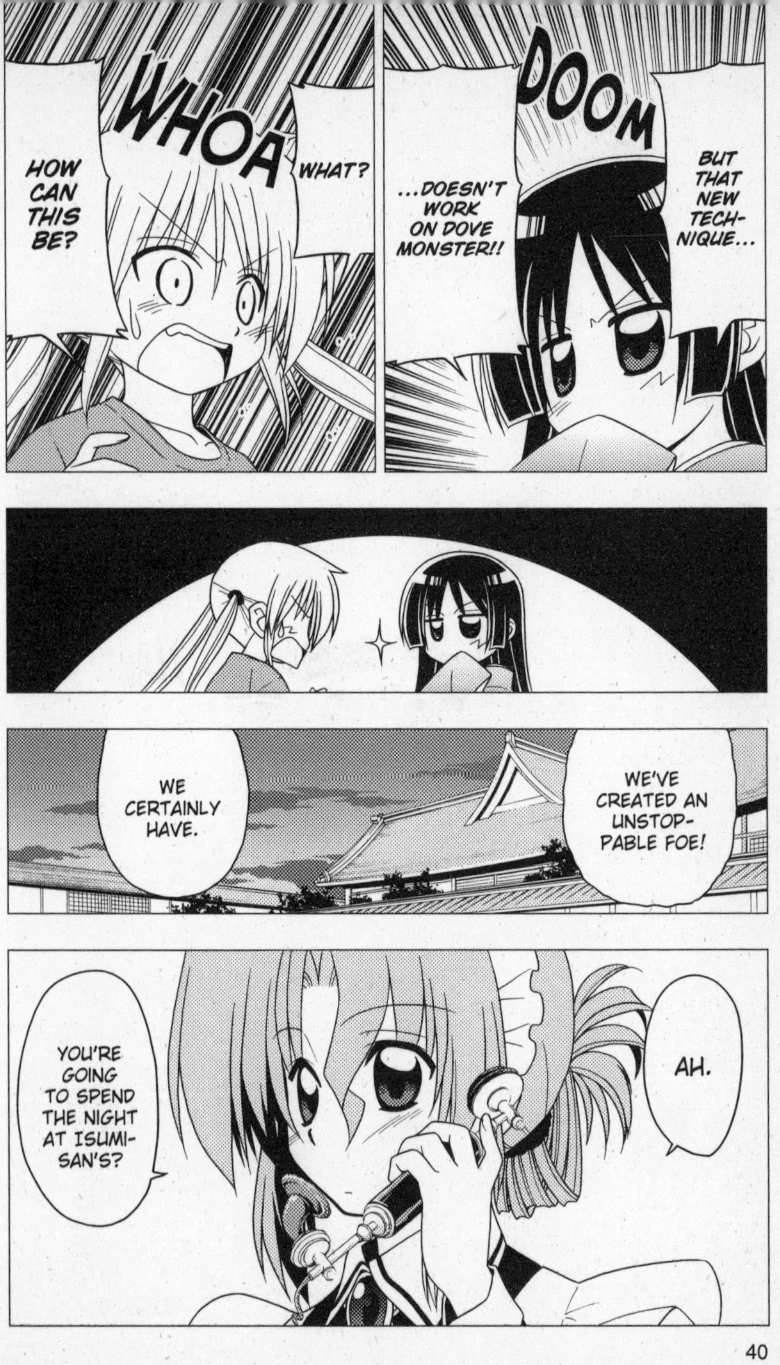
DOOM
BUT THAT NEW TECHNIQUE...
...DOESN'T WORK ON DOVE MONSTER!!
WHOA
WHAT?
HOW CAN THIS BE?
WE'VE CREATED AN UNSTOPPABLE FOE!
WE CERTAINLY HAVE.
AH.
YOU'RE GOING TO SPEND THE NIGHT AT ISUMI-SAN'S?

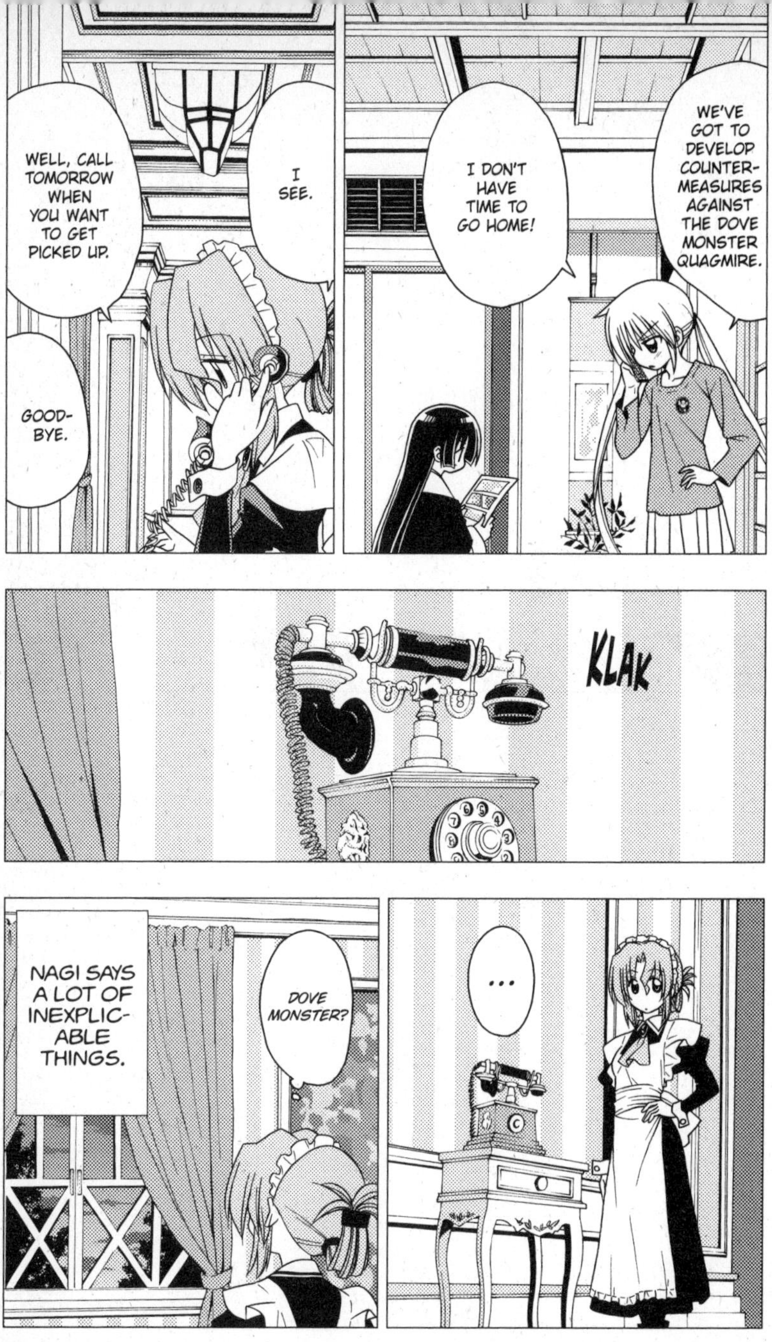
WE'VE GOT TO DEVELOP COUNTER-MEASURES AGAINST THE DOVE MONSTER QUAGMIRE.
I DON'T HAVE TIME TO GO HOME!
I SEE.
WELL, CALL TOMORROW WHEN YOU WANT TO GET PICKED UP.
GOOD-BYE.
KLAK
...
DOVE MONSTER?
NAGI SAYS A LOT OF INEXPLIC-ABLE THINGS.

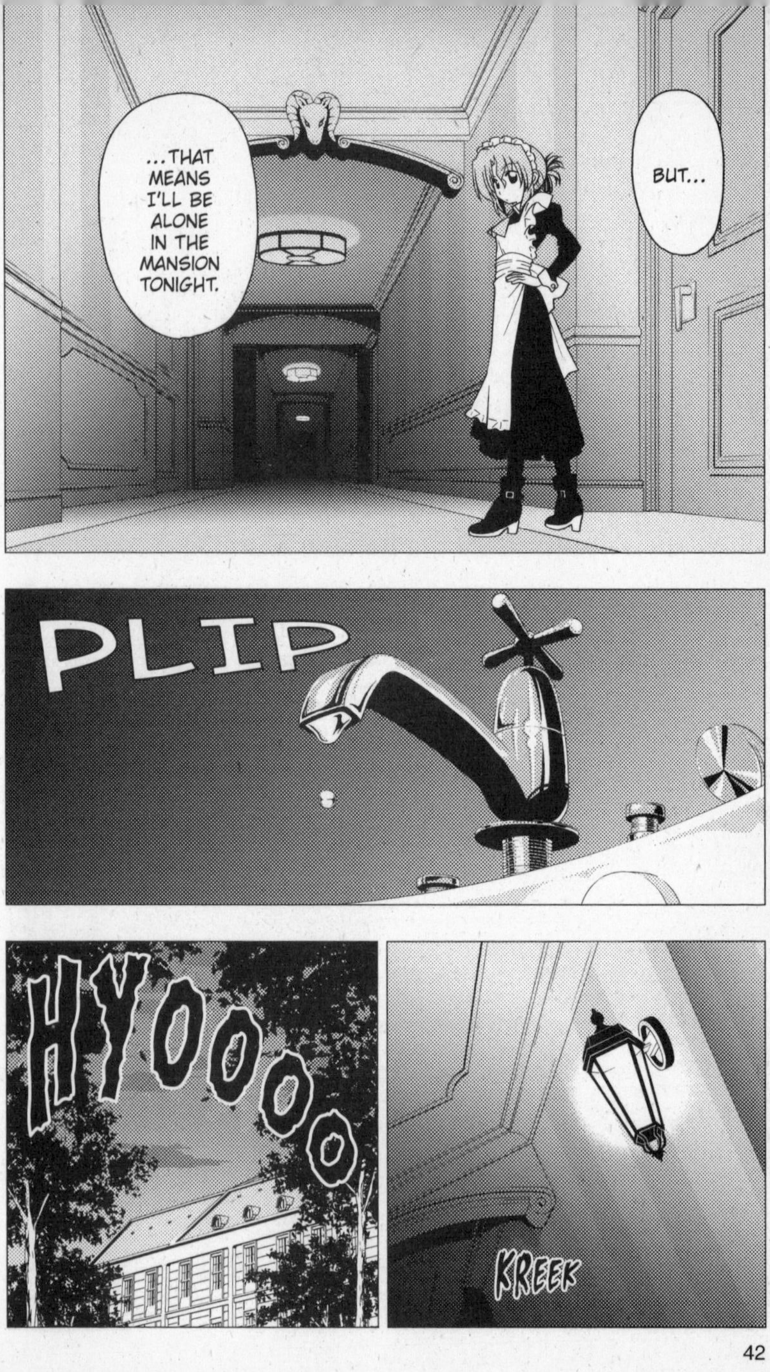
BUT...
...THAT MEANS I'LL BE ALONE IN THE MANSION TONIGHT.
PLIP
KREEK
HYOOOO

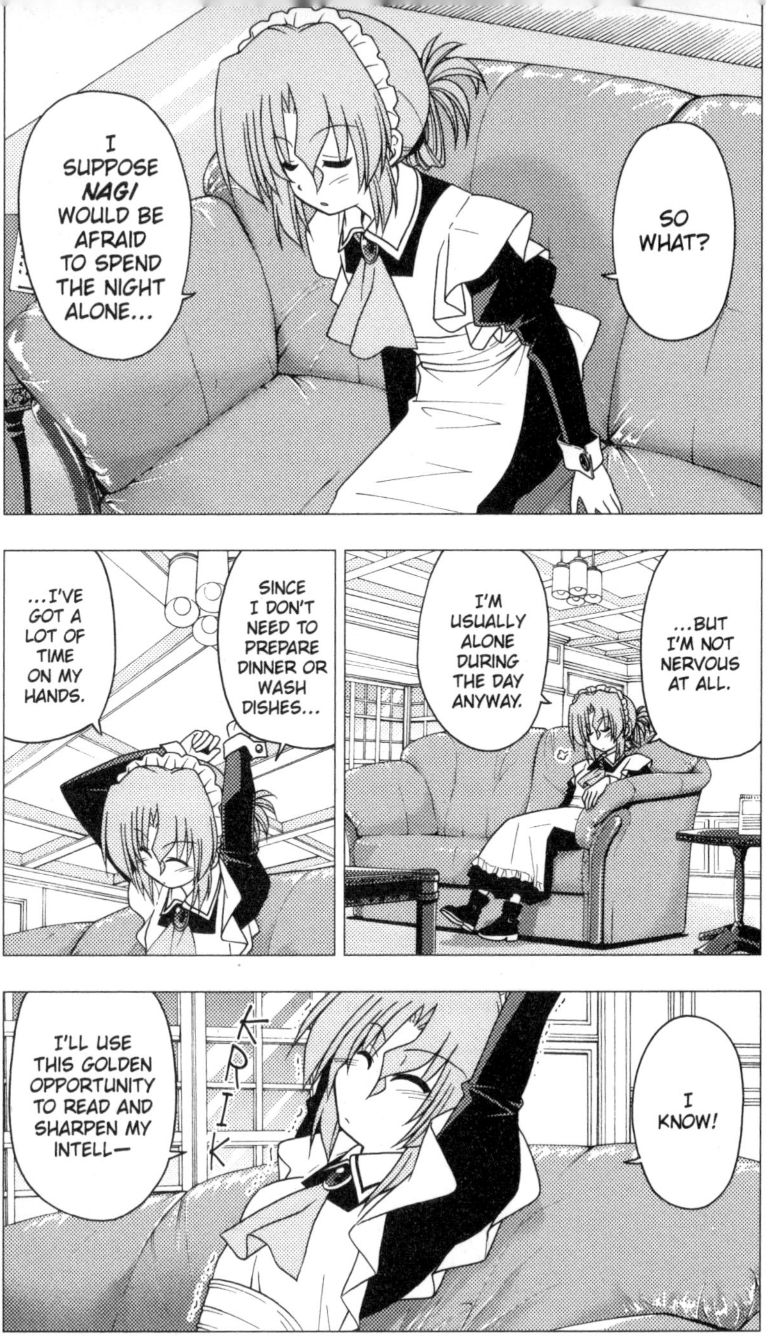
I SUPPOSE NAGI WOULD BE AFRAID TO SPEND THE NIGHT ALONE...
SO WHAT?
...BUT I'M NOT NERVOUS AT ALL.
I'M USUALLY ALONE DURING THE DAY ANYWAY.
SINCE I DON'T NEED TO PREPARE DINNER OR WASH DISHES...
...I'VE GOT A LOT OF TIME ON MY HANDS.
I KNOW!
KRIK
I'LL USE THIS GOLDEN OPPORTUNITY TO READ AND SHARPEN MY INTELL—

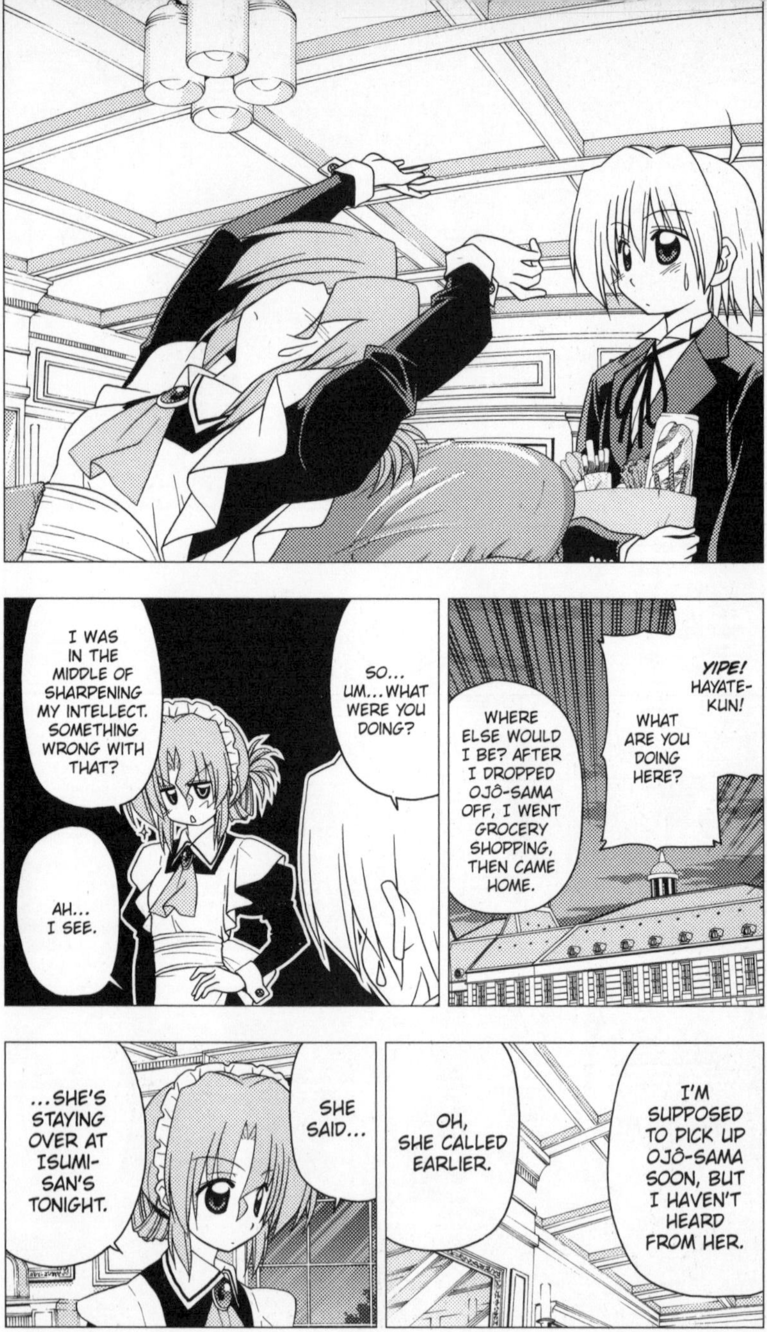
YIPE! HAYATE-KUN! WHAT ARE YOU DOING HERE?
WHERE ELSE WOULD I BE? AFTER I DROPPED OJÔ-SAMA OFF, I WENT GROCERY SHOPPING, THEN CAME HOME.
SO... UM...WHAT WERE YOU DOING?
I WAS IN THE MIDDLE OF SHARPENING MY INTELLECT. SOMETHING WRONG WITH THAT?
AH... I SEE.
I'M SUPPOSED TO PICK UP OJÔ-SAMA SOON, BUT I HAVEN'T HEARD FROM HER.
OH, SHE CALLED EARLIER.
SHE SAID...
...SHE'S STAYING OVER AT ISUMI-SAN'S TONIGHT.

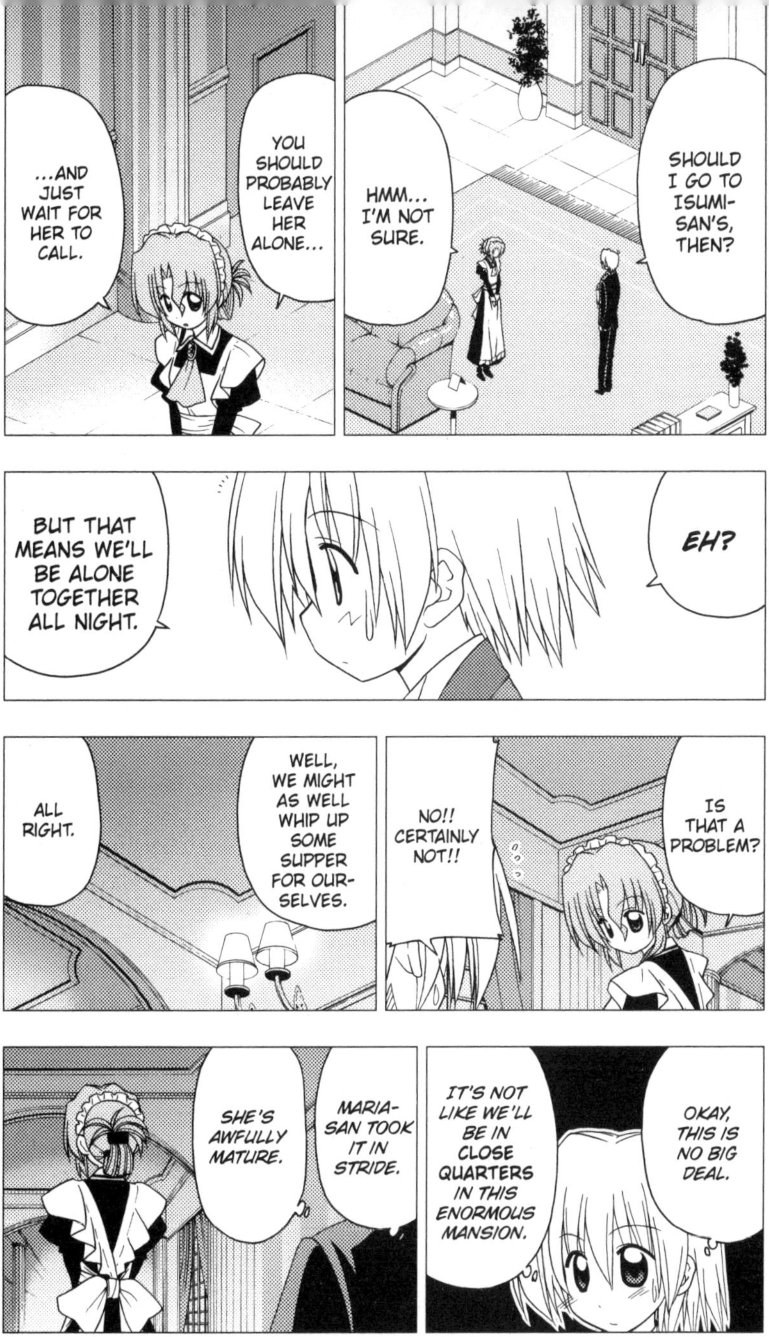
SHOULD I GO TO ISUMI-SAN'S, THEN?
HMM... I'M NOT SURE.
YOU SHOULD PROBABLY LEAVE HER ALONE...
...AND JUST WAIT FOR HER TO CALL.
EH?
BUT THAT MEANS WE'LL BE ALONE TOGETHER ALL NIGHT.
IS THAT A PROBLEM?
NO!! CERTAINLY NOT!!
WELL, WE MIGHT AS WELL WHIP UP SOME SUPPER FOR OUR-SELVES.
ALL RIGHT.
OKAY, THIS IS NO BIG DEAL.
IT'S NOT LIKE WE'LL BE IN CLOSE QUARTERS IN THIS ENORMOUS MANSION.
MARIA-SAN TOOK IT IN STRIDE.
SHE'S AWFULLY MATURE.

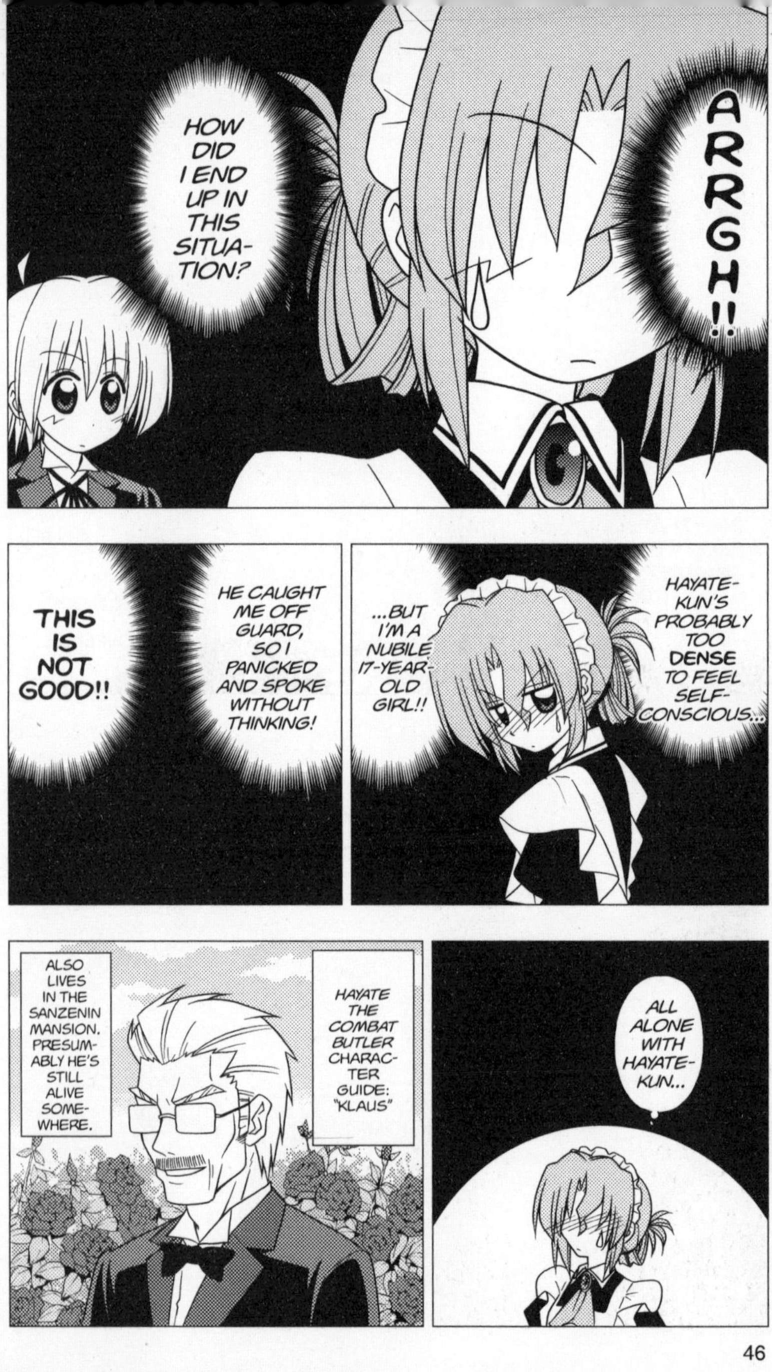
ARRGH!!
HOW DID I END UP IN THIS SITUATION?
HAYATE-KUN'S PROBABLY TOO DENSE TO FEEL SELF-CONSCIOUS...
...BUT I'M A NUBILE 17-YEAR-OLD GIRL!!
HE CAUGHT ME OFF GUARD, SO I PANICKED AND SPOKE WITHOUT THINKING!
THIS IS NOT GOOD!!
ALL ALONE WITH HAYATE-KUN...
HAYATE THE COMBAT BUTLER CHARACTER GUIDE: "KLAUS"
ALSO LIVES IN THE SANZENIN MANSION. PRESUMABLY HE'S STILL ALIVE SOMEWHERE.

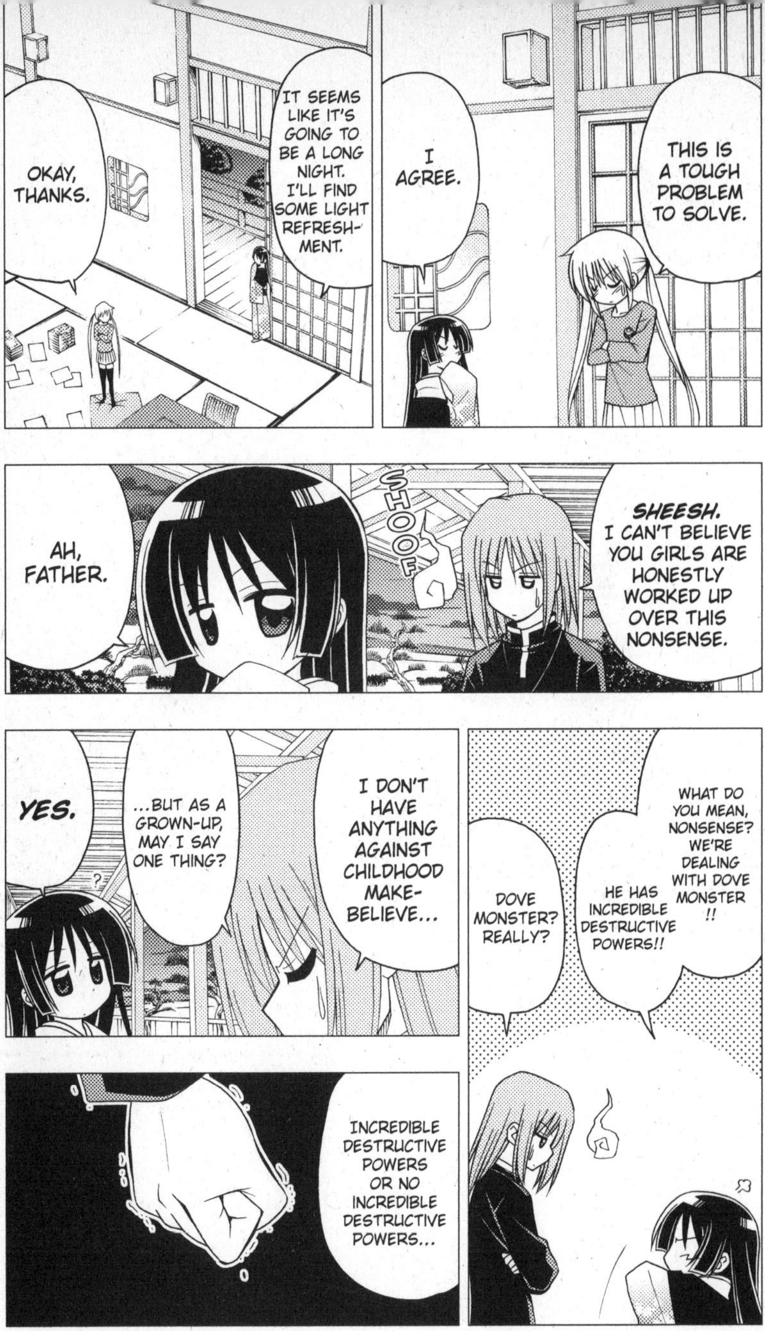
THIS IS A TOUGH PROBLEM TO SOLVE.
I AGREE.
IT SEEMS LIKE IT'S GOING TO BE A LONG NIGHT. I'LL FIND SOME LIGHT REFRESHMENT.
OKAY, THANKS.
SHEESH. I CAN'T BELIEVE YOU GIRLS ARE HONESTLY WORKED UP OVER THIS NONSENSE.
SHOOF
AH, FATHER.
WHAT DO YOU MEAN, NONSENSE? WE'RE DEALING WITH DOVE MONSTER!!
HE HAS INCREDIBLE DESTRUCTIVE POWERS!!
DOVE MONSTER? REALLY?
I DON'T HAVE ANYTHING AGAINST CHILDHOOD MAKE-BELIEVE...
...BUT AS A GROWN-UP, MAY I SAY ONE THING?
YES.
?
INCREDIBLE DESTRUCTIVE POWERS OR NO INCREDIBLE DESTRUCTIVE POWERS...

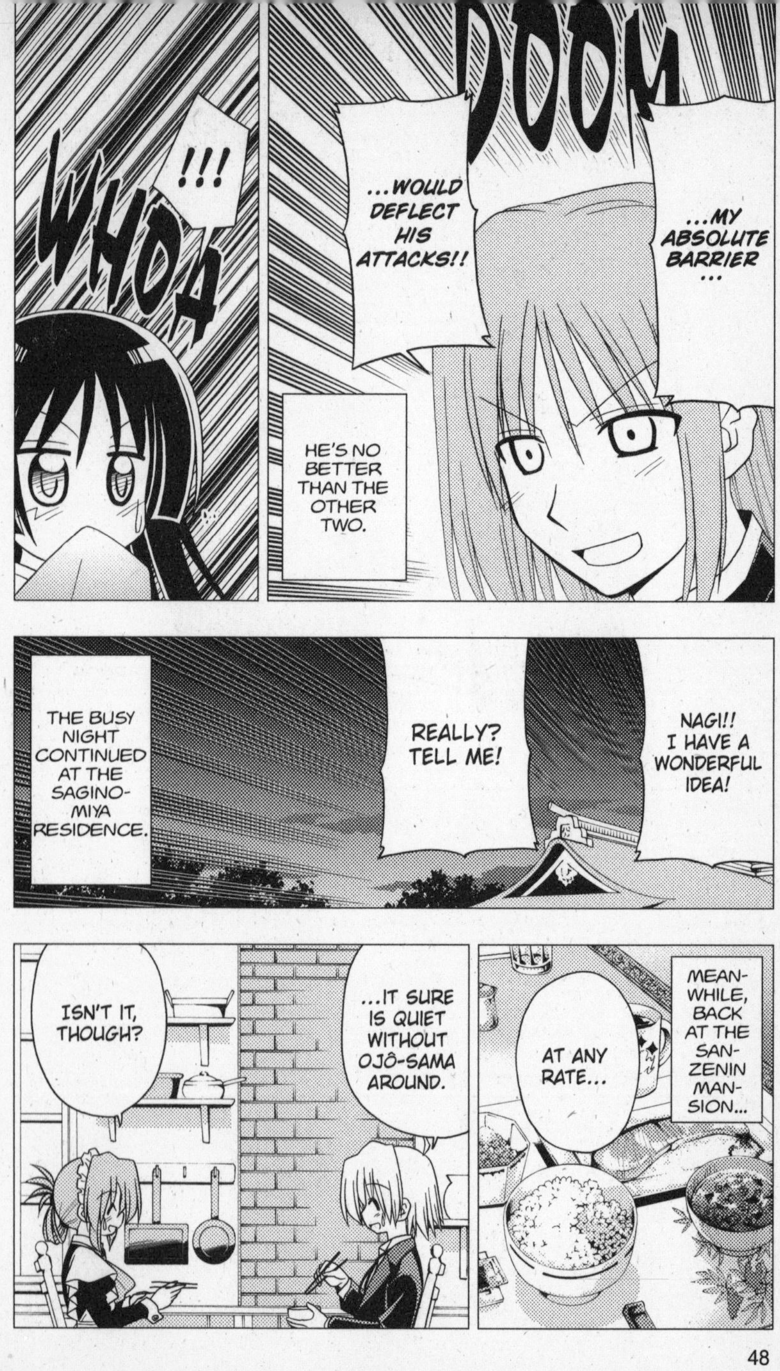
DOOM
...MY ABSOLUTE BARRIER...
...WOULD DEFLECT HIS ATTACKS!!
HE'S NO BETTER THAN THE OTHER TWO.
!!!
WHOA
NAGI!! I HAVE A WONDERFUL IDEA!
REALLY? TELL ME!
THE BUSY NIGHT CONTINUED AT THE SAGINO-MIYA RESIDENCE.
MEAN-WHILE, BACK AT THE SAN-ZENIN MAN-SION...
AT ANY RATE...
...IT SURE IS QUIET WITHOUT OJÔ-SAMA AROUND.
ISN'T IT, THOUGH?

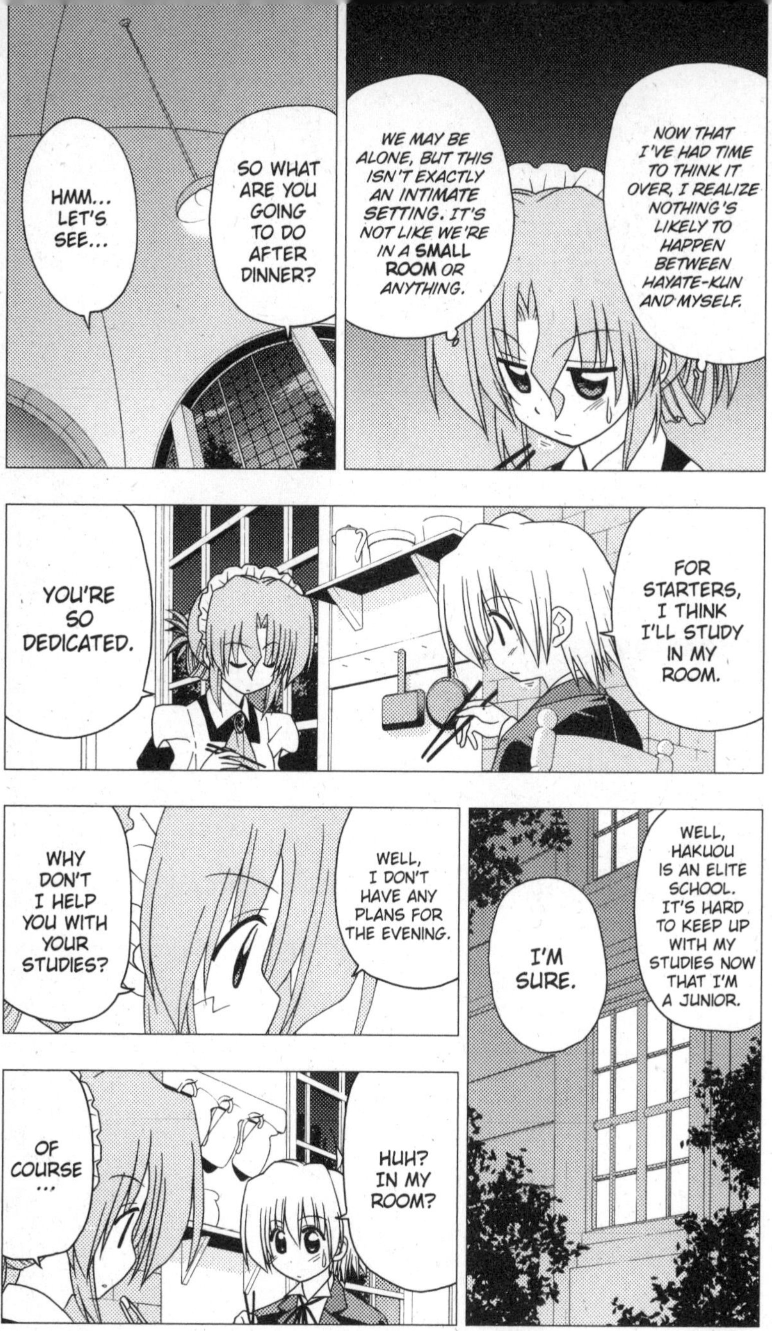
NOW THAT I'VE HAD TIME TO THINK IT OVER, I REALIZE NOTHING'S LIKELY TO HAPPEN BETWEEN HAYATE-KUN AND MYSELF.
WE MAY BE ALONE, BUT THIS ISN'T EXACTLY AN INTIMATE SETTING. IT'S NOT LIKE WE'RE IN A SMALL ROOM OR ANYTHING.
SO WHAT ARE YOU GOING TO DO AFTER DINNER?
HMM... LET'S SEE...
FOR STARTERS, I THINK I'LL STUDY IN MY ROOM.
YOU'RE SO DEDICATED.
WELL, HAKUOU IS AN ELITE SCHOOL. IT'S HARD TO KEEP UP WITH MY STUDIES NOW THAT I'M A JUNIOR.
I'M SURE.
WELL, I DON'T HAVE ANY PLANS FOR THE EVENING.
WHY DON'T I HELP YOU WITH YOUR STUDIES?
HUH? IN MY ROOM?
OF COURSE...

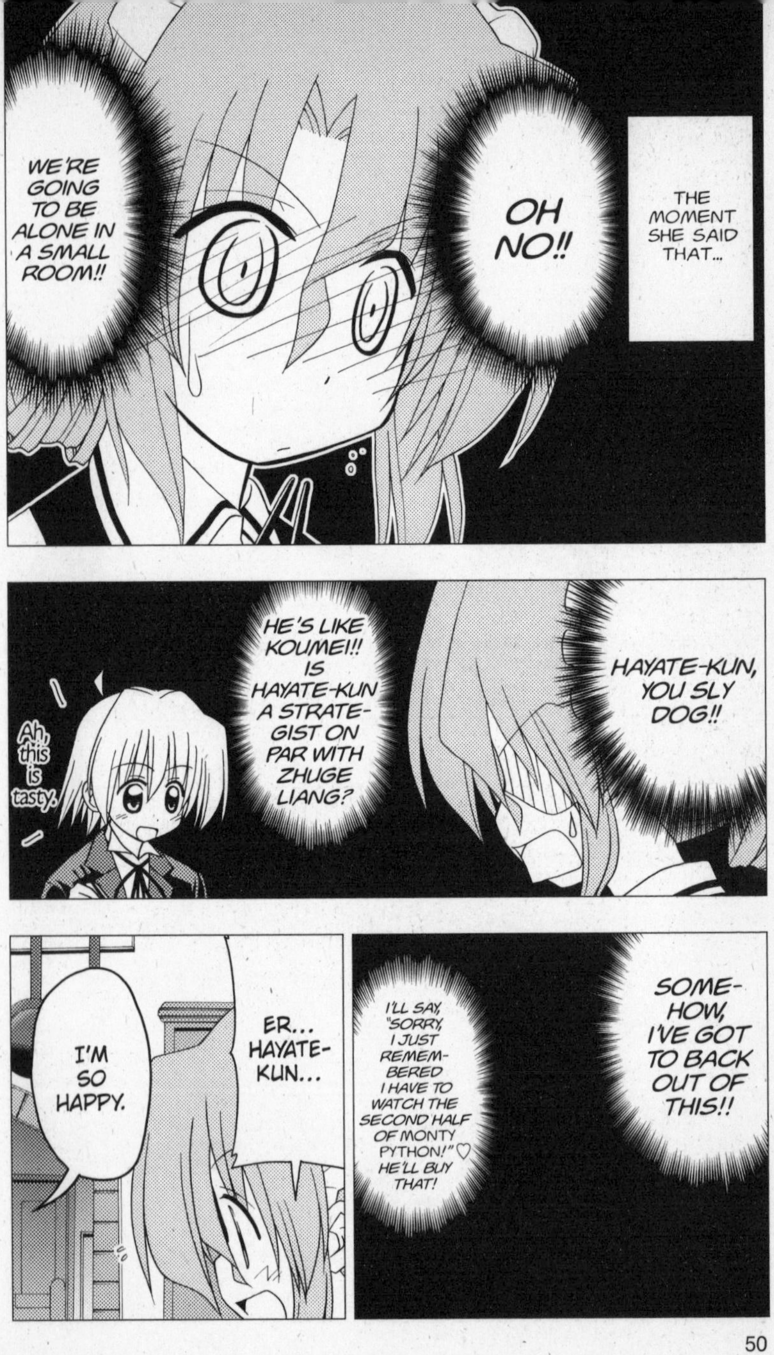
THE MOMENT SHE SAID THAT...
OH NO!!
WE'RE GOING TO BE ALONE IN A SMALL ROOM!!
HAYATE-KUN, YOU SLY DOG!!
HE'S LIKE KOUMEI!! IS HAYATE-KUN A STRATE-GIST ON PAR WITH ZHUGE LIANG?
Ah, this is tasty.
SOME-HOW, I'VE GOT TO BACK OUT OF THIS!!
I'LL SAY, "SORRY, I JUST REMEM-BERED I HAVE TO WATCH THE SECOND HALF OF MONTY PYTHON!"♡ HE'LL BUY THAT!
ER... HAYATE-KUN...
I'M SO HAPPY.

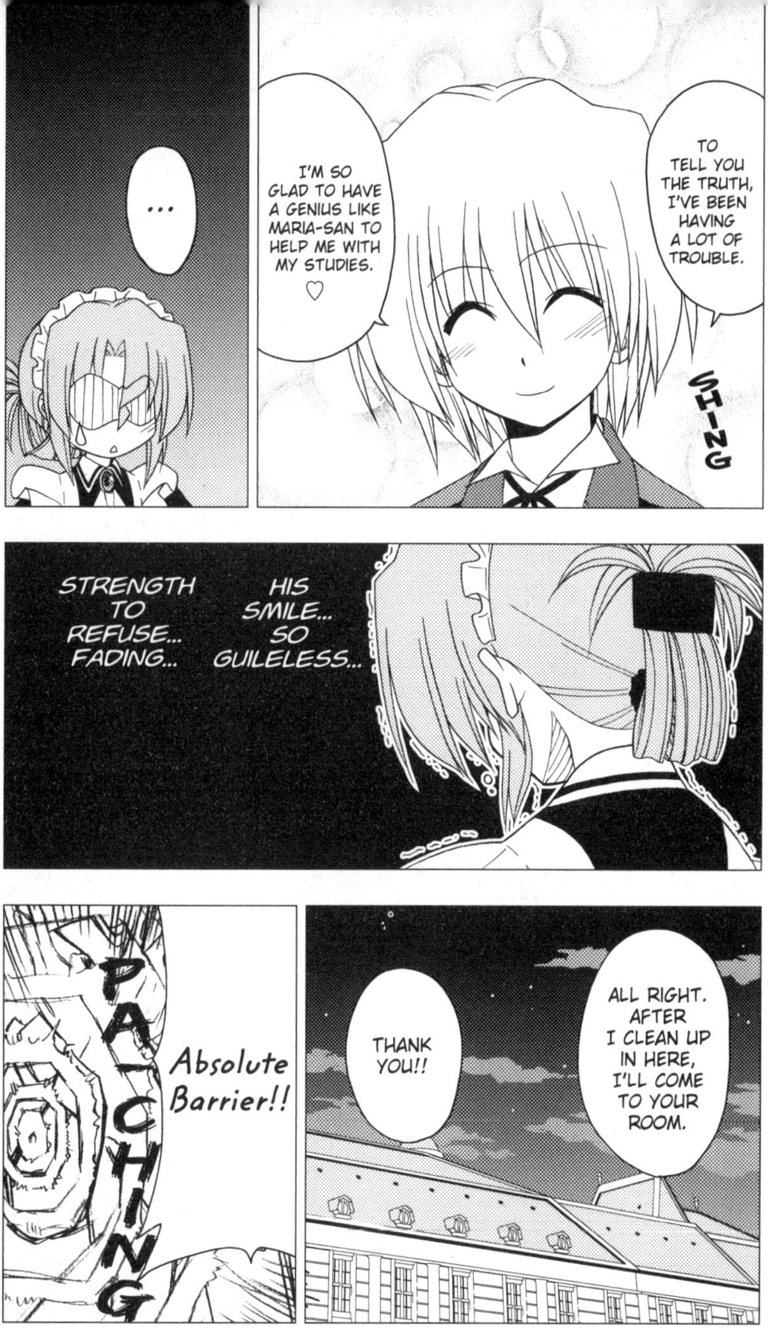
TO TELL YOU THE TRUTH, I'VE BEEN HAVING A LOT OF TROUBLE.
I'M SO GLAD TO HAVE A GENIUS LIKE MARIA-SAN TO HELP ME WITH MY STUDIES. ♡
SHING
...
HIS SMILE... SO GUILELESS...
STRENGTH TO REFUSE... FADING...
ALL RIGHT. AFTER I CLEAN UP IN HERE, I'LL COME TO YOUR ROOM.
THANK YOU!!
Absolute Barrier!!
PA-CHING

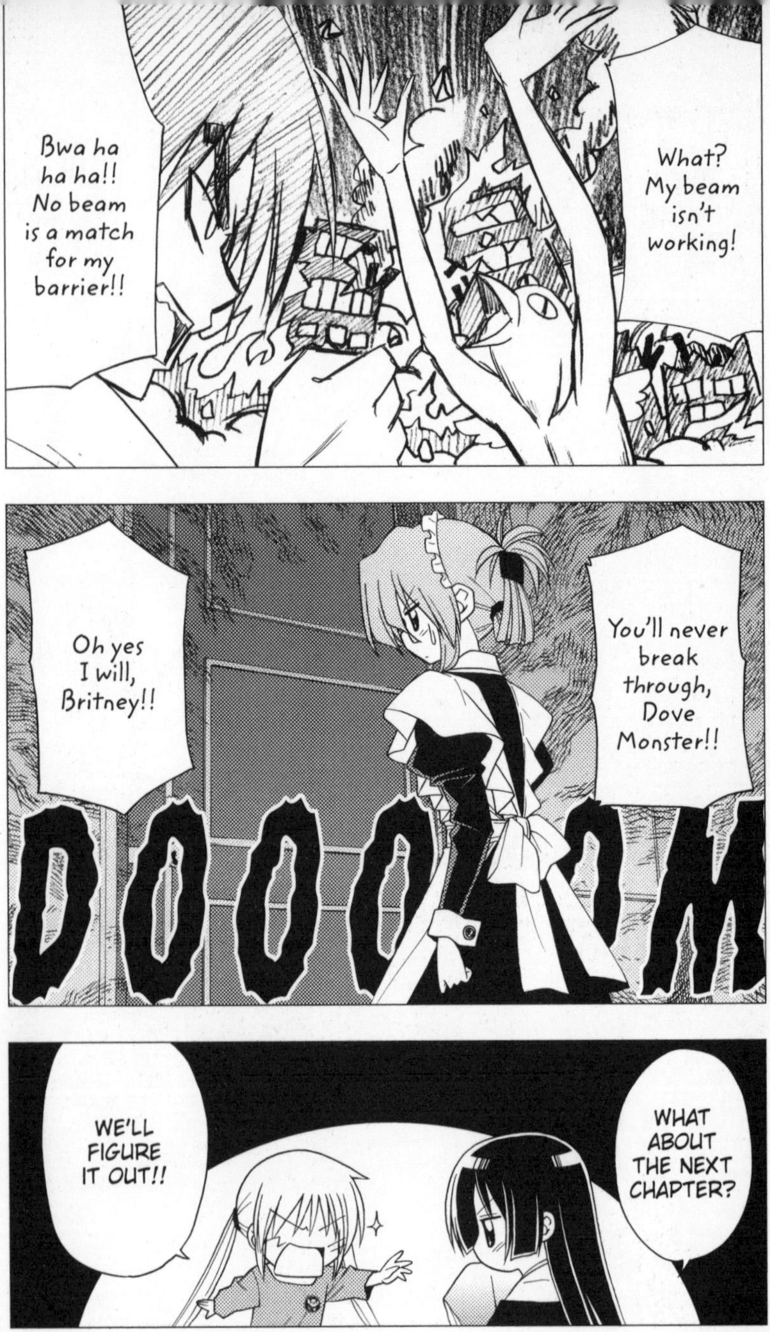

What? My beam isn't working!
Bwa ha ha ha!! No beam is a match for my barrier!!
You'll never break through, Dove Monster!!
Oh yes I will, Britney!!
DOOOOM
WHAT ABOUT THE NEXT CHAPTER?
WE'LL FIGURE IT OUT!!

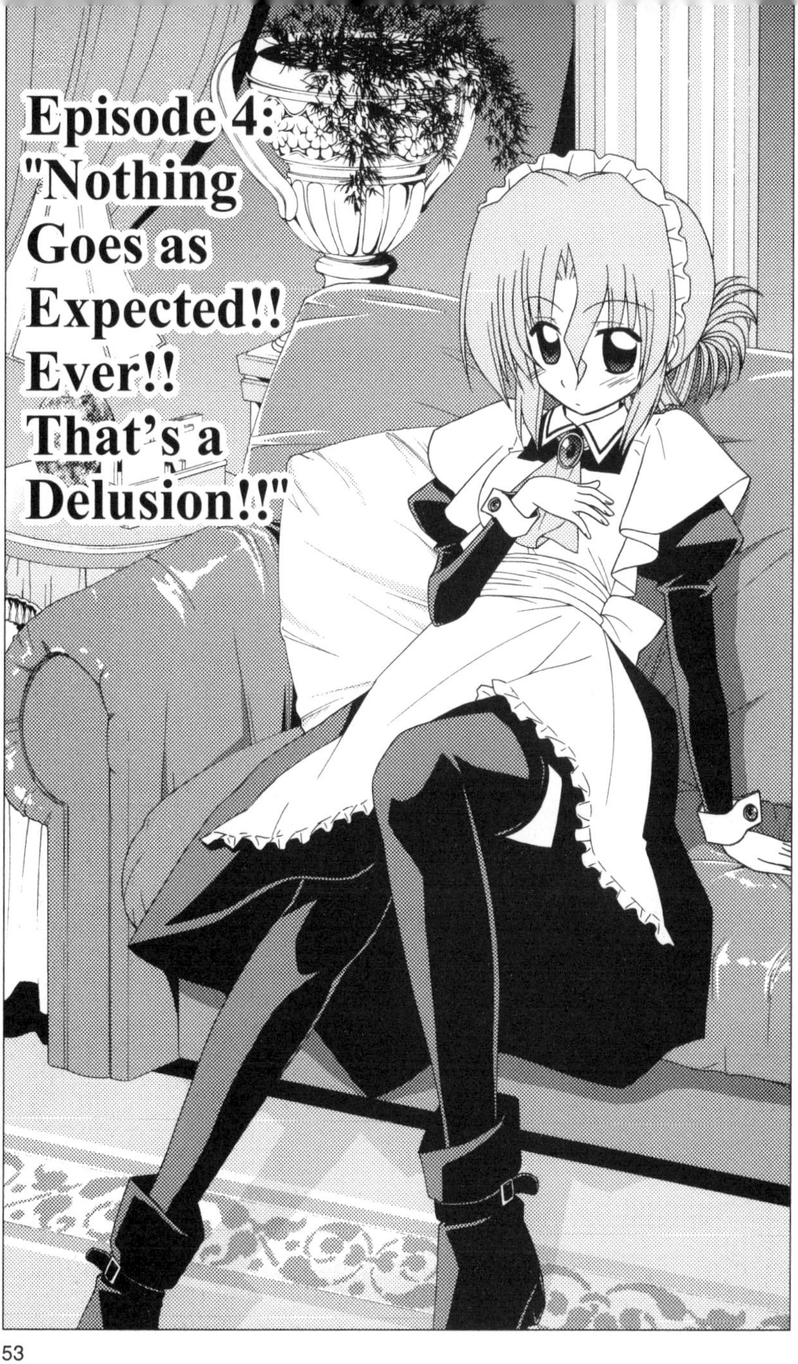
Episode 4: "Nothing Goes as Expected!! Ever!! That's a Delusion!!"

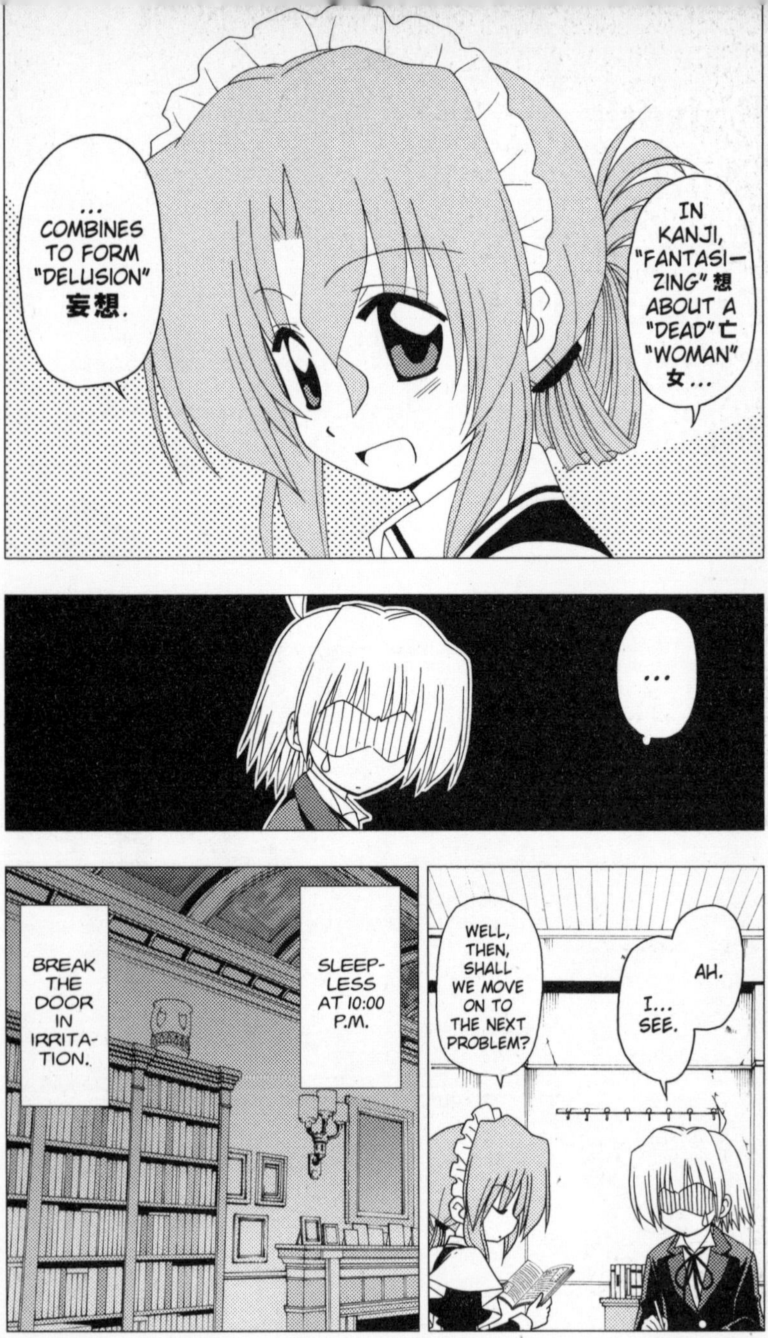
IN KANJI, "FANTASI-ZING" 想 ABOUT A "DEAD" 亡 "WOMAN" 女...
... COMBINES TO FORM "DELUSION" 妄想.
...
AH. I... SEE.
WELL, THEN, SHALL WE MOVE ON TO THE NEXT PROBLEM?
SLEEP-LESS AT 10:00 P.M.
BREAK THE DOOR IN IRRITA-TION..

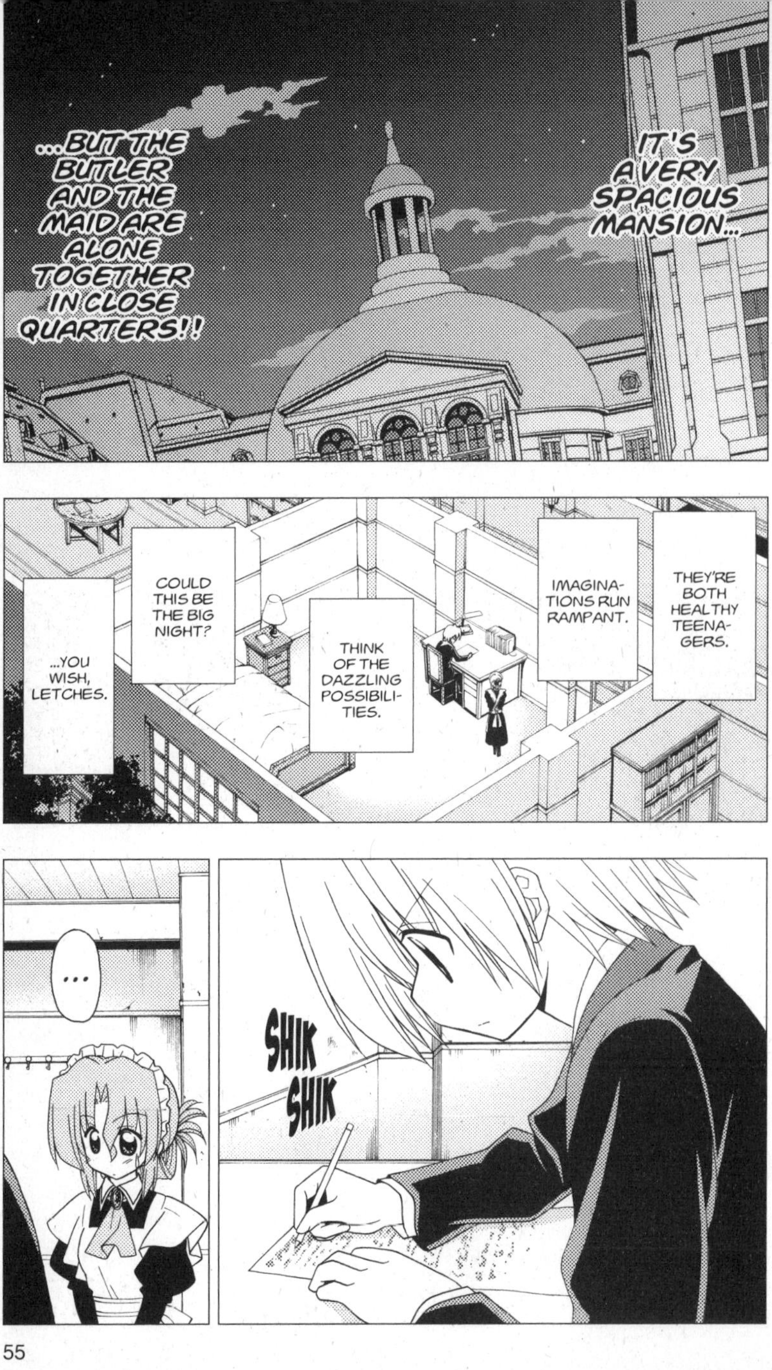
IT'S A VERY SPACIOUS MANSION...
...BUT THE BUTLER AND THE MAID ARE ALONE TOGETHER IN CLOSE QUARTERS!!
THEY'RE BOTH HEALTHY TEENAGERS.
IMAGINATIONS RUN RAMPANT.
THINK OF THE DAZZLING POSSIBILITIES.
COULD THIS BE THE BIG NIGHT?
...YOU WISH, LETCHES.
SHIK SHIK
...

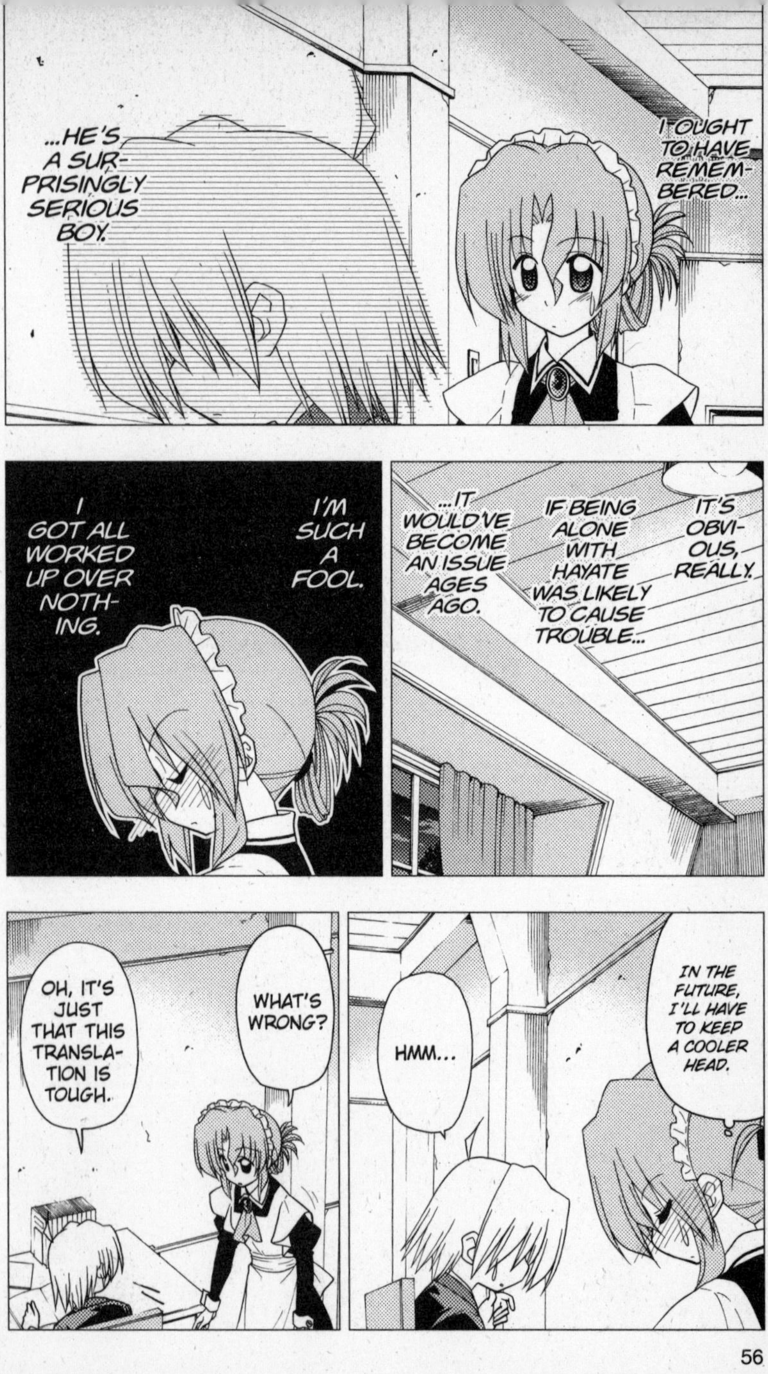
I OUGHT TO HAVE REMEMBERED...
...HE'S A SURPRISINGLY SERIOUS BOY.
IT'S OBVIOUS, REALLY.
IF BEING ALONE WITH HAYATE WAS LIKELY TO CAUSE TROUBLE...
...IT WOULD'VE BECOME AN ISSUE AGES AGO.
I'M SUCH A FOOL.
I GOT ALL WORKED UP OVER NOTHING.
IN THE FUTURE, I'LL HAVE TO KEEP A COOLER HEAD.
HMM...
WHAT'S WRONG?
OH, IT'S JUST THAT THIS TRANSLATION IS TOUGH.

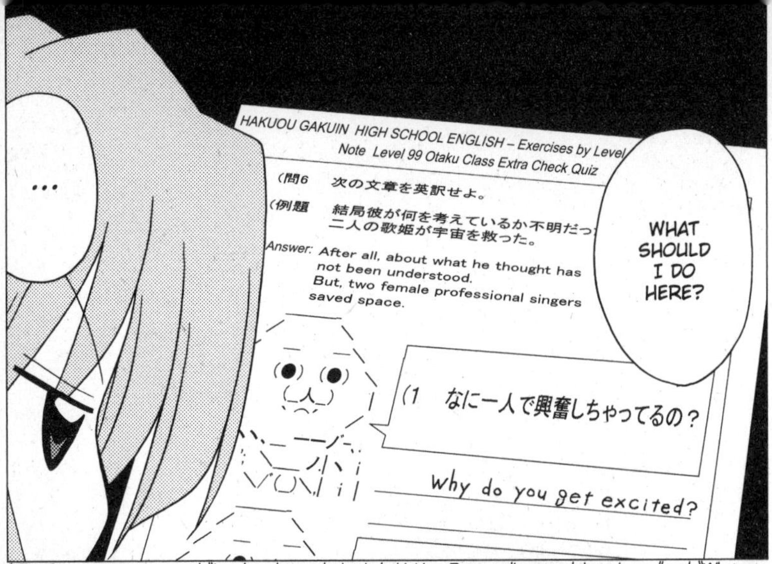
WHAT SHOULD I DO HERE?
HAKUOU GAKUIN HIGH SCHOOL ENGLISH – Exercises by Level
Note Level 99 Otaku Class Extra Check Quiz
(問6 次の文章を英訳せよ。
(例題 結局彼が何を考えているか不明だっ
二人の歌姫が宇宙を救った。
Answer: After all, about what he thought has not been understood.
But, two female professional singers saved space.
(1 なに一人で興奮しちゃってるの？
why do you get excited?
...

*The Japanese sentences read, "I can't understand what he's thinking. But two divas saved the universe," and, "What are you getting all excited about?"

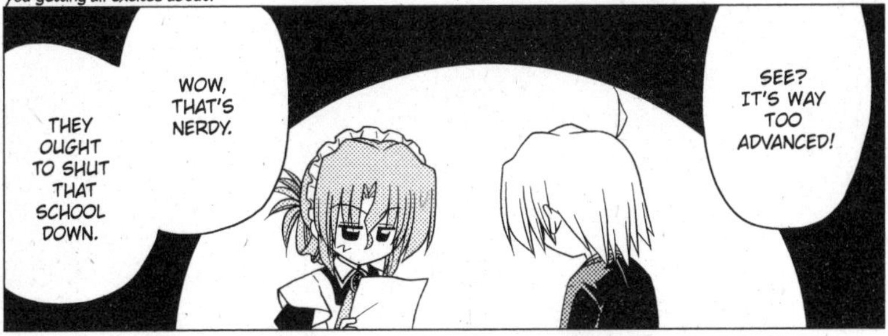
SEE? IT'S WAY TOO ADVANCED!
WOW, THAT'S NERDY.
THEY OUGHT TO SHUT THAT SCHOOL DOWN.

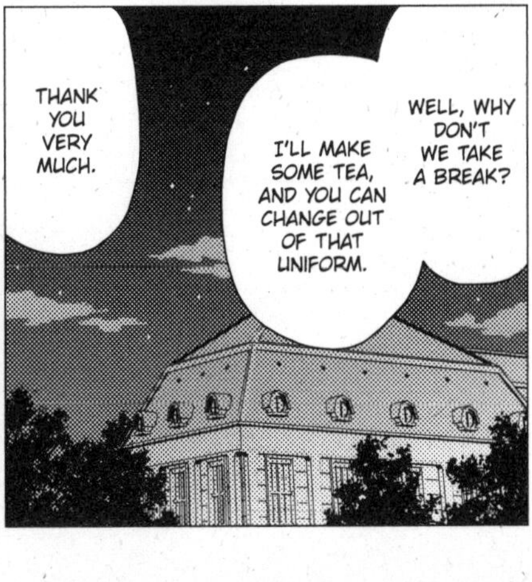
WELL, WHY DON'T WE TAKE A BREAK?
I'LL MAKE SOME TEA, AND YOU CAN CHANGE OUT OF THAT UNIFORM.
THANK YOU VERY MUCH.

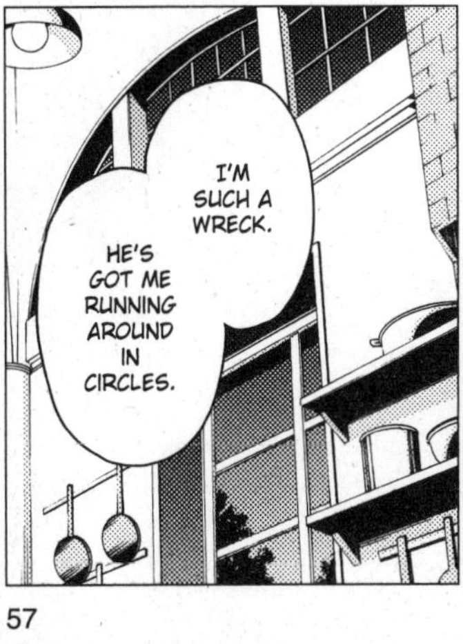
I'M SUCH A WRECK.
HE'S GOT ME RUNNING AROUND IN CIRCLES.

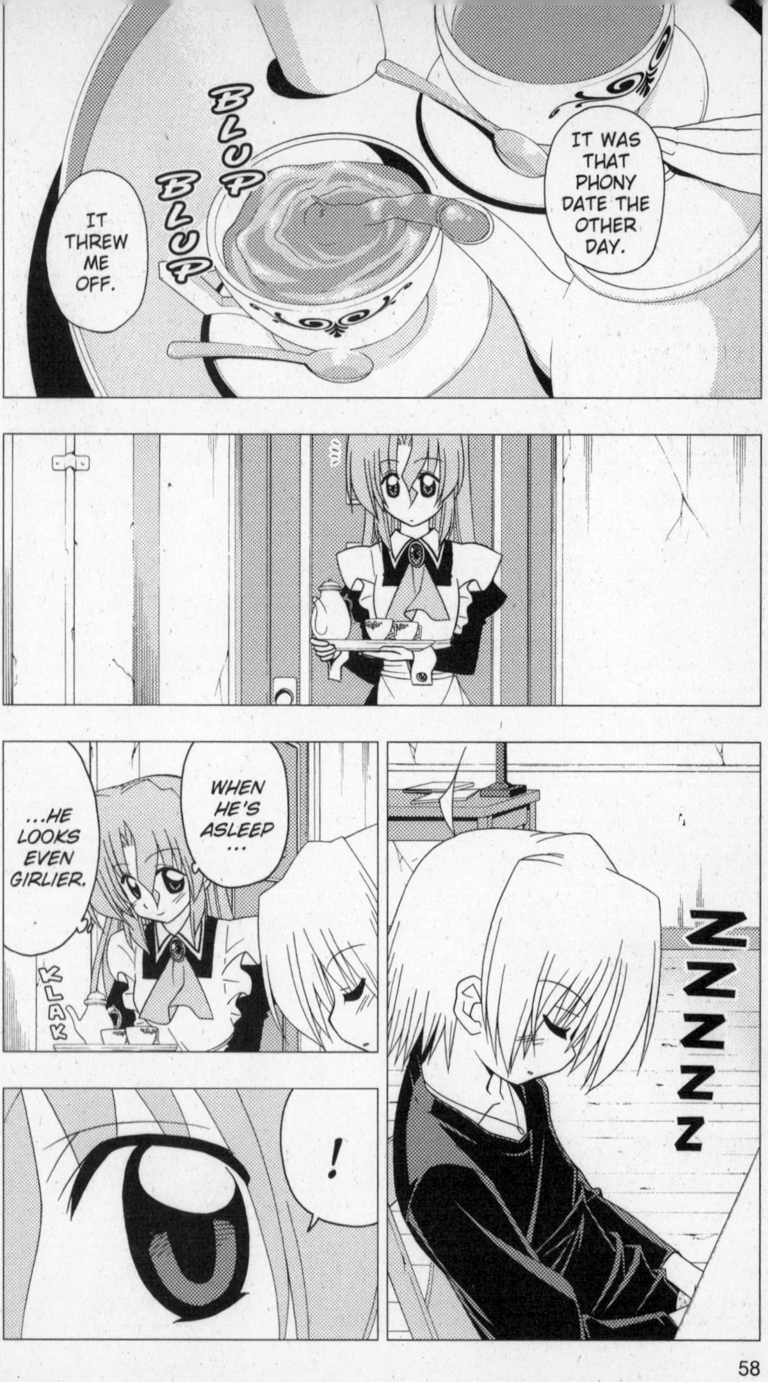
IT WAS THAT PHONY DATE THE OTHER DAY.
BLUP BLUP
IT THREW ME OFF.
ZZZZZ
WHEN HE'S ASLEEP...
...HE LOOKS EVEN GIRLIER.
KLAK
!

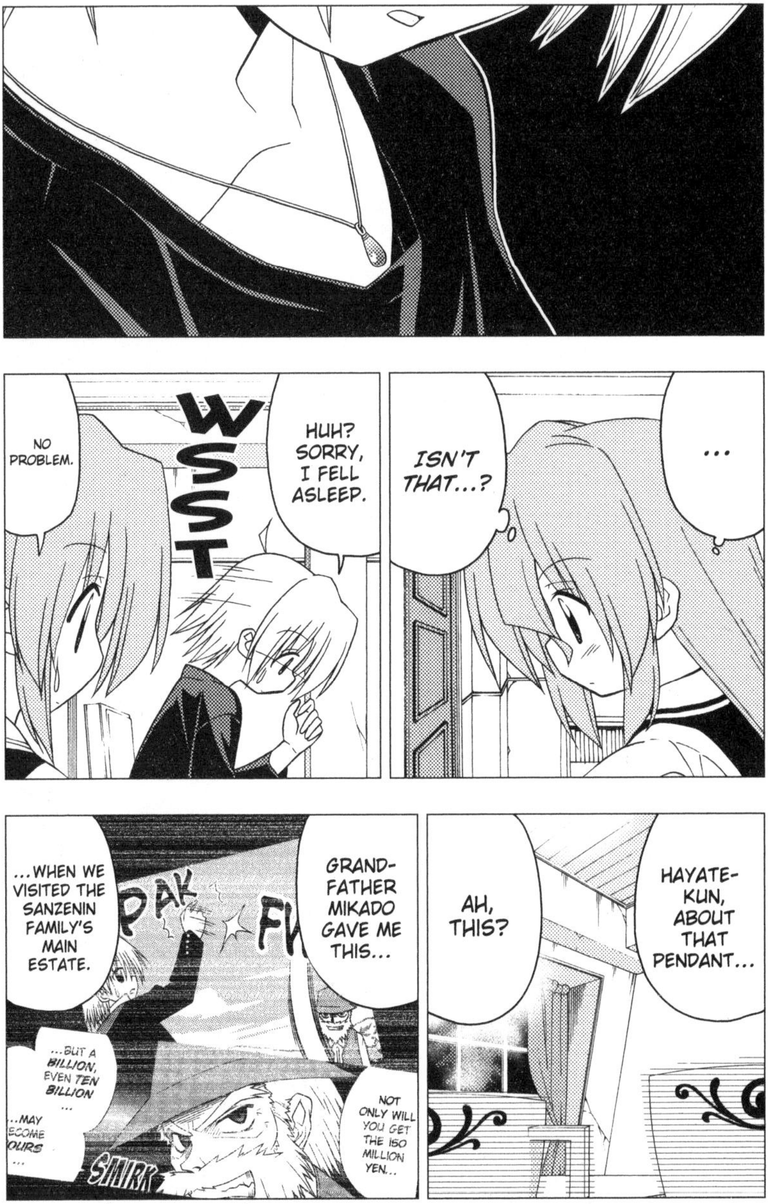
...
ISN'T THAT...?
HUH? SORRY, I FELL ASLEEP.
WSST
NO PROBLEM.
HAYATE-KUN, ABOUT THAT PENDANT...
AH, THIS?
GRANDFATHER MIKADO GAVE ME THIS...
...WHEN WE VISITED THE SANZENIN FAMILY'S MAIN ESTATE.
PAK
NOT ONLY WILL YOU GET THE 150 MILLION YEN...
...BUT A BILLION, EVEN TEN BILLION ...
...MAY ECOME OURS ...
SMIRK

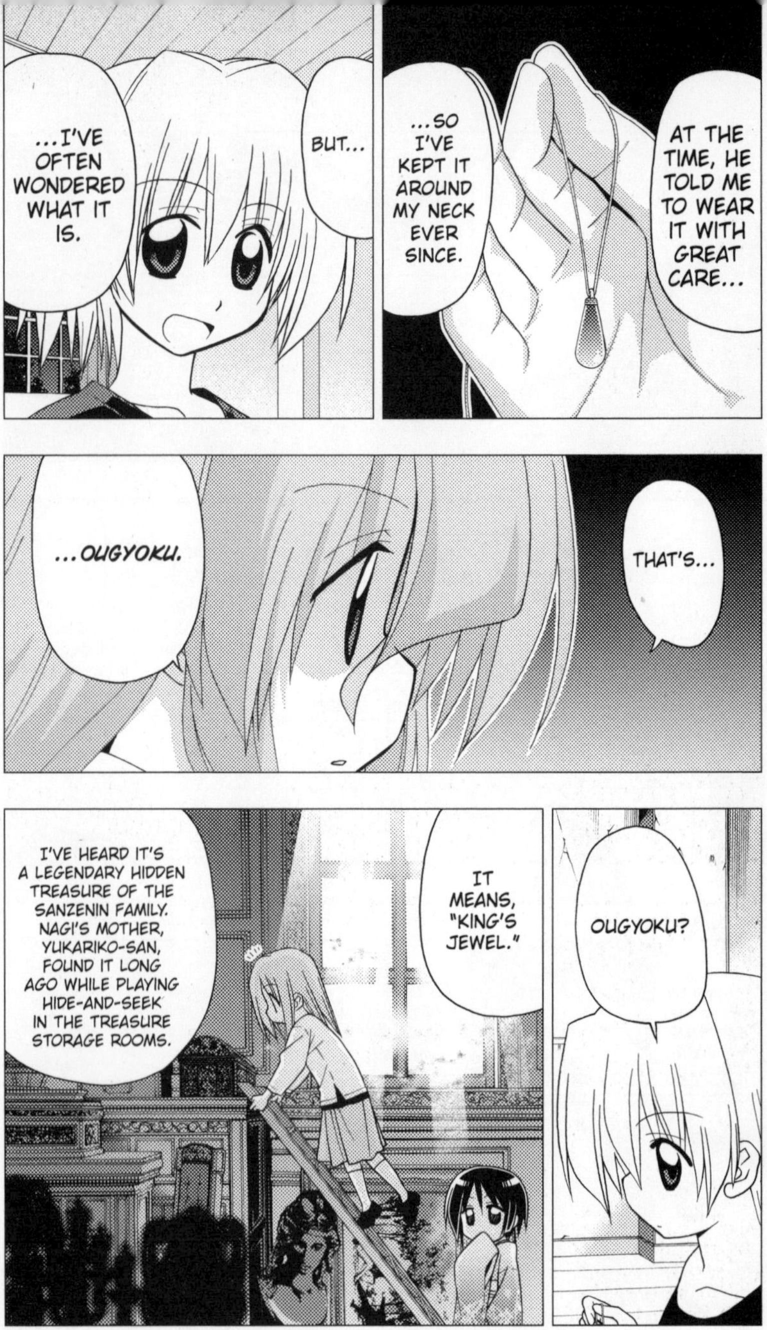
AT THE TIME, HE TOLD ME TO WEAR IT WITH GREAT CARE...
...SO I'VE KEPT IT AROUND MY NECK EVER SINCE.
BUT...
...I'VE OFTEN WONDERED WHAT IT IS.
THAT'S...
...OUGYOKU.
OUGYOKU?
IT MEANS, "KING'S JEWEL."
I'VE HEARD IT'S A LEGENDARY HIDDEN TREASURE OF THE SANZENIN FAMILY. NAGI'S MOTHER, YUKARIKO-SAN, FOUND IT LONG AGO WHILE PLAYING HIDE-AND-SEEK IN THE TREASURE STORAGE ROOMS.

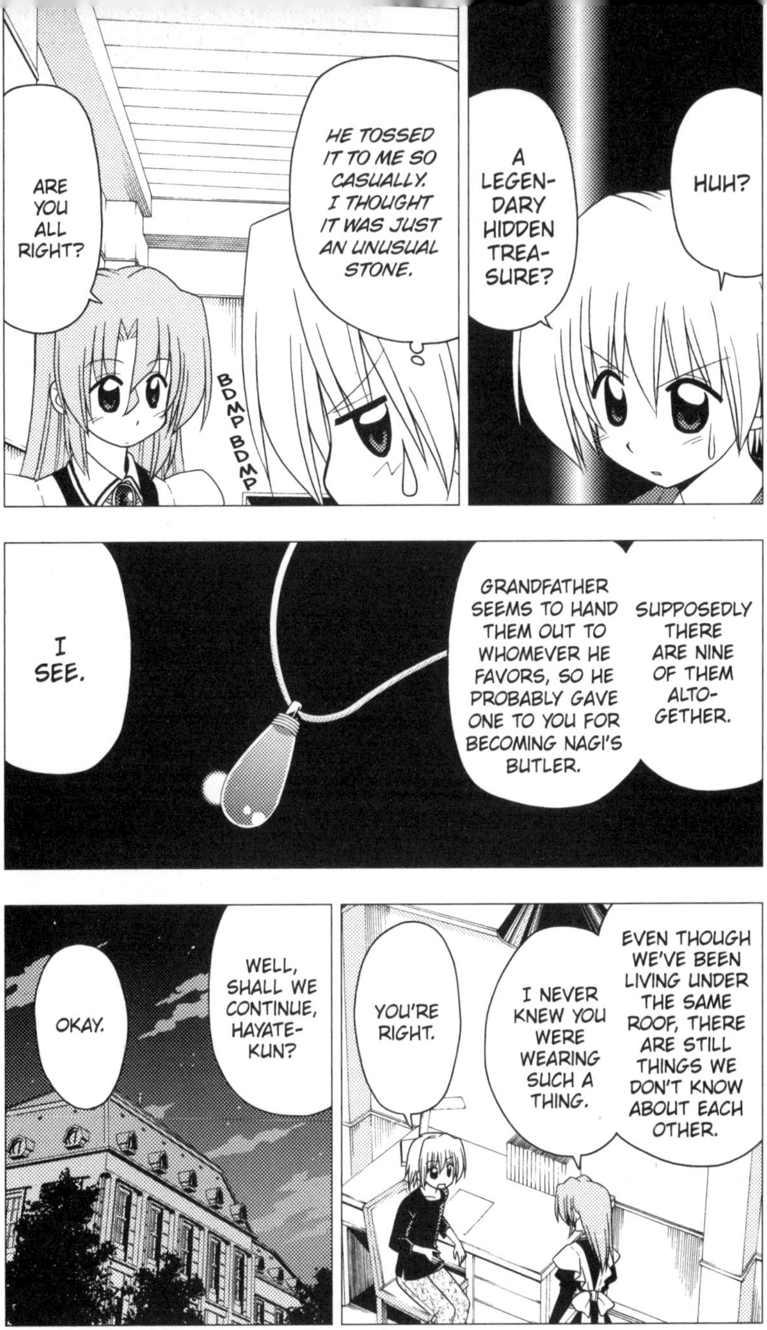
HUH?
A LEGEN-DARY HIDDEN TREA-SURE?
HE TOSSED IT TO ME SO CASUALLY. I THOUGHT IT WAS JUST AN UNUSUAL STONE.
ARE YOU ALL RIGHT?
BDMP BDMP
SUPPOSEDLY THERE ARE NINE OF THEM ALTO-GETHER.
GRANDFATHER SEEMS TO HAND THEM OUT TO WHOMEVER HE FAVORS, SO HE PROBABLY GAVE ONE TO YOU FOR BECOMING NAGI'S BUTLER.
I SEE.
EVEN THOUGH WE'VE BEEN LIVING UNDER THE SAME ROOF, THERE ARE STILL THINGS WE DON'T KNOW ABOUT EACH OTHER.
I NEVER KNEW YOU WERE WEARING SUCH A THING.
YOU'RE RIGHT.
WELL, SHALL WE CONTINUE, HAYATE-KUN?
OKAY.

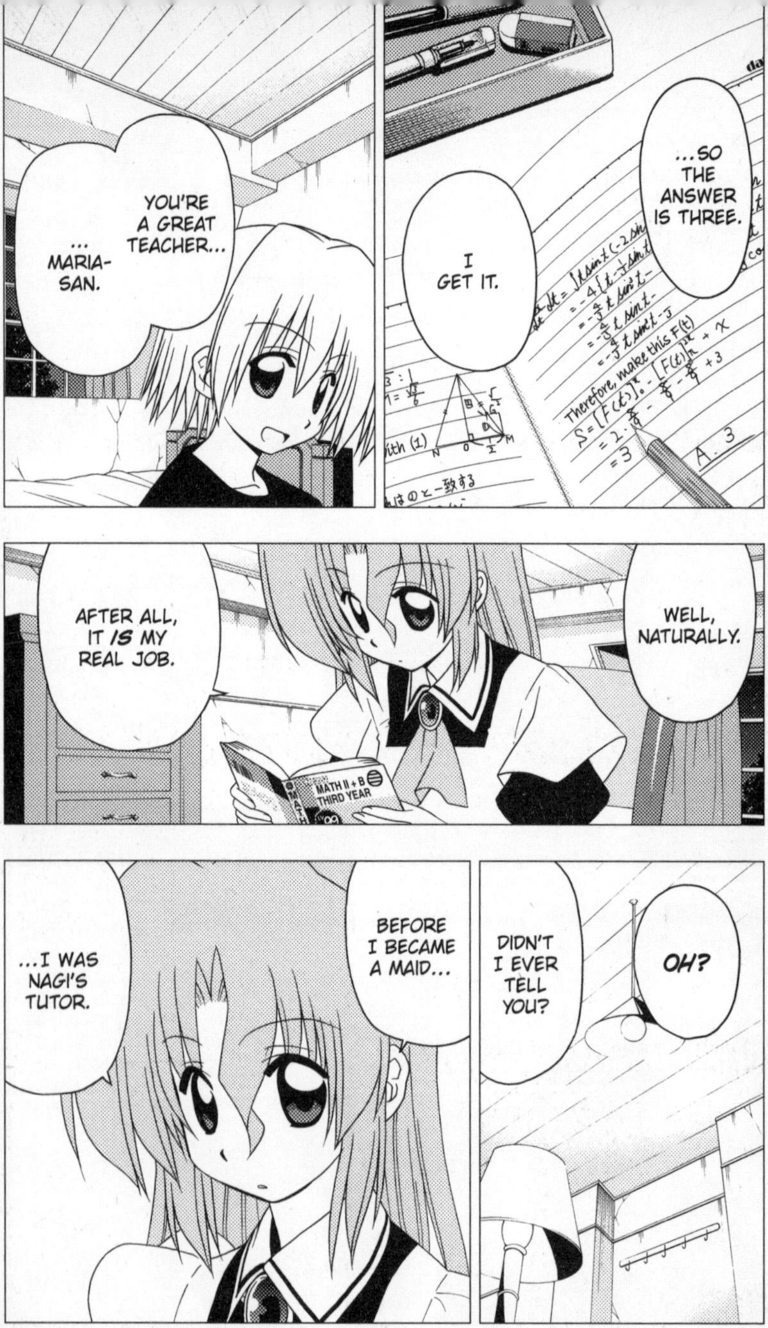
...SO THE ANSWER IS THREE.
I GET IT.
Therefore, make this F(t)
A. 3
YOU'RE A GREAT TEACHER...
...MARIA-SAN.
WELL, NATURALLY.
AFTER ALL, IT *IS* MY REAL JOB.
MATH II + B THIRD YEAR
OH?
DIDN'T I EVER TELL YOU?
BEFORE I BECAME A MAID...
...I WAS NAGI'S TUTOR.

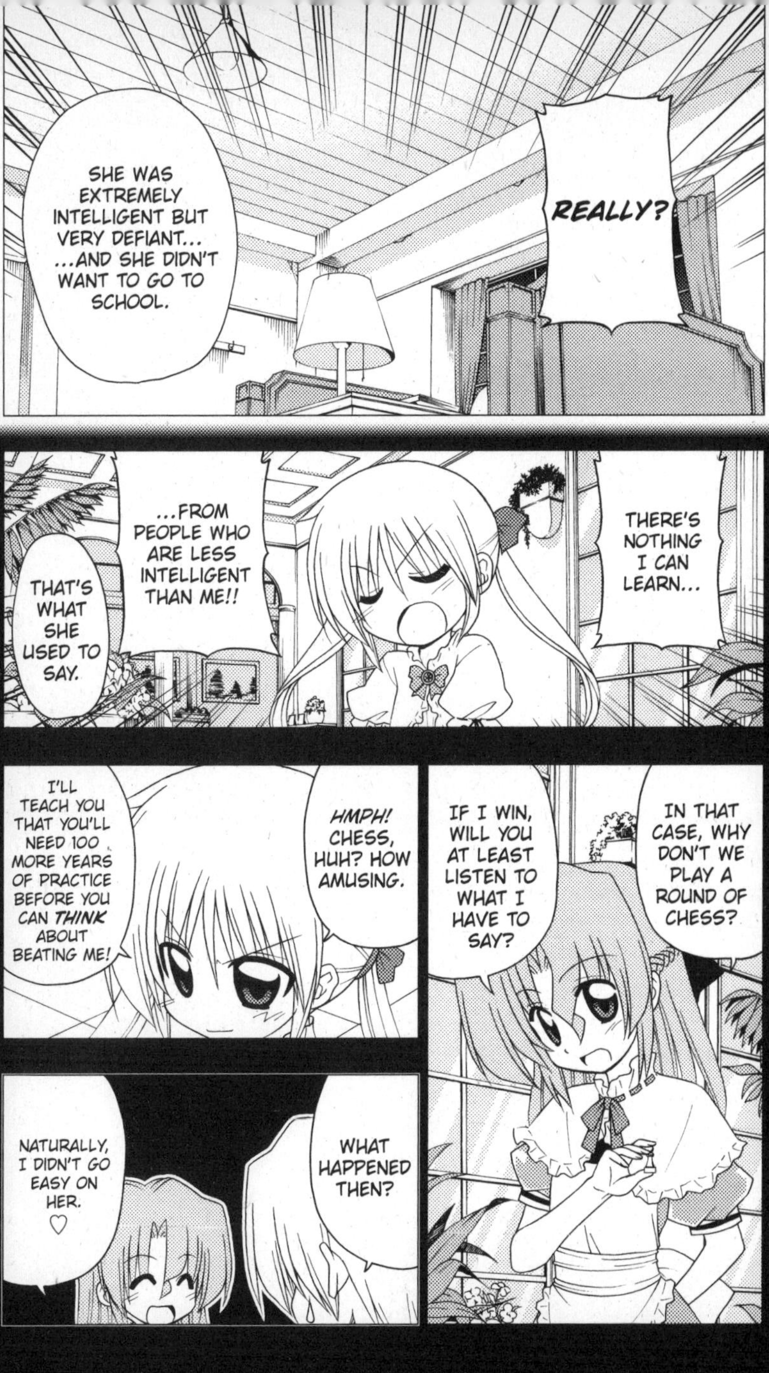
REALLY?
SHE WAS EXTREMELY INTELLIGENT BUT VERY DEFIANT... ...AND SHE DIDN'T WANT TO GO TO SCHOOL.
THERE'S NOTHING I CAN LEARN...
...FROM PEOPLE WHO ARE LESS INTELLIGENT THAN ME!!
THAT'S WHAT SHE USED TO SAY.
IN THAT CASE, WHY DON'T WE PLAY A ROUND OF CHESS?
IF I WIN, WILL YOU AT LEAST LISTEN TO WHAT I HAVE TO SAY?
HMPH! CHESS, HUH? HOW AMUSING.
I'LL TEACH YOU THAT YOU'LL NEED 100 MORE YEARS OF PRACTICE BEFORE YOU CAN THINK ABOUT BEATING ME!
WHAT HAPPENED THEN?
NATURALLY, I DIDN'T GO EASY ON HER. ♡

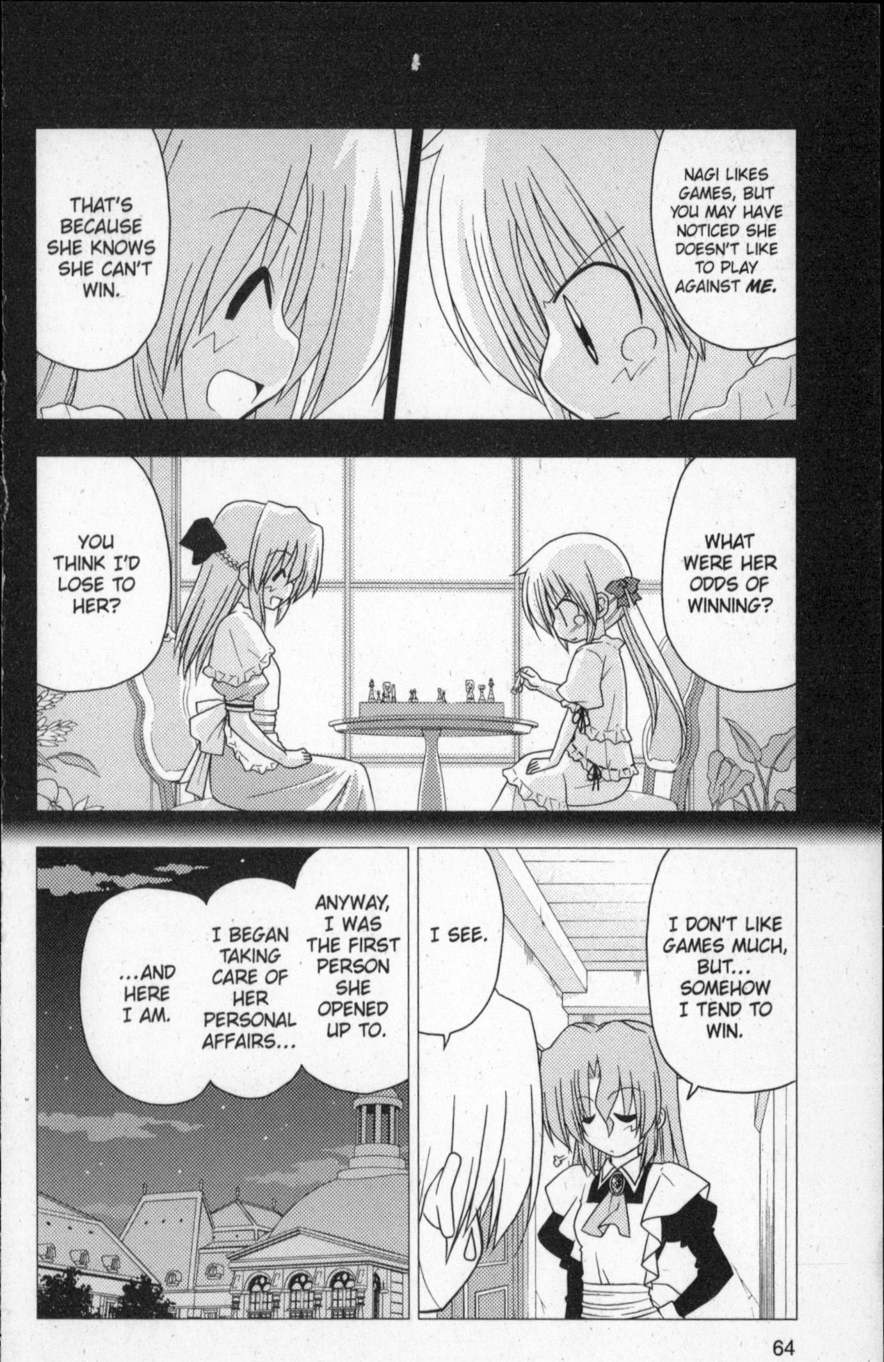
NAGI LIKES GAMES, BUT YOU MAY HAVE NOTICED SHE DOESN'T LIKE TO PLAY AGAINST *ME.*
THAT'S BECAUSE SHE KNOWS SHE CAN'T WIN.
WHAT WERE HER ODDS OF WINNING?
YOU THINK I'D LOSE TO HER?
I DON'T LIKE GAMES MUCH, BUT... SOMEHOW I TEND TO WIN.
I SEE.
ANYWAY, I WAS THE FIRST PERSON SHE OPENED UP TO.
I BEGAN TAKING CARE OF HER PERSONAL AFFAIRS...
...AND HERE I AM.

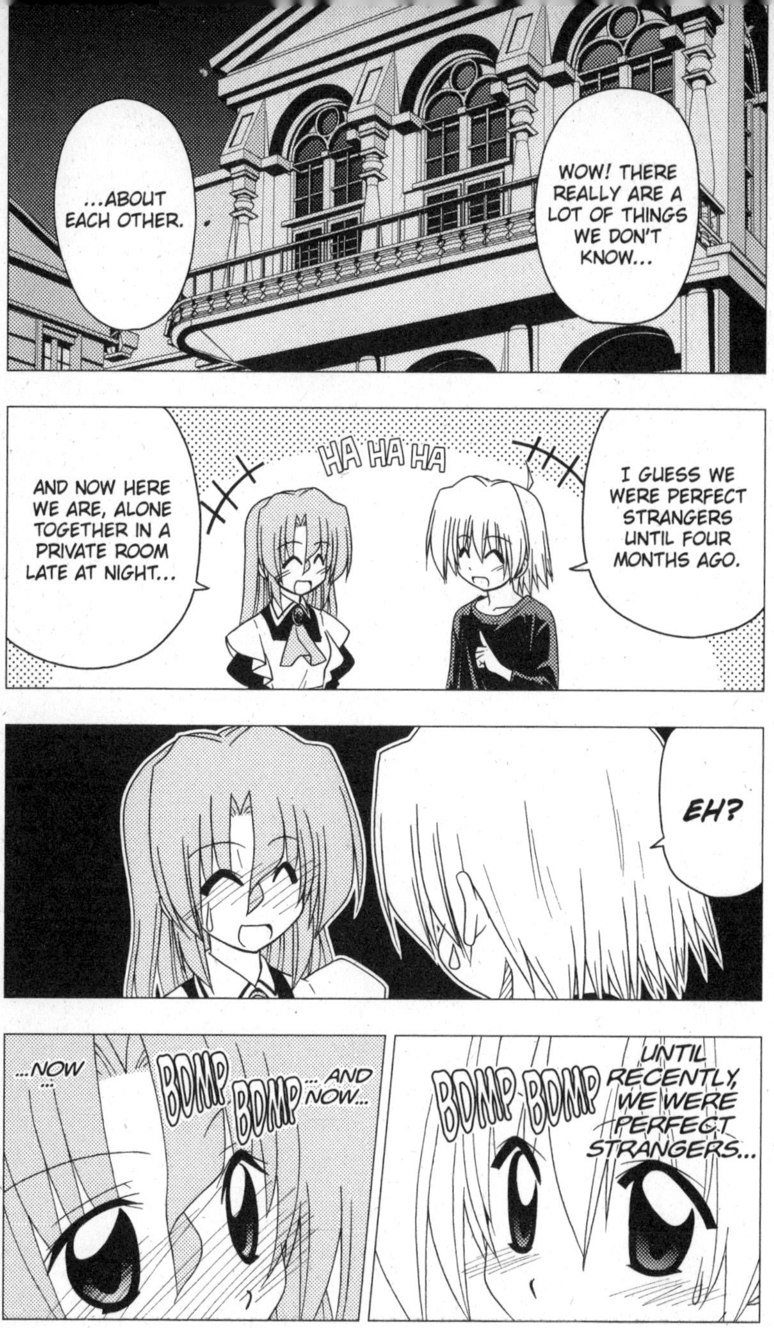
WOW! THERE REALLY ARE A LOT OF THINGS WE DON'T KNOW...
...ABOUT EACH OTHER.
I GUESS WE WERE PERFECT STRANGERS UNTIL FOUR MONTHS AGO.
HA HA HA
AND NOW HERE WE ARE, ALONE TOGETHER IN A PRIVATE ROOM LATE AT NIGHT...
EH?
UNTIL RECENTLY, WE WERE PERFECT STRANGERS...
BDMP BDMP
...AND NOW...
BDMP BDMP
...NOW ...

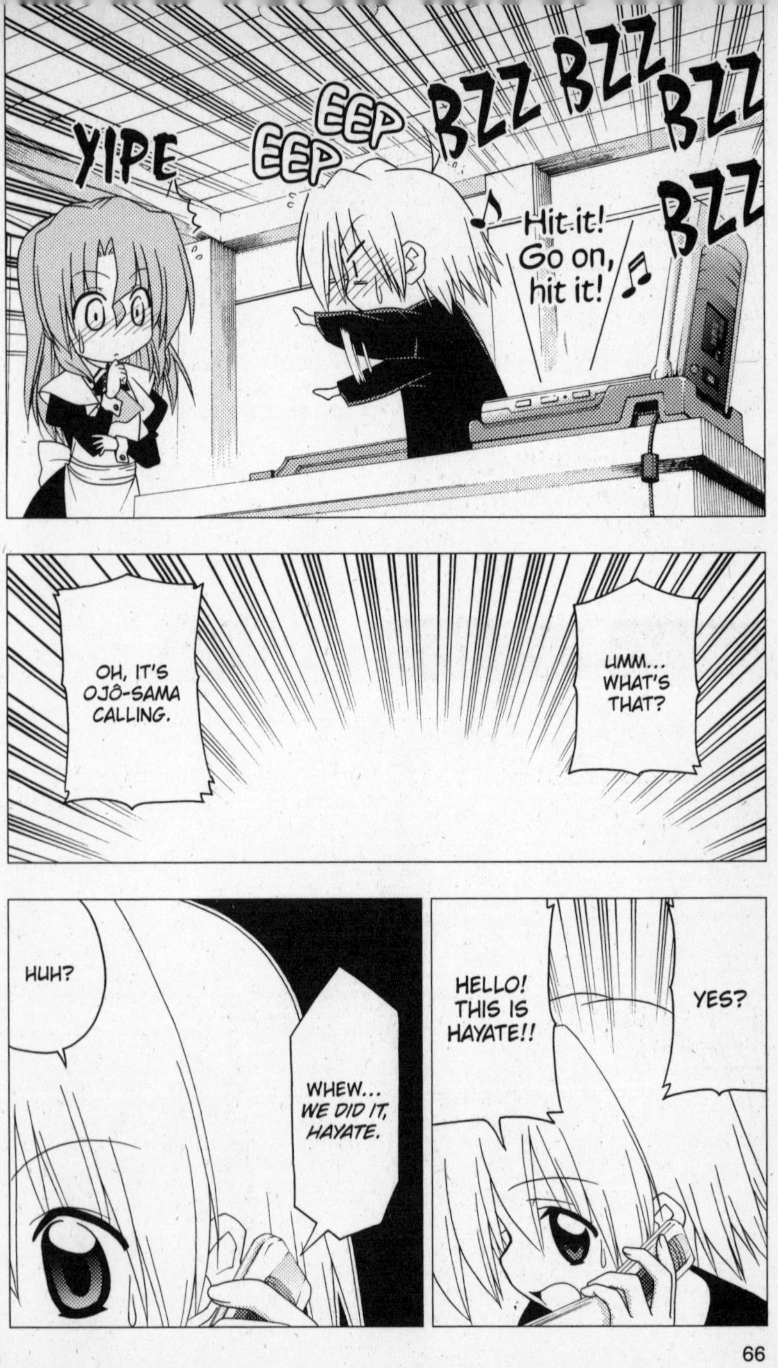
BZZ BZZ BZZ BZZ
Hit it! Go on, hit it!
EEP EEP
YIPE
UMM... WHAT'S THAT?
OH, IT'S OJÔ-SAMA CALLING.
YES?
HELLO! THIS IS HAYATE!!
WHEW... WE DID IT, HAYATE.
HUH?

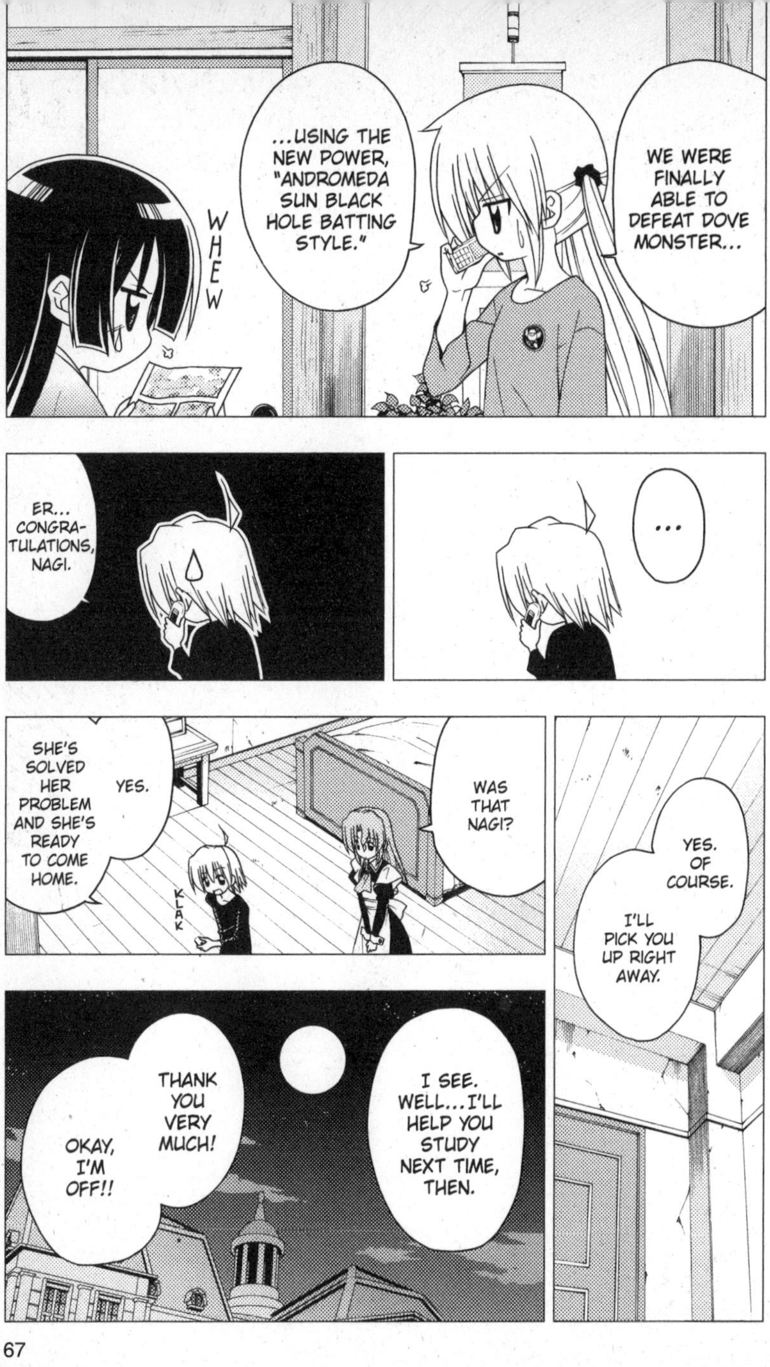
WE WERE FINALLY ABLE TO DEFEAT DOVE MONSTER...
...USING THE NEW POWER, "ANDROMEDA SUN BLACK HOLE BATTING STYLE."
WHEW
...
ER... CONGRA-TULATIONS, NAGI.
YES. OF COURSE.
I'LL PICK YOU UP RIGHT AWAY.
WAS THAT NAGI?
YES.
SHE'S SOLVED HER PROBLEM AND SHE'S READY TO COME HOME.
KLAK
I SEE. WELL...I'LL HELP YOU STUDY NEXT TIME, THEN.
THANK YOU VERY MUCH!
OKAY, I'M OFF!!

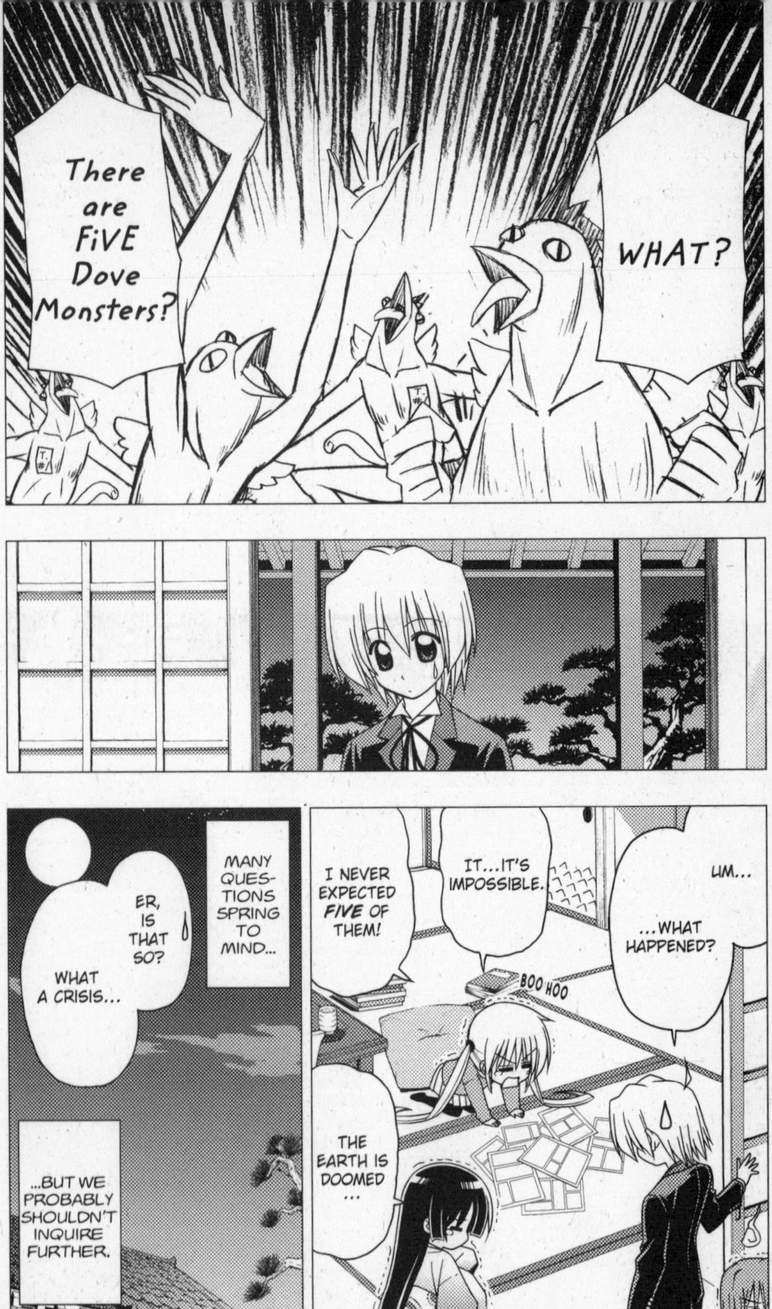
WHAT?
There are FiVE Dove Monsters?
UM...
...WHAT HAPPENED?
IT...IT'S IMPOSSIBLE.
I NEVER EXPECTED FIVE OF THEM!
BOO HOO
THE EARTH IS DOOMED ...
MANY QUESTIONS SPRING TO MIND...
ER, IS THAT SO?
WHAT A CRISIS...
...BUT WE PROBABLY SHOULDN'T INQUIRE FURTHER.

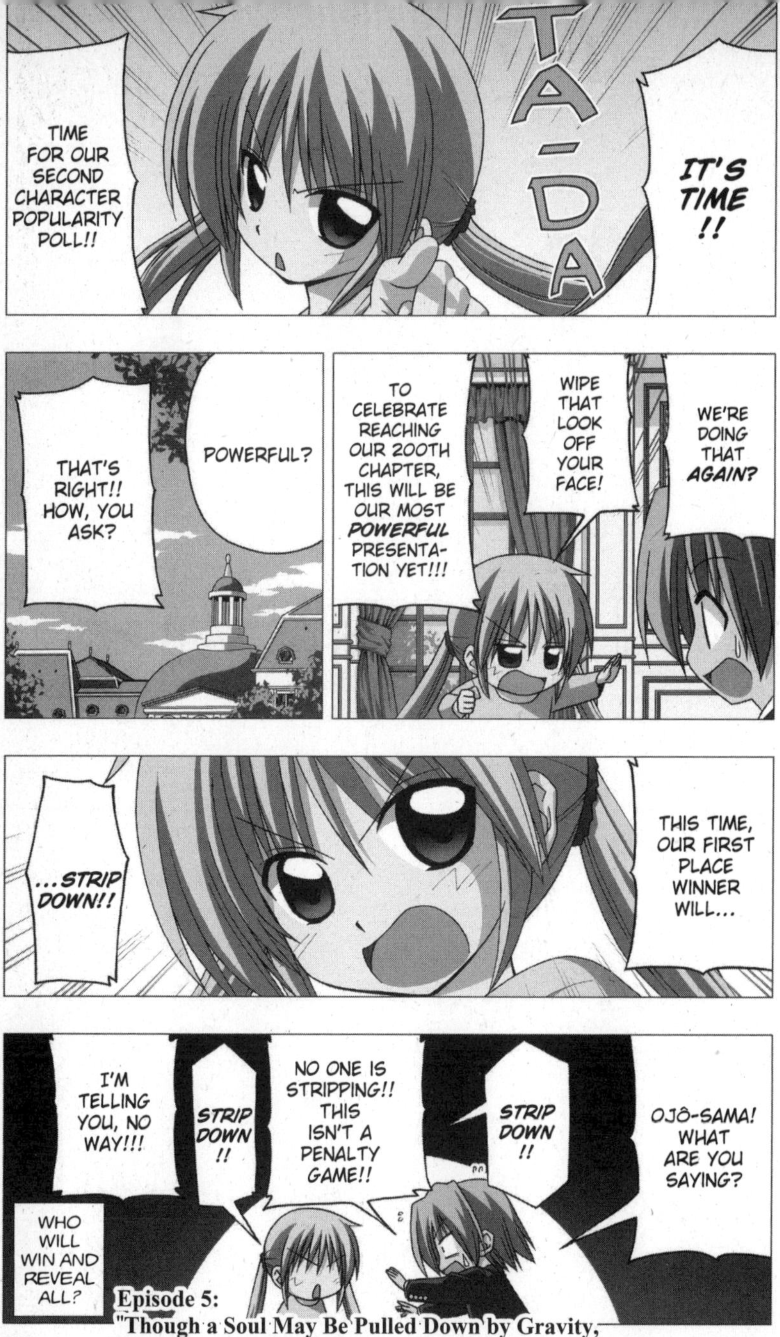
TA-DA
IT'S TIME!!
TIME FOR OUR SECOND CHARACTER POPULARITY POLL!!
WE'RE DOING THAT AGAIN?
WIPE THAT LOOK OFF YOUR FACE!
TO CELEBRATE REACHING OUR 200TH CHAPTER, THIS WILL BE OUR MOST POWERFUL PRESENTATION YET!!!
POWERFUL?
THAT'S RIGHT!! HOW, YOU ASK?
THIS TIME, OUR FIRST PLACE WINNER WILL...
...STRIP DOWN!!
OJÔ-SAMA! WHAT ARE YOU SAYING?
STRIP DOWN!!
NO ONE IS STRIPPING!! THIS ISN'T A PENALTY GAME!!
STRIP DOWN!!
I'M TELLING YOU, NO WAY!!!
WHO WILL WIN AND REVEAL ALL?

Episode 5:
"Though a Soul May Be Pulled Down by Gravity, A Human Being Can Still Fly Out of Narita"

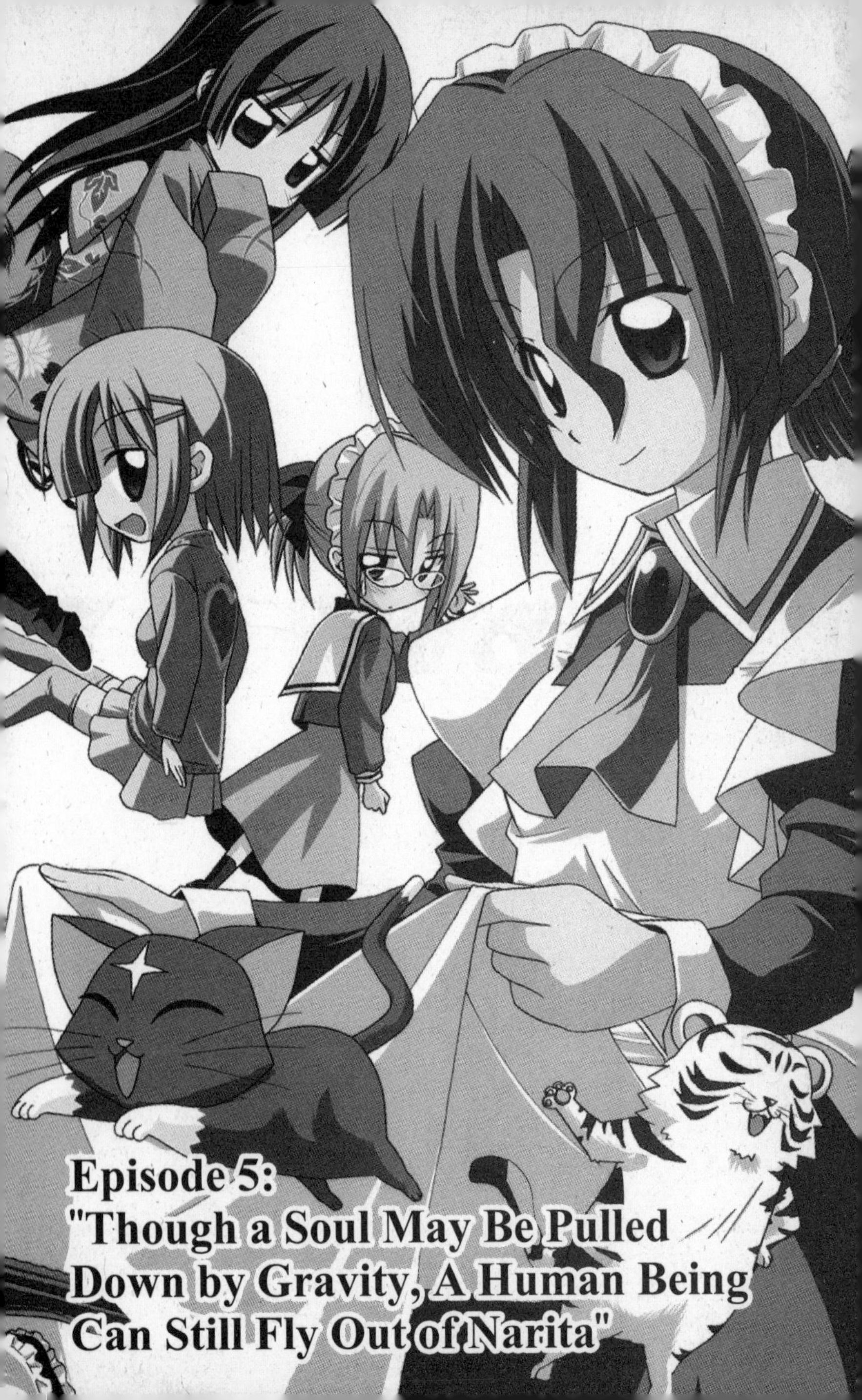

Episode 5: "Though a Soul May Be Pulled Down by Gravity, A Human Being Can Still Fly Out of Narita"

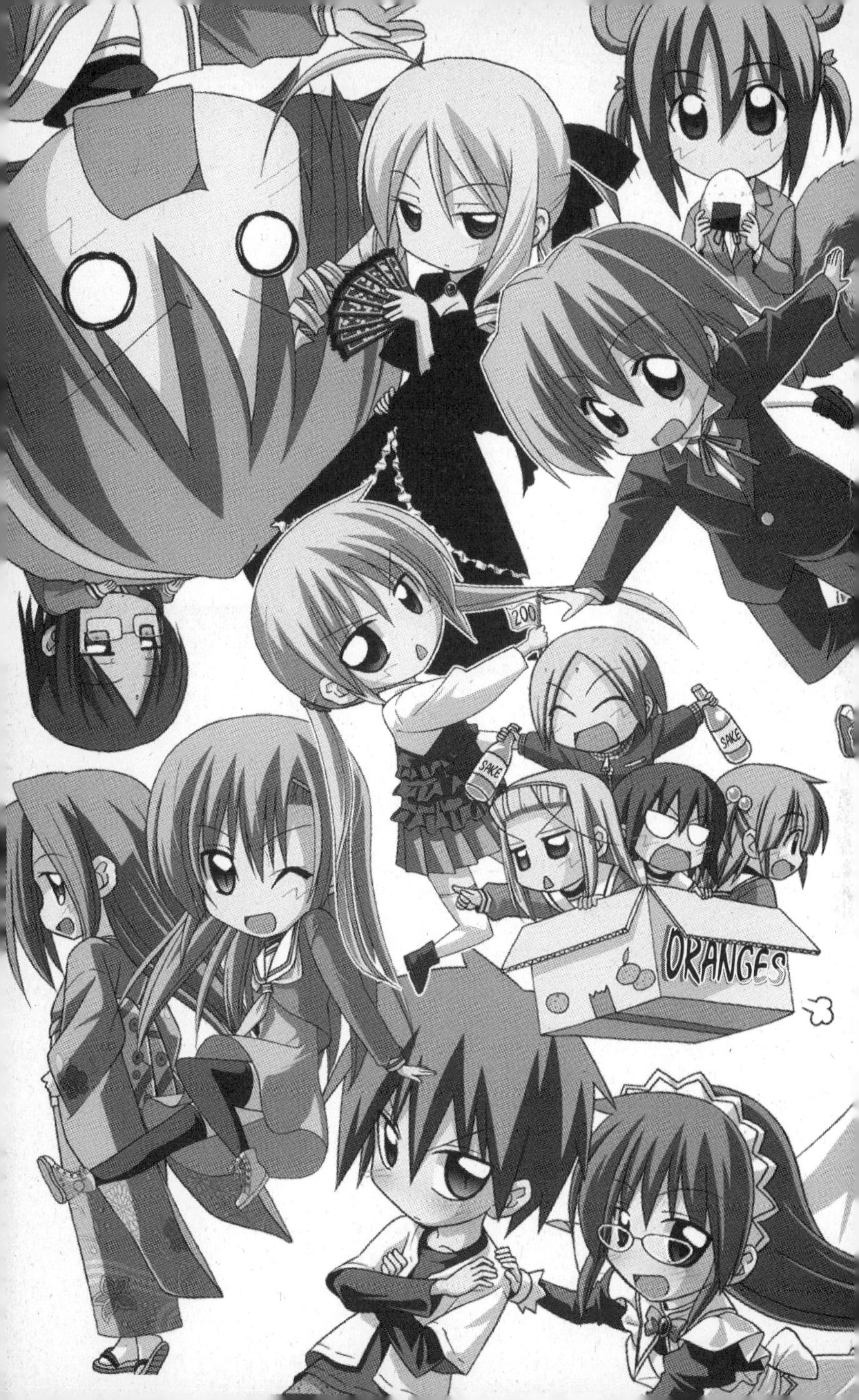
200
SAKE
SAKE
ORANGES

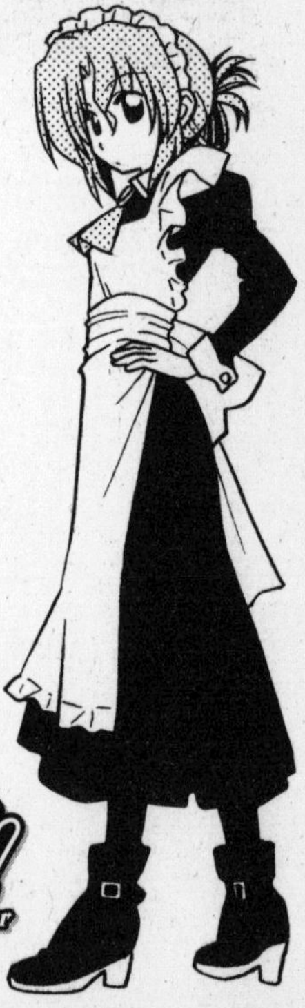

ハヤテのごとく!
Hayate the combat butler

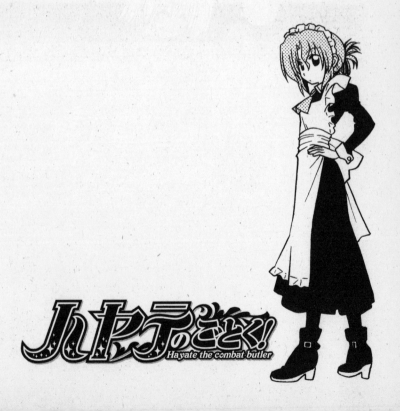

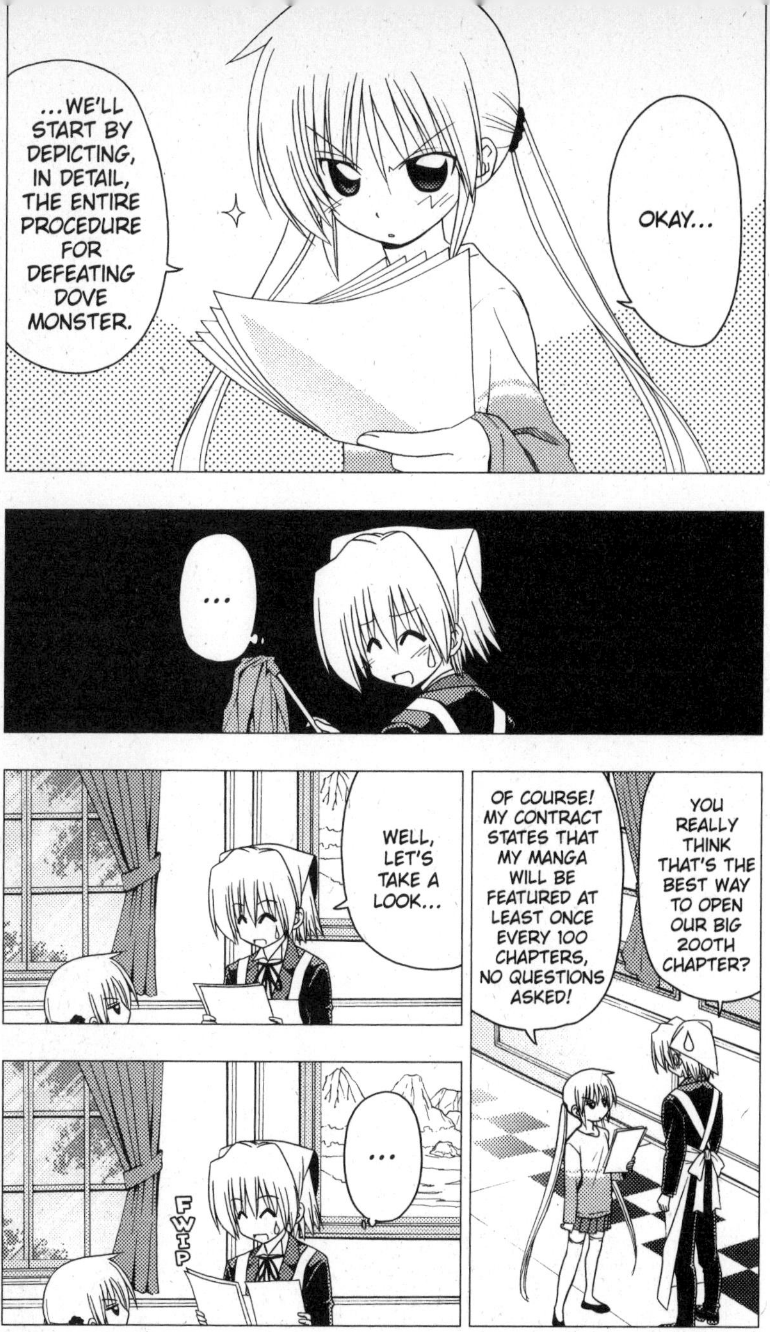
OKAY...
...WE'LL START BY DEPICTING, IN DETAIL, THE ENTIRE PROCEDURE FOR DEFEATING DOVE MONSTER.
...
YOU REALLY THINK THAT'S THE BEST WAY TO OPEN OUR BIG 200TH CHAPTER?
OF COURSE! MY CONTRACT STATES THAT MY MANGA WILL BE FEATURED AT LEAST ONCE EVERY 100 CHAPTERS, NO QUESTIONS ASKED!
WELL, LET'S TAKE A LOOK...
...
FWIP

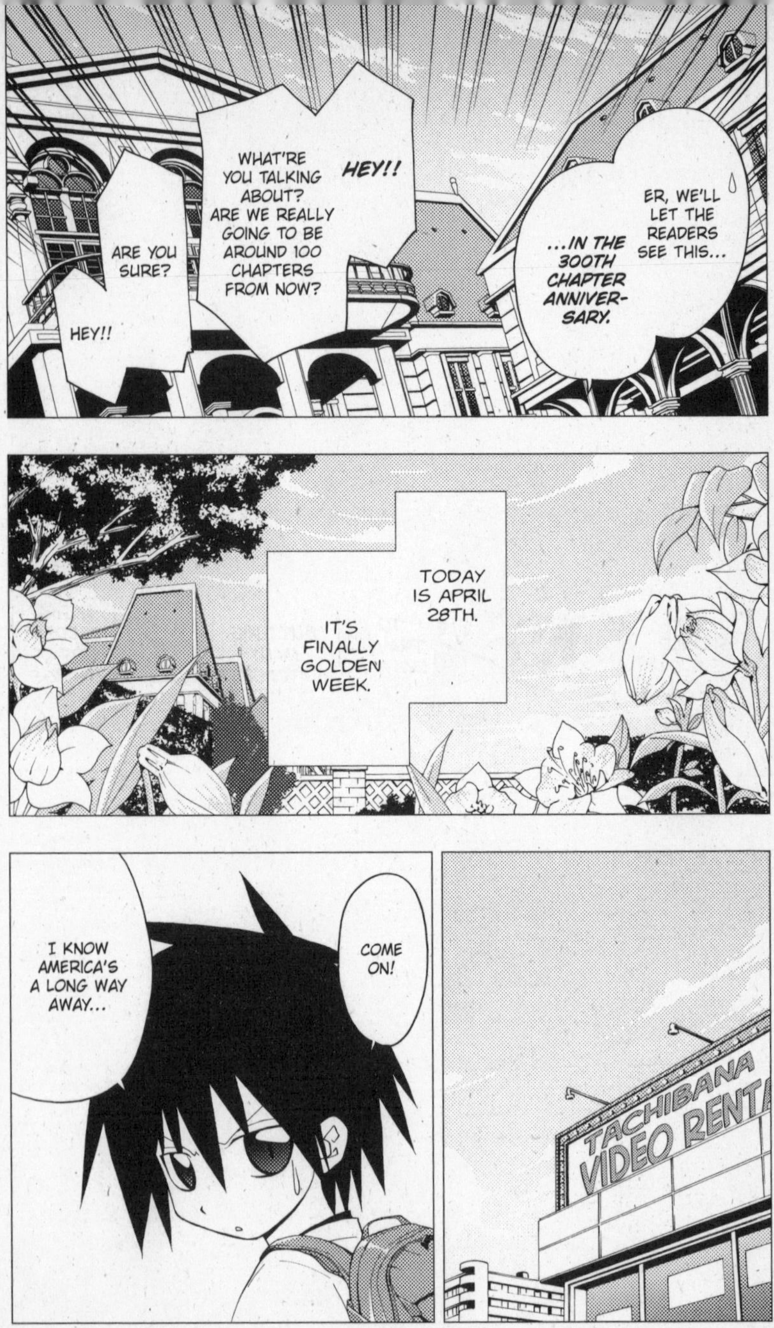
ER, WE'LL LET THE READERS SEE THIS...
...IN THE 300TH CHAPTER ANNIVERSARY.
HEY!!
WHAT'RE YOU TALKING ABOUT? ARE WE REALLY GOING TO BE AROUND 100 CHAPTERS FROM NOW?
ARE YOU SURE?
HEY!!
TODAY IS APRIL 28TH.
IT'S FINALLY GOLDEN WEEK.
TACHIBANA
VIDEO RENTA
COME ON!
I KNOW AMERICA'S A LONG WAY AWAY...

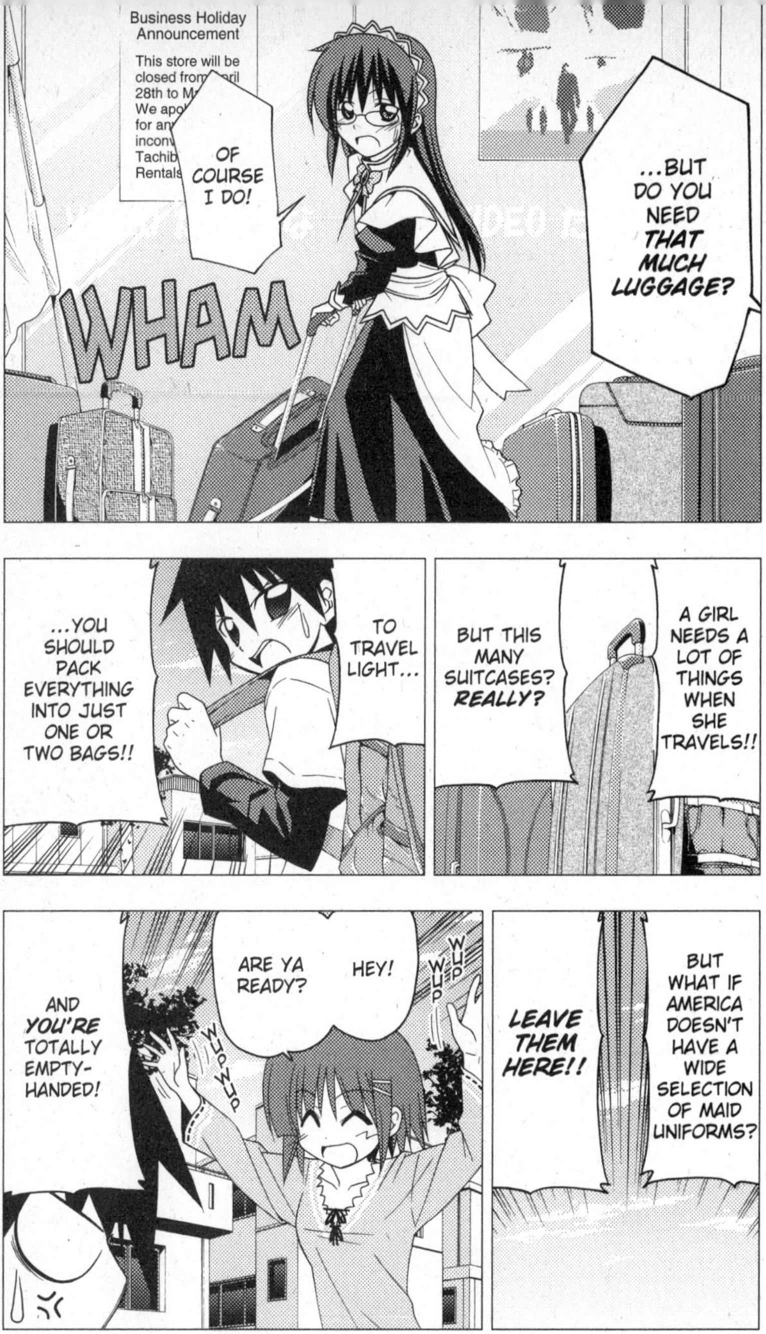
...BUT DO YOU NEED THAT MUCH LUGGAGE?
OF COURSE I DO!
WHAM
Business Holiday Announcement
This store will be closed from
28th to M
We apol
for an
inconv
Tachib
Rentals
A GIRL NEEDS A LOT OF THINGS WHEN SHE TRAVELS!!
BUT THIS MANY SUITCASES? REALLY?
TO TRAVEL LIGHT...
...YOU SHOULD PACK EVERYTHING INTO JUST ONE OR TWO BAGS!!
BUT WHAT IF AMERICA DOESN'T HAVE A WIDE SELECTION OF MAID UNIFORMS?
LEAVE THEM HERE!!
HEY!
ARE YA READY?
WUP WUP
WUP WUP
AND YOU'RE TOTALLY EMPTY-HANDED!

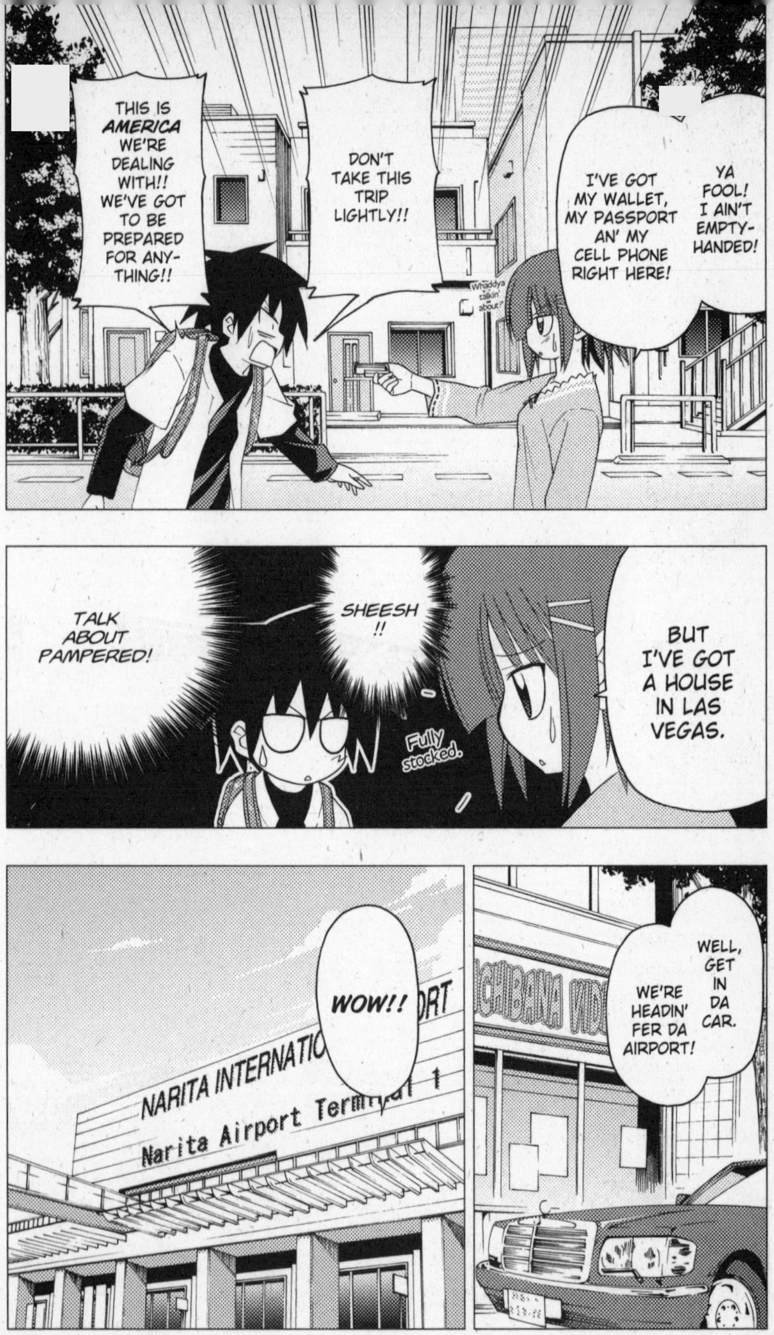
YA FOOL! I AIN'T EMPTY-HANDED!
I'VE GOT MY WALLET, MY PASSPORT AN' MY CELL PHONE RIGHT HERE!
DON'T TAKE THIS TRIP LIGHTLY!!
THIS IS AMERICA WE'RE DEALING WITH!! WE'VE GOT TO BE PREPARED FOR ANY-THING!!
Whaddya talkin' about?
BUT I'VE GOT A HOUSE IN LAS VEGAS.
SHEESH!!
Fully stocked.
TALK ABOUT PAMPERED!
WELL, GET IN DA CAR.
WE'RE HEADIN' FER DA AIRPORT!
WOW!!

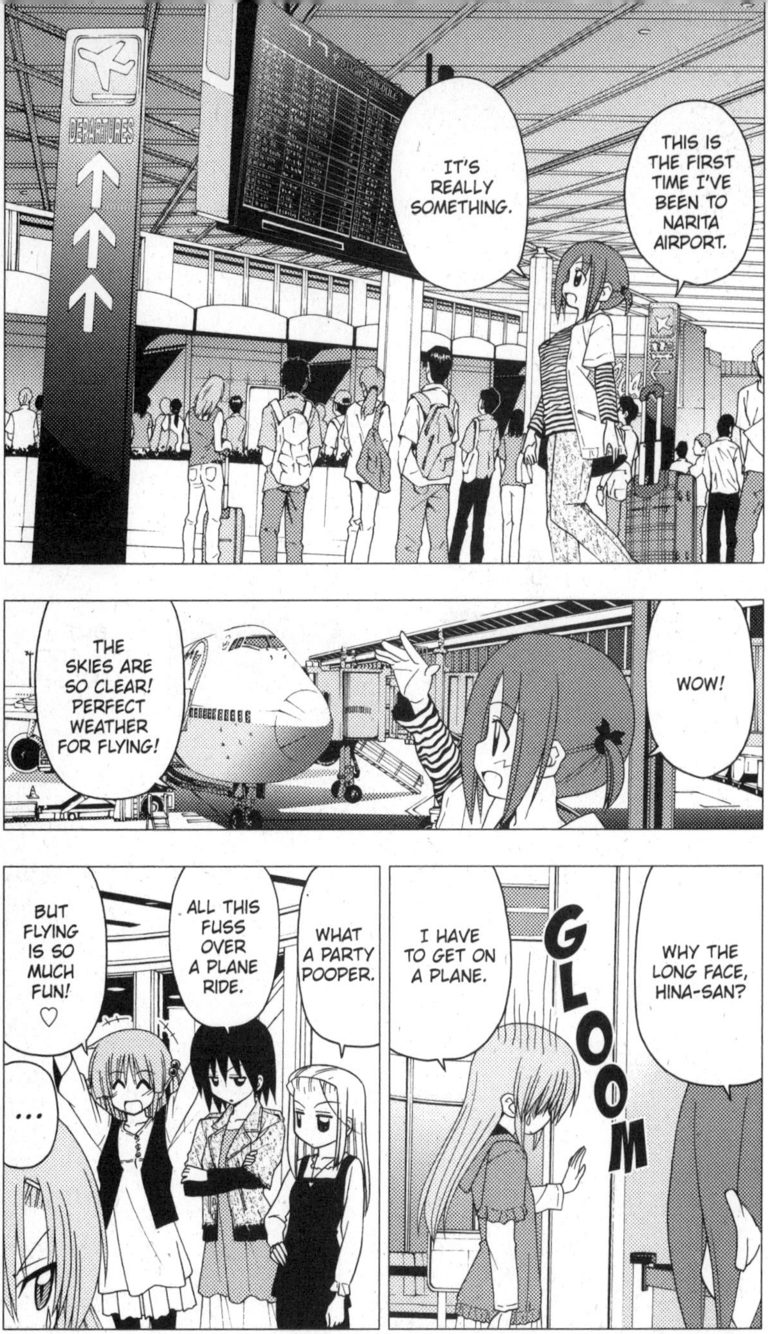
THIS IS THE FIRST TIME I'VE BEEN TO NARITA AIRPORT.
IT'S REALLY SOMETHING.
DEPARTURES
WOW!
THE SKIES ARE SO CLEAR! PERFECT WEATHER FOR FLYING!
WHY THE LONG FACE, HINA-SAN?
GLOOM
I HAVE TO GET ON A PLANE.
WHAT A PARTY POOPER.
ALL THIS FUSS OVER A PLANE RIDE.
BUT FLYING IS SO MUCH FUN! ♡
...

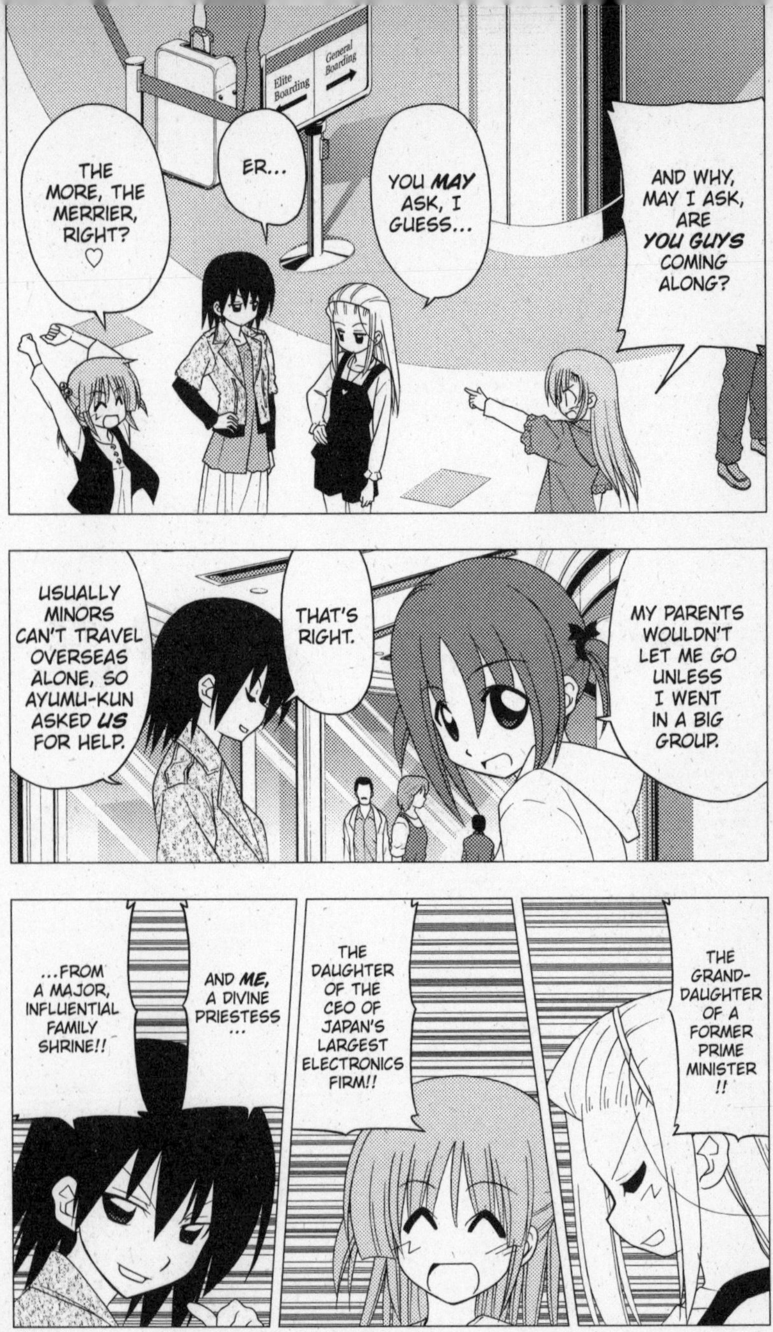
General Boarding
Elite Boarding
AND WHY, MAY I ASK, ARE YOU GUYS COMING ALONG?
YOU MAY ASK, I GUESS...
ER...
THE MORE, THE MERRIER, RIGHT? ♡
MY PARENTS WOULDN'T LET ME GO UNLESS I WENT IN A BIG GROUP.
THAT'S RIGHT.
USUALLY MINORS CAN'T TRAVEL OVERSEAS ALONE, SO AYUMU-KUN ASKED US FOR HELP.
THE GRAND-DAUGHTER OF A FORMER PRIME MINISTER !!
THE DAUGHTER OF THE CEO OF JAPAN'S LARGEST ELECTRONICS FIRM!!
AND ME, A DIVINE PRIESTESS ...
...FROM A MAJOR, INFLUENTIAL FAMILY SHRINE!!

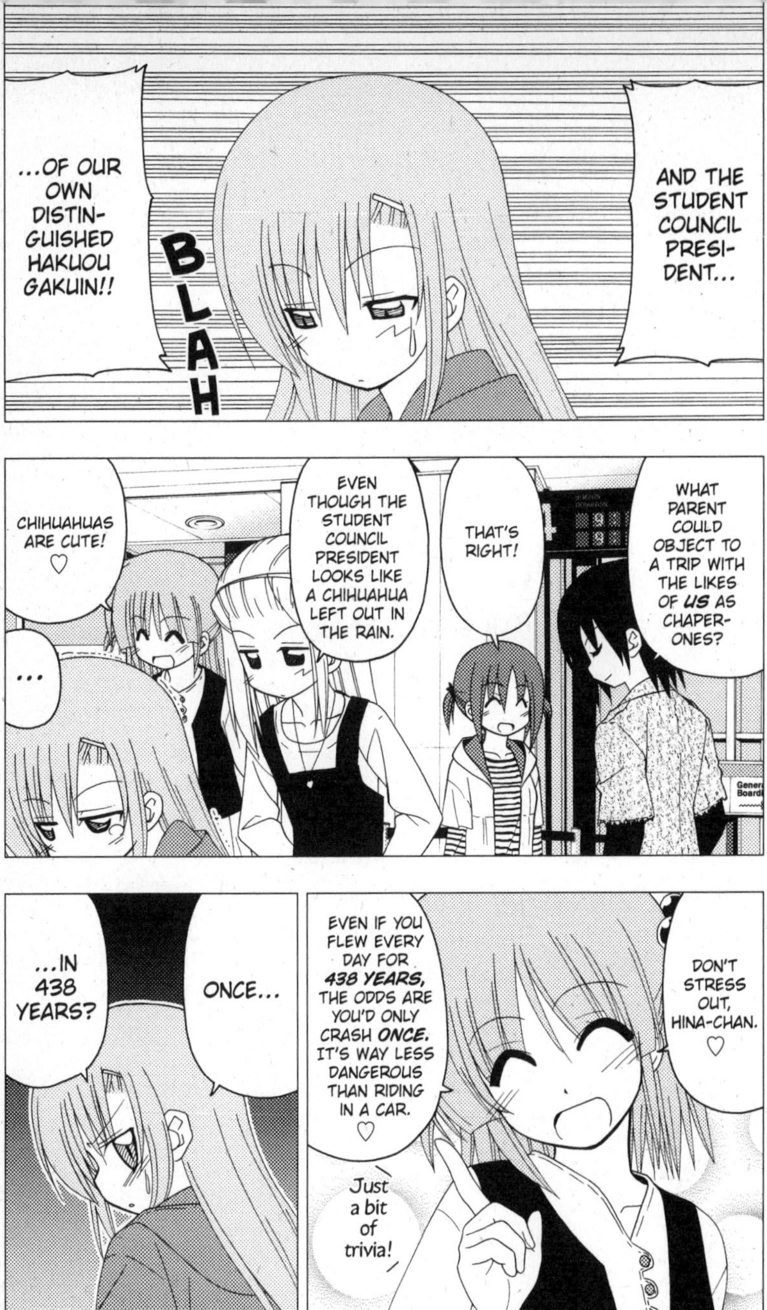
AND THE STUDENT COUNCIL PRESIDENT...
...OF OUR OWN DISTINGUISHED HAKUOU GAKUIN!!
BLAH
WHAT PARENT COULD OBJECT TO A TRIP WITH THE LIKES OF *US* AS CHAPERONES?
THAT'S RIGHT!
EVEN THOUGH THE STUDENT COUNCIL PRESIDENT LOOKS LIKE A CHIHUAHUA LEFT OUT IN THE RAIN.
CHIHUAHUAS ARE CUTE! ♡
...
DON'T STRESS OUT, HINA-CHAN. ♡
EVEN IF YOU FLEW EVERY DAY FOR ***438 YEARS,*** THE ODDS ARE YOU'D ONLY CRASH ***ONCE.*** IT'S WAY LESS DANGEROUS THAN RIDING IN A CAR. ♡
Just a bit of trivia!
ONCE...
...IN 438 YEARS?

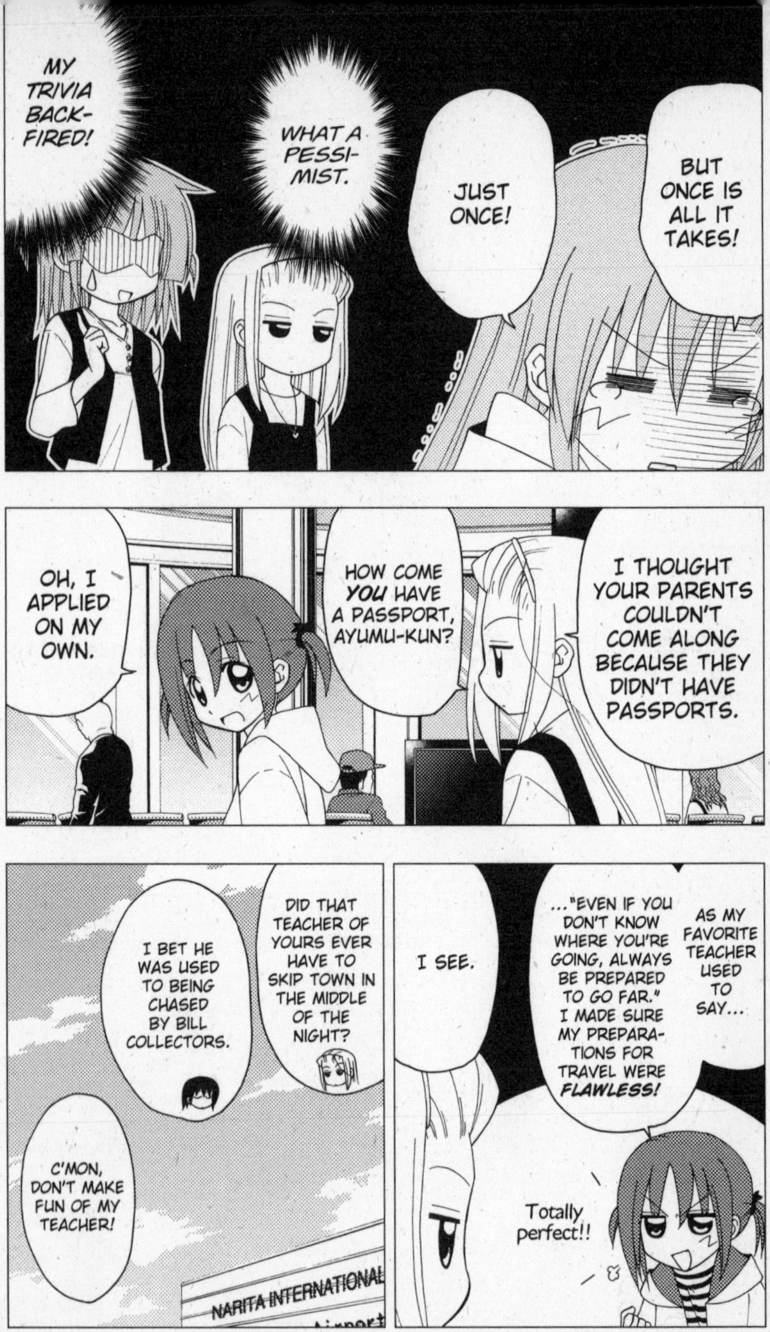
BUT ONCE IS ALL IT TAKES!
JUST ONCE!
WHAT A PESSI-MIST.
MY TRIVIA BACK-FIRED!
I THOUGHT YOUR PARENTS COULDN'T COME ALONG BECAUSE THEY DIDN'T HAVE PASSPORTS.
HOW COME *YOU* HAVE A PASSPORT, AYUMU-KUN?
OH, I APPLIED ON MY OWN.
AS MY FAVORITE TEACHER USED TO SAY...
..."EVEN IF YOU DON'T KNOW WHERE YOU'RE GOING, ALWAYS BE PREPARED TO GO FAR." I MADE SURE MY PREPARA-TIONS FOR TRAVEL WERE ***FLAWLESS!***
I SEE.
Totally perfect!!
DID THAT TEACHER OF YOURS EVER HAVE TO SKIP TOWN IN THE MIDDLE OF THE NIGHT?
I BET HE WAS USED TO BEING CHASED BY BILL COLLECTORS.
C'MON, DON'T MAKE FUN OF MY TEACHER!
NARITA INTERNATIONAL

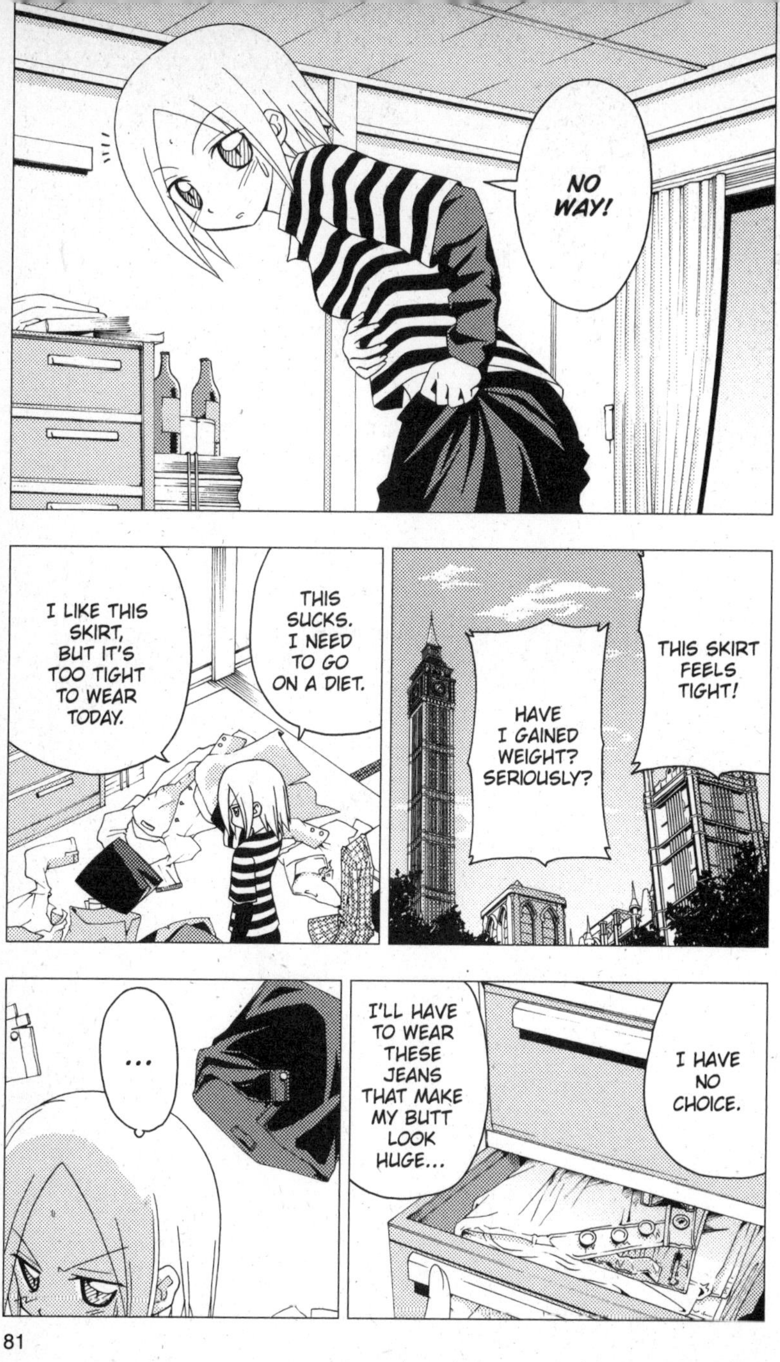
NO WAY!
THIS SKIRT FEELS TIGHT!
HAVE I GAINED WEIGHT? SERIOUSLY?
THIS SUCKS. I NEED TO GO ON A DIET.
I LIKE THIS SKIRT, BUT IT'S TOO TIGHT TO WEAR TODAY.
I HAVE NO CHOICE.
I'LL HAVE TO WEAR THESE JEANS THAT MAKE MY BUTT LOOK HUGE...
...

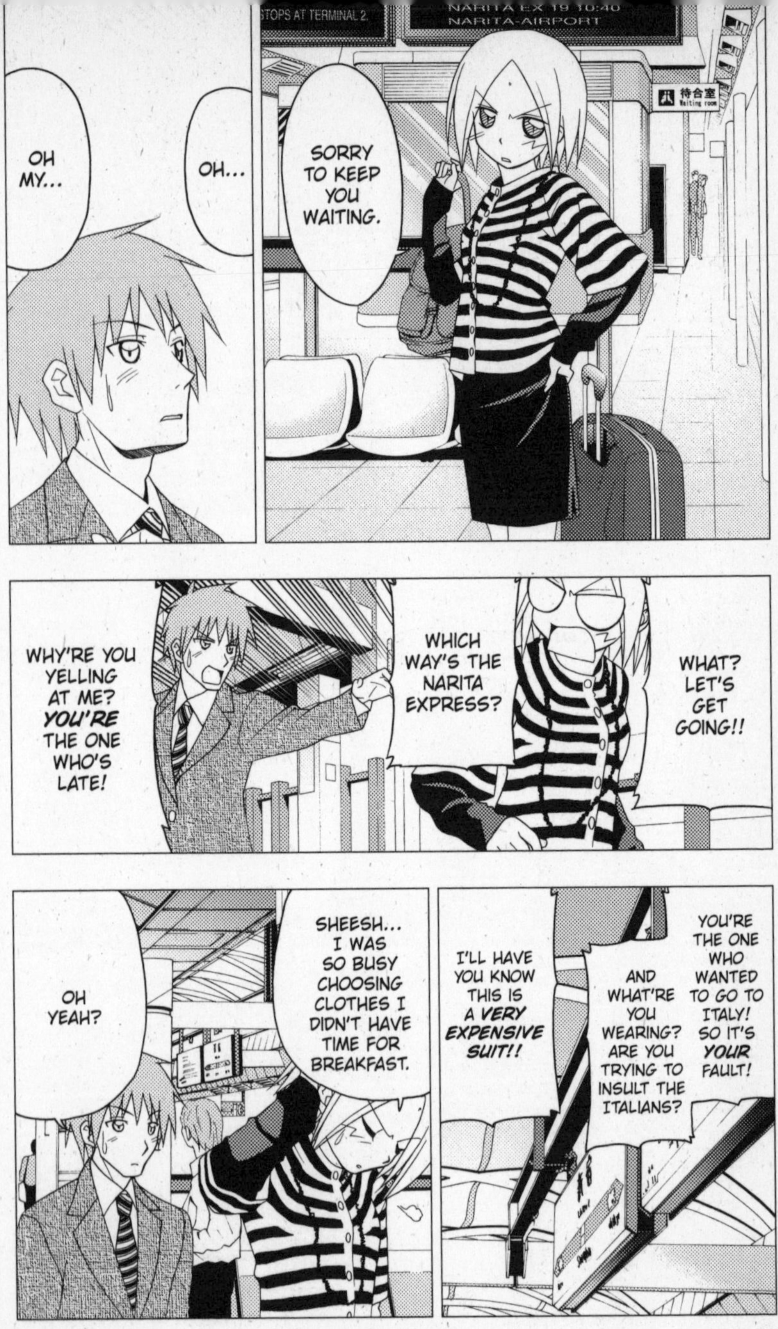
STOPS AT TERMINAL 2.
NARITA EX 19 10:40
NARITA-AIRPORT
待合室 Waiting room
SORRY TO KEEP YOU WAITING.
OH...
OH MY...
WHAT? LET'S GET GOING!!
WHICH WAY'S THE NARITA EXPRESS?
WHY'RE YOU YELLING AT ME? YOU'RE THE ONE WHO'S LATE!
YOU'RE THE ONE WHO WANTED TO GO TO ITALY! SO IT'S YOUR FAULT!
AND WHAT'RE YOU WEARING? ARE YOU TRYING TO INSULT THE ITALIANS?
I'LL HAVE YOU KNOW THIS IS A VERY EXPENSIVE SUIT!!
SHEESH... I WAS SO BUSY CHOOSING CLOTHES I DIDN'T HAVE TIME FOR BREAKFAST.
OH YEAH?

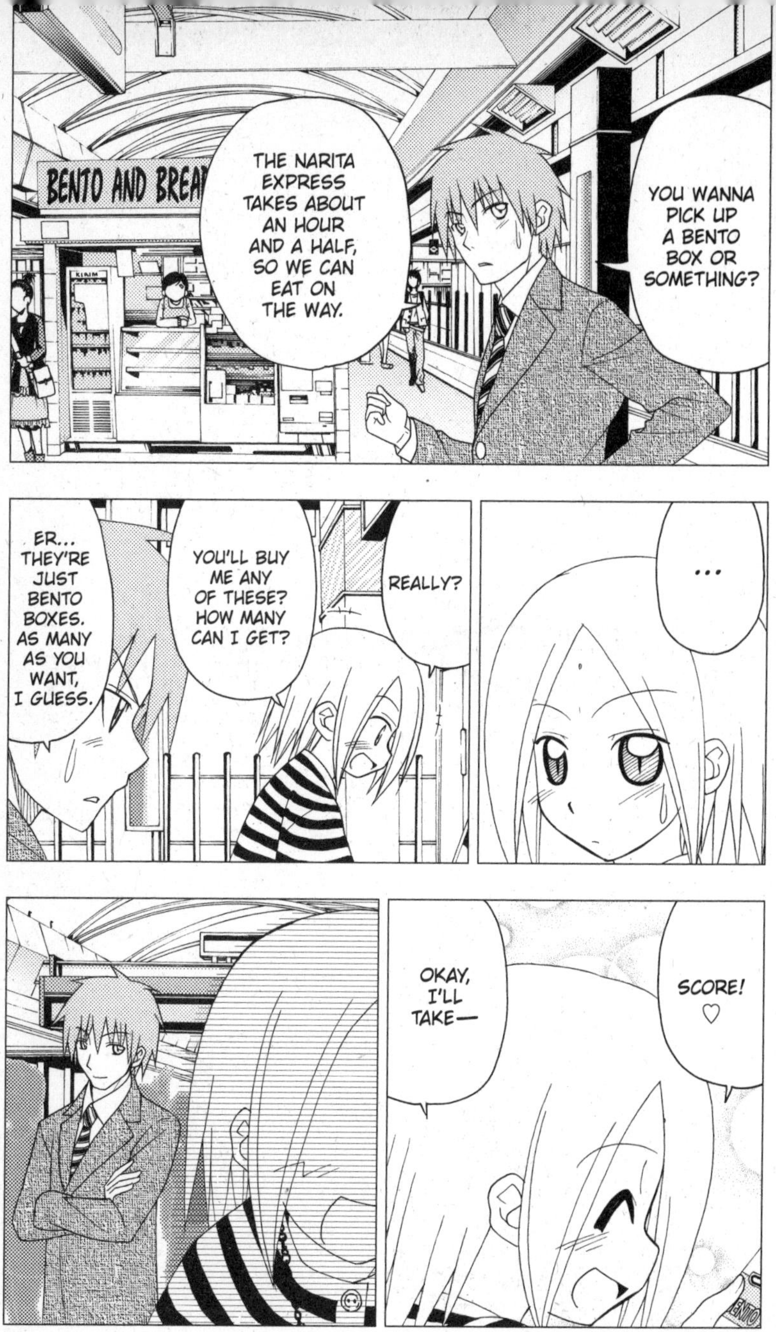
YOU WANNA PICK UP A BENTO BOX OR SOMETHING?
THE NARITA EXPRESS TAKES ABOUT AN HOUR AND A HALF, SO WE CAN EAT ON THE WAY.
...
REALLY?
YOU'LL BUY ME ANY OF THESE? HOW MANY CAN I GET?
ER... THEY'RE JUST BENTO BOXES. AS MANY AS YOU WANT, I GUESS.
SCORE! ♡
OKAY, I'LL TAKE—

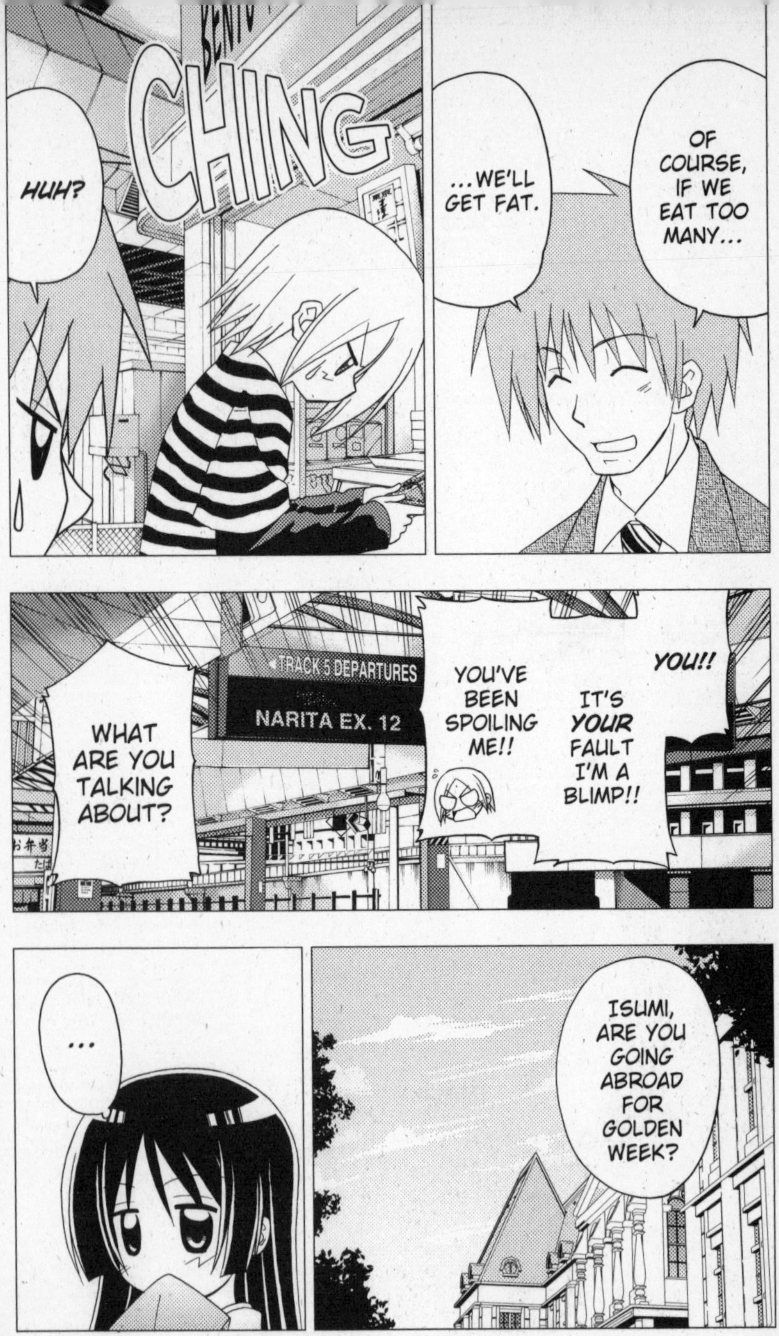
OF COURSE, IF WE EAT TOO MANY...
...WE'LL GET FAT.
CHING
HUH?
YOU!!
IT'S YOUR FAULT I'M A BLIMP!!
YOU'VE BEEN SPOILING ME!!
TRACK 5 DEPARTURES
NARITA EX. 12
WHAT ARE YOU TALKING ABOUT?
ISUMI, ARE YOU GOING ABROAD FOR GOLDEN WEEK?
...

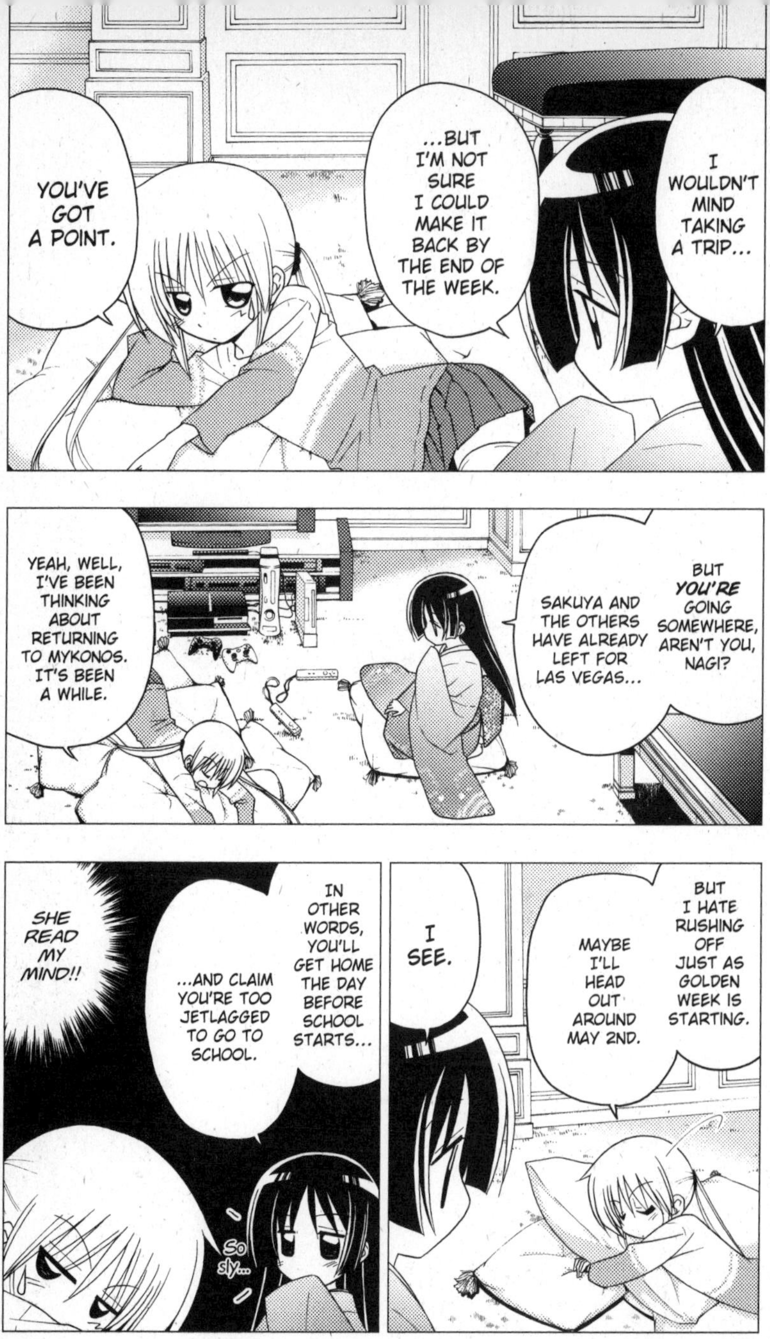
I WOULDN'T MIND TAKING A TRIP...
...BUT I'M NOT SURE I COULD MAKE IT BACK BY THE END OF THE WEEK.
YOU'VE GOT A POINT.
BUT *YOU'RE* GOING SOMEWHERE, AREN'T YOU, NAGI?
SAKUYA AND THE OTHERS HAVE ALREADY LEFT FOR LAS VEGAS...
YEAH, WELL, I'VE BEEN THINKING ABOUT RETURNING TO MYKONOS. IT'S BEEN A WHILE.
BUT I HATE RUSHING OFF JUST AS GOLDEN WEEK IS STARTING.
MAYBE I'LL HEAD OUT AROUND MAY 2ND.
I SEE.
IN OTHER WORDS, YOU'LL GET HOME THE DAY BEFORE SCHOOL STARTS...
...AND CLAIM YOU'RE TOO JETLAGGED TO GO TO SCHOOL.
SHE READ MY MIND!!
So sly...

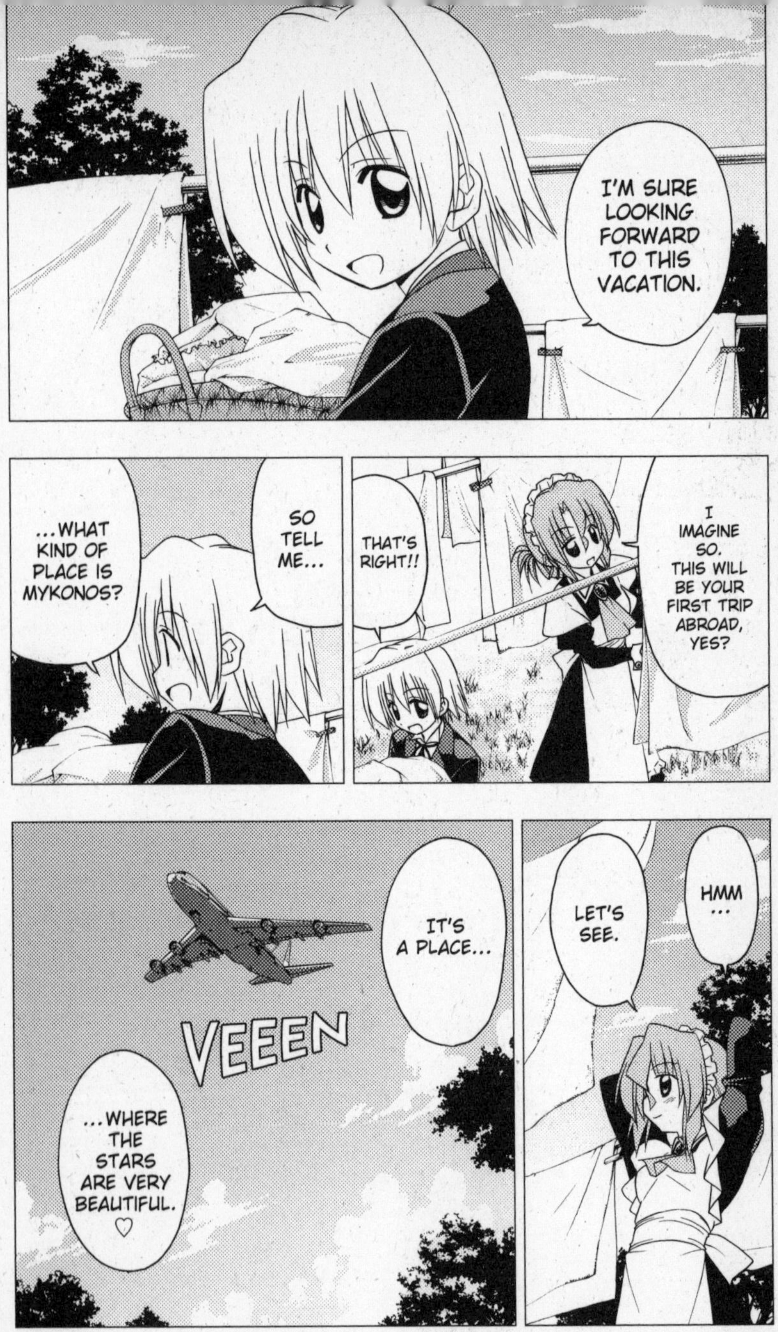
I'M SURE LOOKING FORWARD TO THIS VACATION.
I IMAGINE SO. THIS WILL BE YOUR FIRST TRIP ABROAD, YES?
THAT'S RIGHT!!
SO TELL ME...
...WHAT KIND OF PLACE IS MYKONOS?
HMM...
LET'S SEE.
IT'S A PLACE...
VEEEN
...WHERE THE STARS ARE VERY BEAUTIFUL. ♡

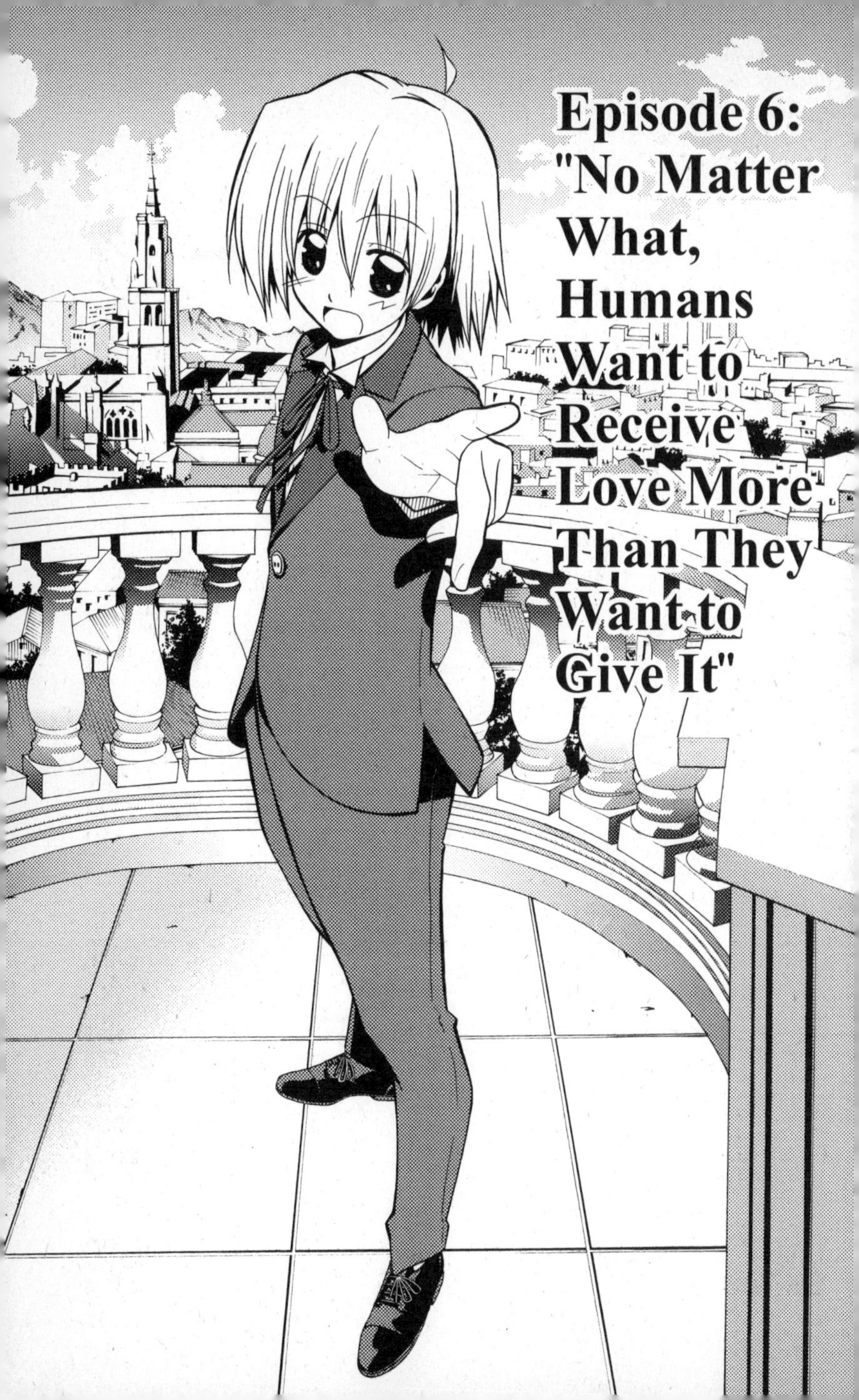
Episode 6:
"No Matter What, Humans Want to Receive Love More Than They Want to Give It"

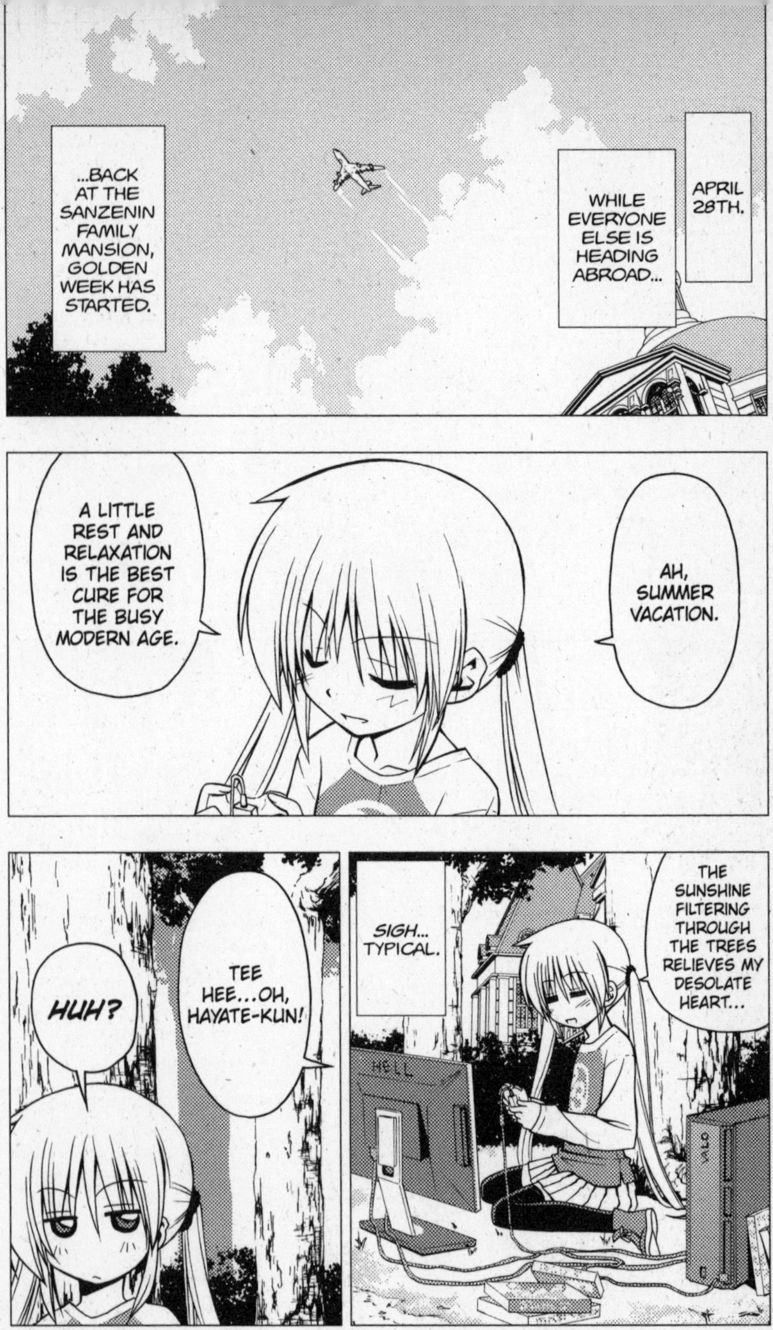
APRIL 28TH.
WHILE EVERYONE ELSE IS HEADING ABROAD...
...BACK AT THE SANZENIN FAMILY MANSION, GOLDEN WEEK HAS STARTED.
AH, SUMMER VACATION.
A LITTLE REST AND RELAXATION IS THE BEST CURE FOR THE BUSY MODERN AGE.
THE SUNSHINE FILTERING THROUGH THE TREES RELIEVES MY DESOLATE HEART...
SIGH... TYPICAL.
HELL
TEE HEE...OH, HAYATE-KUN!
HUH?

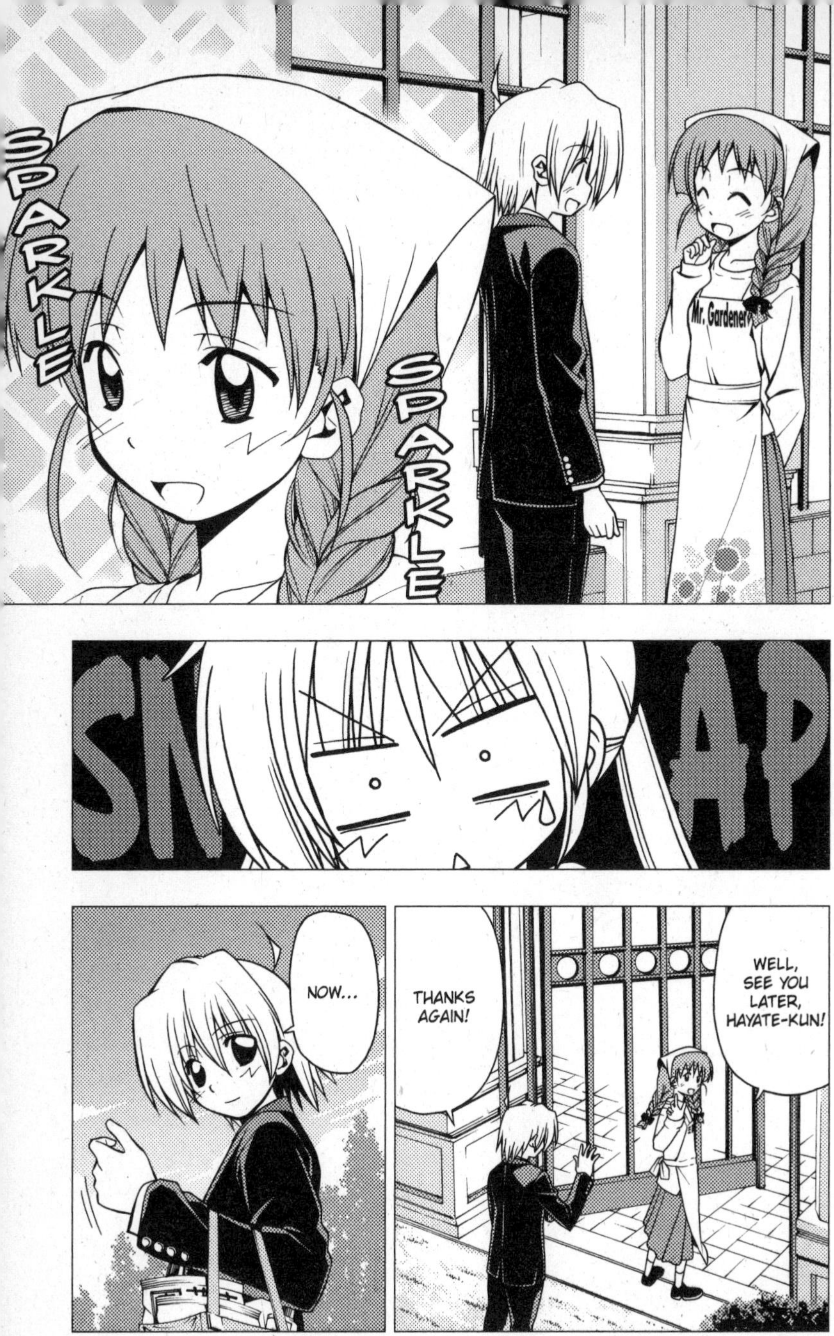
SPARKLE
SPARKLE
Mr. Gardener
SN AP
WELL, SEE YOU LATER, HAYATE-KUN!
THANKS AGAIN!
NOW...

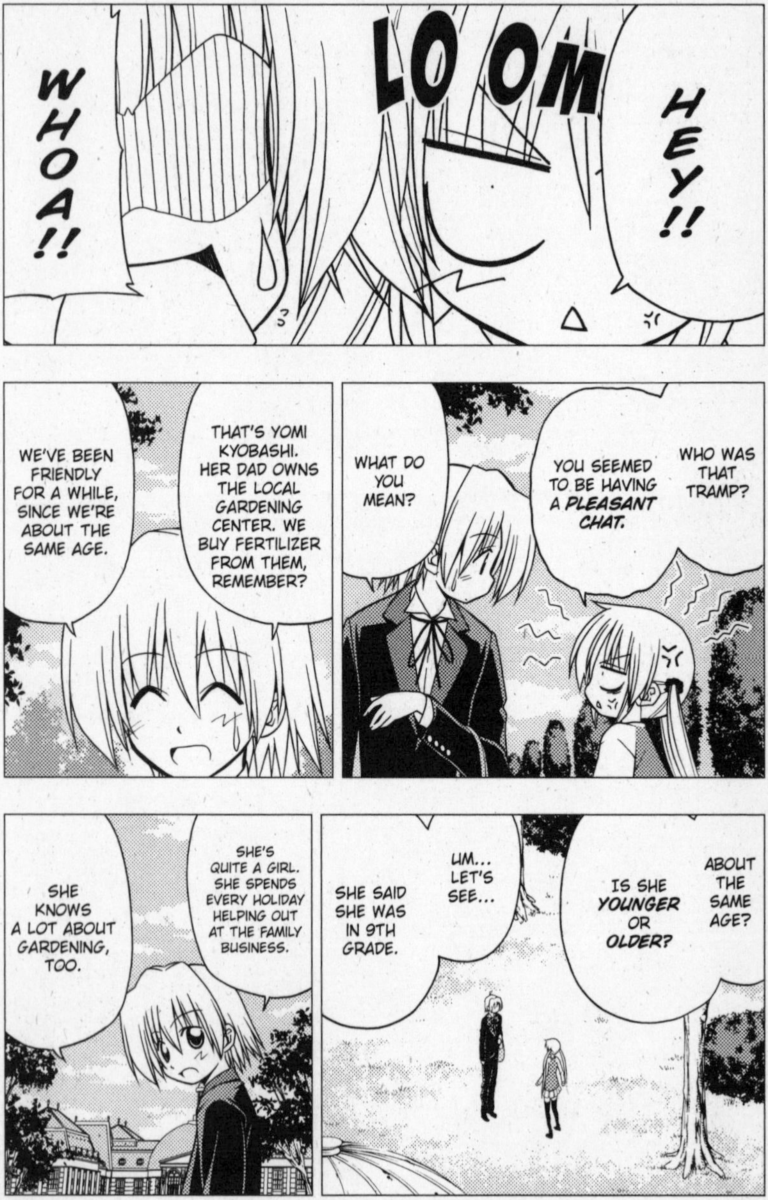
HEY!!
LOOM
WHOA!!
WHO WAS THAT TRAMP?
YOU SEEMED TO BE HAVING A PLEASANT CHAT.
WHAT DO YOU MEAN?
THAT'S YOMI KYOBASHI. HER DAD OWNS THE LOCAL GARDENING CENTER. WE BUY FERTILIZER FROM THEM, REMEMBER?
WE'VE BEEN FRIENDLY FOR A WHILE, SINCE WE'RE ABOUT THE SAME AGE.
ABOUT THE SAME AGE?
IS SHE YOUNGER OR OLDER?
UM... LET'S SEE...
SHE SAID SHE WAS IN 9TH GRADE.
SHE'S QUITE A GIRL. SHE SPENDS EVERY HOLIDAY HELPING OUT AT THE FAMILY BUSINESS.
SHE KNOWS A LOT ABOUT GARDENING, TOO.

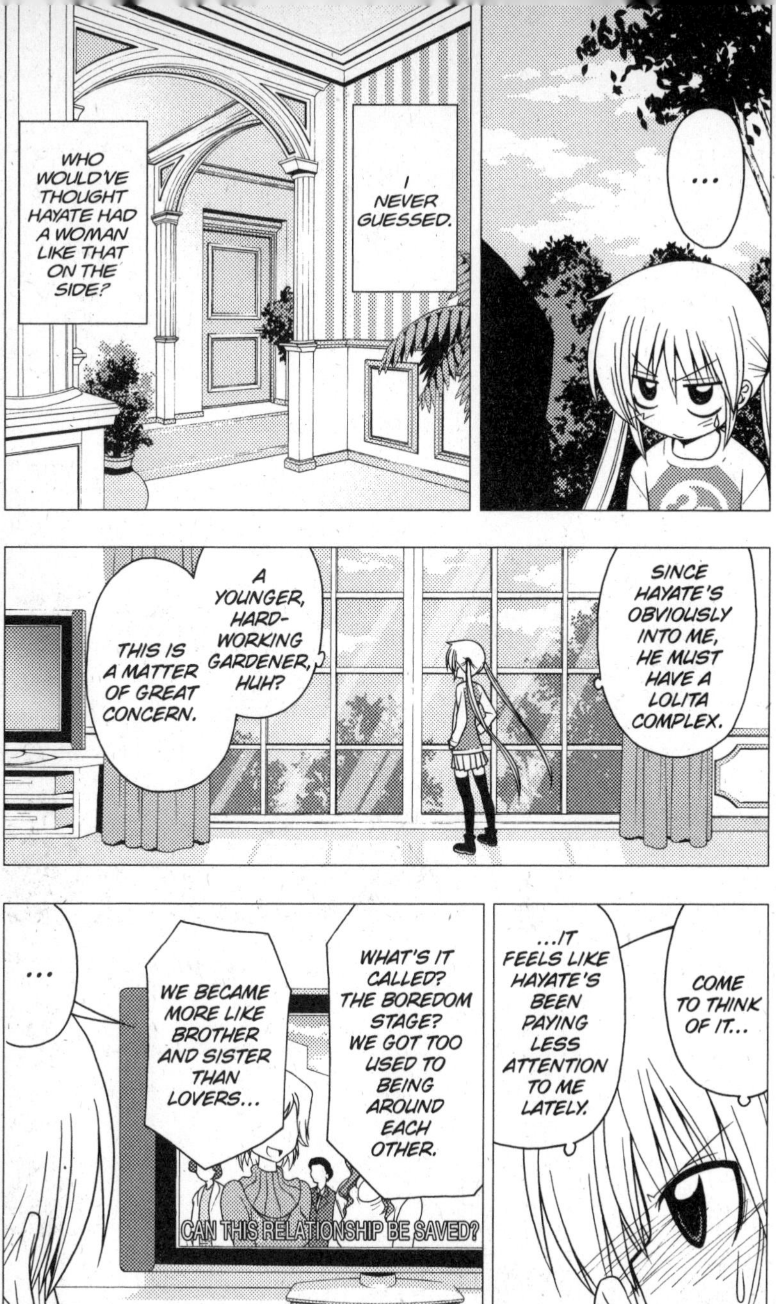
...
I NEVER GUESSED.
WHO WOULD'VE THOUGHT HAYATE HAD A WOMAN LIKE THAT ON THE SIDE?
SINCE HAYATE'S OBVIOUSLY INTO ME, HE MUST HAVE A LOLITA COMPLEX.
A YOUNGER, HARD-WORKING GARDENER, HUH?
THIS IS A MATTER OF GREAT CONCERN.
COME TO THINK OF IT...
...IT FEELS LIKE HAYATE'S BEEN PAYING LESS ATTENTION TO ME LATELY.
WHAT'S IT CALLED? THE BOREDOM STAGE? WE GOT TOO USED TO BEING AROUND EACH OTHER.
WE BECAME MORE LIKE BROTHER AND SISTER THAN LOVERS...
CAN THIS RELATIONSHIP BE SAVED?
...

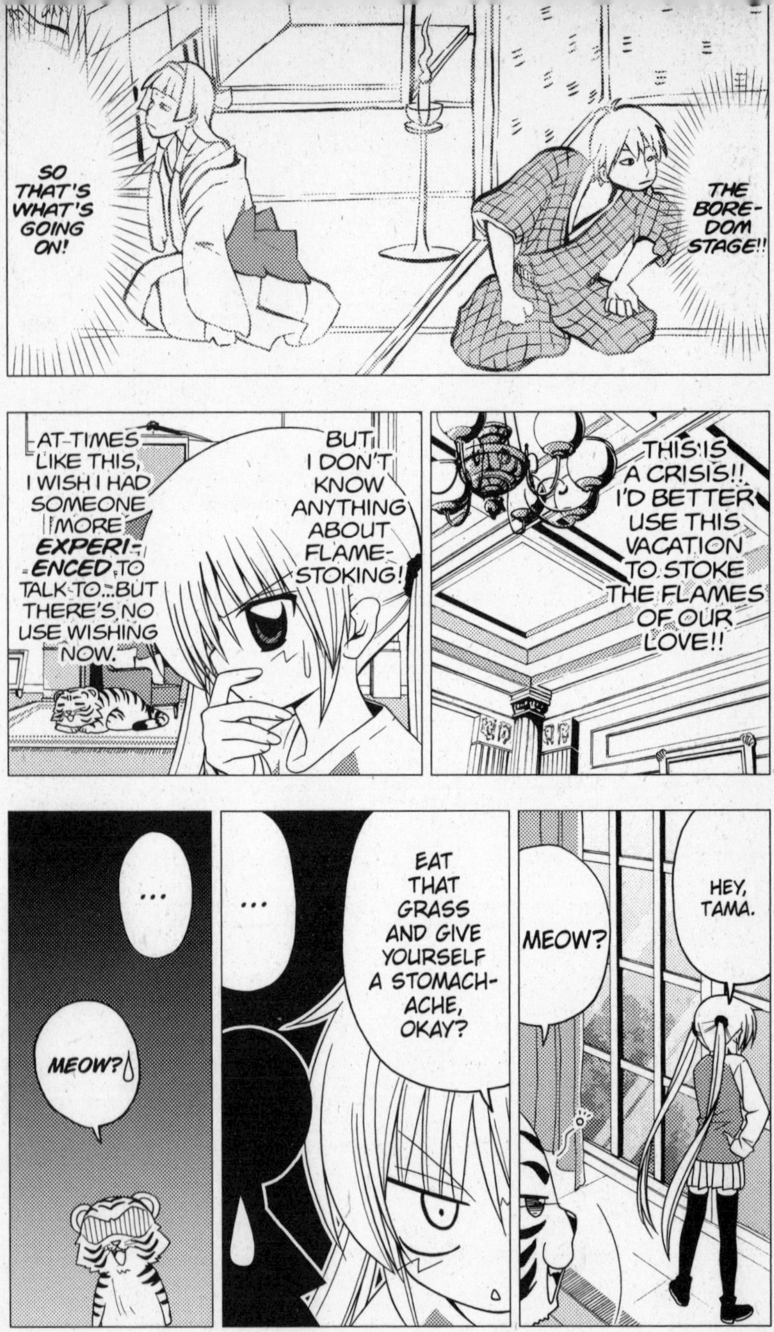
THE BOREDOM STAGE!!
SO THAT'S WHAT'S GOING ON!
THIS IS A CRISIS!! I'D BETTER USE THIS VACATION TO STOKE THE FLAMES OF OUR LOVE!!
BUT I DON'T KNOW ANYTHING ABOUT FLAME-STOKING!
AT TIMES LIKE THIS, I WISH I HAD SOMEONE MORE *EXPERIENCED* TO TALK TO...BUT THERE'S NO USE WISHING NOW.
HEY, TAMA.
MEOW?
EAT THAT GRASS AND GIVE YOURSELF A STOMACHACHE, OKAY?
...
...
MEOW?

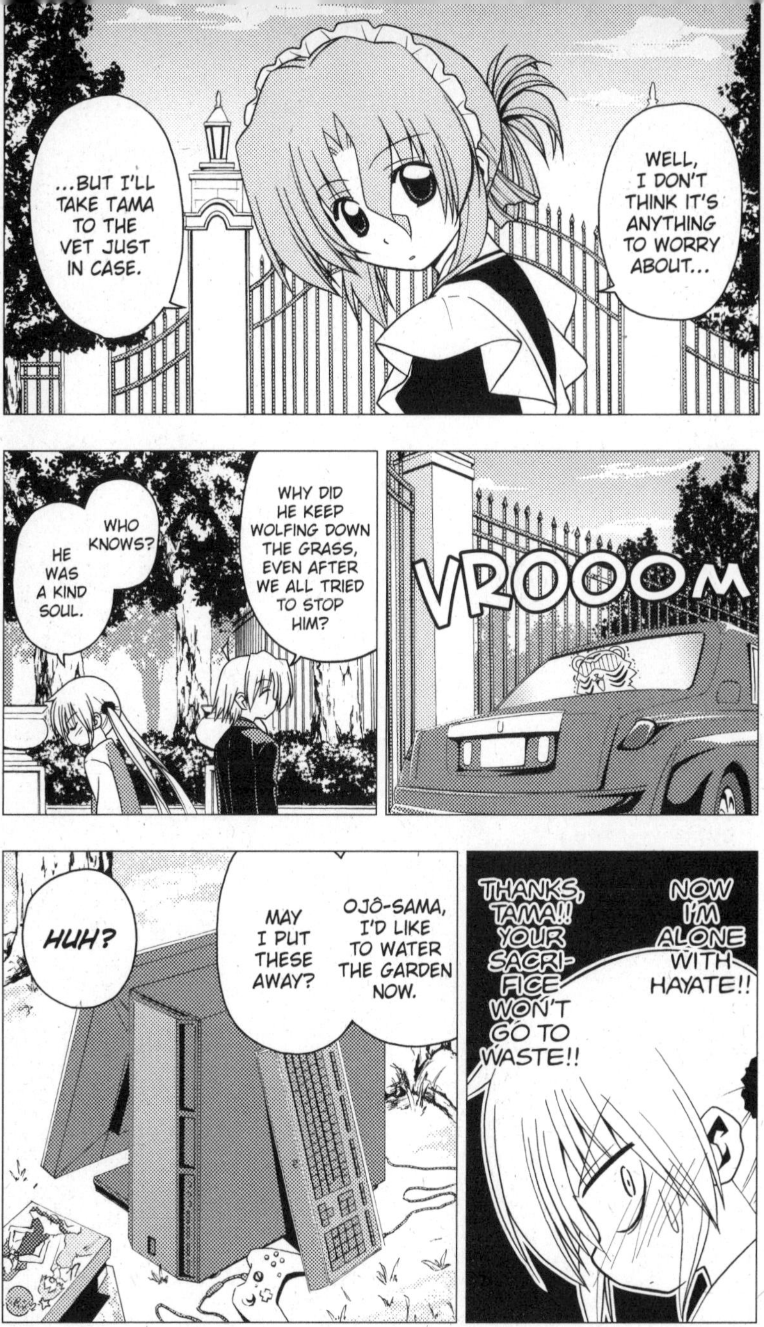
WELL, I DON'T THINK IT'S ANYTHING TO WORRY ABOUT...
...BUT I'LL TAKE TAMA TO THE VET JUST IN CASE.
VROOOM
WHY DID HE KEEP WOLFING DOWN THE GRASS, EVEN AFTER WE ALL TRIED TO STOP HIM?
WHO KNOWS? HE WAS A KIND SOUL.
NOW I'M ALONE WITH HAYATE!!
THANKS, TAMA!! YOUR SACRI-FICE WON'T GO TO WASTE!!
OJÔ-SAMA, I'D LIKE TO WATER THE GARDEN NOW.
MAY I PUT THESE AWAY?
HUH?

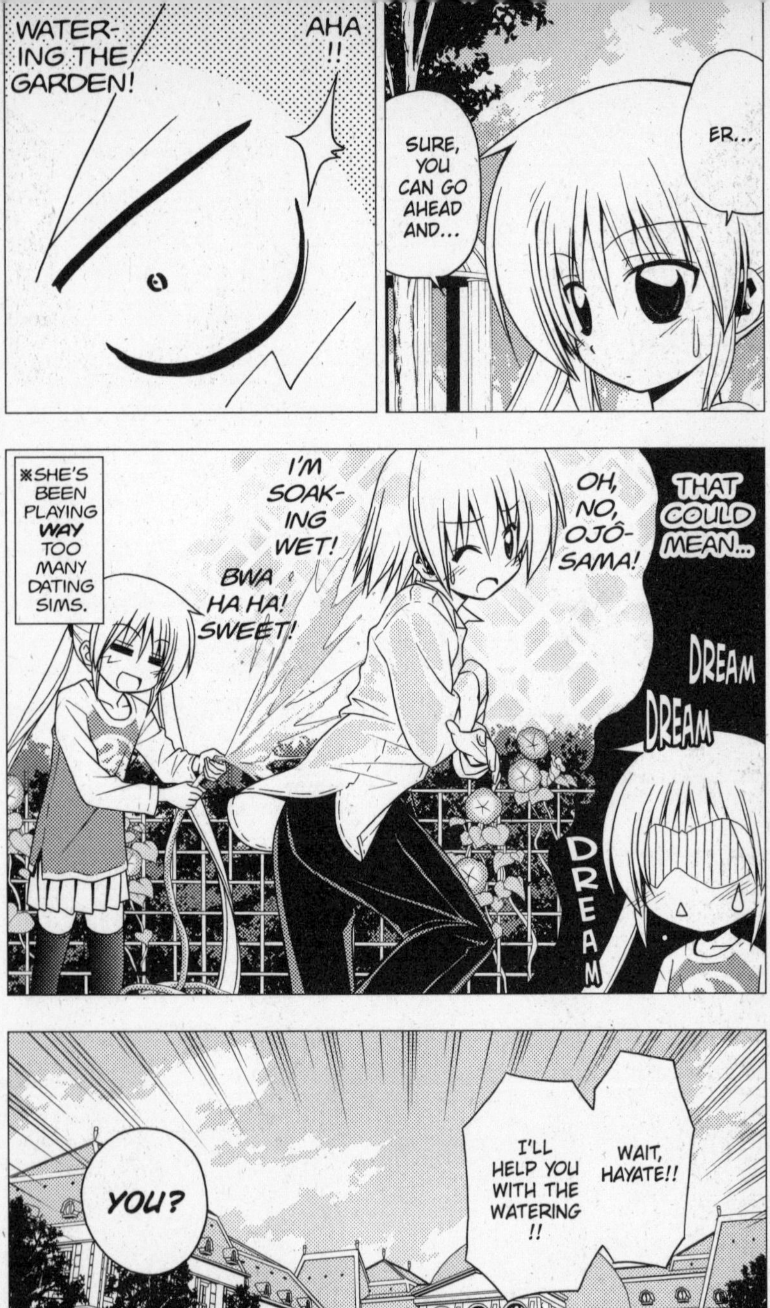
ER...
SURE, YOU CAN GO AHEAD AND...
AHA!!
WATERING THE GARDEN!
THAT COULD MEAN...
OH, NO, OJÔ-SAMA!
I'M SOAKING WET!
BWA HA HA! SWEET!
DREAM
DREAM
DREAM
※SHE'S BEEN PLAYING **WAY** TOO MANY DATING SIMS.
WAIT, HAYATE!!
I'LL HELP YOU WITH THE WATERING!!
YOU?

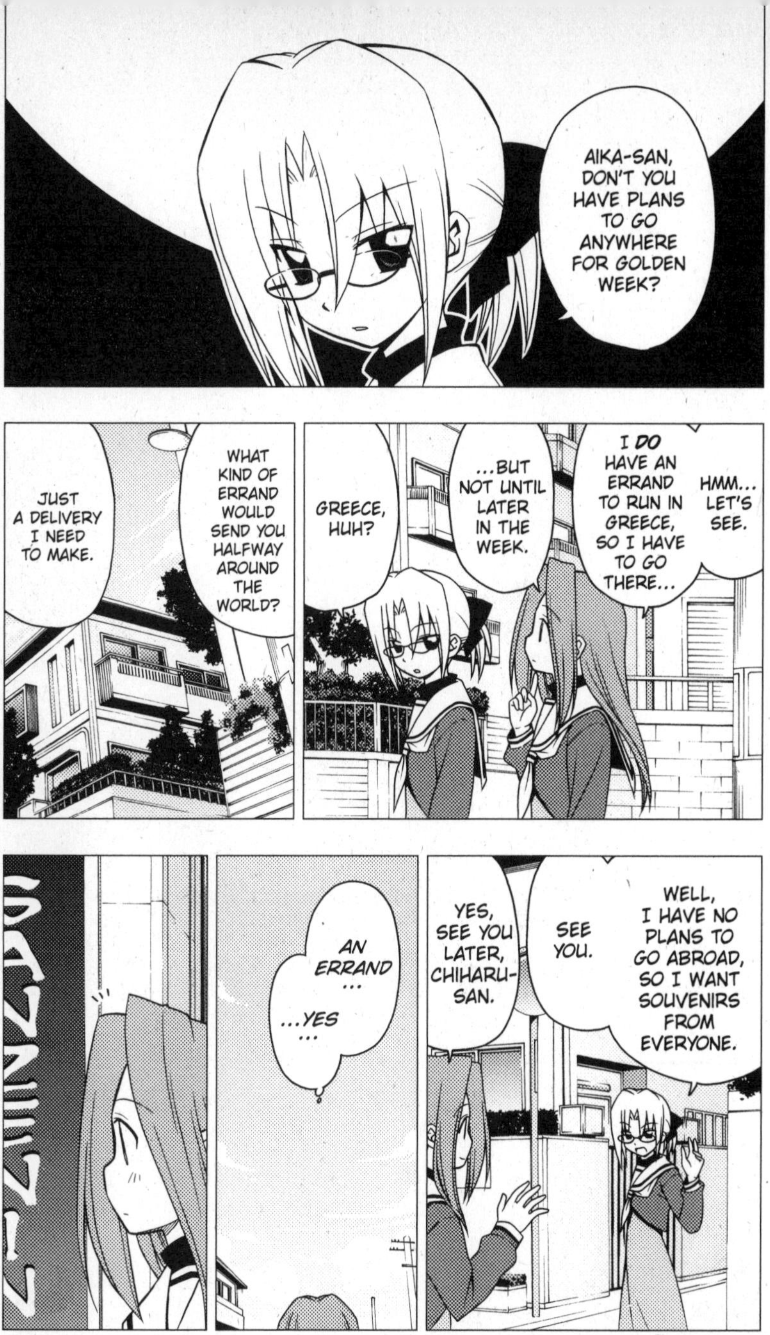
AIKA-SAN, DON'T YOU HAVE PLANS TO GO ANYWHERE FOR GOLDEN WEEK?
HMM... LET'S SEE.
I *DO* HAVE AN ERRAND TO RUN IN GREECE, SO I HAVE TO GO THERE...
...BUT NOT UNTIL LATER IN THE WEEK.
GREECE, HUH?
WHAT KIND OF ERRAND WOULD SEND YOU HALFWAY AROUND THE WORLD?
JUST A DELIVERY I NEED TO MAKE.
WELL, I HAVE NO PLANS TO GO ABROAD, SO I WANT SOUVENIRS FROM EVERYONE.
SEE YOU.
YES, SEE YOU LATER, CHIHARU-SAN.
AN ERRAND...
...YES...

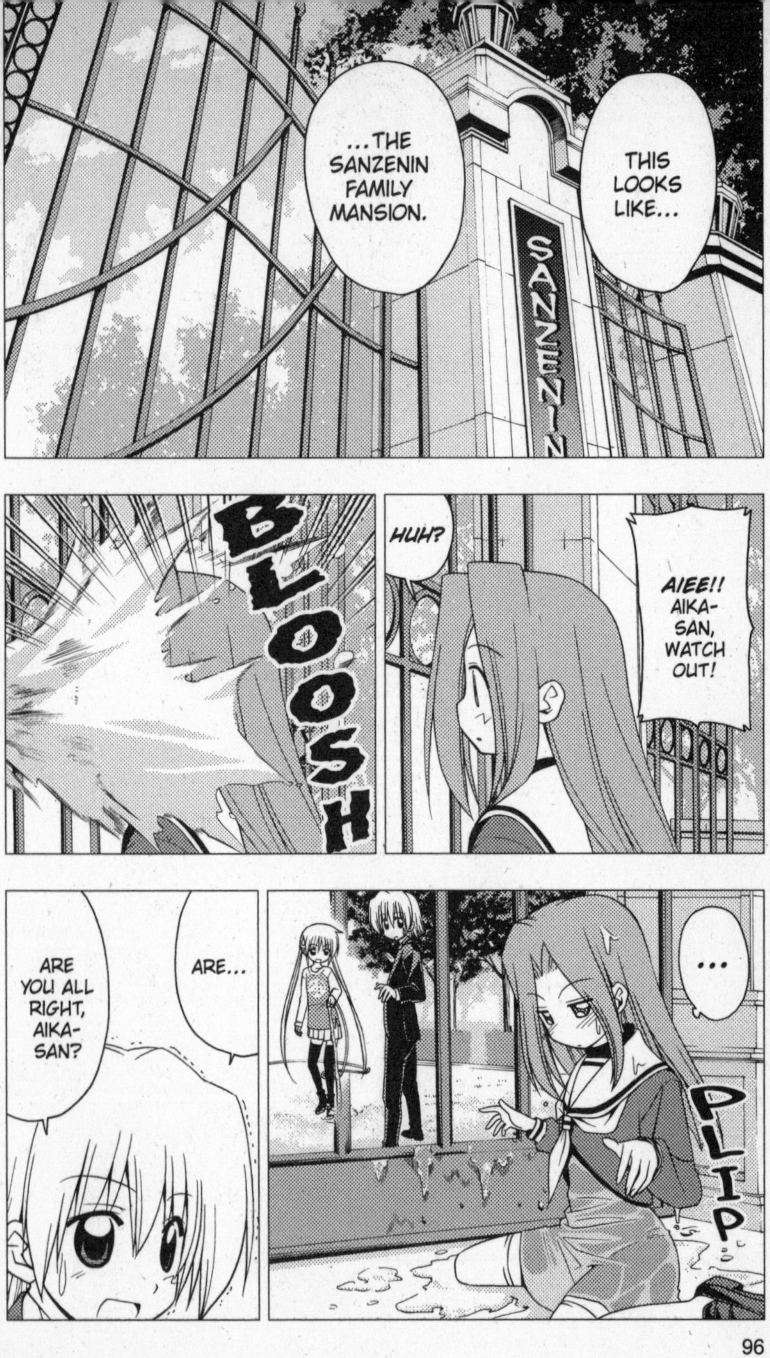
THIS LOOKS LIKE...
...THE SANZENIN FAMILY MANSION.
SANZENIN
AIEE!! AIKA-SAN, WATCH OUT!
HUH?
BLOOSH
...
PLIP
ARE...
ARE YOU ALL RIGHT, AIKA-SAN?

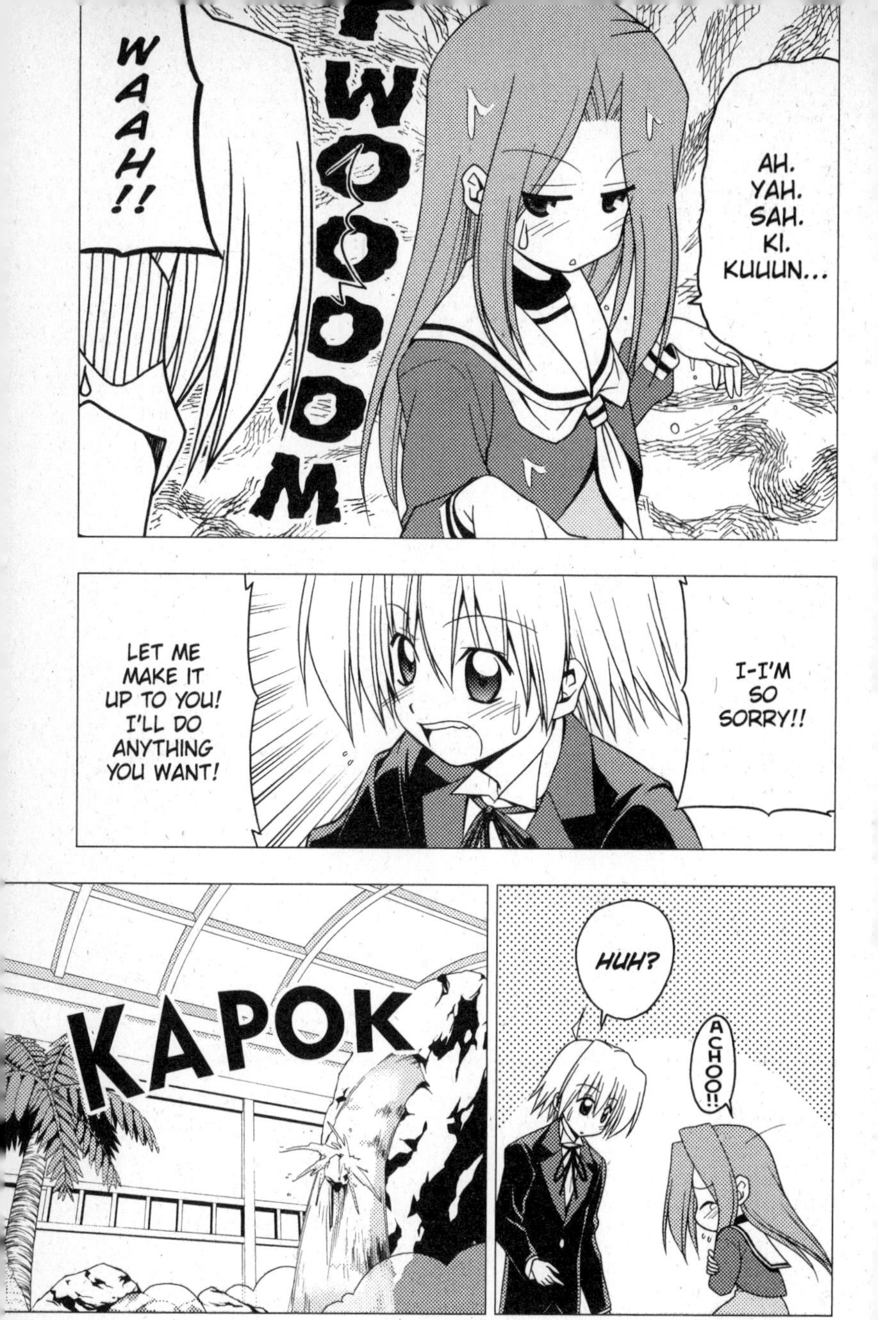
AH. YAH. SAH. KI. KUUUN...
WOOOOM
WAAH!!
I-I'M SO SORRY!!
LET ME MAKE IT UP TO YOU! I'LL DO ANYTHING YOU WANT!
HUH?
ACHOO!!
KAPOK

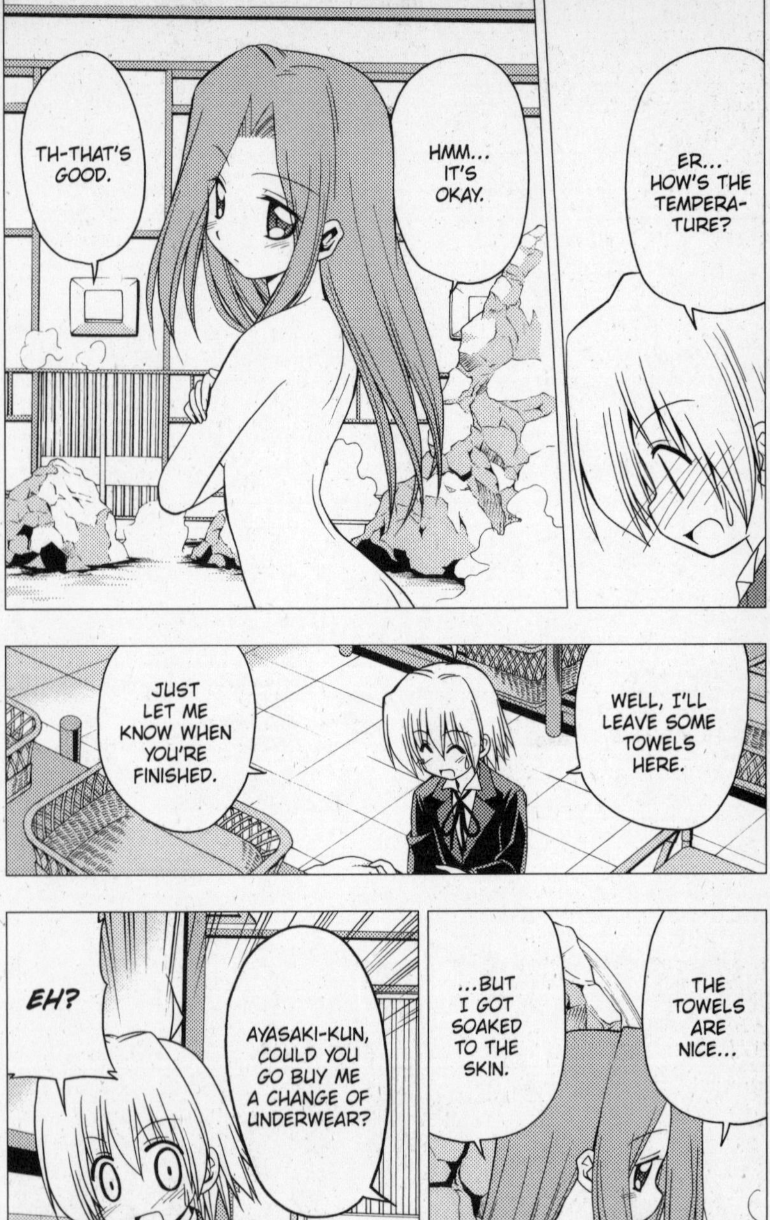
ER... HOW'S THE TEMPERA-TURE?
HMM... IT'S OKAY.
TH-THAT'S GOOD.
WELL, I'LL LEAVE SOME TOWELS HERE.
JUST LET ME KNOW WHEN YOU'RE FINISHED.
THE TOWELS ARE NICE...
...BUT I GOT SOAKED TO THE SKIN.
AYASAKI-KUN, COULD YOU GO BUY ME A CHANGE OF UNDERWEAR?
EH?

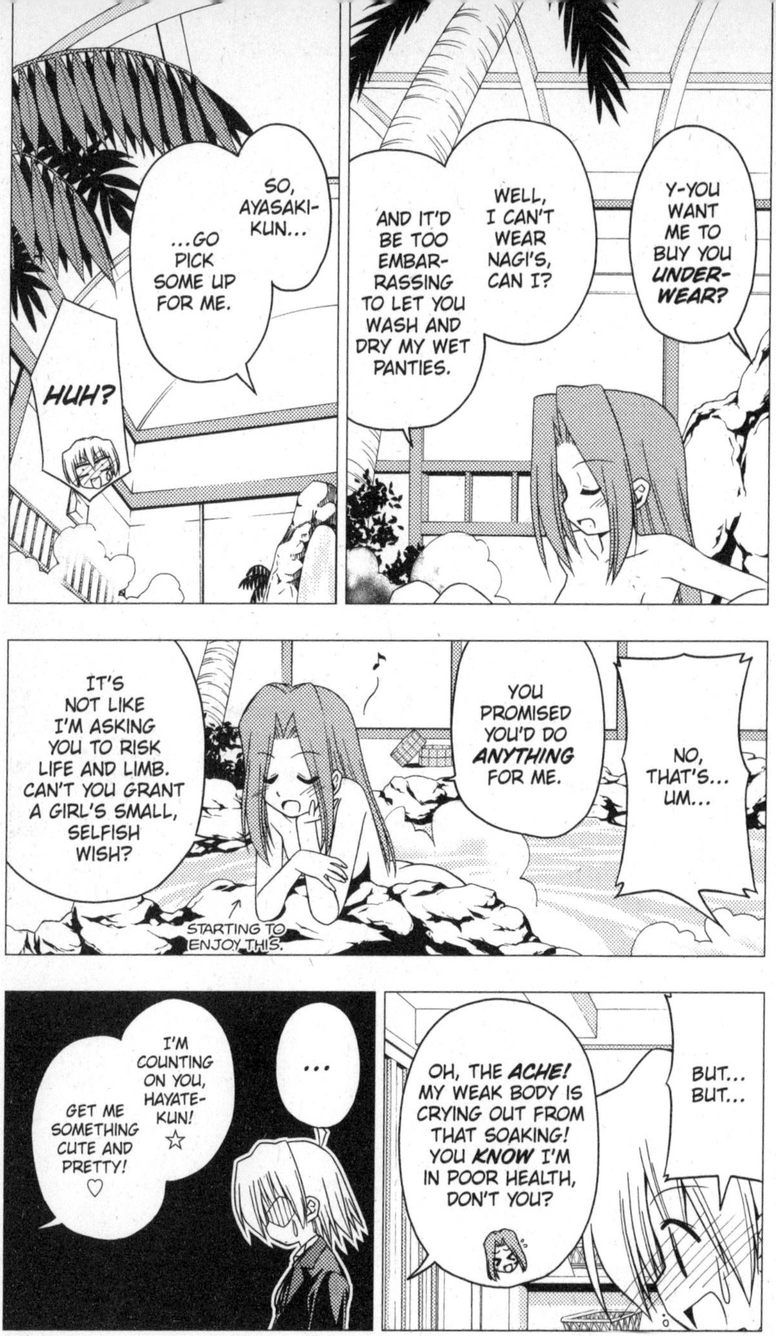
Y-YOU WANT ME TO BUY YOU UNDERWEAR?
WELL, I CAN'T WEAR NAGI'S, CAN I?
AND IT'D BE TOO EMBARRASSING TO LET YOU WASH AND DRY MY WET PANTIES.
SO, AYASAKI-KUN...
...GO PICK SOME UP FOR ME.
HUH?
NO, THAT'S... UM...
YOU PROMISED YOU'D DO ANYTHING FOR ME.
IT'S NOT LIKE I'M ASKING YOU TO RISK LIFE AND LIMB. CAN'T YOU GRANT A GIRL'S SMALL, SELFISH WISH?
STARTING TO ENJOY THIS.
BUT... BUT...
OH, THE ACHE! MY WEAK BODY IS CRYING OUT FROM THAT SOAKING! YOU KNOW I'M IN POOR HEALTH, DON'T YOU?
...
I'M COUNTING ON YOU, HAYATE-KUN! ☆
GET ME SOMETHING CUTE AND PRETTY! ♡

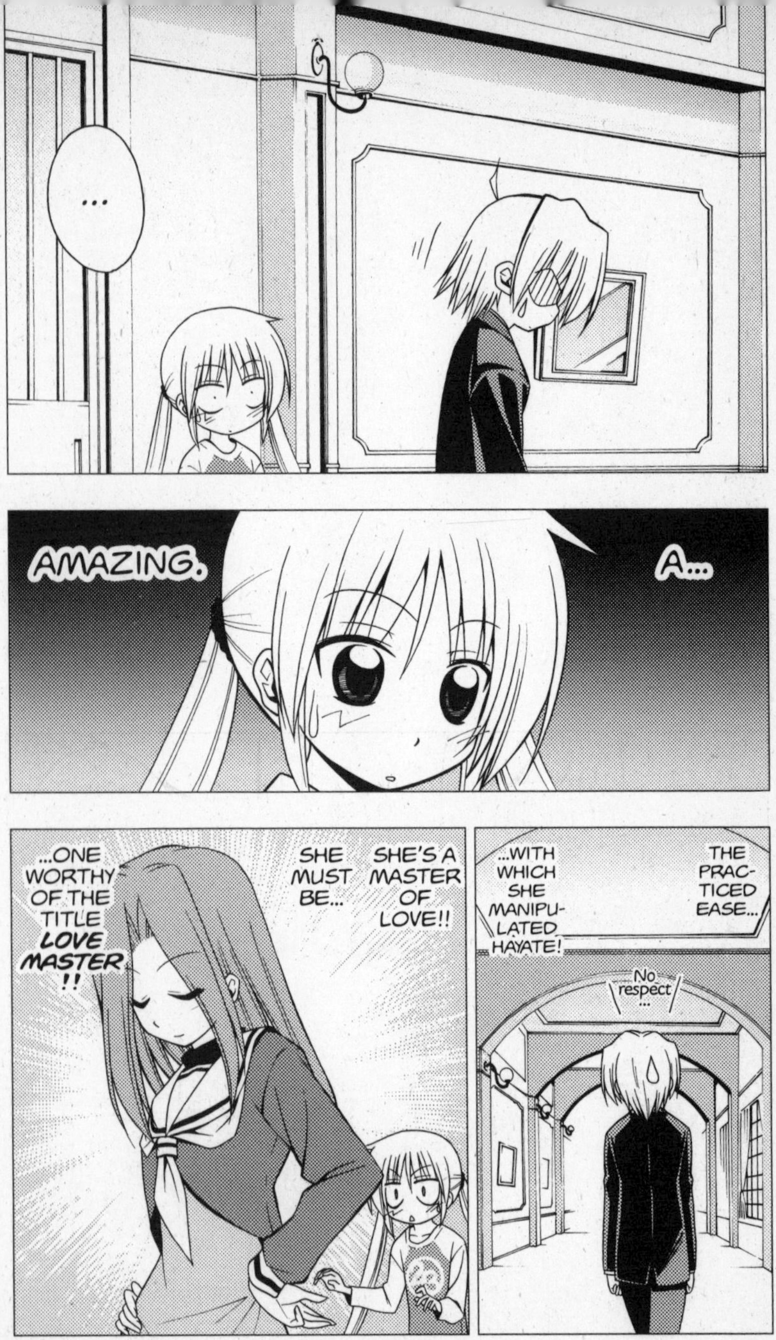
...
A...
AMAZING.
THE PRACTICED EASE...
...WITH WHICH SHE MANIPULATED HAYATE!
No respect...
SHE'S A MASTER OF LOVE!!
SHE MUST BE...
...ONE WORTHY OF THE TITLE LOVE MASTER!!

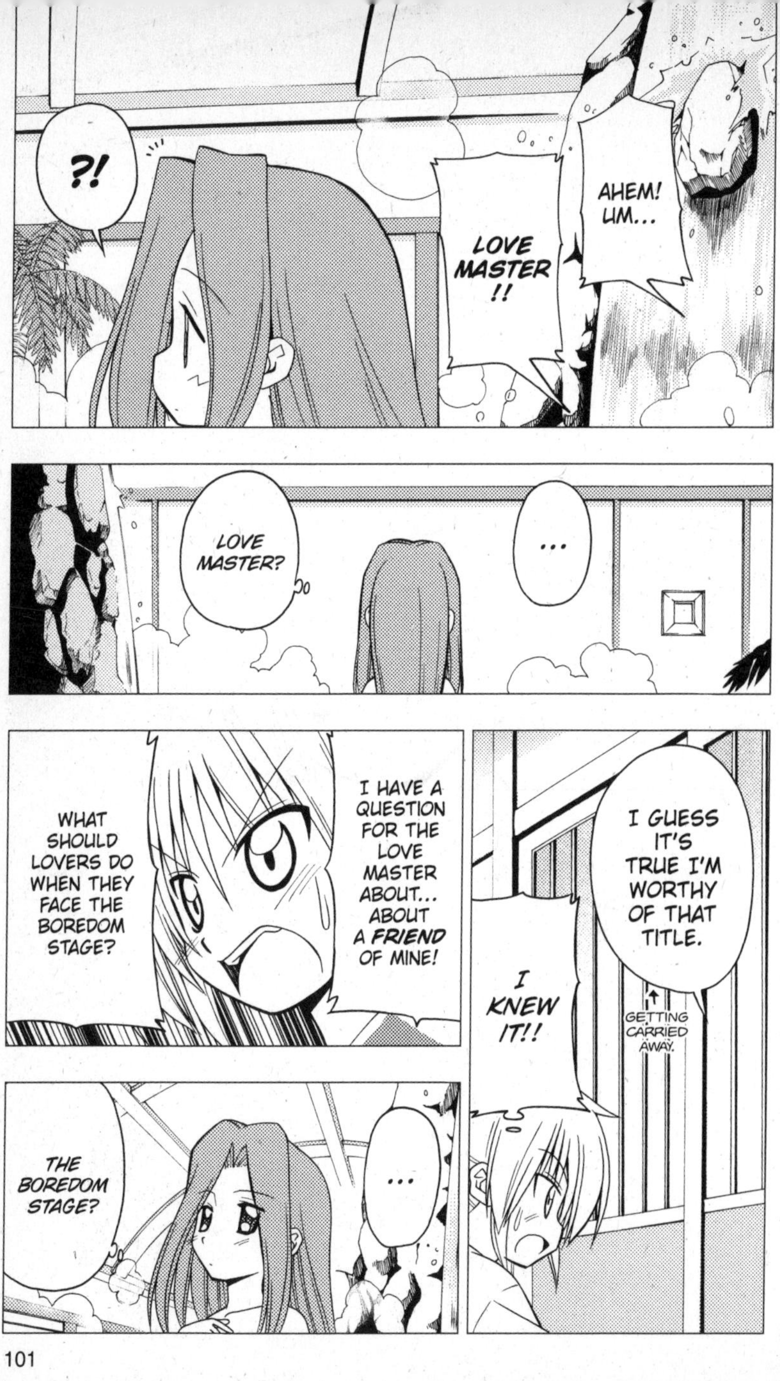
AHEM! UM...
LOVE MASTER!!
?!
...
LOVE MASTER?
I GUESS IT'S TRUE I'M WORTHY OF THAT TITLE.
I KNEW IT!!
GETTING CARRIED AWAY.
I HAVE A QUESTION FOR THE LOVE MASTER ABOUT... ABOUT A FRIEND OF MINE!
WHAT SHOULD LOVERS DO WHEN THEY FACE THE BOREDOM STAGE?
...
THE BOREDOM STAGE?

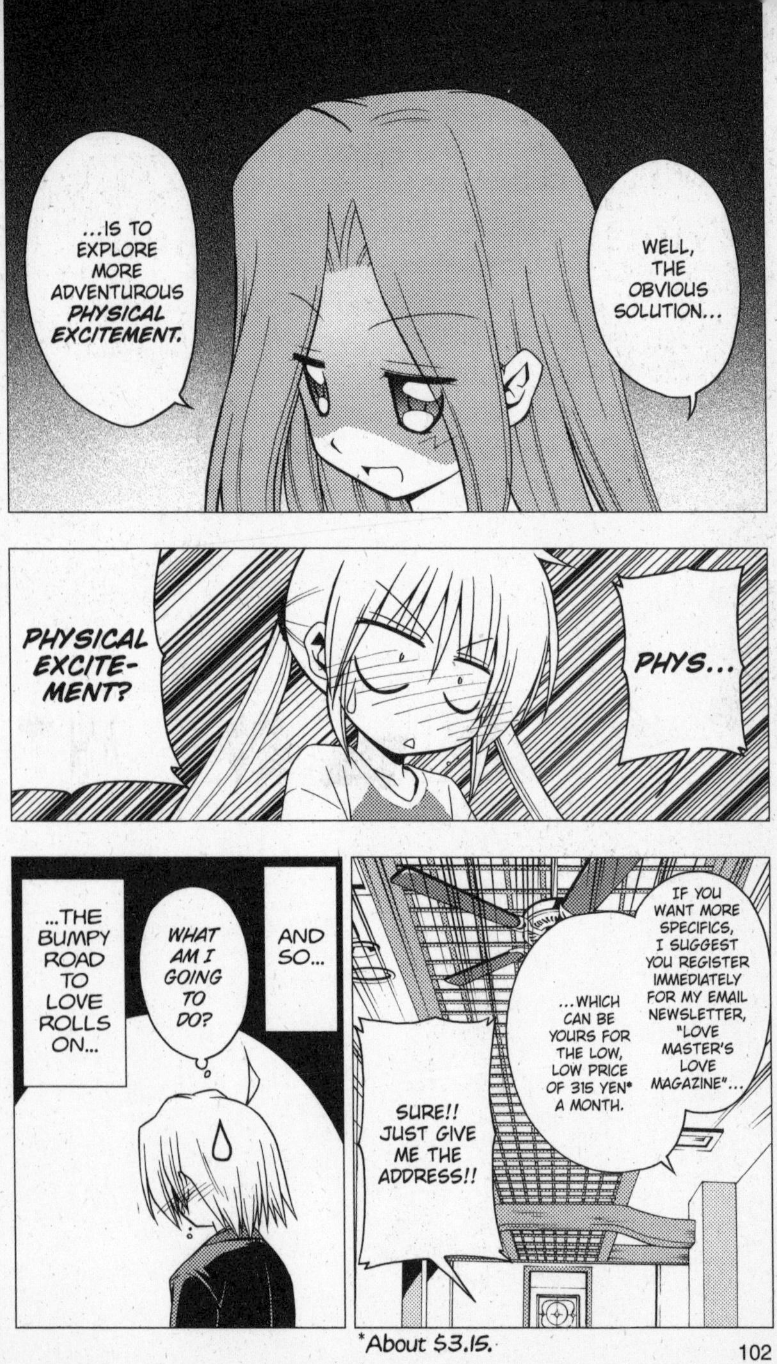
WELL, THE OBVIOUS SOLUTION...
...IS TO EXPLORE MORE ADVENTUROUS PHYSICAL EXCITEMENT.
PHYS...
PHYSICAL EXCITE-MENT?
IF YOU WANT MORE SPECIFICS, I SUGGEST YOU REGISTER IMMEDIATELY FOR MY EMAIL NEWSLETTER, "LOVE MASTER'S LOVE MAGAZINE"...
...WHICH CAN BE YOURS FOR THE LOW, LOW PRICE OF 315 YEN* A MONTH.
SURE!! JUST GIVE ME THE ADDRESS!!
AND SO...
WHAT AM I GOING TO DO?
...THE BUMPY ROAD TO LOVE ROLLS ON...

*About $3.15.

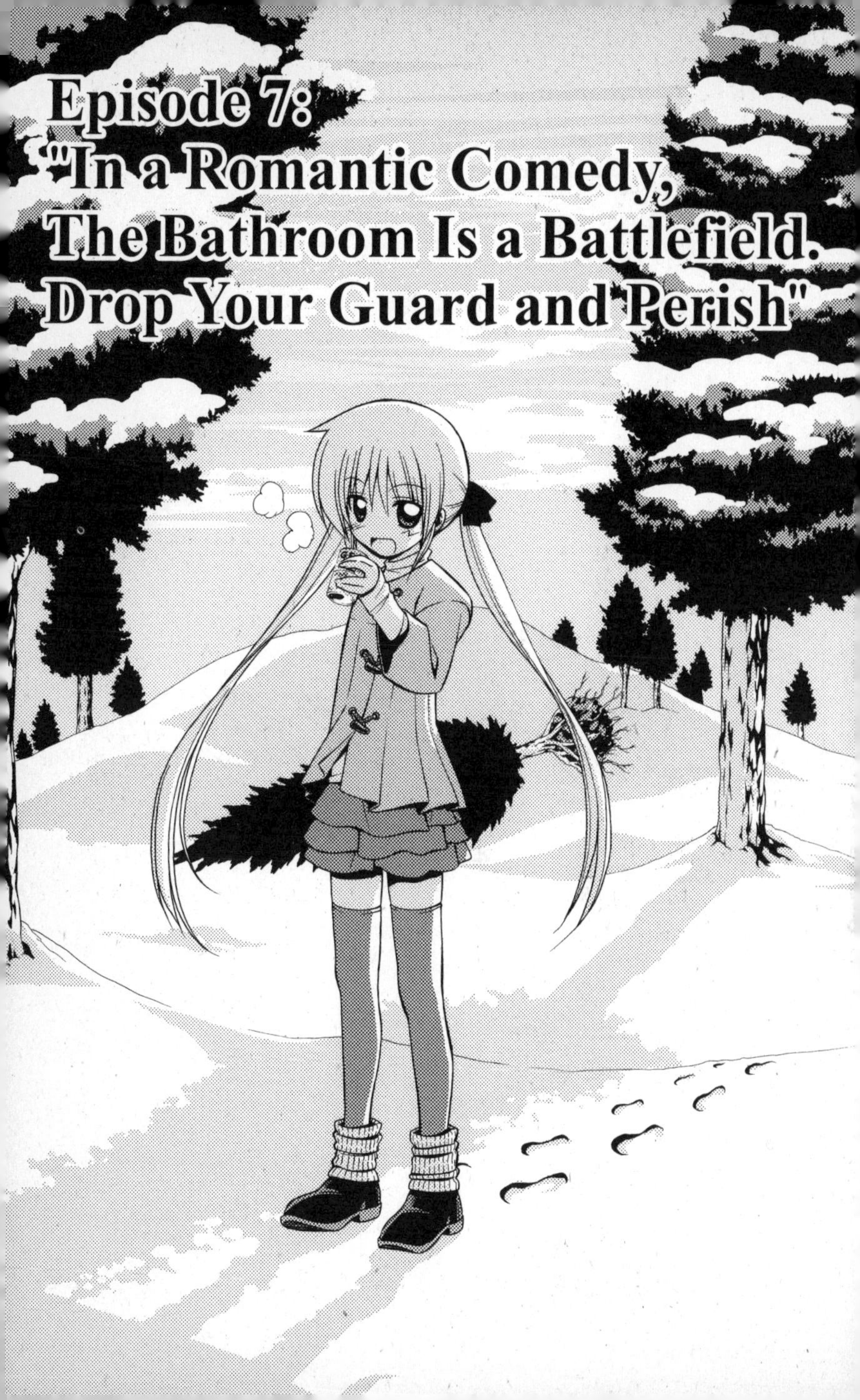
Episode 7:
"In a Romantic Comedy,
The Bathroom Is a Battlefield.
Drop Your Guard and Perish"

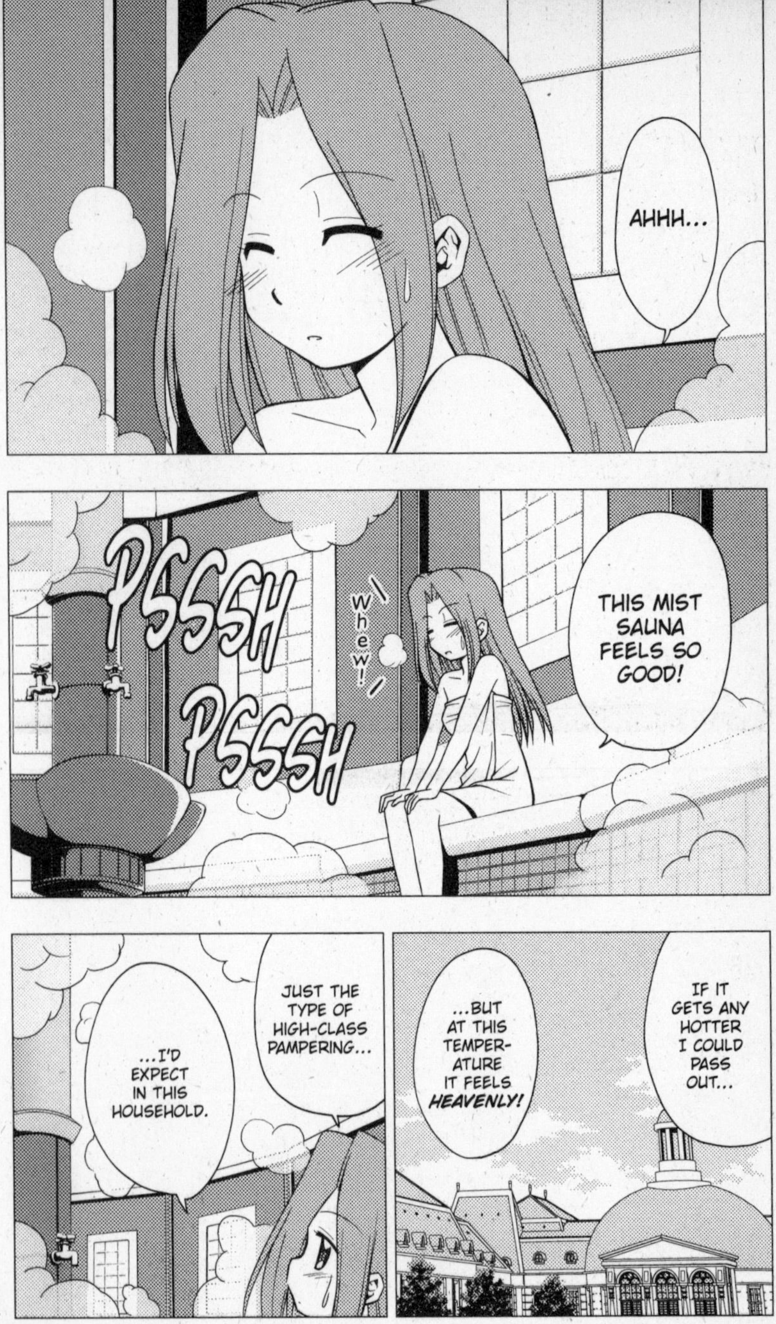
AHHH...
THIS MIST SAUNA FEELS SO GOOD!
Whew!
PSSSH PSSSH
IF IT GETS ANY HOTTER I COULD PASS OUT...
...BUT AT THIS TEMPER-ATURE IT FEELS *HEAVENLY!*
JUST THE TYPE OF HIGH-CLASS PAMPERING...
...I'D EXPECT IN THIS HOUSEHOLD.

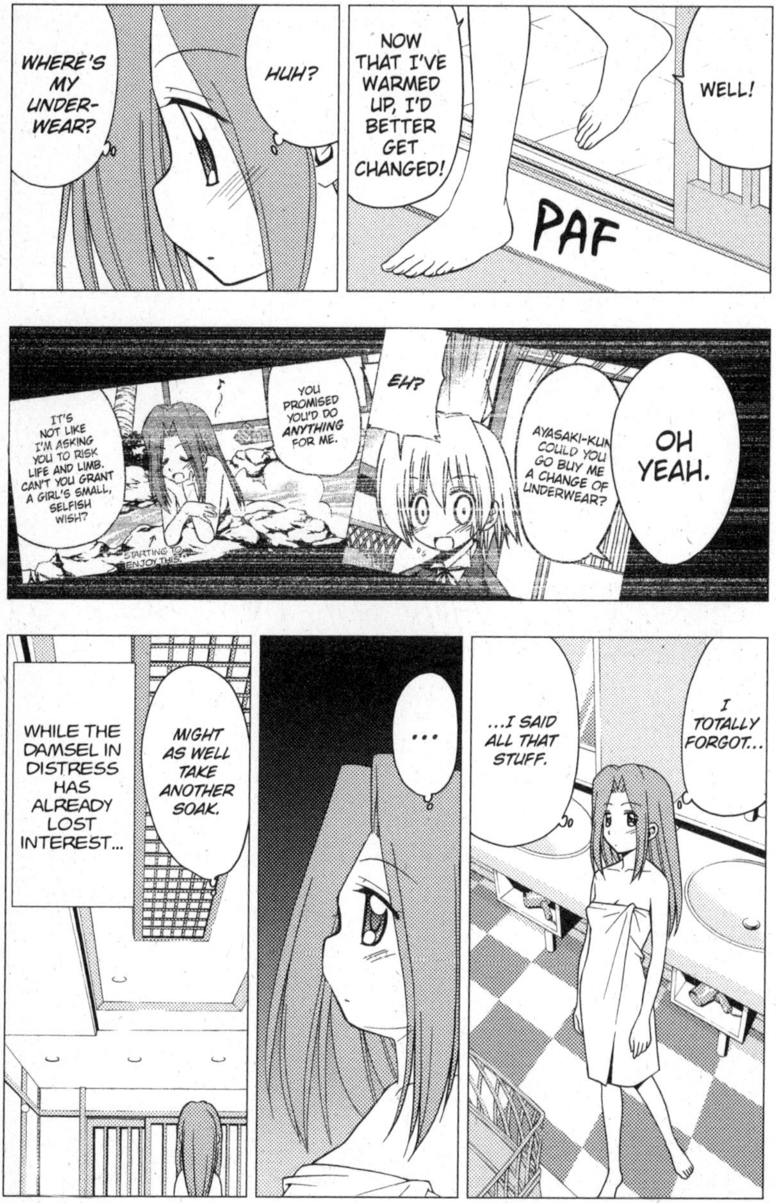

WELL!
NOW THAT I'VE WARMED UP, I'D BETTER GET CHANGED!
PAF
HUH?
WHERE'S MY UNDERWEAR?
OH YEAH.
AYASAKI-KUN COULD YOU GO BUY ME A CHANGE OF UNDERWEAR?
EH?
YOU PROMISED YOU'D DO ANYTHING FOR ME.
IT'S NOT LIKE I'M ASKING YOU TO RISK LIFE AND LIMB. CAN'T YOU GRANT A GIRL'S SMALL, SELFISH WISH?
STARTING TO ENJOY THIS.
I TOTALLY FORGOT...
...I SAID ALL THAT STUFF.
...
MIGHT AS WELL TAKE ANOTHER SOAK.
WHILE THE DAMSEL IN DISTRESS HAS ALREADY LOST INTEREST...

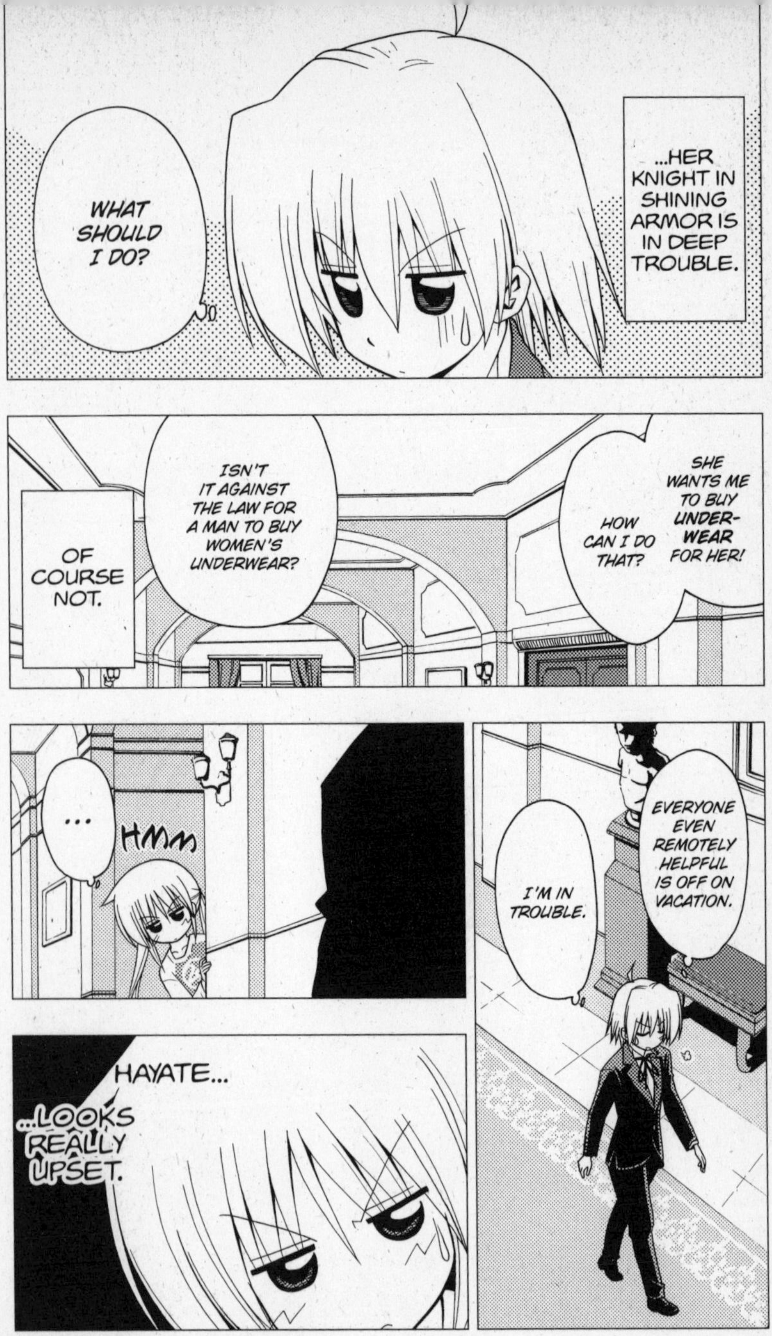
...HER KNIGHT IN SHINING ARMOR IS IN DEEP TROUBLE.
WHAT SHOULD I DO?
SHE WANTS ME TO BUY UNDER-WEAR FOR HER!
HOW CAN I DO THAT?
ISN'T IT AGAINST THE LAW FOR A MAN TO BUY WOMEN'S UNDERWEAR?
OF COURSE NOT.
EVERYONE EVEN REMOTELY HELPFUL IS OFF ON VACATION.
I'M IN TROUBLE.
...
HMM
HAYATE...
...LOOKS REALLY UPSET.

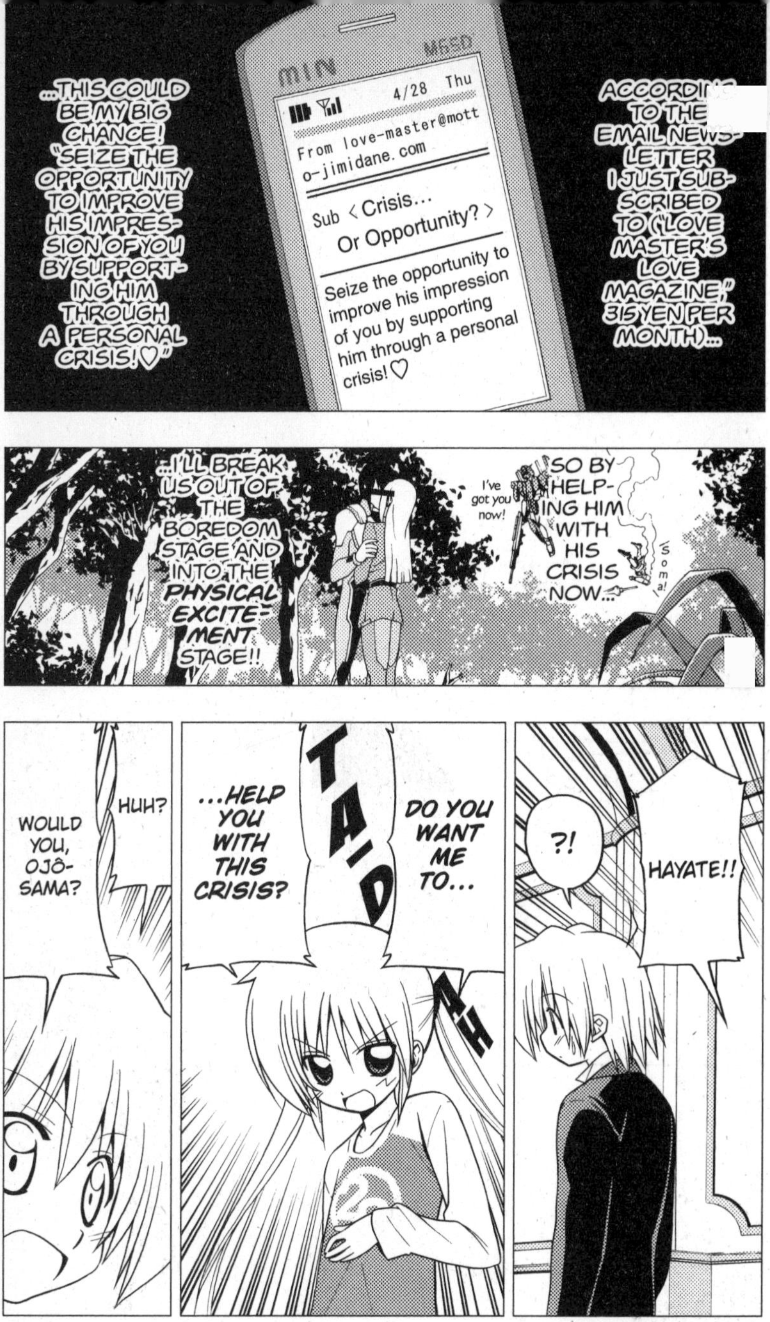

ACCORDI
TO THE EMAIL NEWS-LETTER I JUST SUB-SCRIBED TO ("LOVE MASTER'S LOVE MAGAZINE," 315 YEN PER MONTH)...
MIN
M65D
4/28 Thu
From love-master@motto-jimidane.com
Sub < Crisis... Or Opportunity? >
Seize the opportunity to improve his impression of you by supporting him through a personal crisis! ♡
...THIS COULD BE MY BIG CHANCE! "SEIZE THE OPPORTUNITY TO IMPROVE HIS IMPRES-SION OF YOU BY SUPPORT-ING HIM THROUGH A PERSONAL CRISIS! ♡"
SO BY HELP-ING HIM WITH HIS CRISIS NOW...
Soma!
I've got you now!
...I'LL BREAK US OUT OF THE BOREDOM STAGE AND INTO THE PHYSICAL EXCITE-MENT STAGE!!
HAYATE!!
?!
DO YOU WANT ME TO...
TA-DAH
...HELP YOU WITH THIS CRISIS?
HUH?
WOULD YOU, OJÔ-SAMA?

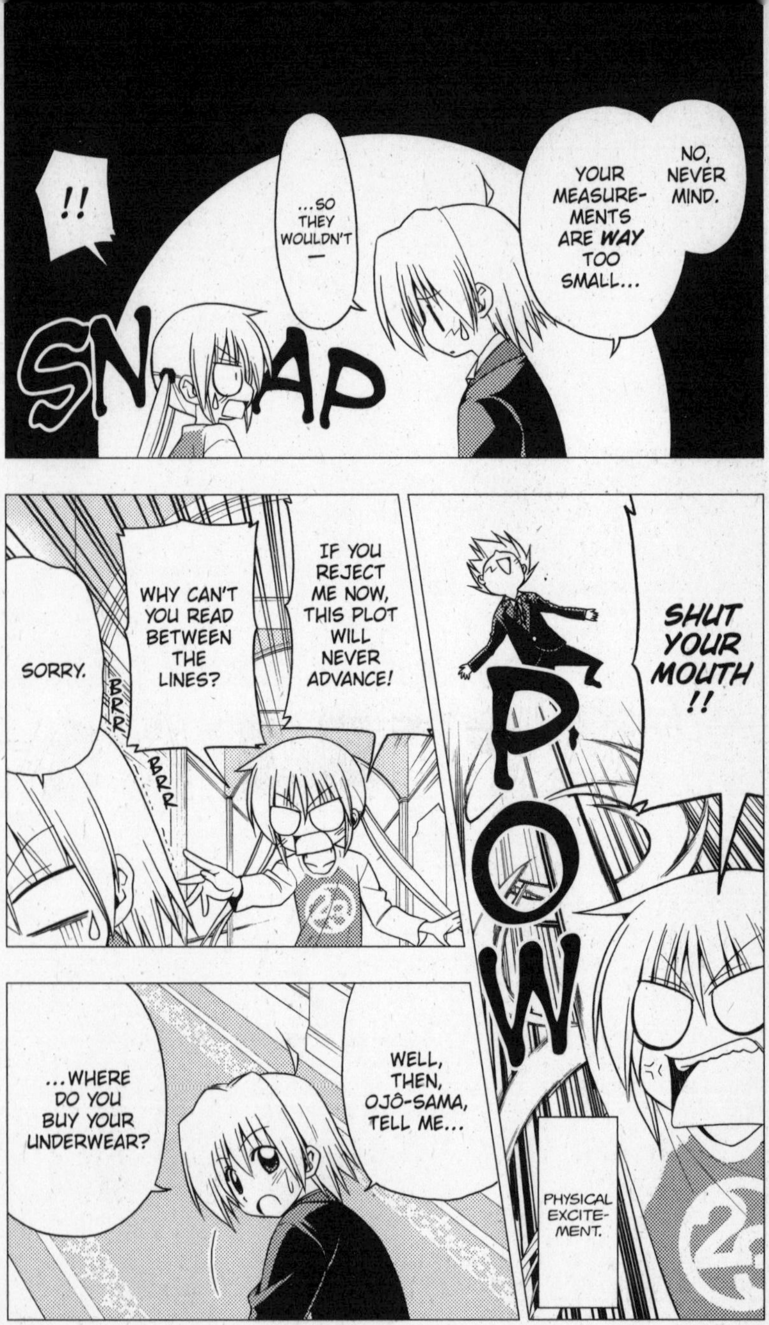
NO, NEVER MIND.
YOUR MEASUREMENTS ARE WAY TOO SMALL...
...SO THEY WOULDN'T—
!!
SNAP
SHUT YOUR MOUTH!!
POW
PHYSICAL EXCITEMENT.
IF YOU REJECT ME NOW, THIS PLOT WILL NEVER ADVANCE!
WHY CAN'T YOU READ BETWEEN THE LINES?
BRR
BRR
SORRY.
WELL, THEN, OJÔ-SAMA, TELL ME...
...WHERE DO YOU BUY YOUR UNDERWEAR?

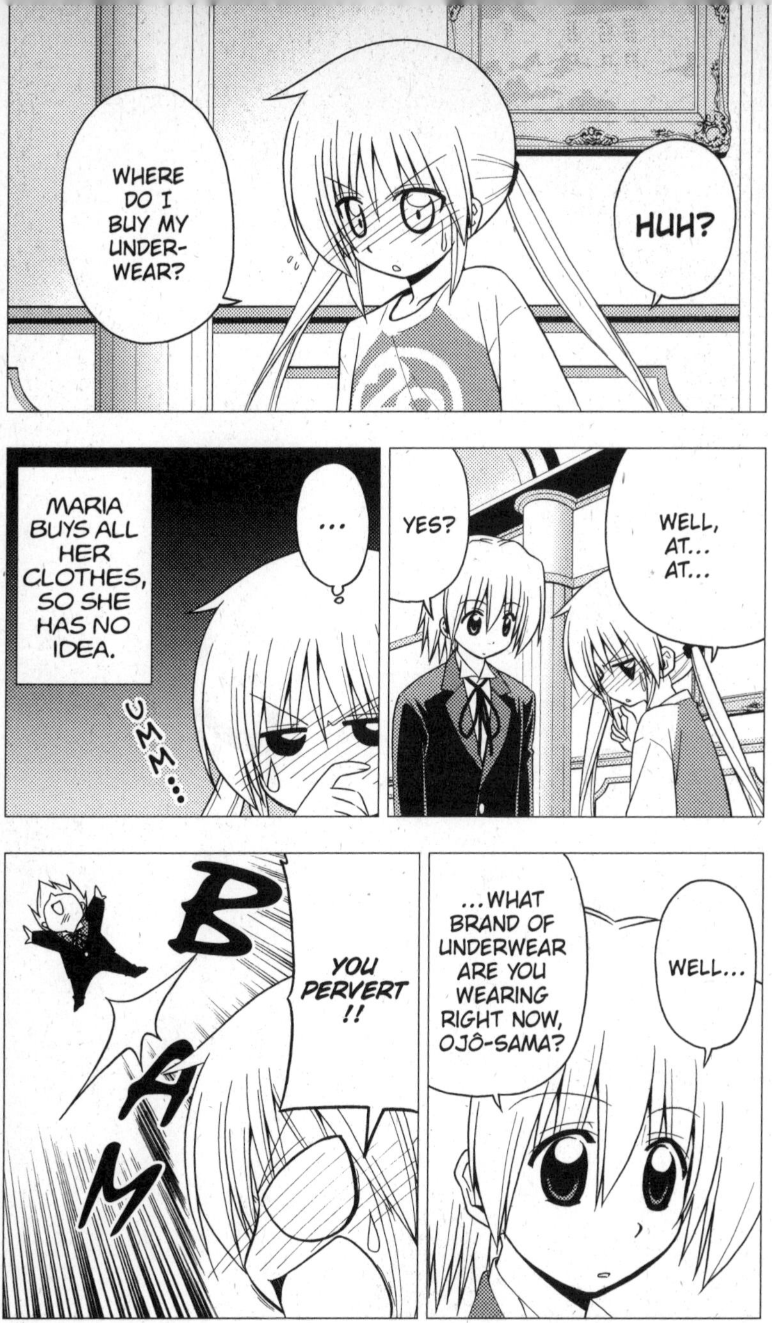
HUH?
WHERE DO I BUY MY UNDER-WEAR?
WELL, AT... AT...
YES?
...
MARIA BUYS ALL HER CLOTHES, SO SHE HAS NO IDEA.
UMM...
WELL...
...WHAT BRAND OF UNDERWEAR ARE YOU WEARING RIGHT NOW, OJÔ-SAMA?
YOU PERVERT!!
BAM

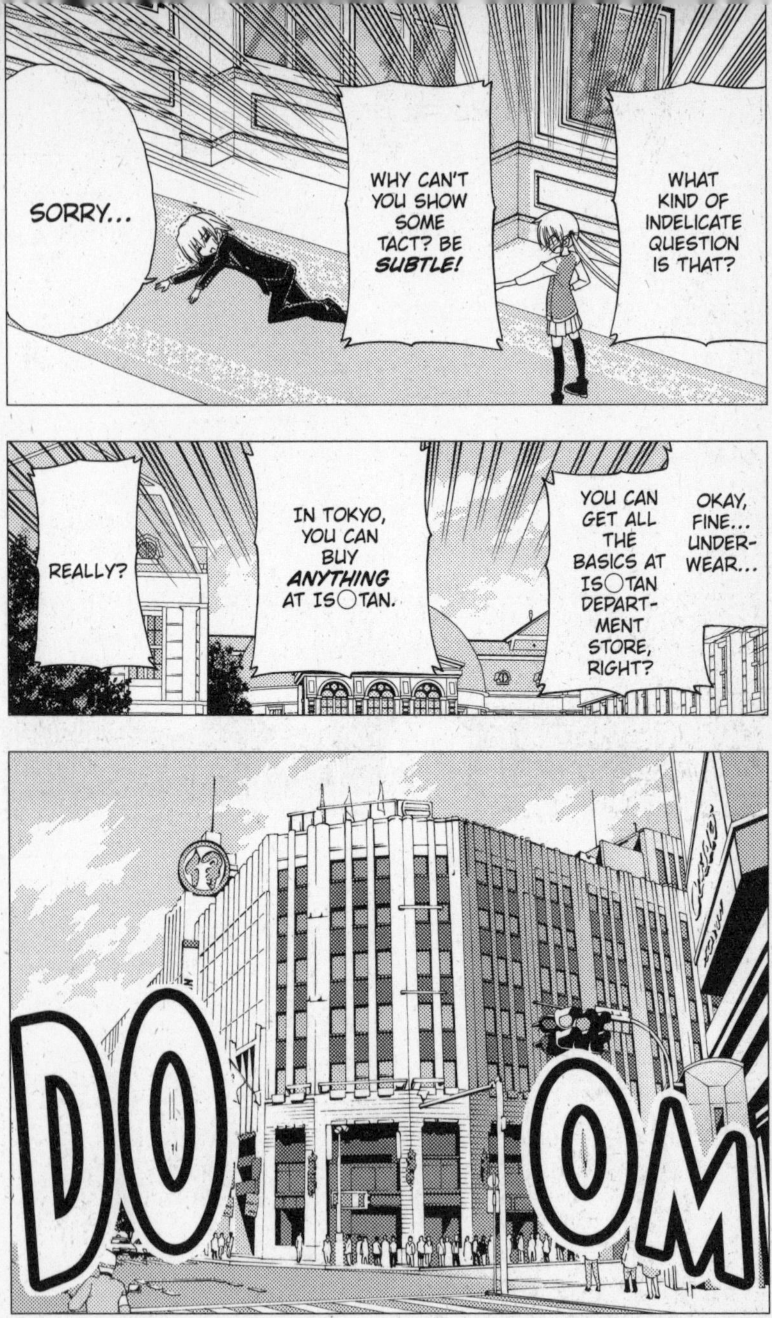
WHAT KIND OF INDELICATE QUESTION IS THAT?
WHY CAN'T YOU SHOW SOME TACT? BE SUBTLE!
SORRY...
OKAY, FINE... UNDERWEAR...
YOU CAN GET ALL THE BASICS AT IS○TAN DEPARTMENT STORE, RIGHT?
IN TOKYO, YOU CAN BUY ANYTHING AT IS○TAN.
REALLY?
DOOM

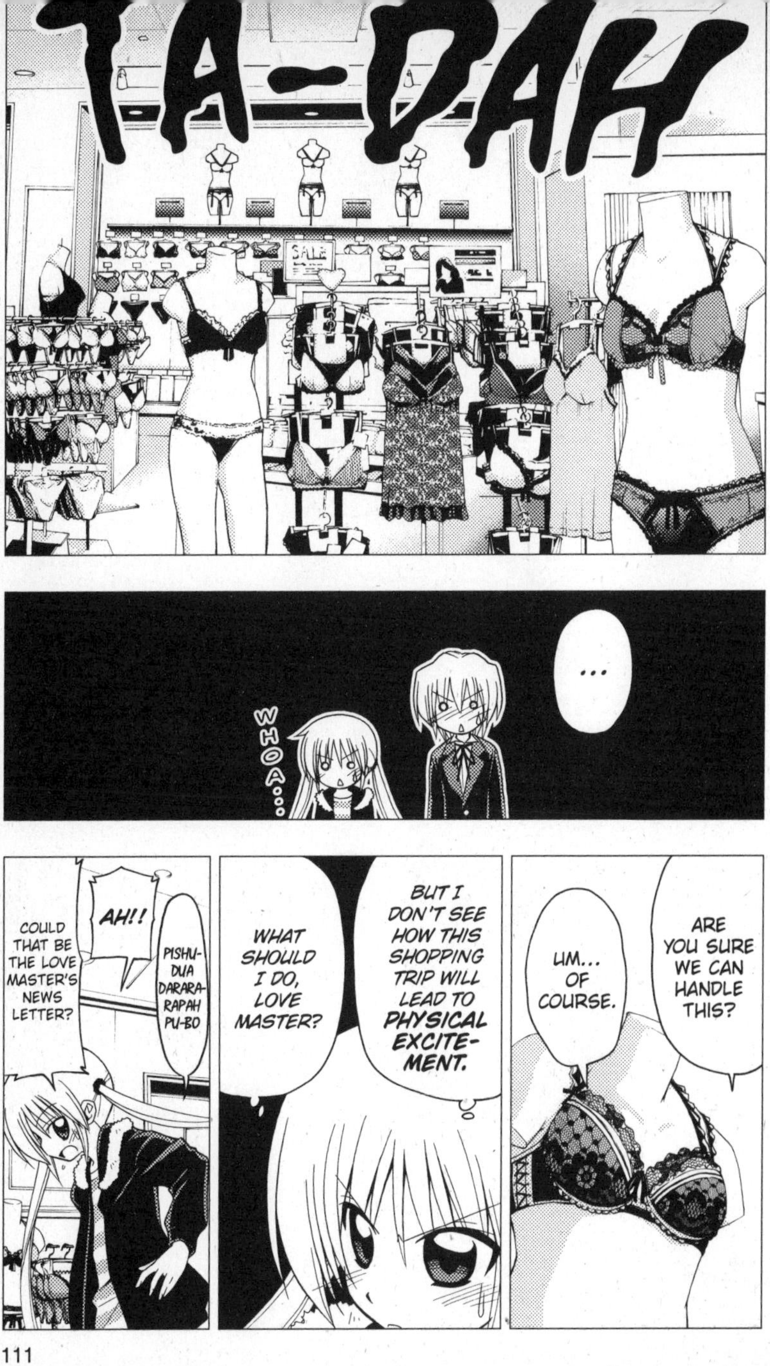
TA-DAH
...
WHOA...
ARE YOU SURE WE CAN HANDLE THIS?
UM... OF COURSE.
BUT I DON'T SEE HOW THIS SHOPPING TRIP WILL LEAD TO PHYSICAL EXCITE-MENT.
WHAT SHOULD I DO, LOVE MASTER?
PISHU-DUA DARARA-RAPAH PU-BO
AH!!
COULD THAT BE THE LOVE MASTER'S NEWS LETTER?

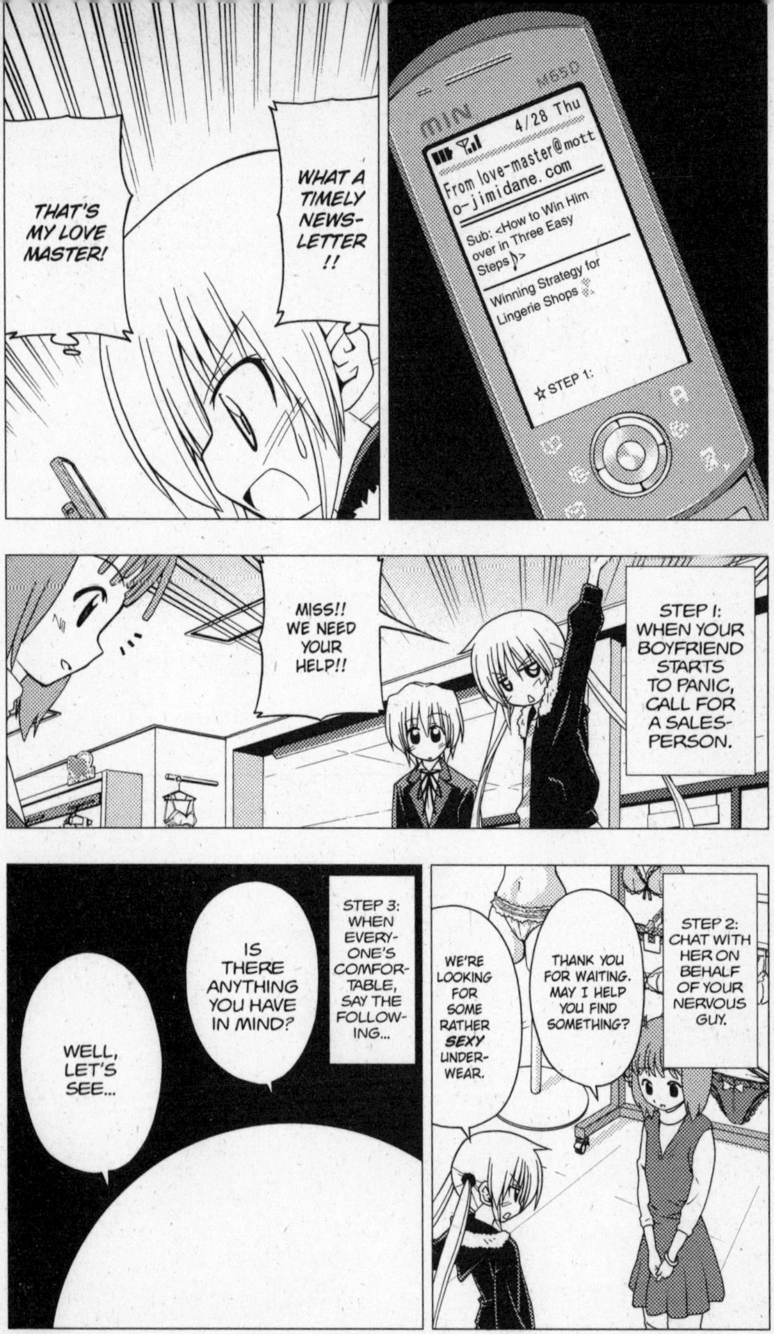
4/28 Thu
From love-master@mott
o-jimidane.com
Sub: <How to Win Him over in Three Easy Steps♪>
Winning Strategy for Lingerie Shops
☆STEP 1:
WHAT A TIMELY NEWSLETTER!!
THAT'S MY LOVE MASTER!
STEP 1: WHEN YOUR BOYFRIEND STARTS TO PANIC, CALL FOR A SALESPERSON.
MISS!! WE NEED YOUR HELP!!
...
STEP 2: CHAT WITH HER ON BEHALF OF YOUR NERVOUS GUY.
THANK YOU FOR WAITING. MAY I HELP YOU FIND SOMETHING?
WE'RE LOOKING FOR SOME RATHER ***SEXY*** UNDERWEAR.
STEP 3: WHEN EVERYONE'S COMFORTABLE, SAY THE FOLLOWING...
IS THERE ANYTHING YOU HAVE IN MIND?
WELL, LET'S SEE...

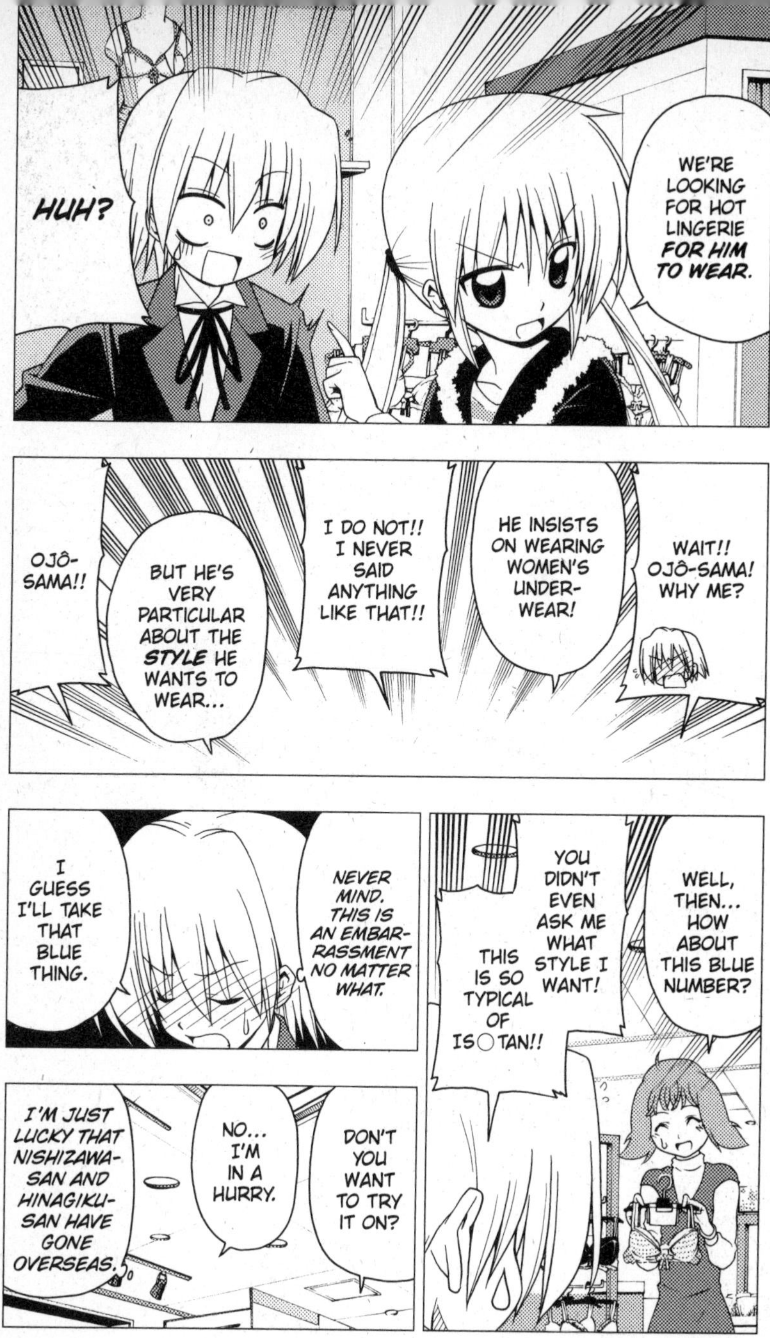
WE'RE LOOKING FOR HOT LINGERIE **FOR HIM TO WEAR**.
HUH?
WAIT!! OJÔ-SAMA! WHY ME?
HE INSISTS ON WEARING WOMEN'S UNDER-WEAR!
I DO NOT!! I NEVER SAID ANYTHING LIKE THAT!!
BUT HE'S VERY PARTICULAR ABOUT THE **STYLE** HE WANTS TO WEAR...
OJÔ-SAMA!!
WELL, THEN... HOW ABOUT THIS BLUE NUMBER?
YOU DIDN'T EVEN ASK ME WHAT STYLE I WANT!
THIS IS SO TYPICAL OF IS○TAN!!
NEVER MIND. THIS IS AN EMBARRASSMENT NO MATTER WHAT.
I GUESS I'LL TAKE THAT BLUE THING.
DON'T YOU WANT TO TRY IT ON?
NO... I'M IN A HURRY.
I'M JUST LUCKY THAT NISHIZAWA-SAN AND HINAGIKU-SAN HAVE GONE OVERSEAS.

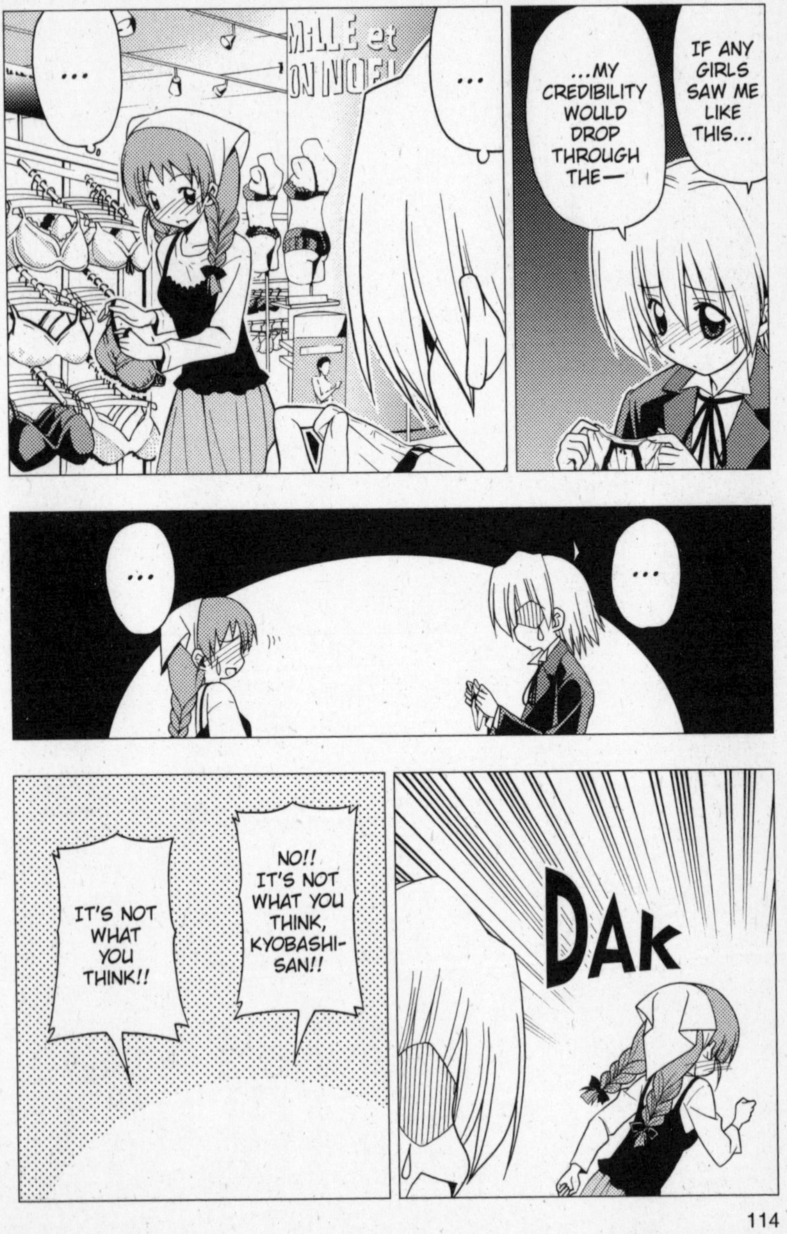
IF ANY GIRLS SAW ME LIKE THIS...
...MY CREDIBILITY WOULD DROP THROUGH THE—
...
MiLLE et UN NOEL
...
...
...
DAk
NO!! IT'S NOT WHAT YOU THINK, KYOBASHI-SAN!!
IT'S NOT WHAT YOU THINK!!

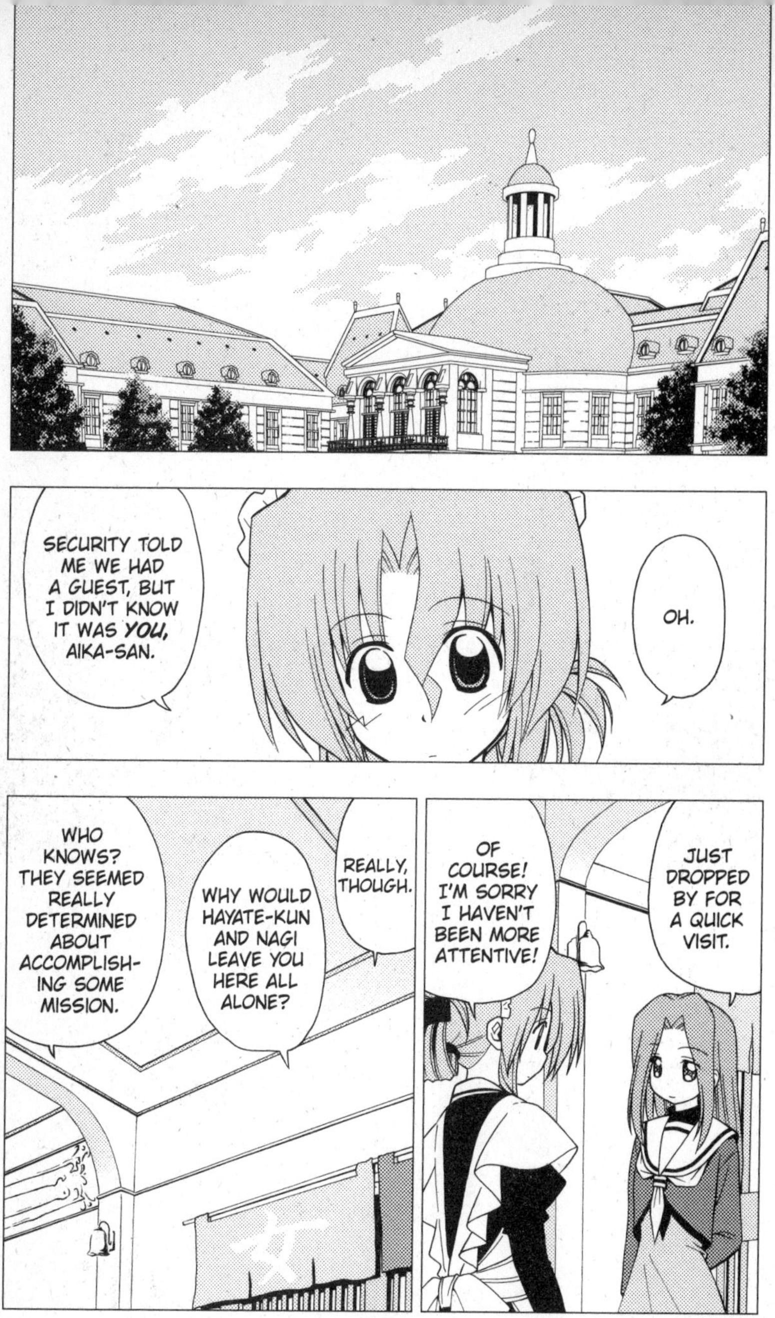
OH.
SECURITY TOLD ME WE HAD A GUEST, BUT I DIDN'T KNOW IT WAS *YOU,* AIKA-SAN.
JUST DROPPED BY FOR A QUICK VISIT.
OF COURSE! I'M SORRY I HAVEN'T BEEN MORE ATTENTIVE!
REALLY, THOUGH.
WHY WOULD HAYATE-KUN AND NAGI LEAVE YOU HERE ALL ALONE?
WHO KNOWS? THEY SEEMED REALLY DETERMINED ABOUT ACCOMPLISH-ING SOME MISSION.

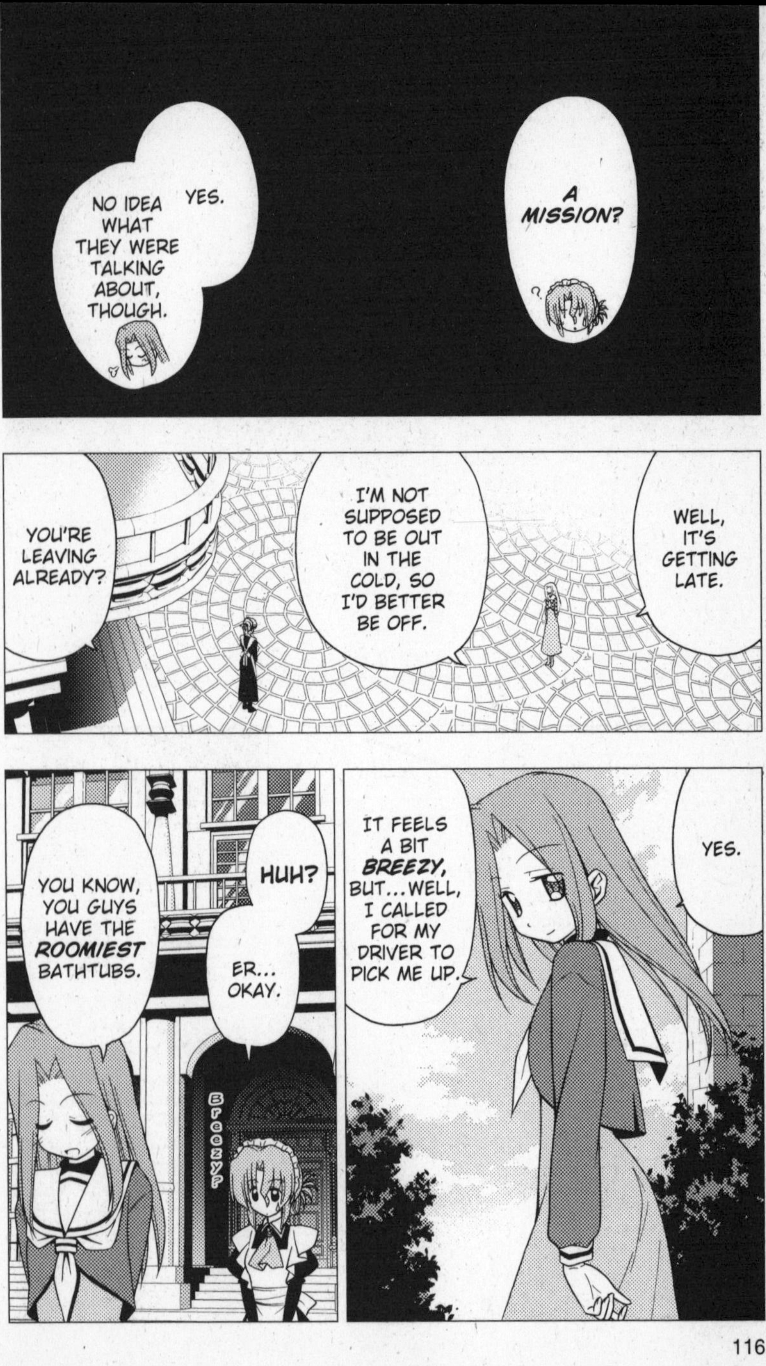
A MISSION?
YES.
NO IDEA WHAT THEY WERE TALKING ABOUT, THOUGH.
WELL, IT'S GETTING LATE.
I'M NOT SUPPOSED TO BE OUT IN THE COLD, SO I'D BETTER BE OFF.
YOU'RE LEAVING ALREADY?
YES.
IT FEELS A BIT BREEZY, BUT...WELL, I CALLED FOR MY DRIVER TO PICK ME UP.
HUH?
ER... OKAY.
YOU KNOW, YOU GUYS HAVE THE ROOMIEST BATHTUBS.
Breezy?

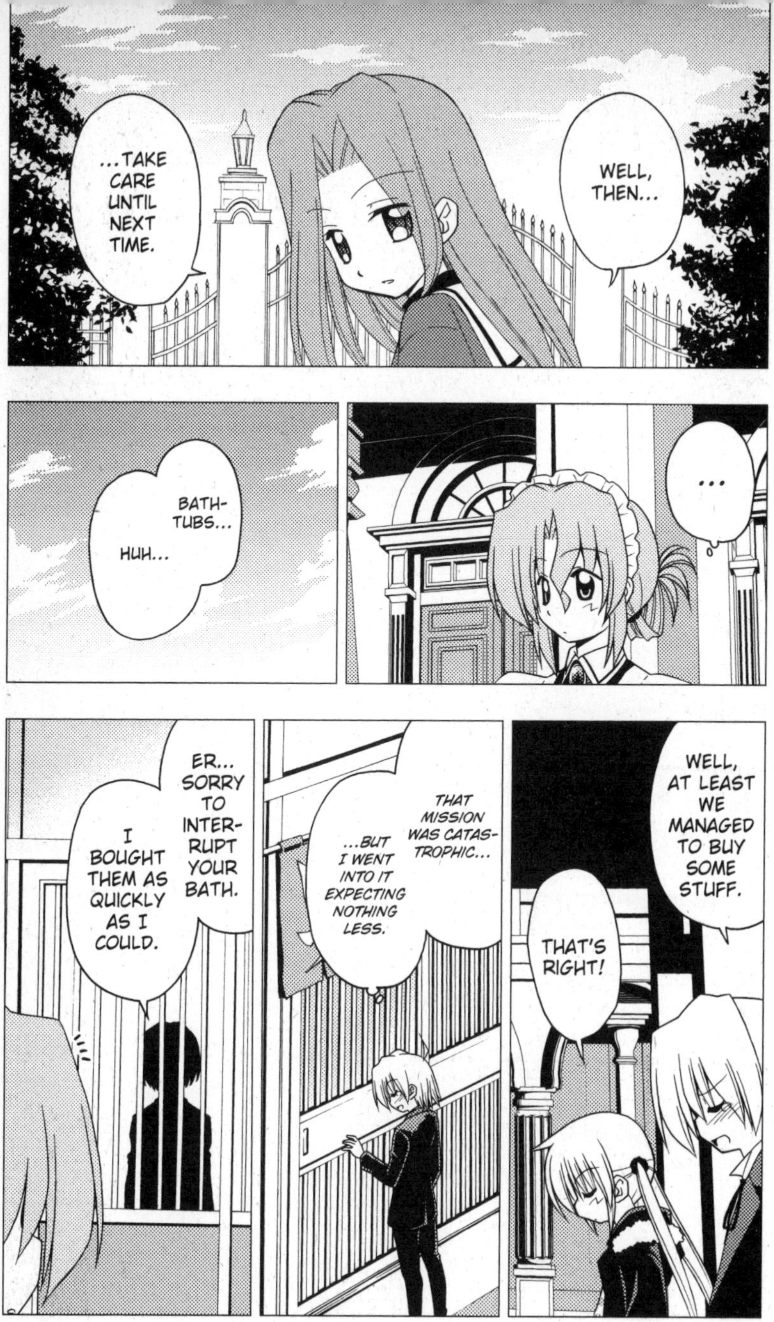
WELL, THEN...
...TAKE CARE UNTIL NEXT TIME.
...
BATH-TUBS... HUH...
WELL, AT LEAST WE MANAGED TO BUY SOME STUFF.
THAT'S RIGHT!
THAT MISSION WAS CATAS-TROPHIC...
...BUT I WENT INTO IT EXPECTING NOTHING LESS.
ER... SORRY TO INTER-RUPT YOUR BATH.
I BOUGHT THEM AS QUICKLY AS I COULD.

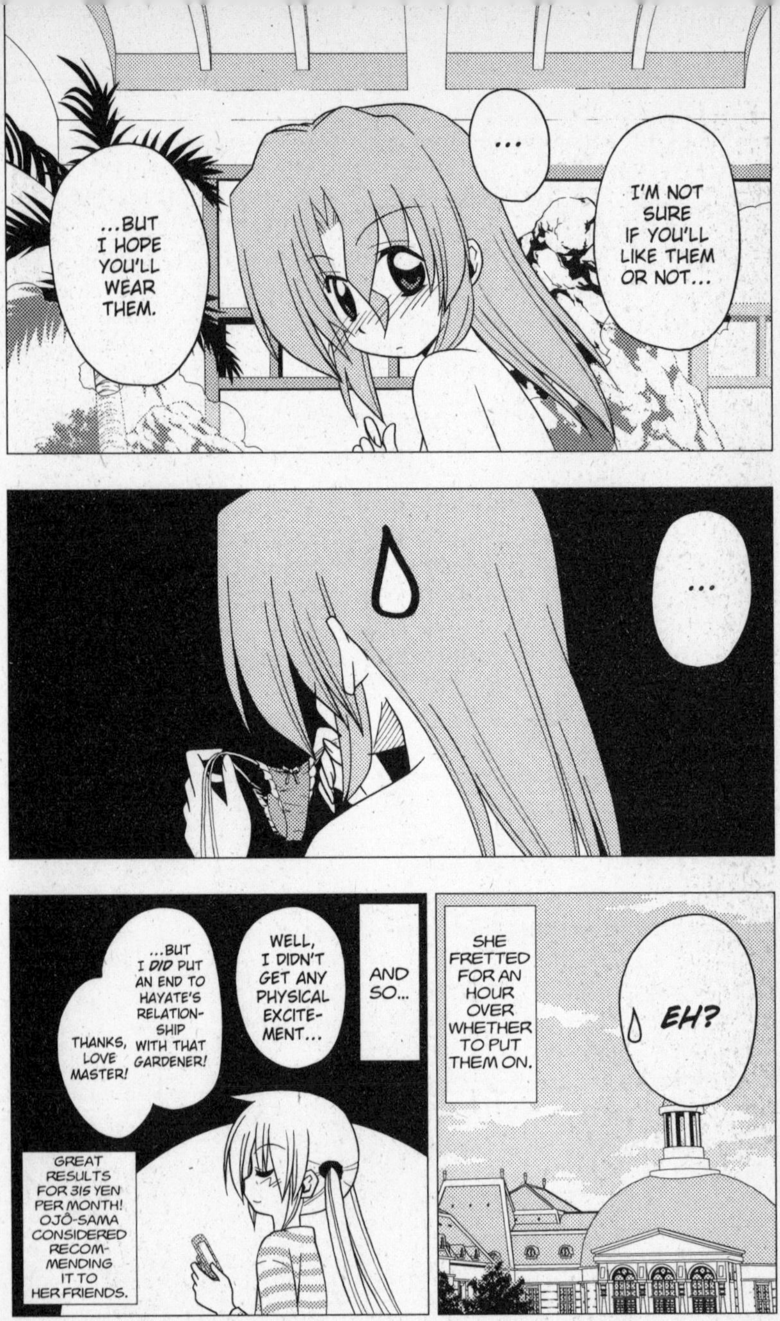
I'M NOT SURE IF YOU'LL LIKE THEM OR NOT...
...
...BUT I HOPE YOU'LL WEAR THEM.
...
EH?
SHE FRETTED FOR AN HOUR OVER WHETHER TO PUT THEM ON.
AND SO...
WELL, I DIDN'T GET ANY PHYSICAL EXCITEMENT...
...BUT I *DID* PUT AN END TO HAYATE'S RELATIONSHIP WITH THAT GARDENER!
THANKS, LOVE MASTER!
GREAT RESULTS FOR 315 YEN PER MONTH! OJÔ-SAMA CONSIDERED RECOMMENDING IT TO HER FRIENDS.

Episode 8: "You Can Earn More by Not Gambling"

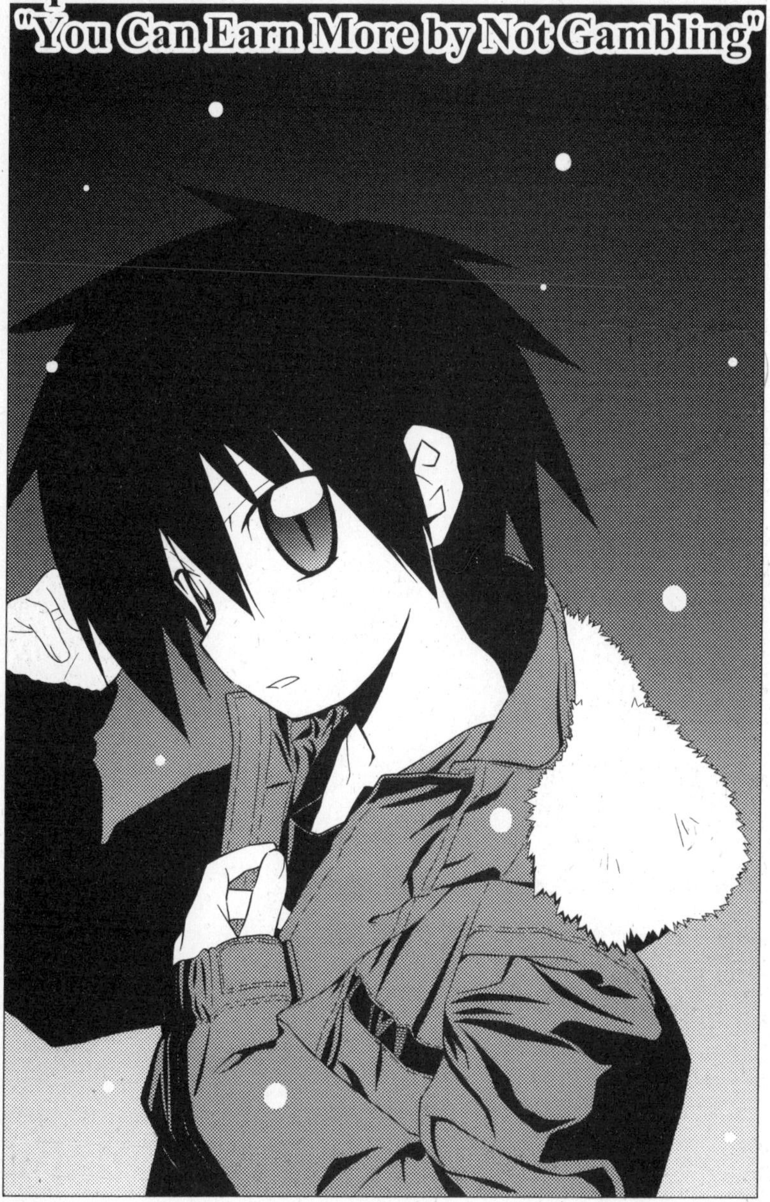

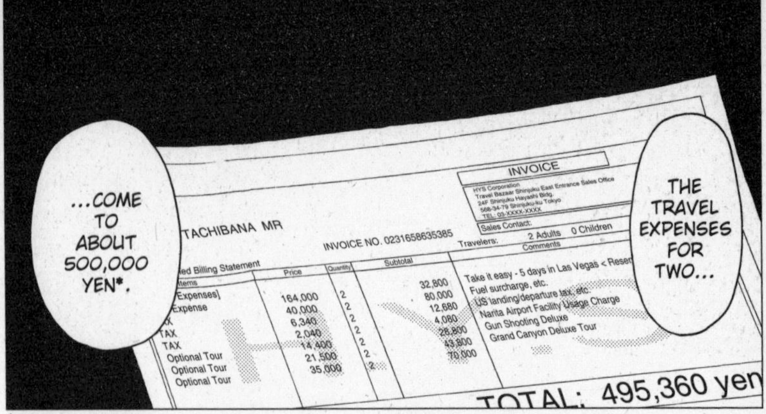
THE TRAVEL EXPENSES FOR TWO...
...COME TO ABOUT 500,000 YEN*.
INVOICE
TACHIBANA MR
INVOICE NO. 0231658635385
TOTAL: 495,360 yen

*About $5,000.

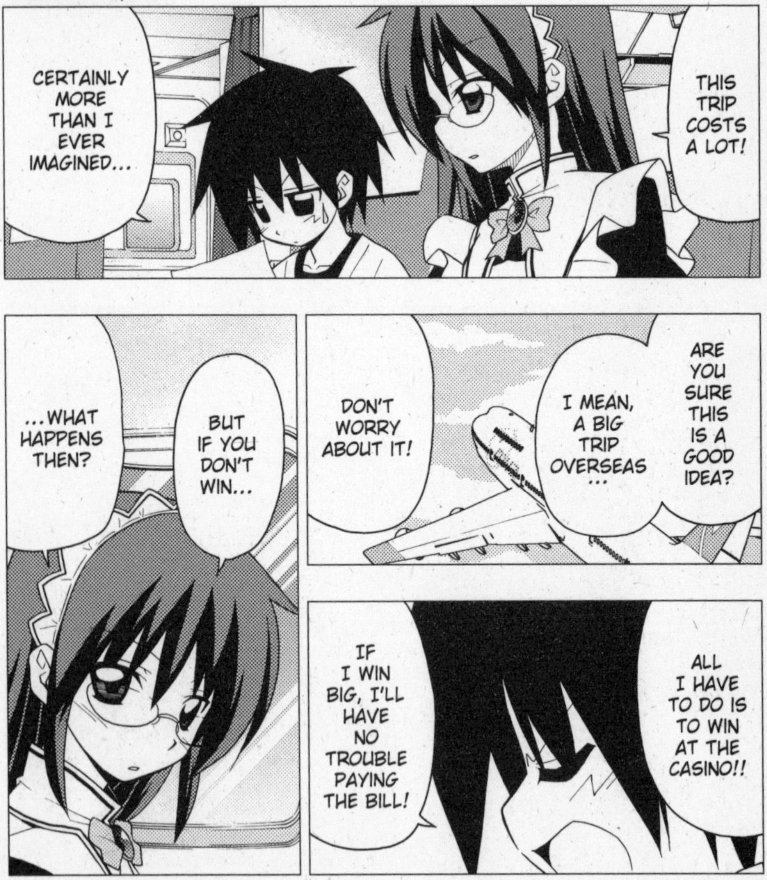
THIS TRIP COSTS A LOT!
CERTAINLY MORE THAN I EVER IMAGINED...
ARE YOU SURE THIS IS A GOOD IDEA?
I MEAN, A BIG TRIP OVERSEAS...
DON'T WORRY ABOUT IT!
ALL I HAVE TO DO IS TO WIN AT THE CASINO!!
IF I WIN BIG, I'LL HAVE NO TROUBLE PAYING THE BILL!
BUT IF YOU DON'T WIN...
...WHAT HAPPENS THEN?

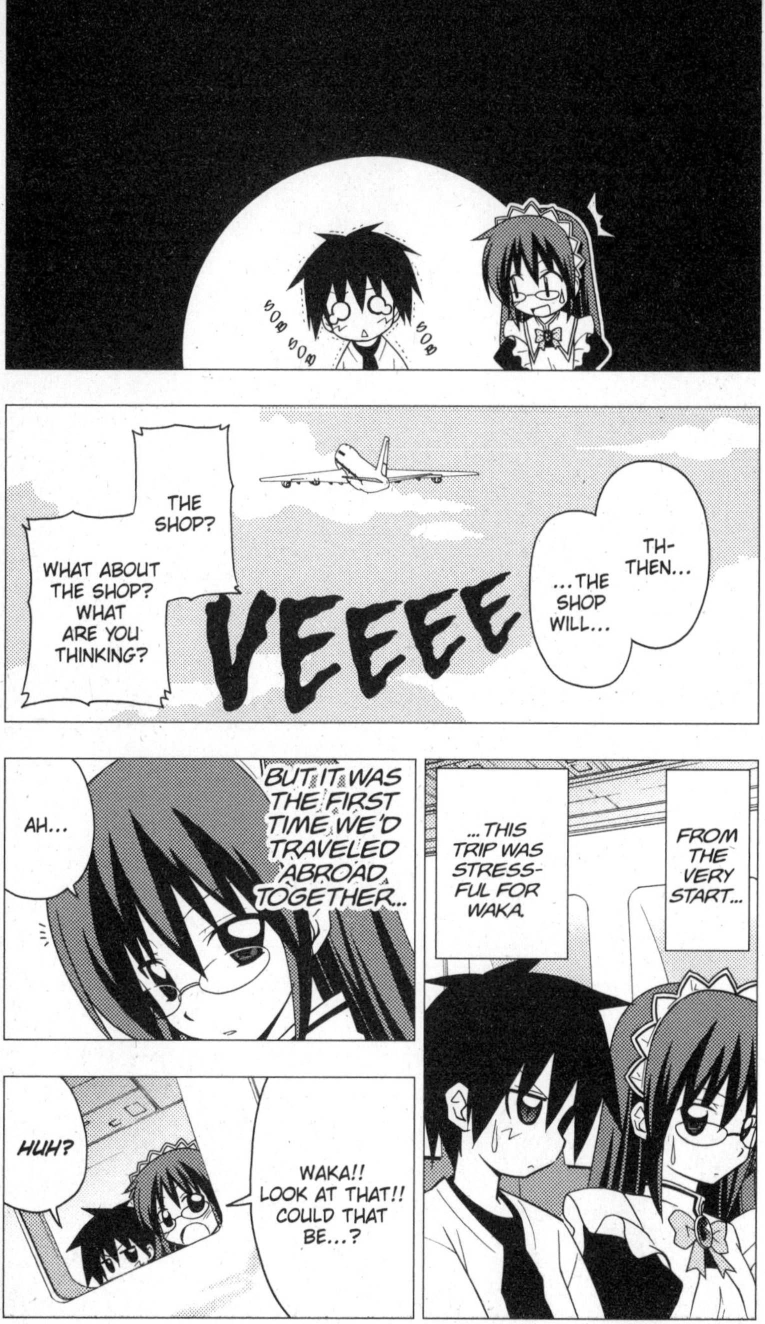
TH- THEN...
...THE SHOP WILL...
VEEEE
THE SHOP?
WHAT ABOUT THE SHOP? WHAT ARE YOU THINKING?
FROM THE VERY START...
...THIS TRIP WAS STRESS-FUL FOR WAKA.
BUT IT WAS THE FIRST TIME WE'D TRAVELED ABROAD TOGETHER...
AH...
WAKA!! LOOK AT THAT!! COULD THAT BE...?
HUH?

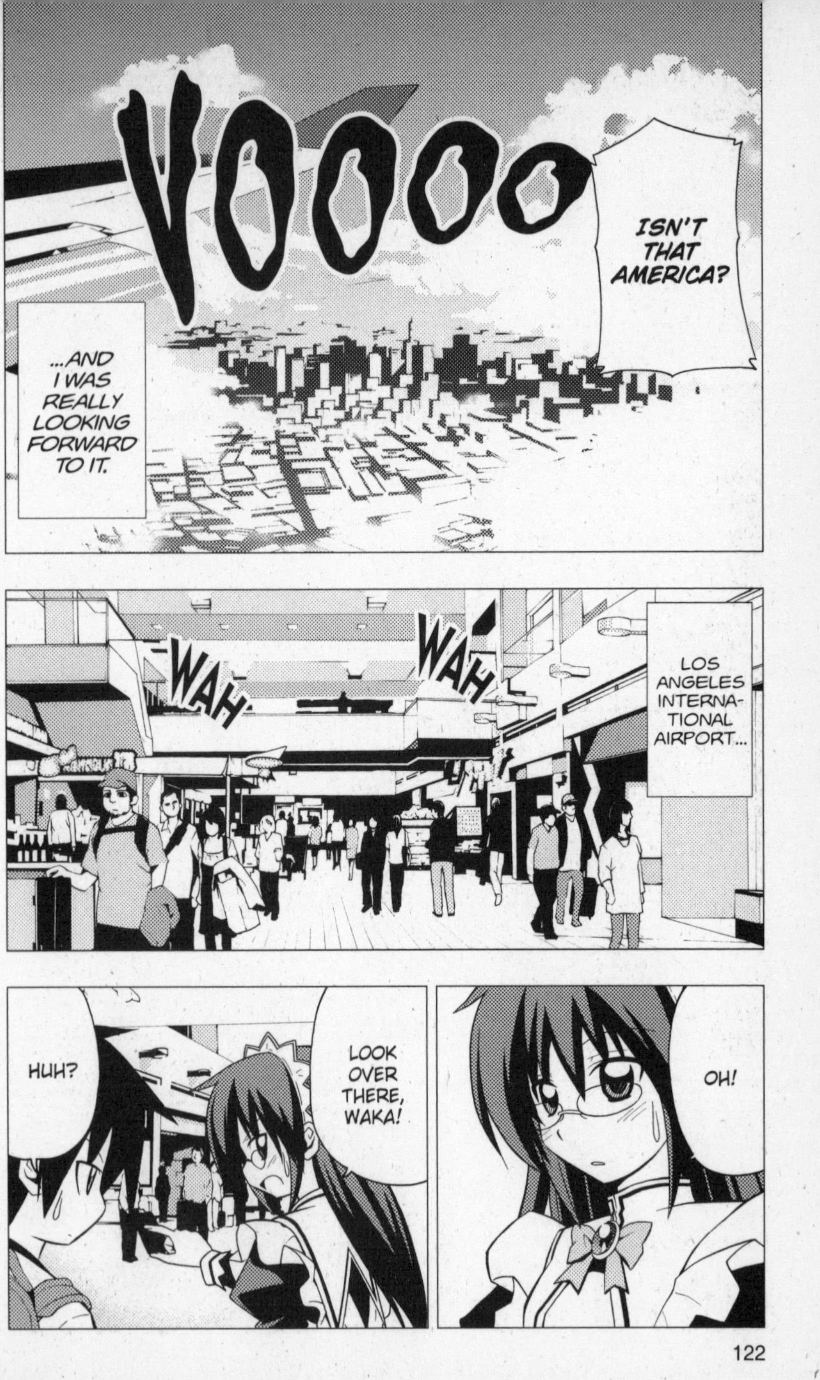
ISN'T THAT AMERICA?
VOOOO
...AND I WAS REALLY LOOKING FORWARD TO IT.
LOS ANGELES INTERNATIONAL AIRPORT...
WAH
WAH
OH!
LOOK OVER THERE, WAKA!
HUH?

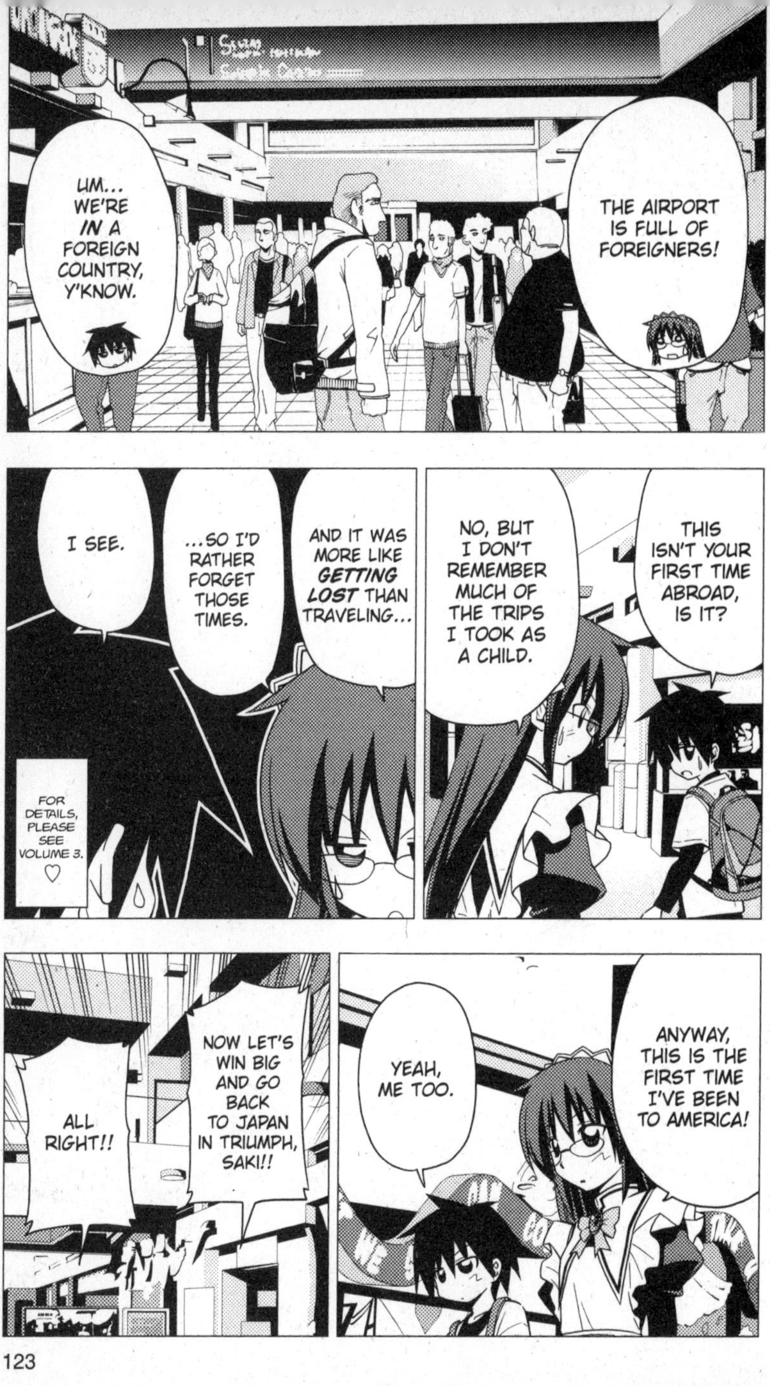
THE AIRPORT IS FULL OF FOREIGNERS!
UM... WE'RE *IN* A FOREIGN COUNTRY, Y'KNOW.
THIS ISN'T YOUR FIRST TIME ABROAD, IS IT?
NO, BUT I DON'T REMEMBER MUCH OF THE TRIPS I TOOK AS A CHILD.
AND IT WAS MORE LIKE *GETTING LOST* THAN TRAVELING...
...SO I'D RATHER FORGET THOSE TIMES.
I SEE.
FOR DETAILS, PLEASE SEE VOLUME 3. ♡
ANYWAY, THIS IS THE FIRST TIME I'VE BEEN TO AMERICA!
YEAH, ME TOO.
NOW LET'S WIN BIG AND GO BACK TO JAPAN IN TRIUMPH, SAKI!!
ALL RIGHT!!

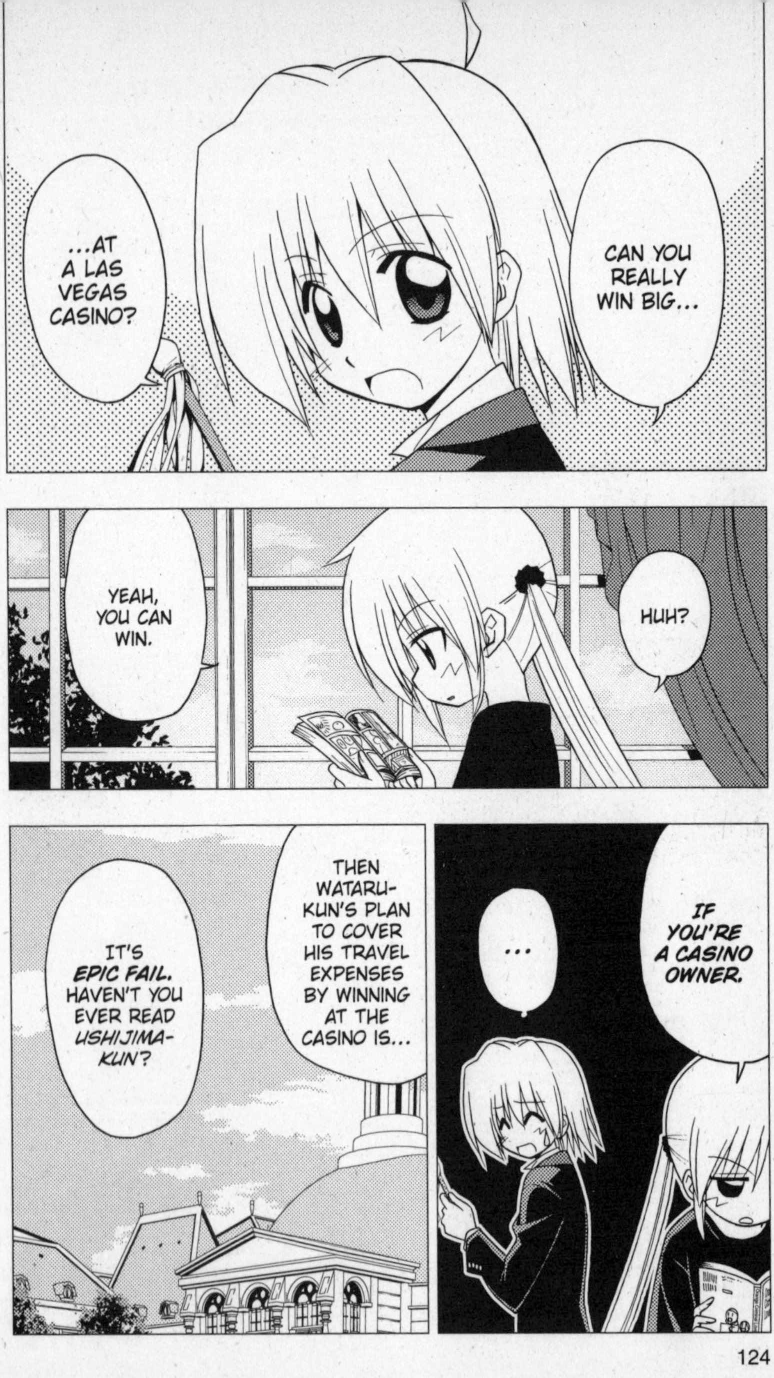
CAN YOU REALLY WIN BIG...
...AT A LAS VEGAS CASINO?
HUH?
YEAH, YOU CAN WIN.
IF YOU'RE A CASINO OWNER.
...
THEN WATARU-KUN'S PLAN TO COVER HIS TRAVEL EXPENSES BY WINNING AT THE CASINO IS...
IT'S EPIC FAIL. HAVEN'T YOU EVER READ USHIJIMA-KUN?

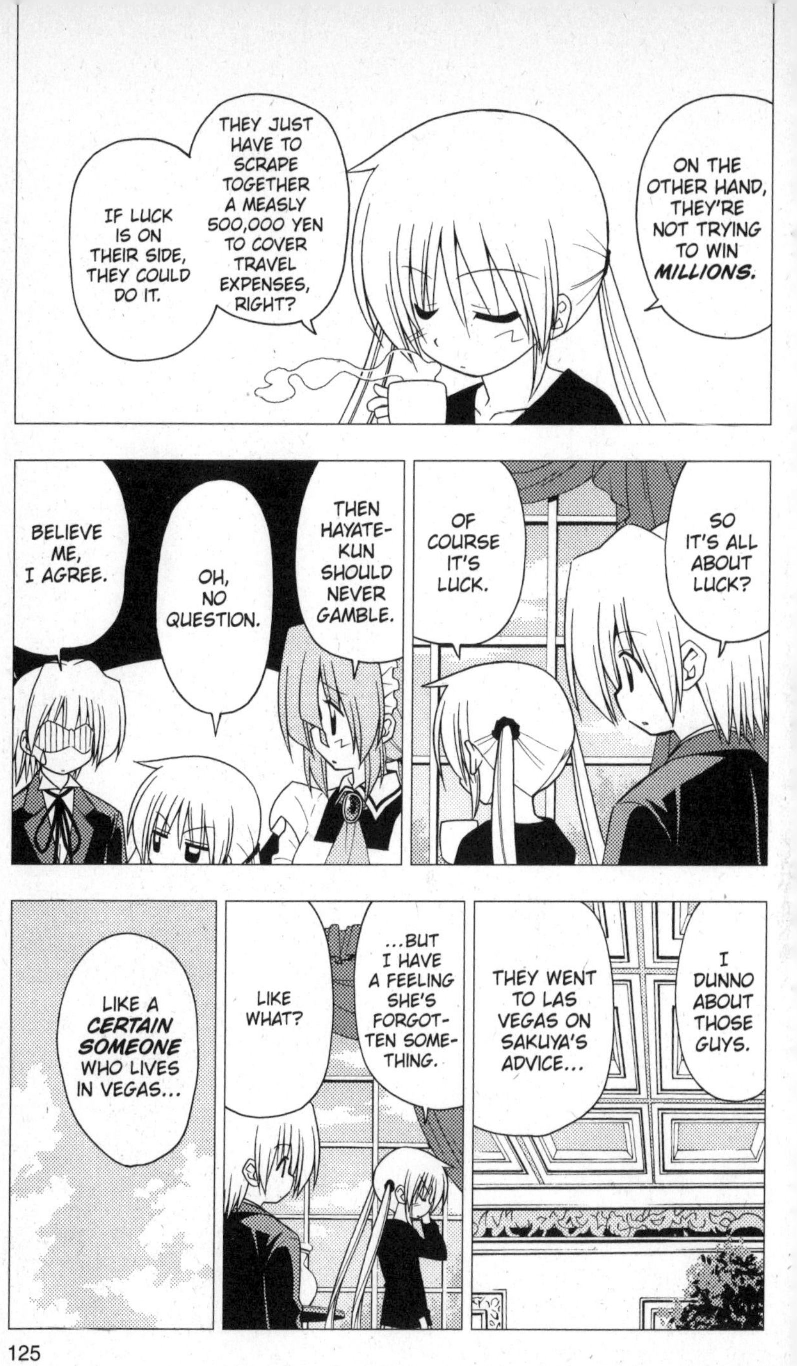
ON THE OTHER HAND, THEY'RE NOT TRYING TO WIN *MILLIONS.*
THEY JUST HAVE TO SCRAPE TOGETHER A MEASLY 500,000 YEN TO COVER TRAVEL EXPENSES, RIGHT?
IF LUCK IS ON THEIR SIDE, THEY COULD DO IT.
SO IT'S ALL ABOUT LUCK?
OF COURSE IT'S LUCK.
THEN HAYATE-KUN SHOULD NEVER GAMBLE.
OH, NO QUESTION.
BELIEVE ME, I AGREE.
I DUNNO ABOUT THOSE GUYS.
THEY WENT TO LAS VEGAS ON SAKUYA'S ADVICE...
...BUT I HAVE A FEELING SHE'S FORGOT-TEN SOME-THING.
LIKE WHAT?
LIKE A *CERTAIN SOMEONE* WHO LIVES IN VEGAS...

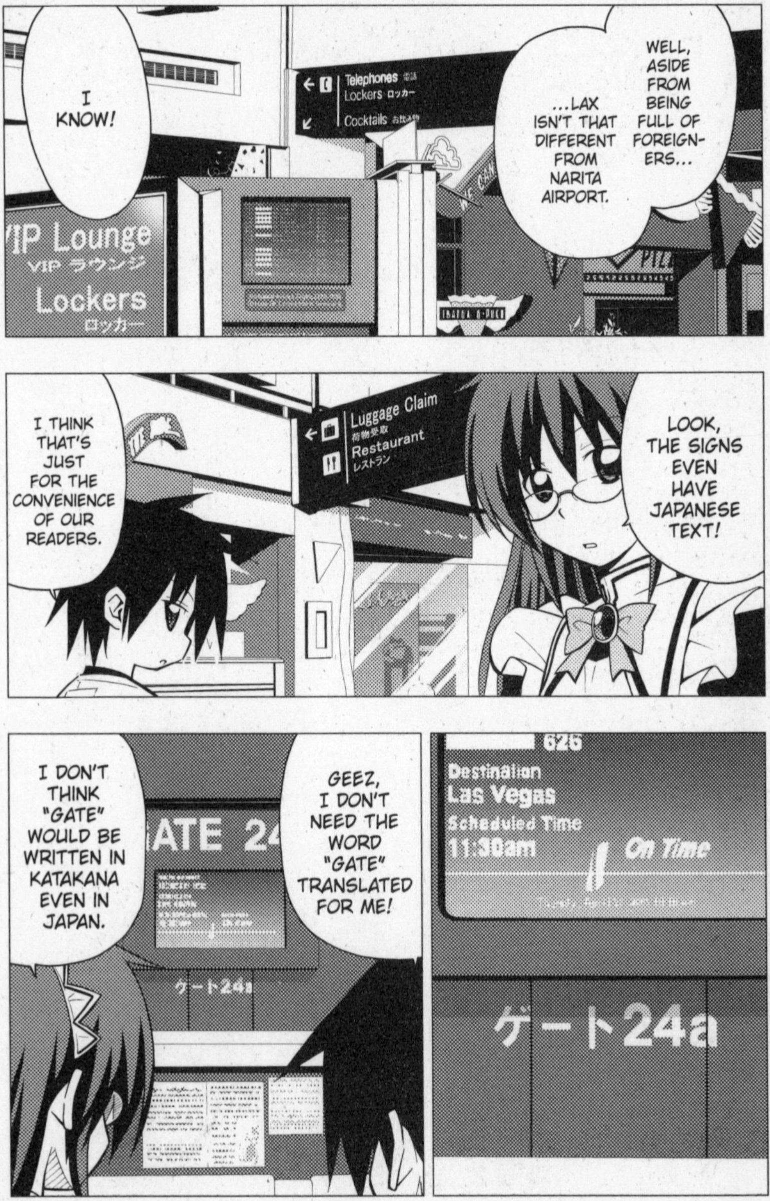
WELL, ASIDE FROM BEING FULL OF FOREIGNERS...
...LAX ISN'T THAT DIFFERENT FROM NARITA AIRPORT.
Telephones 電話
Lockers ロッカー
Cocktails お飲み物
I KNOW!
VIP Lounge
VIP ラウンジ
Lockers
ロッカー
LOOK, THE SIGNS EVEN HAVE JAPANESE TEXT!
Luggage Claim
荷物受取
Restaurant
レストラン
I THINK THAT'S JUST FOR THE CONVENIENCE OF OUR READERS.
626
Destination
Las Vegas
Scheduled Time
11:30am
On Time
ゲート24a
GEEZ, I DON'T NEED THE WORD "GATE" TRANSLATED FOR ME!
I DON'T THINK "GATE" WOULD BE WRITTEN IN KATAKANA EVEN IN JAPAN.
ゲート24a

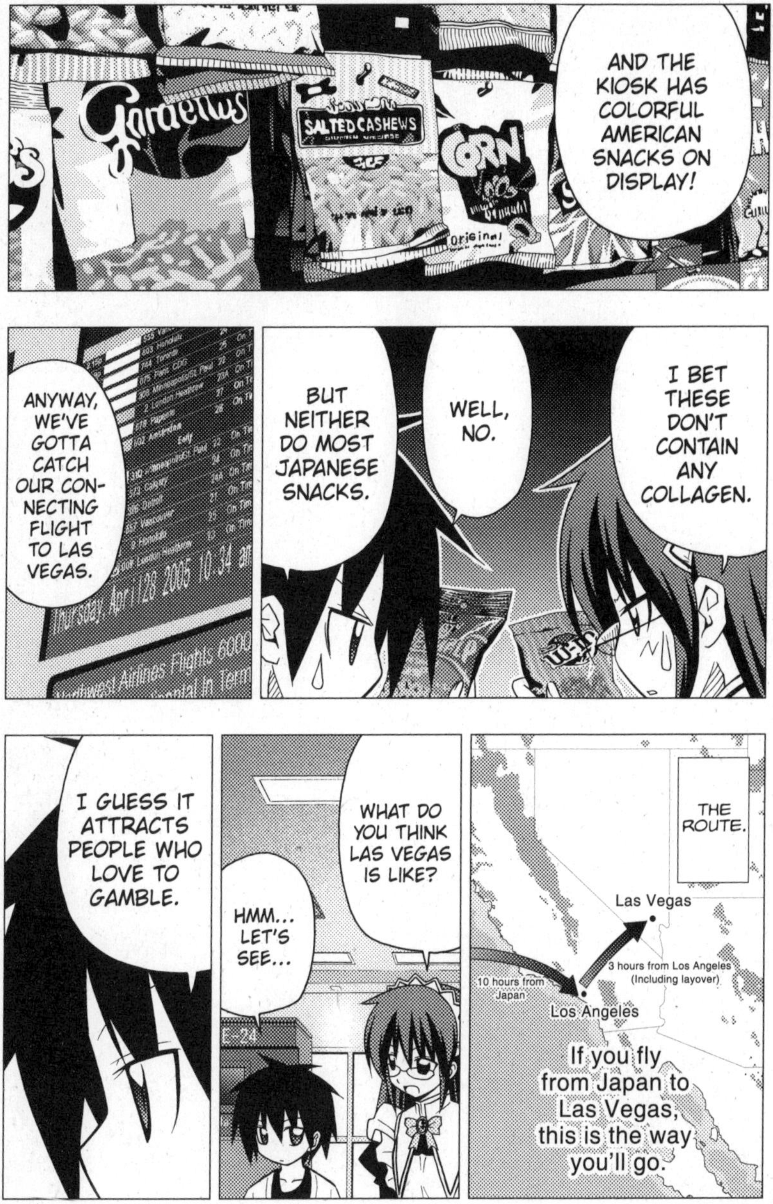
AND THE KIOSK HAS COLORFUL AMERICAN SNACKS ON DISPLAY!
SALTED CASHEWS
I BET THESE DON'T CONTAIN ANY COLLAGEN.
WELL, NO.
BUT NEITHER DO MOST JAPANESE SNACKS.
ANYWAY, WE'VE GOTTA CATCH OUR CON-NECTING FLIGHT TO LAS VEGAS.
THE ROUTE.
Las Vegas
3 hours from Los Angeles (Including layover)
10 hours from Japan
Los Angeles
If you fly from Japan to Las Vegas, this is the way you'll go.
WHAT DO YOU THINK LAS VEGAS IS LIKE?
HMM... LET'S SEE...
I GUESS IT ATTRACTS PEOPLE WHO LOVE TO GAMBLE.

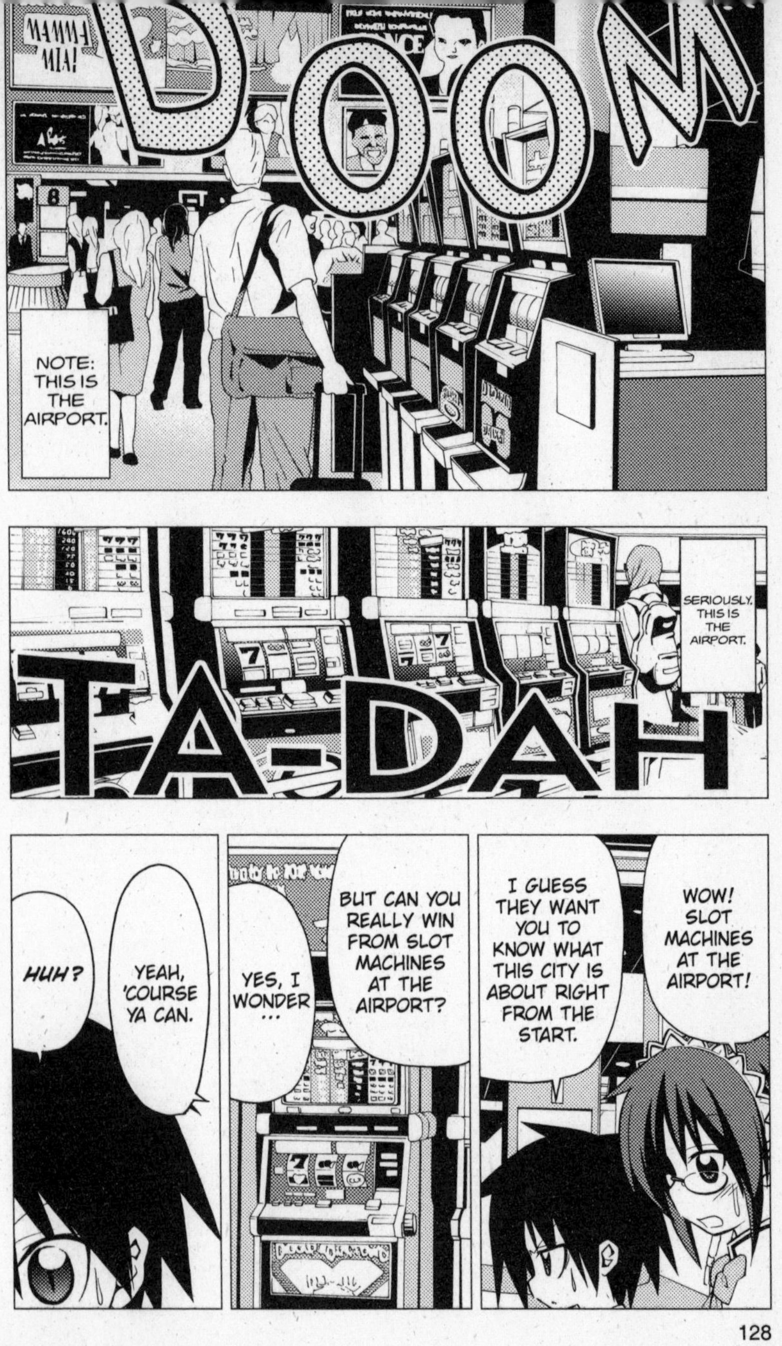
MAMMA MIA!
DOOM
NOTE: THIS IS THE AIRPORT.
SERIOUSLY. THIS IS THE AIRPORT.
TA-DAH
WOW! SLOT MACHINES AT THE AIRPORT!
I GUESS THEY WANT YOU TO KNOW WHAT THIS CITY IS ABOUT RIGHT FROM THE START.
BUT CAN YOU REALLY WIN FROM SLOT MACHINES AT THE AIRPORT?
YES, I WONDER...
YEAH, 'COURSE YA CAN.
HUH?

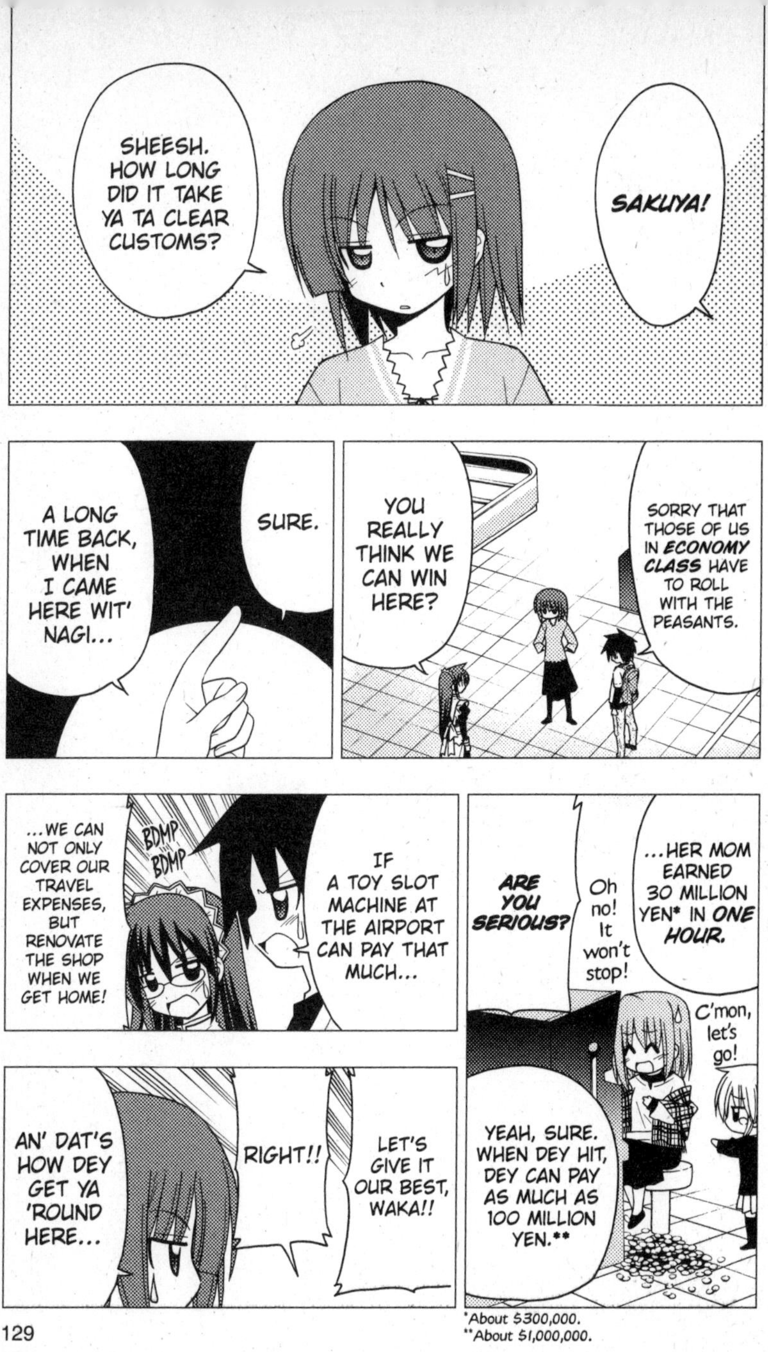
SAKUYA!
SHEESH. HOW LONG DID IT TAKE YA TA CLEAR CUSTOMS?
SORRY THAT THOSE OF US IN ECONOMY CLASS HAVE TO ROLL WITH THE PEASANTS.
YOU REALLY THINK WE CAN WIN HERE?
SURE.
A LONG TIME BACK, WHEN I CAME HERE WIT' NAGI...
...HER MOM EARNED 30 MILLION YEN* IN ONE HOUR.
Oh no! It won't stop!
ARE YOU SERIOUS?
C'mon, let's go!
YEAH, SURE. WHEN DEY HIT, DEY CAN PAY AS MUCH AS 100 MILLION YEN.**
IF A TOY SLOT MACHINE AT THE AIRPORT CAN PAY THAT MUCH...
BDMP BDMP
...WE CAN NOT ONLY COVER OUR TRAVEL EXPENSES, BUT RENOVATE THE SHOP WHEN WE GET HOME!
LET'S GIVE IT OUR BEST, WAKA!!
RIGHT!!
AN' DAT'S HOW DEY GET YA 'ROUND HERE...

*About $300,000.
**About $1,000,000.

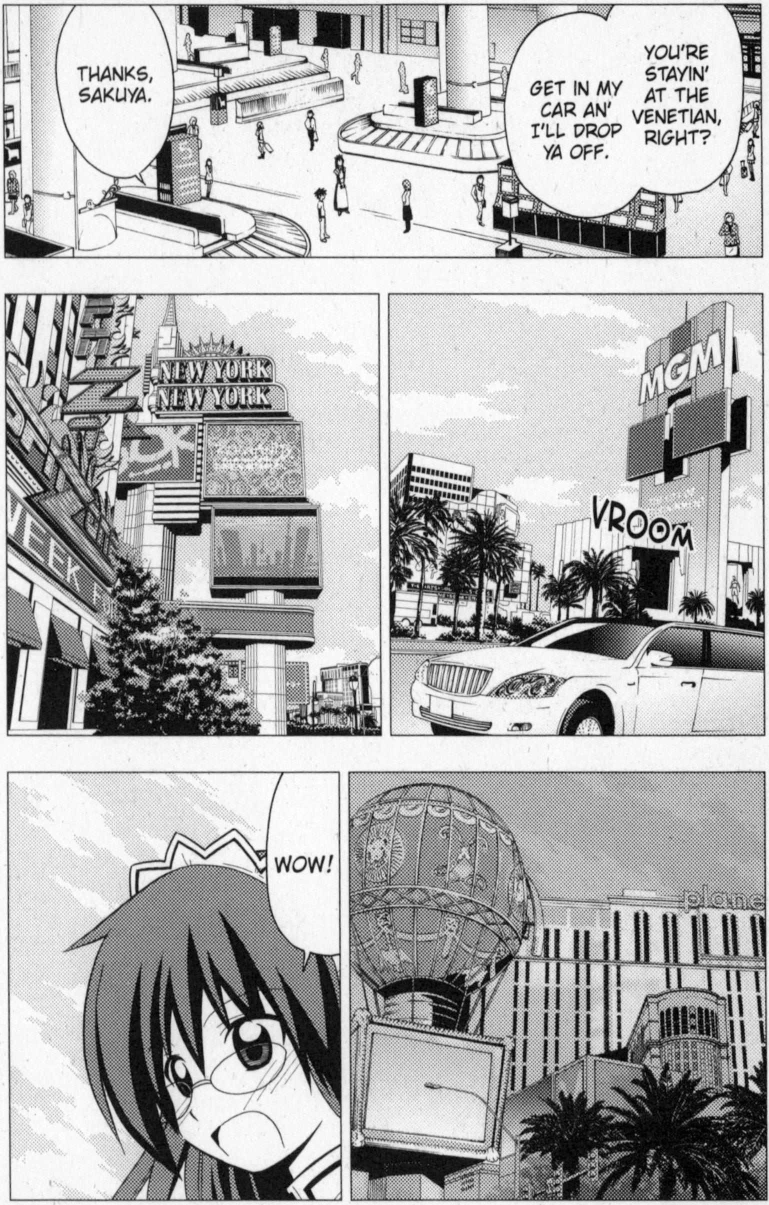
YOU'RE STAYIN' AT THE VENETIAN, RIGHT?
GET IN MY CAR AN' I'LL DROP YA OFF.
THANKS, SAKUYA.
MGM
VROOM
NEW YORK NEW YORK
WOW!

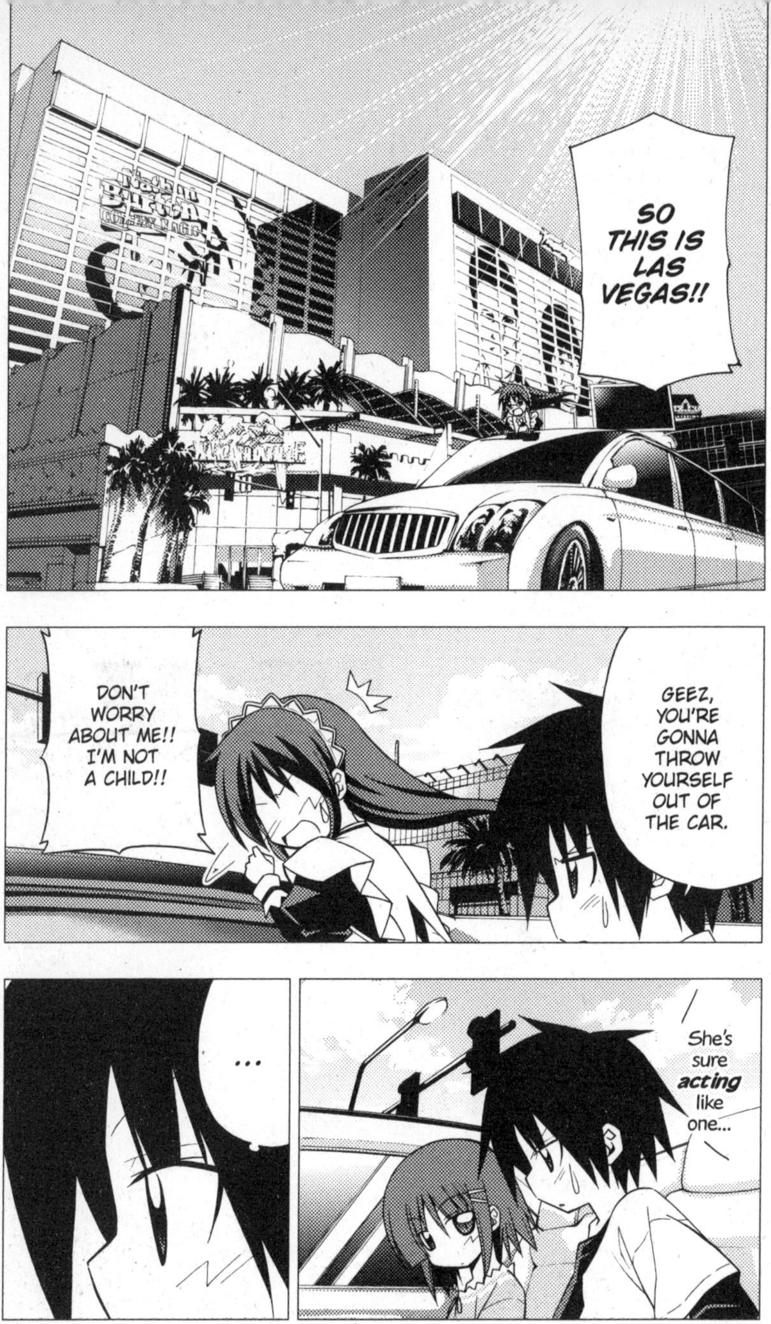
SO THIS IS LAS VEGAS!!
GEEZ, YOU'RE GONNA THROW YOURSELF OUT OF THE CAR.
DON'T WORRY ABOUT ME!! I'M NOT A CHILD!!
She's sure acting like one...
...

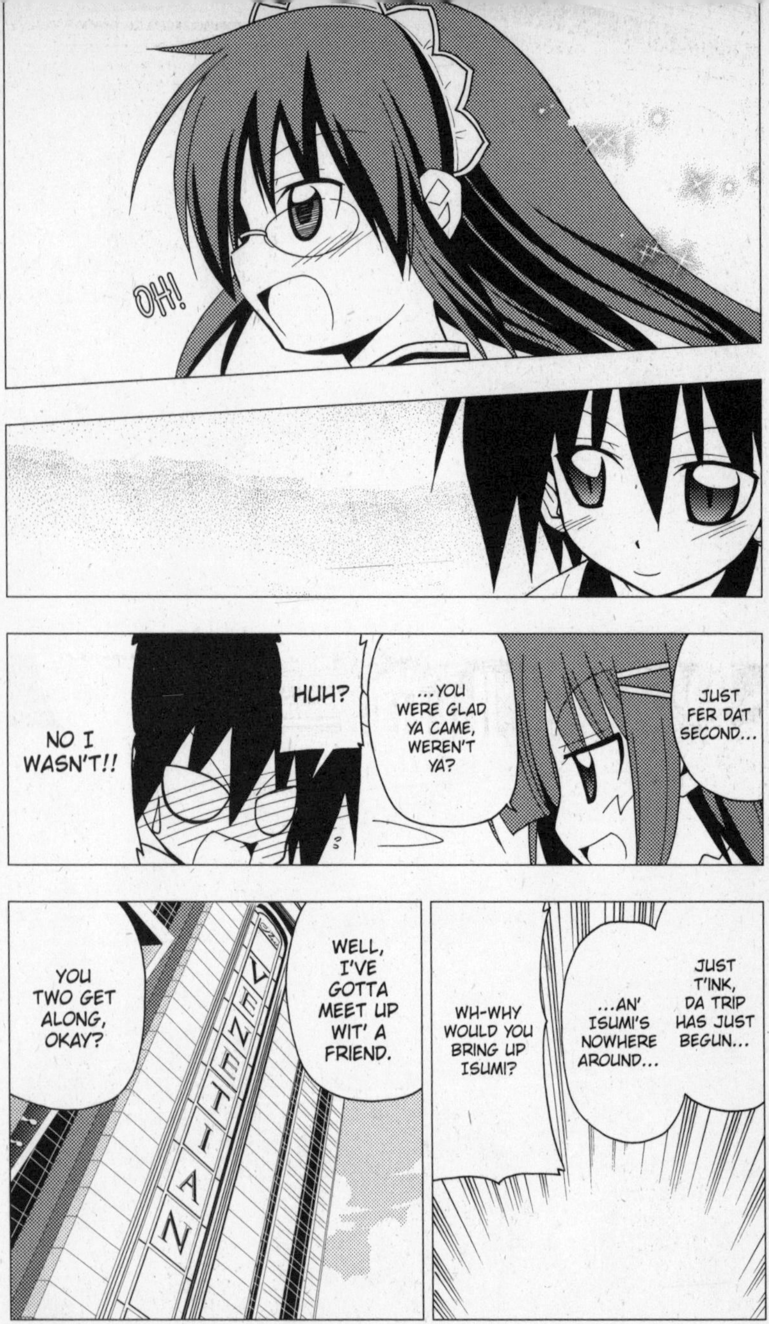
OH!
JUST FER DAT SECOND...
...YOU WERE GLAD YA CAME, WEREN'T YA?
HUH?
NO I WASN'T!!
JUST T'INK, DA TRIP HAS JUST BEGUN...
...AN' ISUMI'S NOWHERE AROUND...
WH-WHY WOULD YOU BRING UP ISUMI?
WELL, I'VE GOTTA MEET UP WIT' A FRIEND.
VENETIAN
YOU TWO GET ALONG, OKAY?

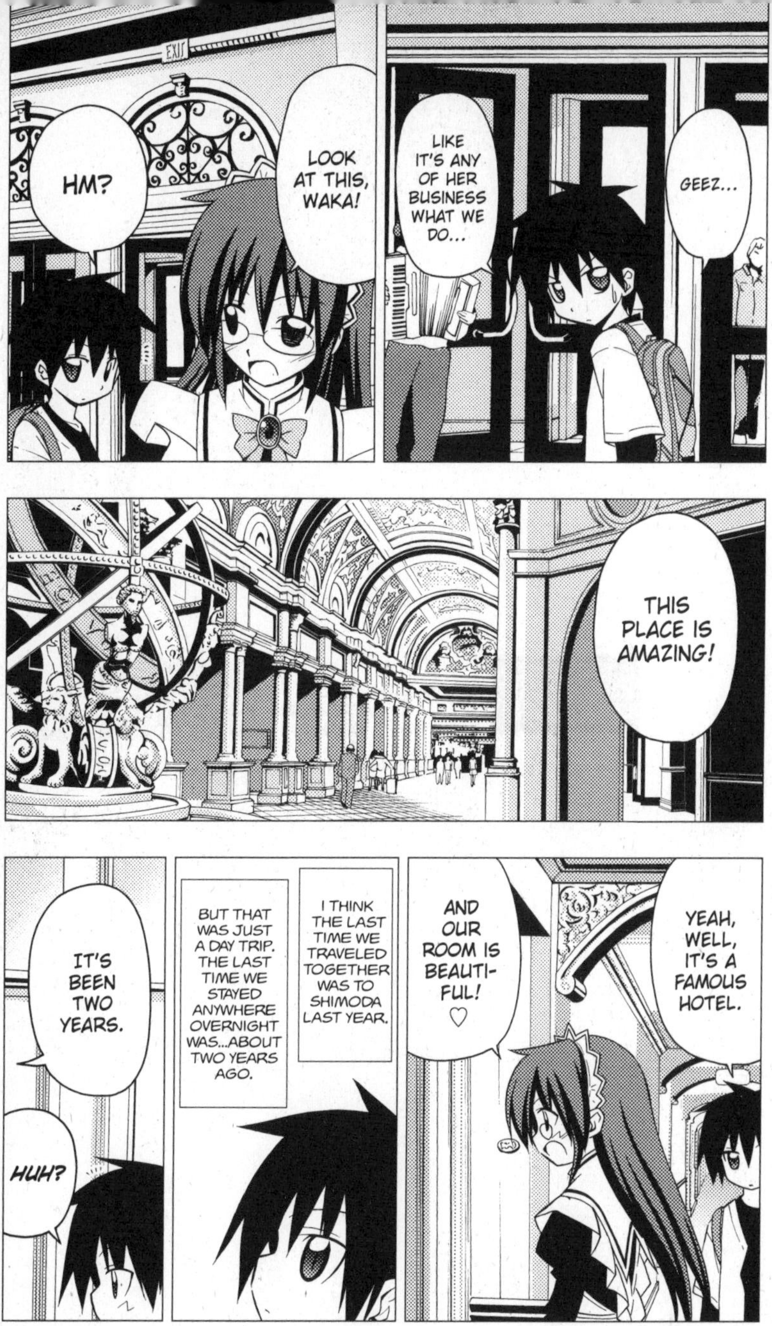
GEEZ...
LIKE IT'S ANY OF HER BUSINESS WHAT WE DO...
LOOK AT THIS, WAKA!
HM?
THIS PLACE IS AMAZING!
YEAH, WELL, IT'S A FAMOUS HOTEL.
AND OUR ROOM IS BEAUTIFUL! ♡
I THINK THE LAST TIME WE TRAVELED TOGETHER WAS TO SHIMODA LAST YEAR.
BUT THAT WAS JUST A DAY TRIP. THE LAST TIME WE STAYED ANYWHERE OVERNIGHT WAS...ABOUT TWO YEARS AGO.
IT'S BEEN TWO YEARS.
HUH?

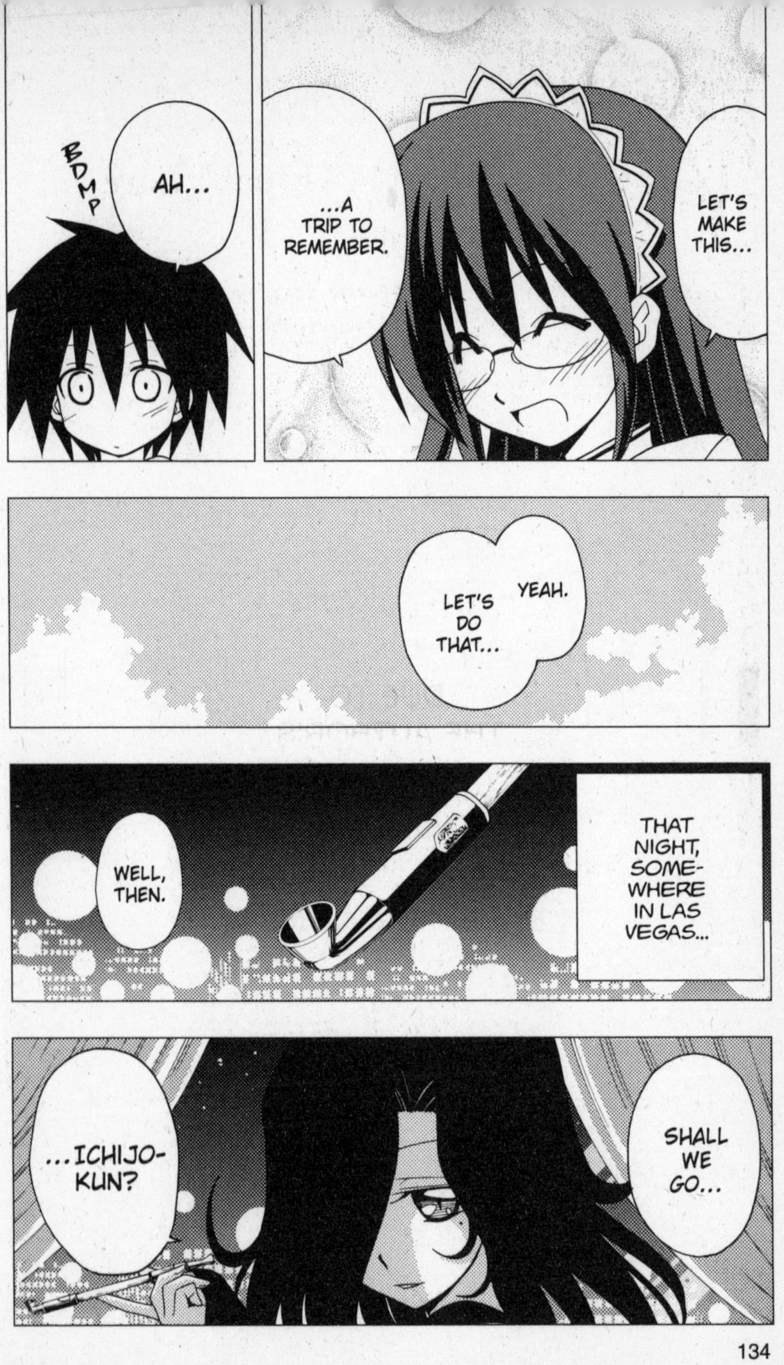
LET'S MAKE THIS...
...A TRIP TO REMEMBER.
AH...
BDMP
YEAH.
LET'S DO THAT...
THAT NIGHT, SOMEWHERE IN LAS VEGAS...
WELL, THEN.
SHALL WE GO...
...ICHIJO-KUN?

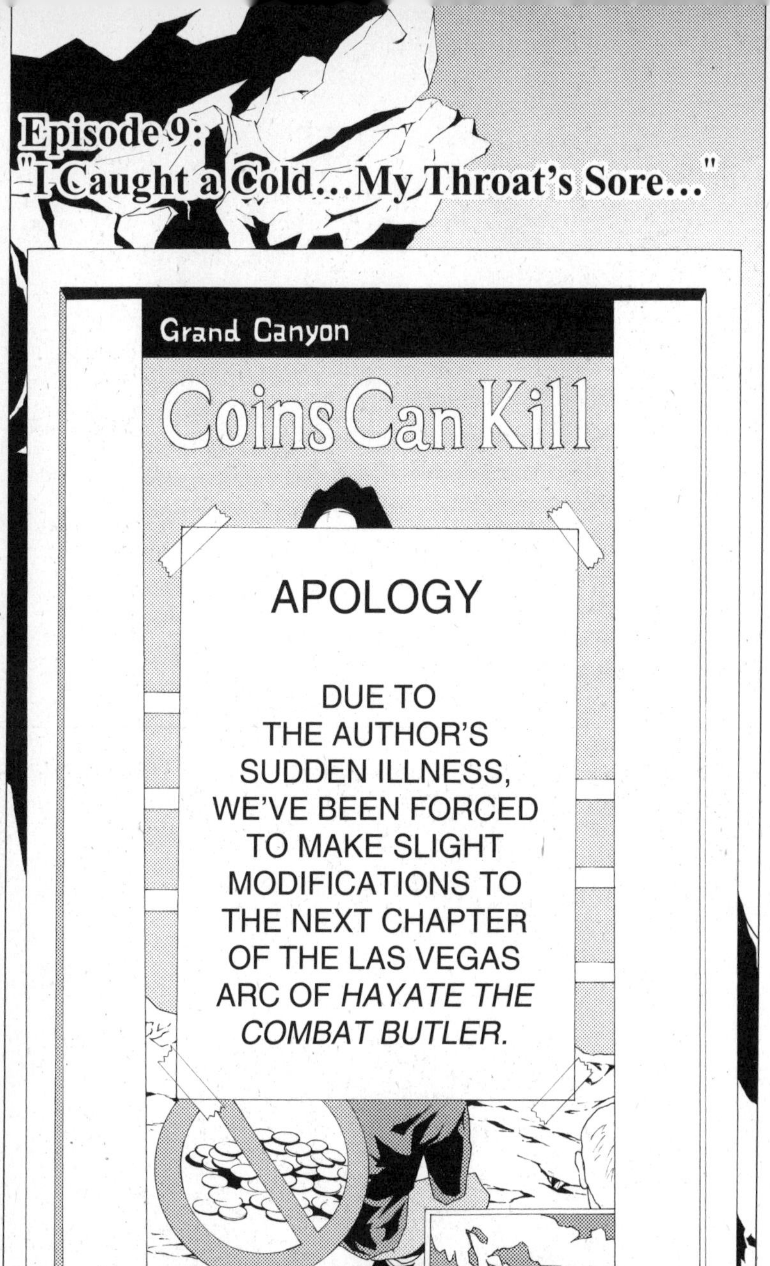
Episode 9:
"I Caught a Cold...My Throat's Sore..."
Grand Canyon
Coins Can Kill
APOLOGY
DUE TO THE AUTHOR'S SUDDEN ILLNESS, WE'VE BEEN FORCED TO MAKE SLIGHT MODIFICATIONS TO THE NEXT CHAPTER OF THE LAS VEGAS ARC OF *HAYATE THE COMBAT BUTLER.*

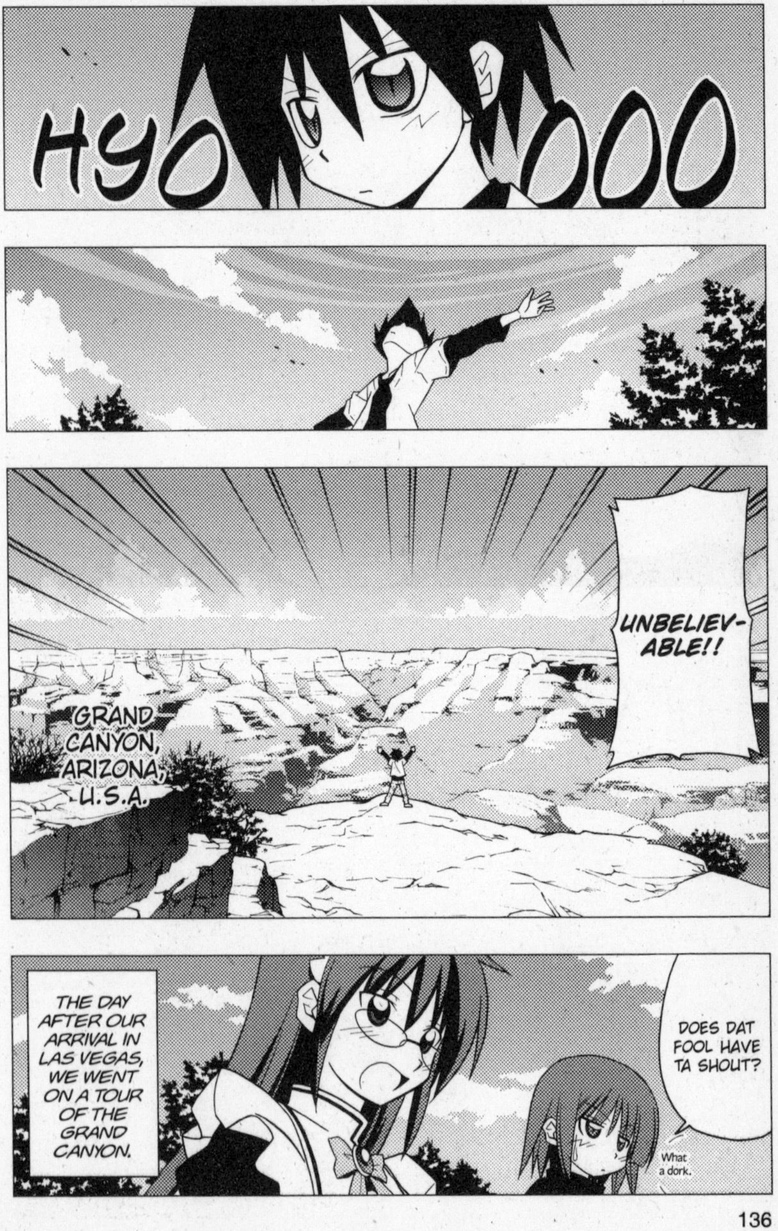
HYOOOO
UNBELIEV-ABLE!!
GRAND CANYON, ARIZONA, U.S.A.
DOES DAT FOOL HAVE TA SHOUT?
What a dork.
THE DAY AFTER OUR ARRIVAL IN LAS VEGAS, WE WENT ON A TOUR OF THE GRAND CANYON.

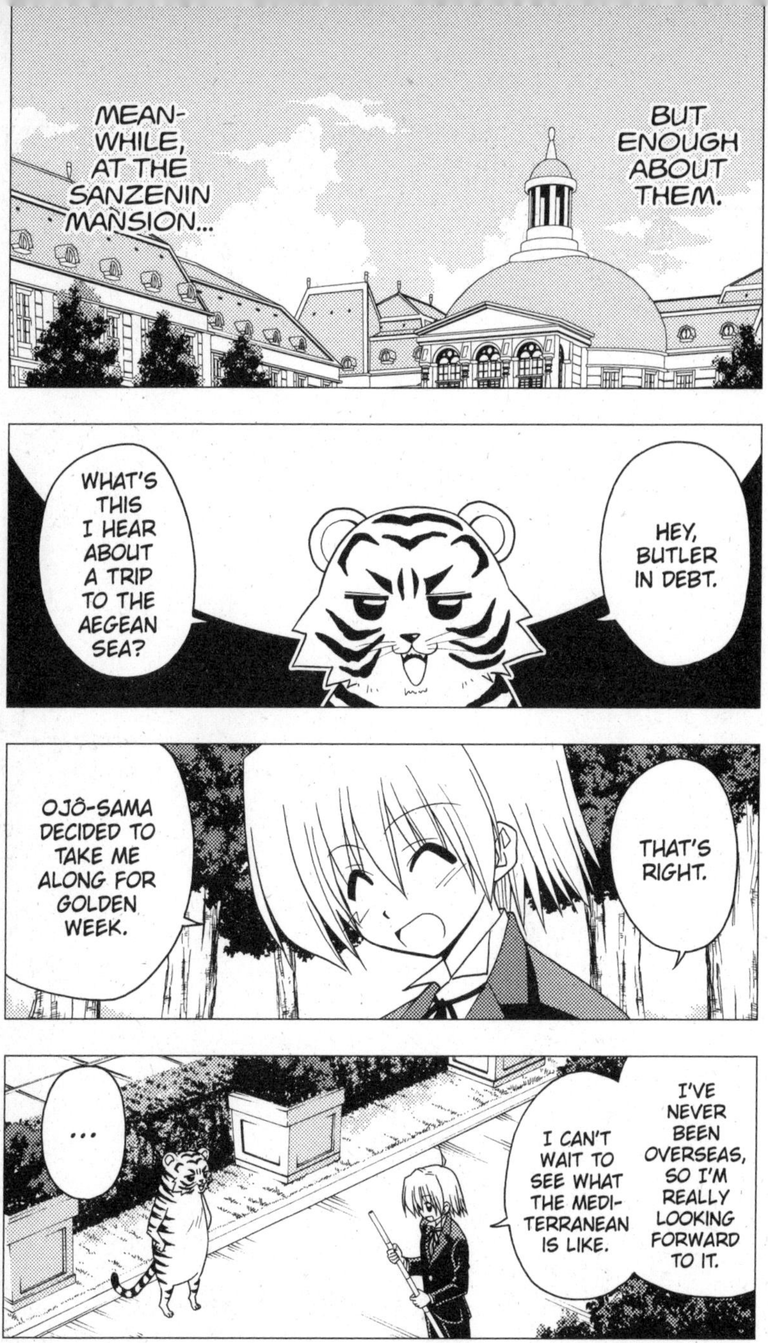
BUT ENOUGH ABOUT THEM.
MEAN-WHILE, AT THE SANZENIN MANSION...
HEY, BUTLER IN DEBT.
WHAT'S THIS I HEAR ABOUT A TRIP TO THE AEGEAN SEA?
THAT'S RIGHT.
OJÔ-SAMA DECIDED TO TAKE ME ALONG FOR GOLDEN WEEK.
I'VE NEVER BEEN OVERSEAS, SO I'M REALLY LOOKING FORWARD TO IT.
I CAN'T WAIT TO SEE WHAT THE MEDI-TERRANEAN IS LIKE.
...

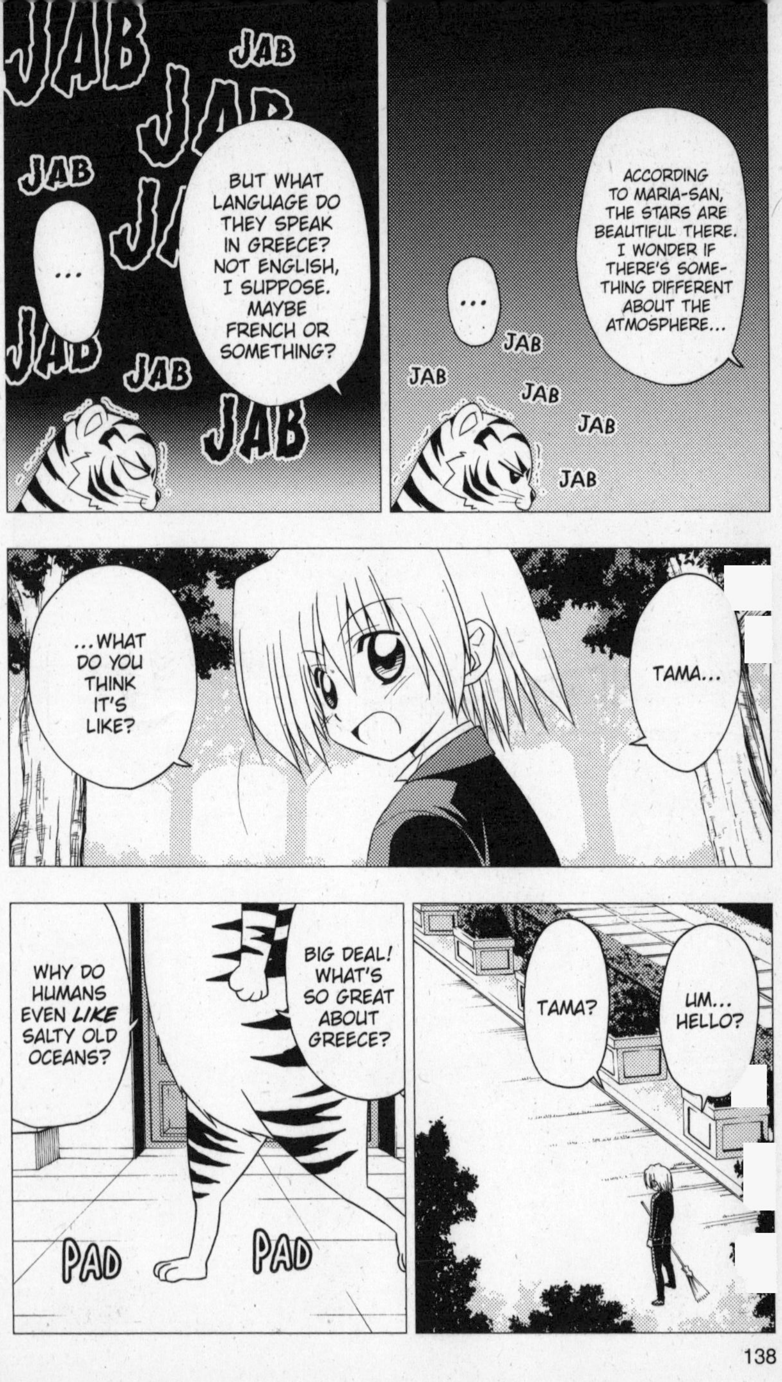
ACCORDING TO MARIA-SAN, THE STARS ARE BEAUTIFUL THERE. I WONDER IF THERE'S SOME-THING DIFFERENT ABOUT THE ATMOSPHERE...
...
JAB
JAB
JAB
JAB
JAB
BUT WHAT LANGUAGE DO THEY SPEAK IN GREECE? NOT ENGLISH, I SUPPOSE. MAYBE FRENCH OR SOMETHING?
...
JAB
JAB
JAB
JAB
JAB
TAMA...
...WHAT DO YOU THINK IT'S LIKE?
UM... HELLO?
TAMA?
BIG DEAL! WHAT'S SO GREAT ABOUT GREECE?
WHY DO HUMANS EVEN *LIKE* SALTY OLD OCEANS?
PAD
PAD

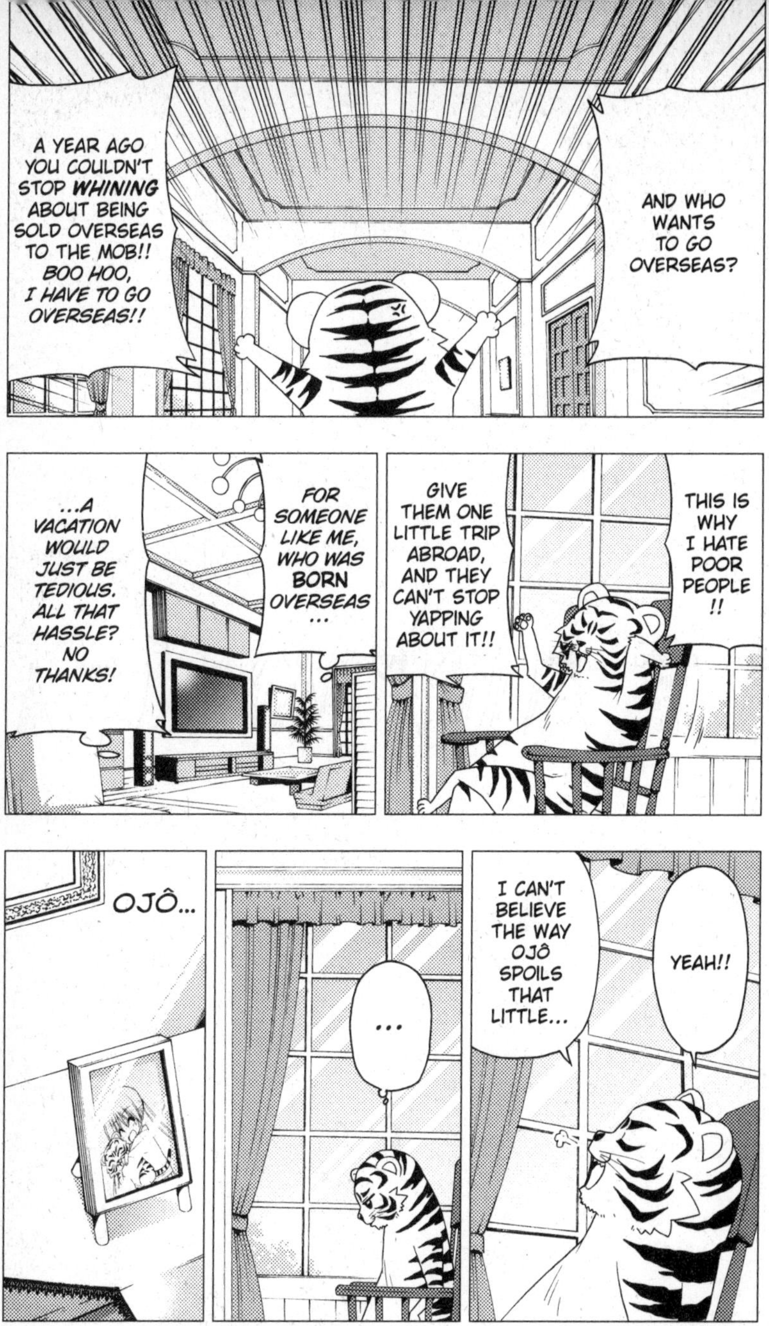
AND WHO WANTS TO GO OVERSEAS?
A YEAR AGO YOU COULDN'T STOP *WHINING* ABOUT BEING SOLD OVERSEAS TO THE MOB!! *BOO HOO, I HAVE TO GO OVERSEAS!!*
THIS IS WHY I HATE POOR PEOPLE!!
GIVE THEM ONE LITTLE TRIP ABROAD, AND THEY CAN'T STOP YAPPING ABOUT IT!!
FOR SOMEONE LIKE ME, WHO WAS BORN *OVERSEAS...*
...A VACATION WOULD JUST BE TEDIOUS. ALL THAT HASSLE? NO THANKS!
YEAH!!
I CAN'T BELIEVE THE WAY OJÔ SPOILS THAT LITTLE...
...
OJÔ...

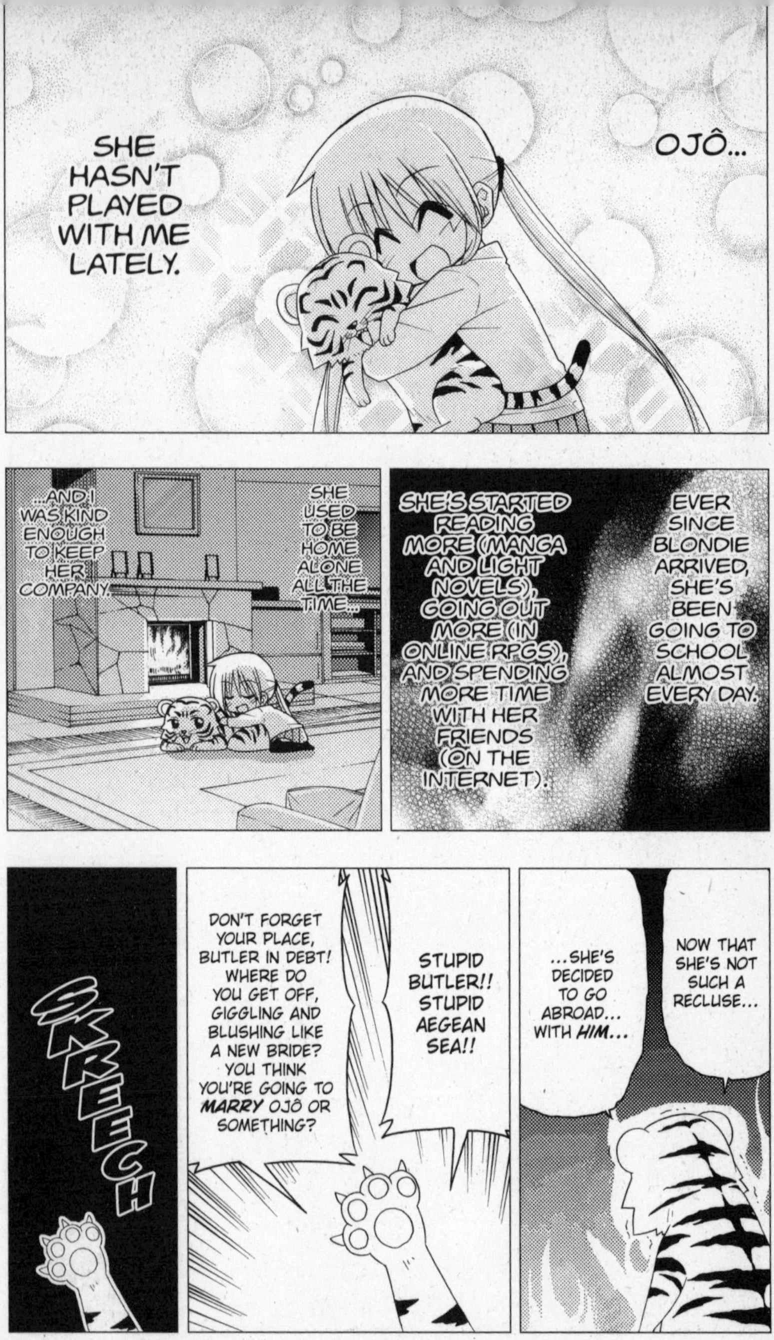
OJÔ...
SHE HASN'T PLAYED WITH ME LATELY.
EVER SINCE BLONDIE ARRIVED, SHE'S BEEN GOING TO SCHOOL ALMOST EVERY DAY.
SHE'S STARTED READING MORE (MANGA AND LIGHT NOVELS), GOING OUT MORE (IN ONLINE RPGS), AND SPENDING MORE TIME WITH HER FRIENDS (ON THE INTERNET).
SHE USED TO BE HOME ALONE ALL THE TIME...
...AND I WAS KIND ENOUGH TO KEEP HER COMPANY.
NOW THAT SHE'S NOT SUCH A RECLUSE...
...SHE'S DECIDED TO GO ABROAD... WITH *HIM*...
STUPID BUTLER!! STUPID AEGEAN SEA!!
DON'T FORGET YOUR PLACE, BUTLER IN DEBT! WHERE DO YOU GET OFF, GIGGLING AND BLUSHING LIKE A NEW BRIDE? YOU THINK YOU'RE GOING TO *MARRY* OJÔ OR SOMETHING?
SKREECH

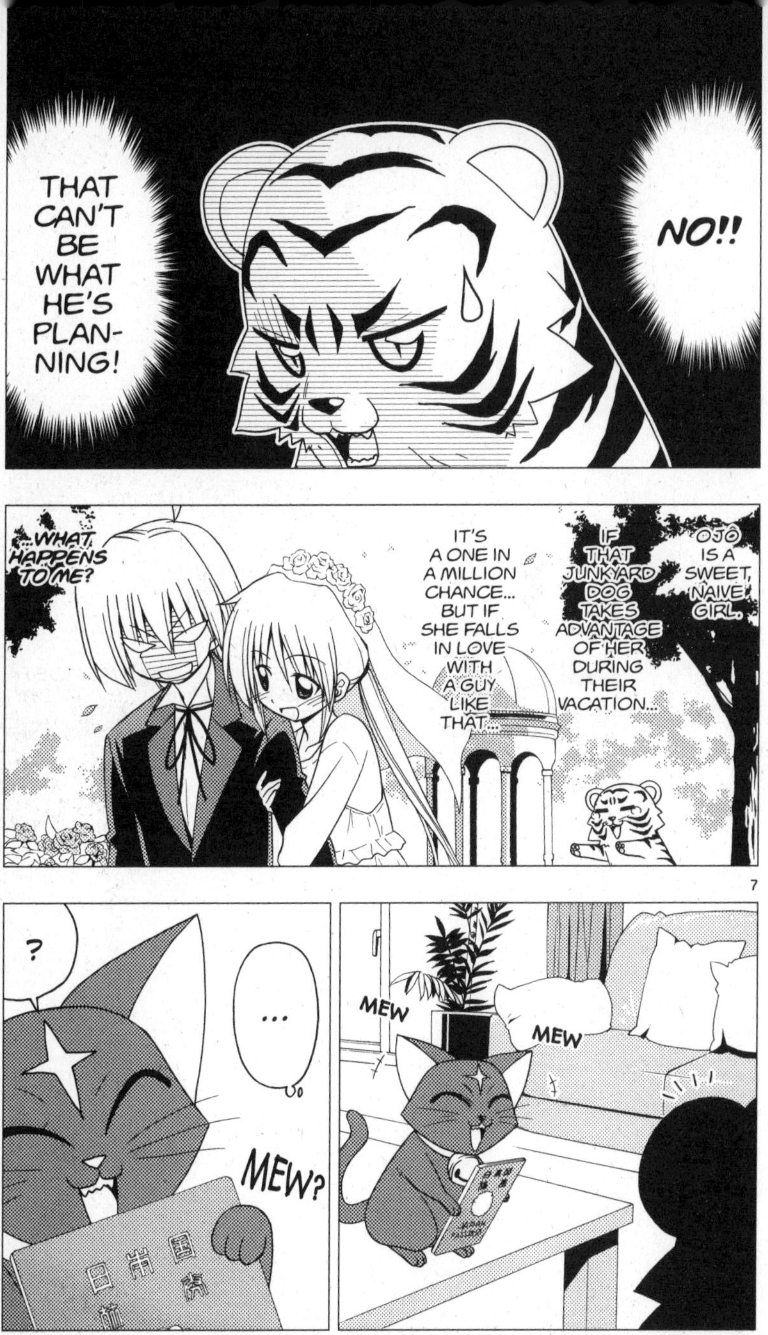
THAT CAN'T BE WHAT HE'S PLAN-NING!
NO!!
OJÔ IS A SWEET, NAIVE GIRL.
IF THAT JUNKYARD DOG TAKES ADVANTAGE OF HER DURING THEIR VACATION...
IT'S A ONE IN A MILLION CHANCE... BUT IF SHE FALLS IN LOVE WITH A GUY LIKE THAT...
...WHAT HAPPENS TO ME?
7
MEW
MEW
?
...
MEW?

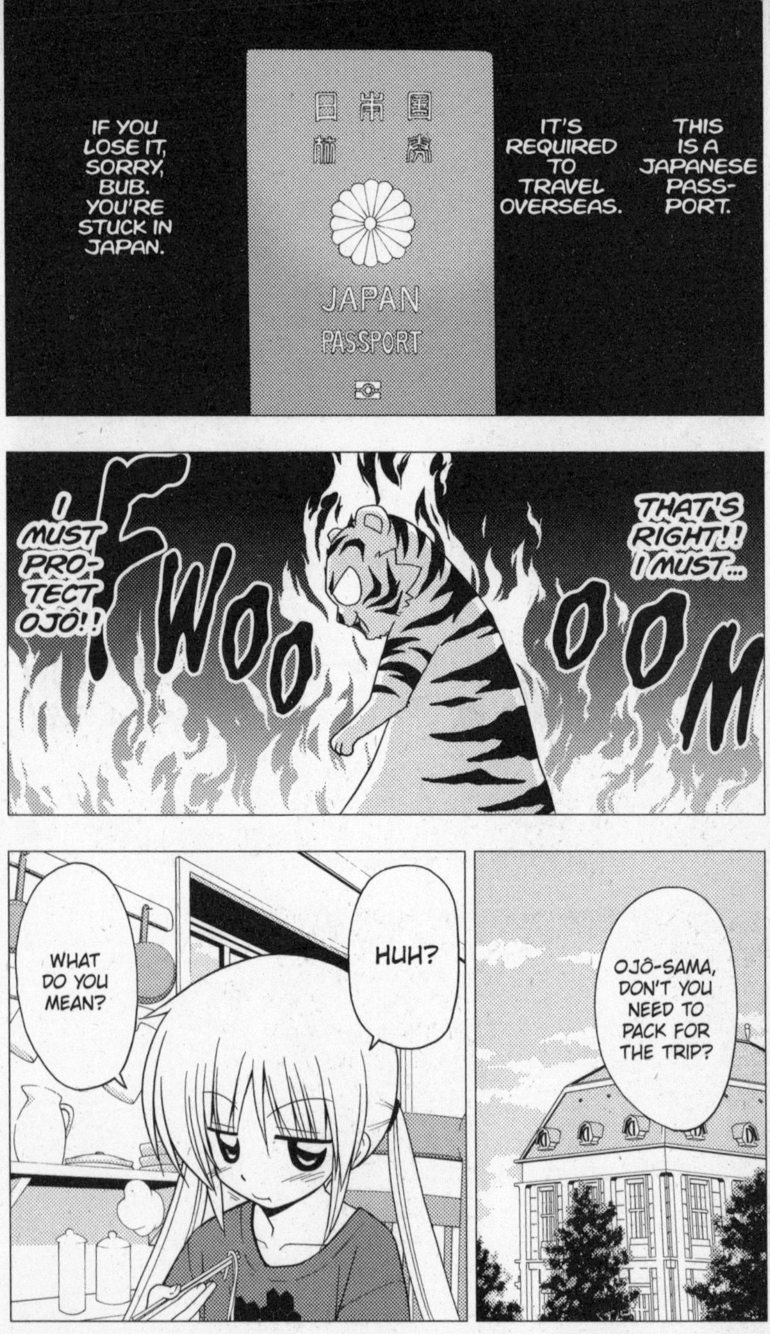
THIS IS A JAPANESE PASS-PORT.
IT'S REQUIRED TO TRAVEL OVERSEAS.
JAPAN
PASSPORT
IF YOU LOSE IT, SORRY, BUB. YOU'RE STUCK IN JAPAN.
THAT'S RIGHT!! I MUST...
FWOOOOOM
I MUST PROTECT OJÔ!!
OJÔ-SAMA, DON'T YOU NEED TO PACK FOR THE TRIP?
HUH?
WHAT DO YOU MEAN?

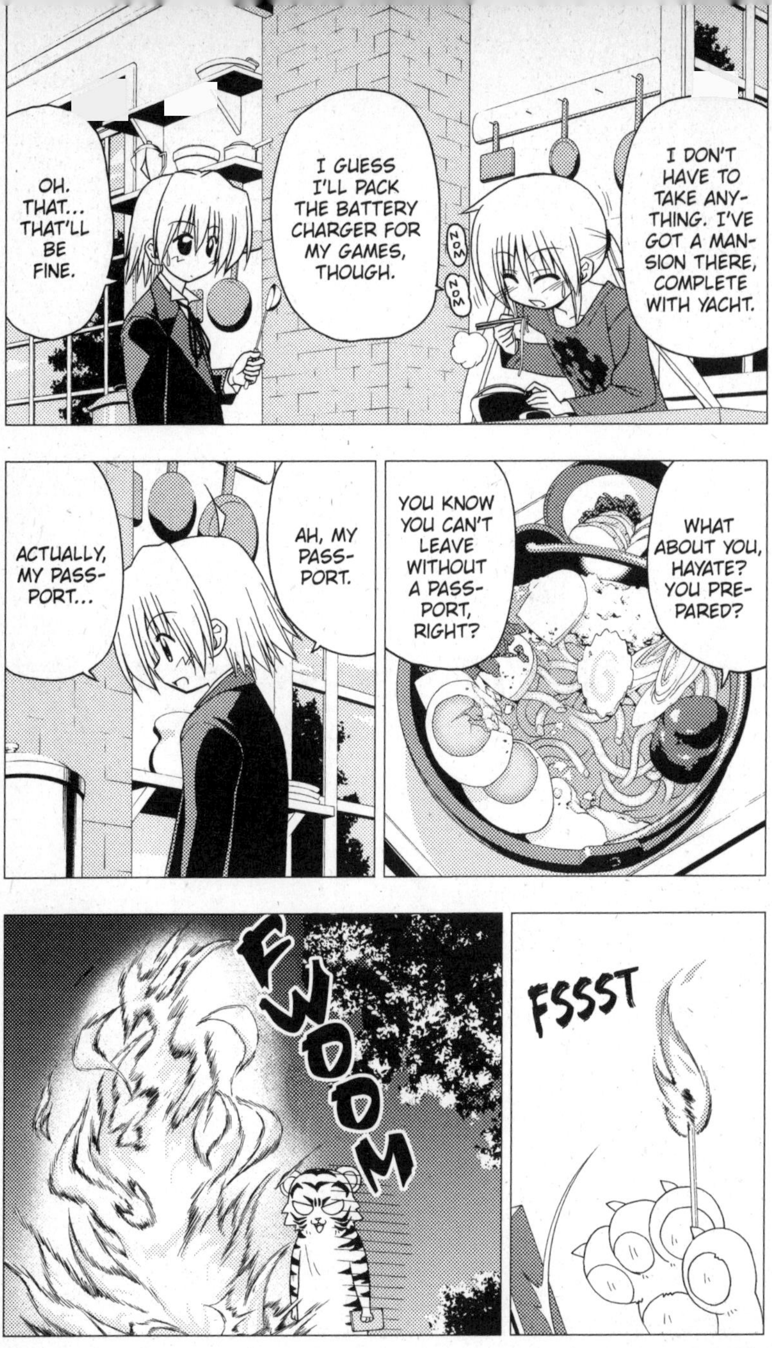
I DON'T HAVE TO TAKE ANYTHING. I'VE GOT A MANSION THERE, COMPLETE WITH YACHT.
NOM
NOM
I GUESS I'LL PACK THE BATTERY CHARGER FOR MY GAMES, THOUGH.
OH. THAT... THAT'LL BE FINE.
WHAT ABOUT YOU, HAYATE? YOU PREPARED?
YOU KNOW YOU CAN'T LEAVE WITHOUT A PASSPORT, RIGHT?
AH, MY PASSPORT.
ACTUALLY, MY PASSPORT...
FSSST
FWOOM

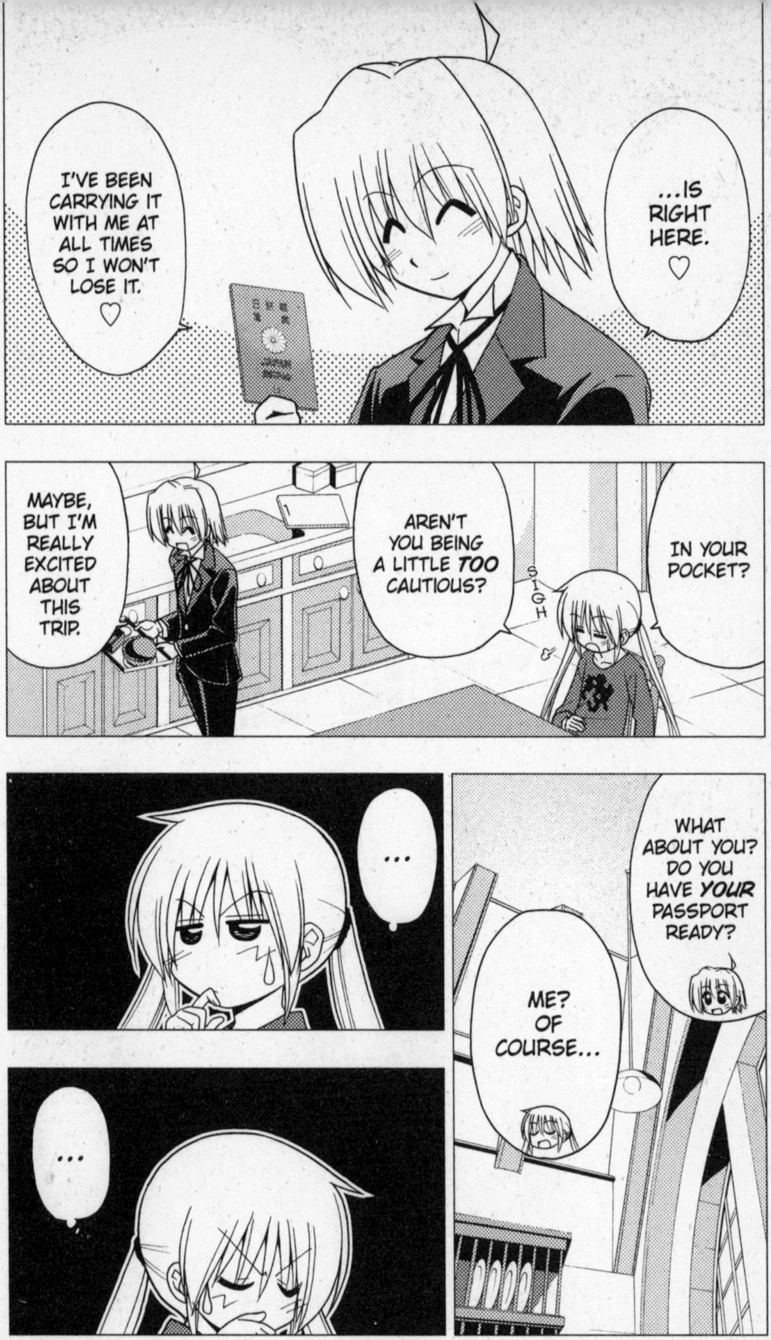
...IS RIGHT HERE. ♡
I'VE BEEN CARRYING IT WITH ME AT ALL TIMES SO I WON'T LOSE IT. ♡
IN YOUR POCKET?
SIGH
AREN'T YOU BEING A LITTLE *TOO* CAUTIOUS?
MAYBE, BUT I'M REALLY EXCITED ABOUT THIS TRIP.
WHAT ABOUT YOU? DO YOU HAVE *YOUR* PASSPORT READY?
ME? OF COURSE...
...
...

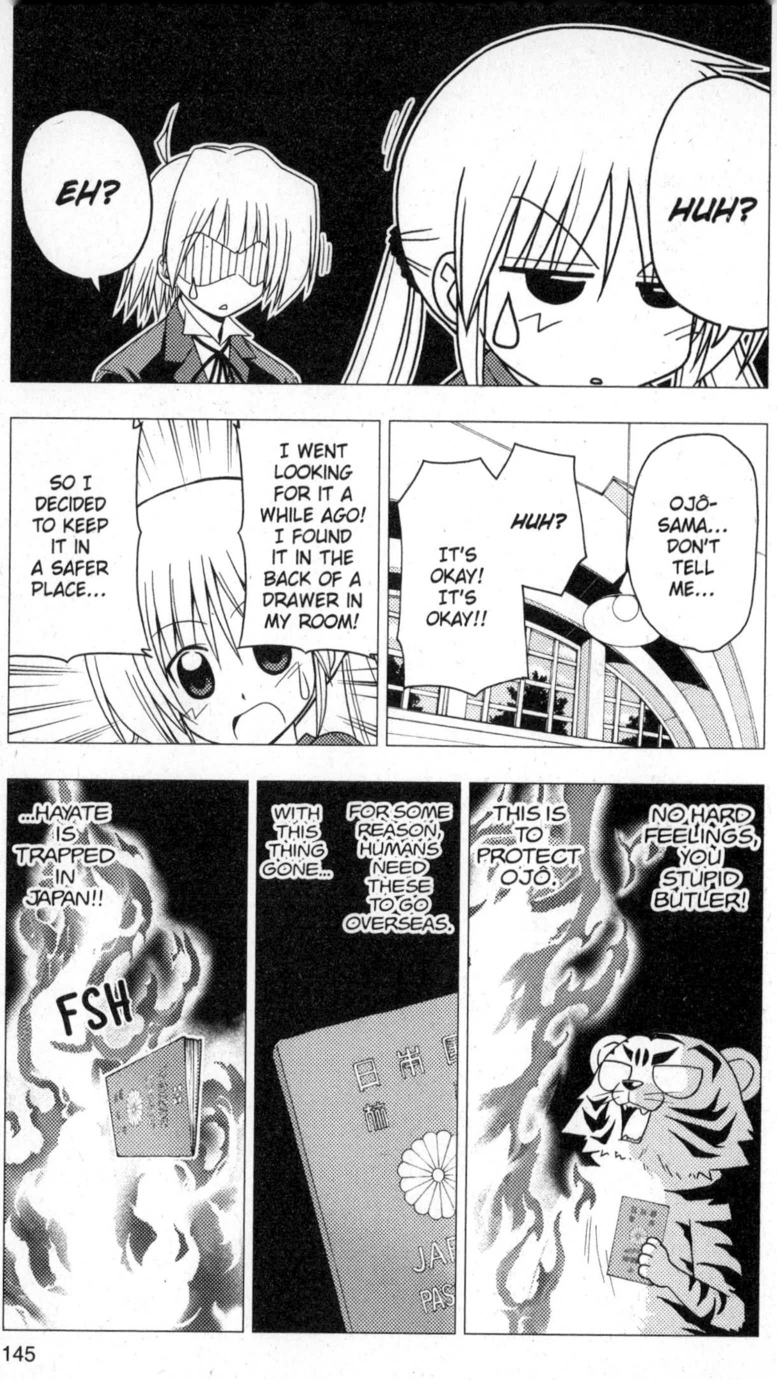
HUH?
EH?
OJÔ-SAMA... DON'T TELL ME...
HUH?
IT'S OKAY! IT'S OKAY!!
I WENT LOOKING FOR IT A WHILE AGO! I FOUND IT IN THE BACK OF A DRAWER IN MY ROOM!
SO I DECIDED TO KEEP IT IN A SAFER PLACE...
NO HARD FEELINGS, YOU STUPID BUTLER!
THIS IS TO PROTECT OJÔ.
FOR SOME REASON, HUMANS NEED THESE TO GO OVERSEAS.
WITH THIS THING GONE...
...HAYATE IS TRAPPED IN JAPAN!!
FSH

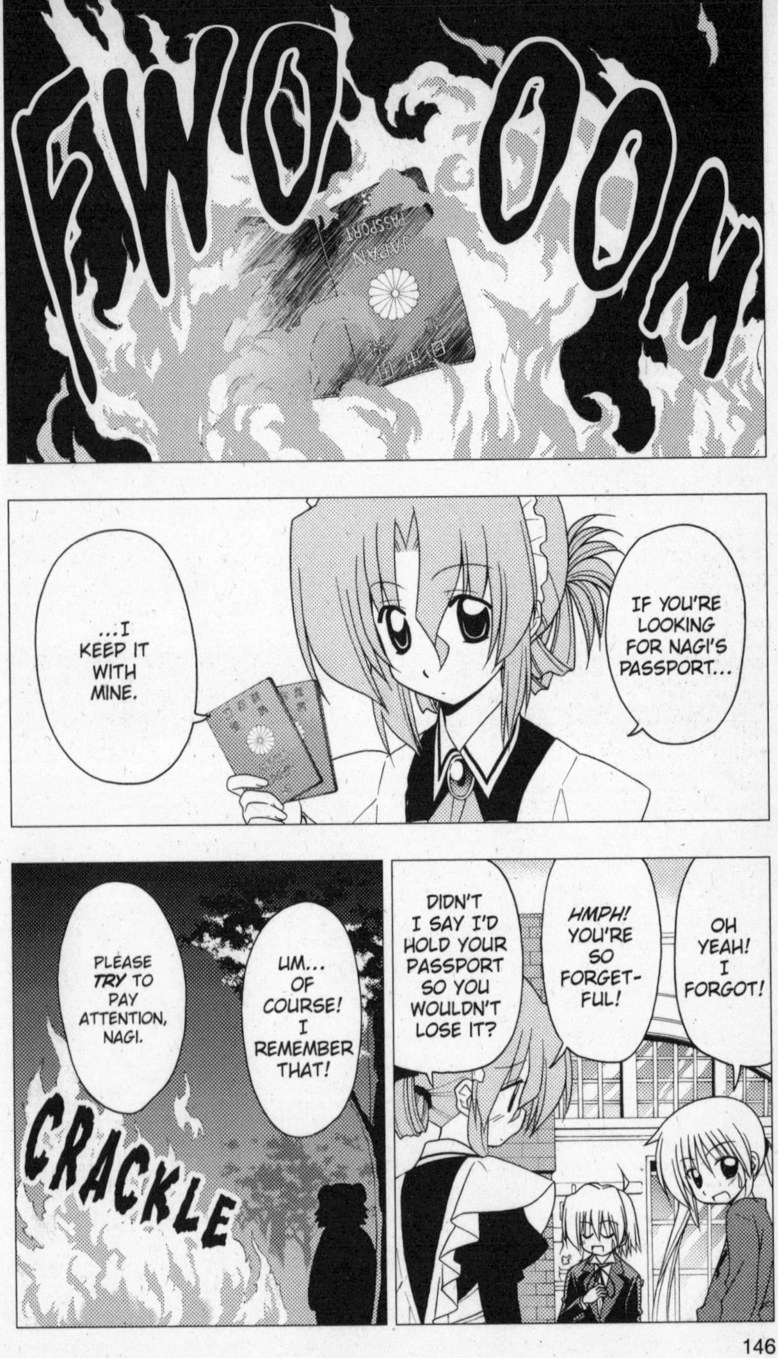
FWO-OOM
IF YOU'RE LOOKING FOR NAGI'S PASSPORT...
...I KEEP IT WITH MINE.
OH YEAH! I FORGOT!
HMPH! YOU'RE SO FORGET-FUL!
DIDN'T I SAY I'D HOLD YOUR PASSPORT SO YOU WOULDN'T LOSE IT?
UM... OF COURSE! I REMEMBER THAT!
PLEASE *TRY* TO PAY ATTENTION, NAGI.
CRACKLE

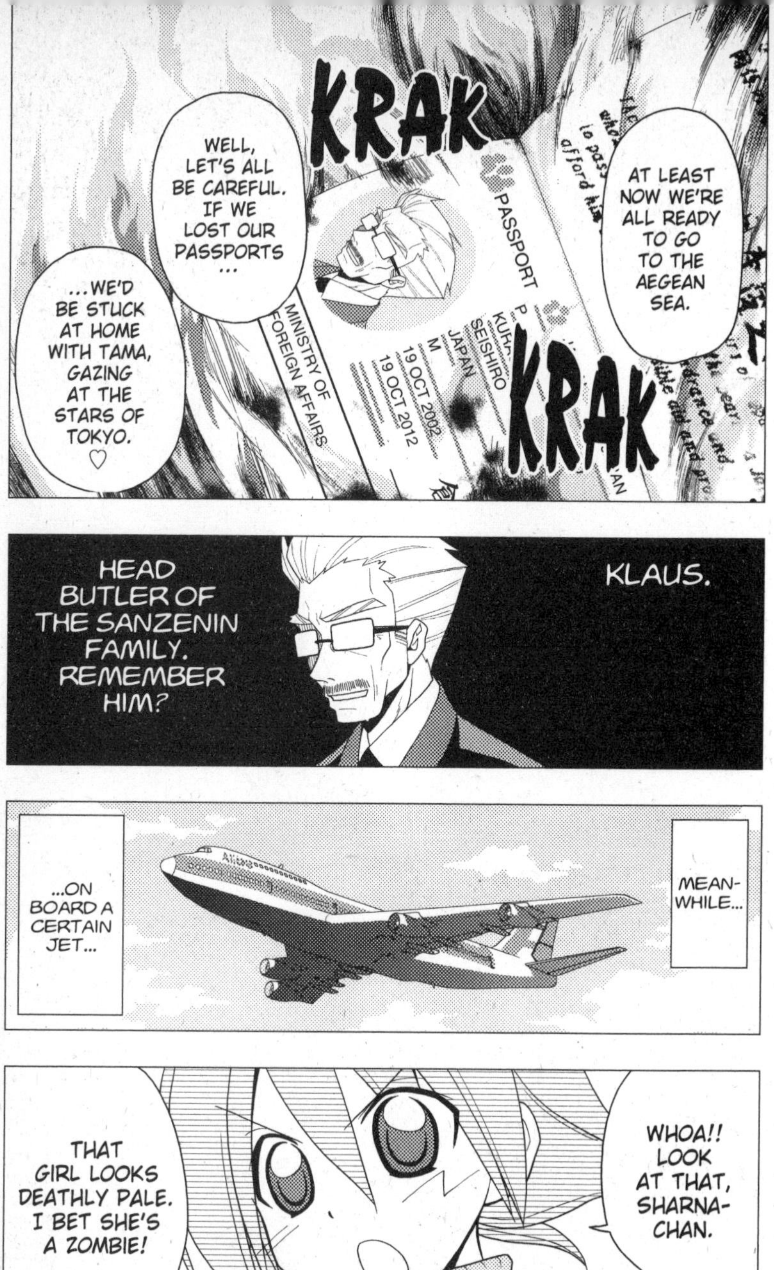
AT LEAST NOW WE'RE ALL READY TO GO TO THE AEGEAN SEA.
KRAK
KRAK
PASSPORT
SEISHIRO
JAPAN
M
19 OCT 2002
19 OCT 2012
MINISTRY OF FOREIGN AFFAIRS
WELL, LET'S ALL BE CAREFUL. IF WE LOST OUR PASSPORTS...
...WE'D BE STUCK AT HOME WITH TAMA, GAZING AT THE STARS OF TOKYO. ♡
KLAUS.
HEAD BUTLER OF THE SANZENIN FAMILY. REMEMBER HIM?
MEAN-WHILE...
...ON BOARD A CERTAIN JET...
WHOA!! LOOK AT THAT, SHARNA-CHAN.
THAT GIRL LOOKS DEATHLY PALE. I BET SHE'S A ZOMBIE!

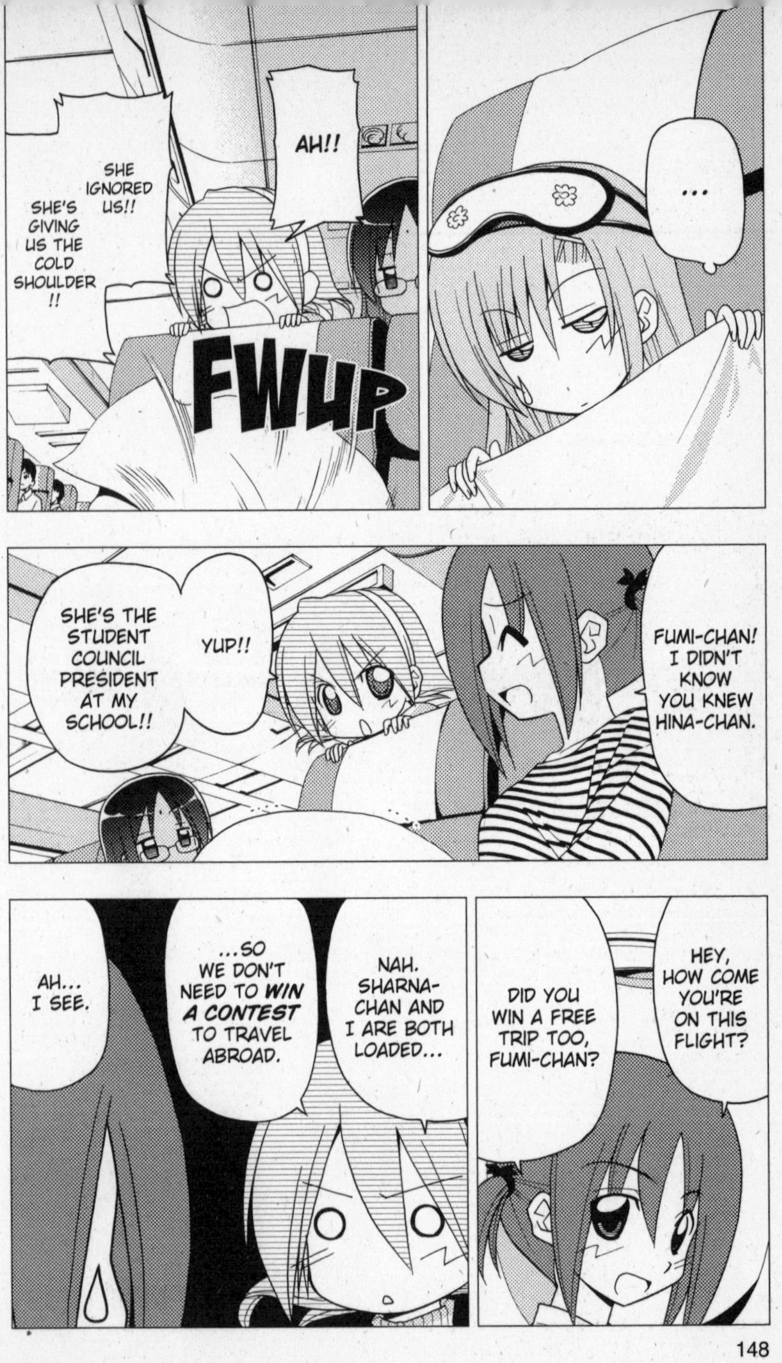
...
AH!!
SHE IGNORED US!!
SHE'S GIVING US THE COLD SHOULDER!!
FWUP
FUMI-CHAN! I DIDN'T KNOW YOU KNEW HINA-CHAN.
YUP!!
SHE'S THE STUDENT COUNCIL PRESIDENT AT MY SCHOOL!!
HEY, HOW COME YOU'RE ON THIS FLIGHT?
DID YOU WIN A FREE TRIP TOO, FUMI-CHAN?
NAH. SHARNA-CHAN AND I ARE BOTH LOADED...
...SO WE DON'T NEED TO ***WIN A CONTEST*** TO TRAVEL ABROAD.
AH... I SEE.

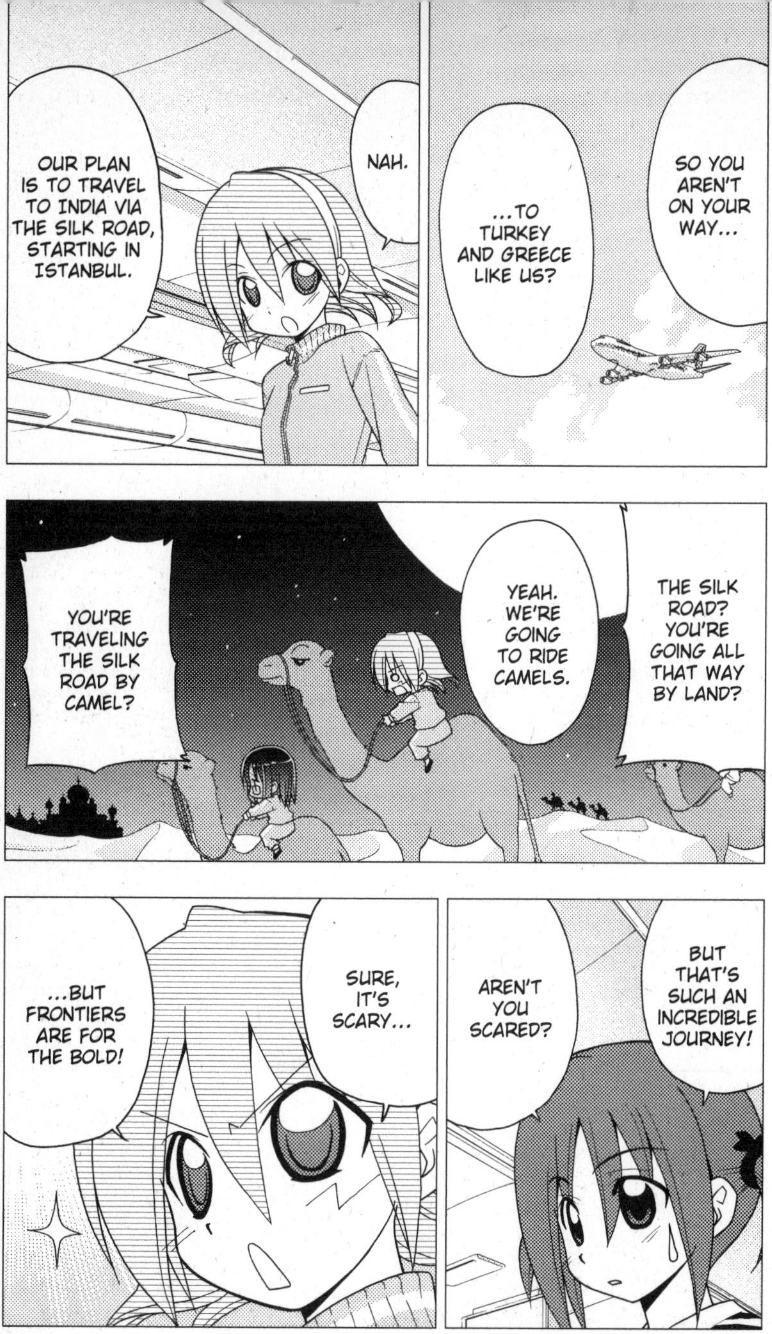
SO YOU AREN'T ON YOUR WAY...
...TO TURKEY AND GREECE LIKE US?
NAH.
OUR PLAN IS TO TRAVEL TO INDIA VIA THE SILK ROAD, STARTING IN ISTANBUL.
THE SILK ROAD? YOU'RE GOING ALL THAT WAY BY LAND?
YEAH. WE'RE GOING TO RIDE CAMELS.
YOU'RE TRAVELING THE SILK ROAD BY CAMEL?
BUT THAT'S SUCH AN INCREDIBLE JOURNEY!
AREN'T YOU SCARED?
SURE, IT'S SCARY...
...BUT FRONTIERS ARE FOR THE BOLD!

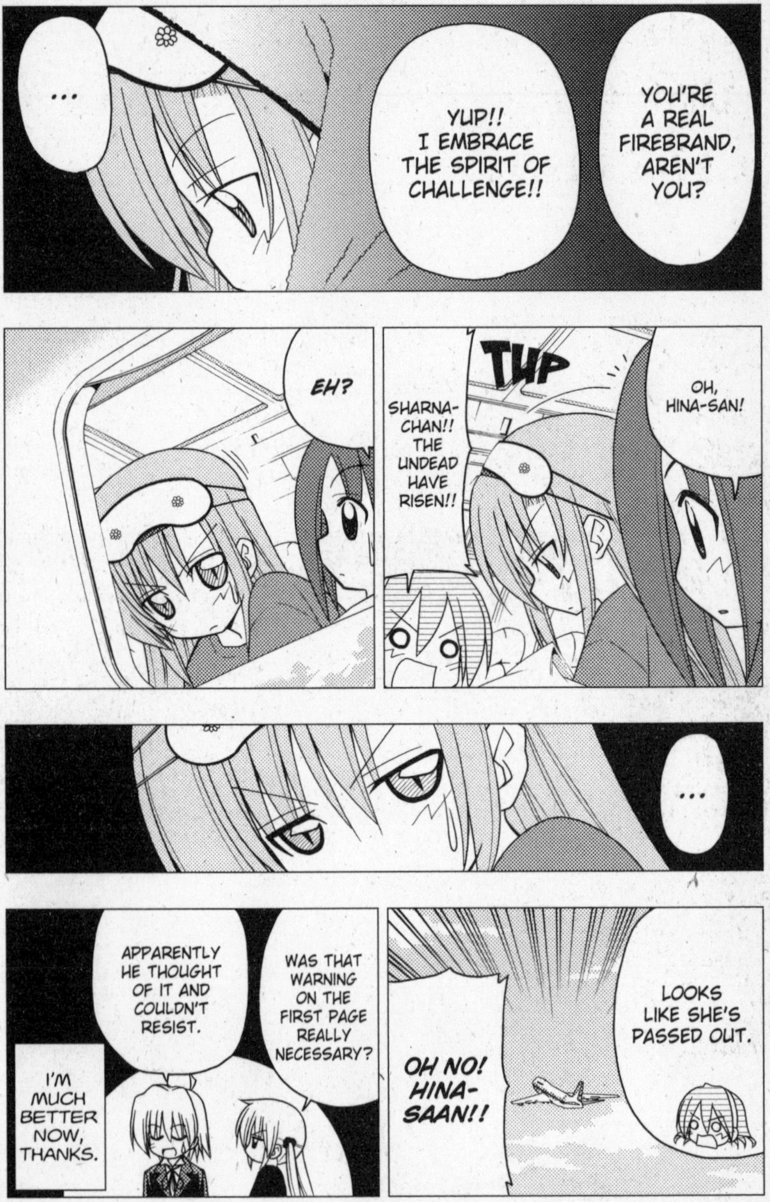
YOU'RE A REAL FIREBRAND, AREN'T YOU?
YUP!! I EMBRACE THE SPIRIT OF CHALLENGE!!
...
OH, HINA-SAN!
THP
SHARNA-CHAN!! THE UNDEAD HAVE RISEN!!
EH?
...
LOOKS LIKE SHE'S PASSED OUT.
OH NO! HINA-SAAN!!
WAS THAT WARNING ON THE FIRST PAGE REALLY NECESSARY?
APPARENTLY HE THOUGHT OF IT AND COULDN'T RESIST.
I'M MUCH BETTER NOW, THANKS.

Episode 10: "I'm Not Going to Say, 'But Look Now—It Wasn't a Dream.'"

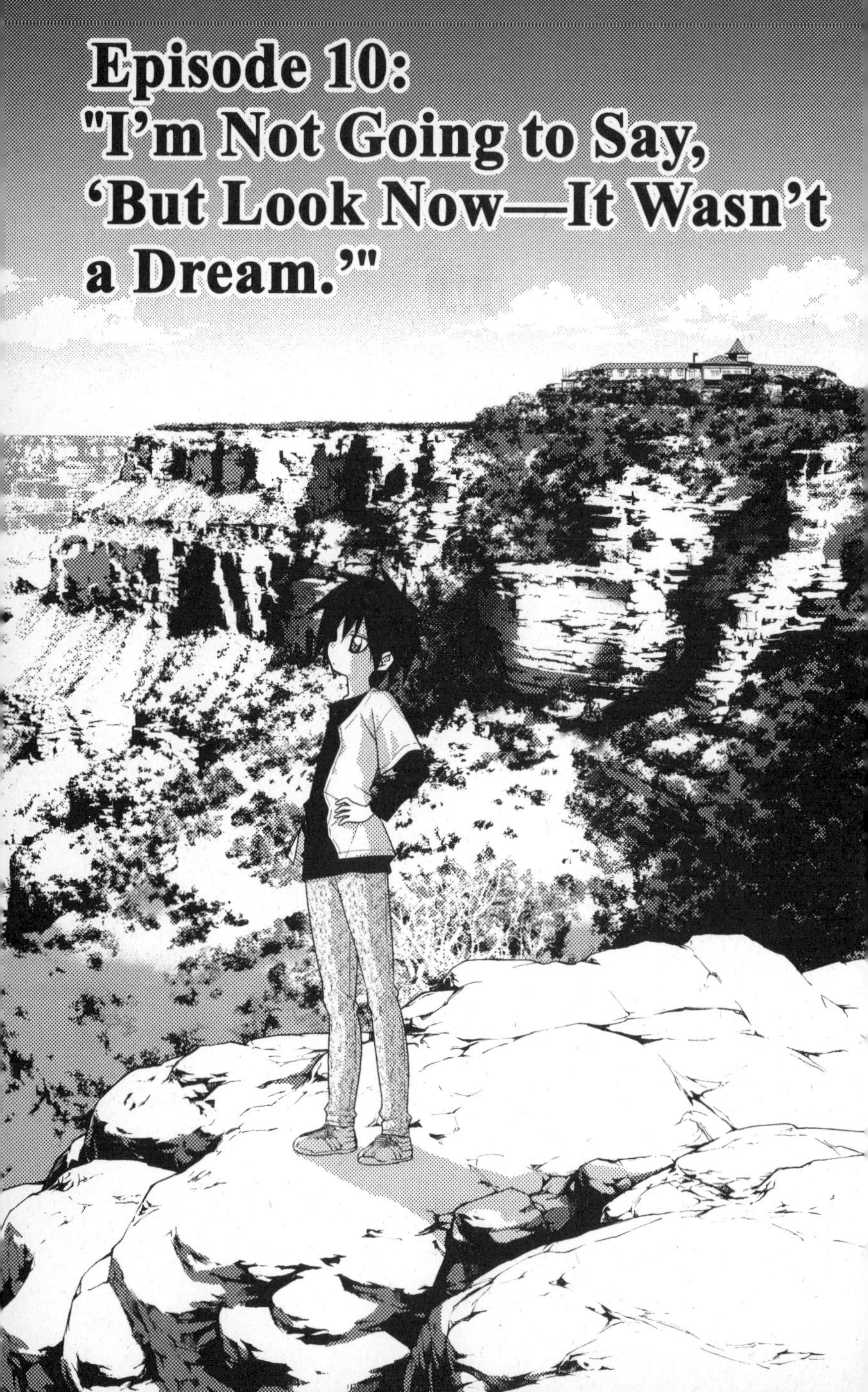

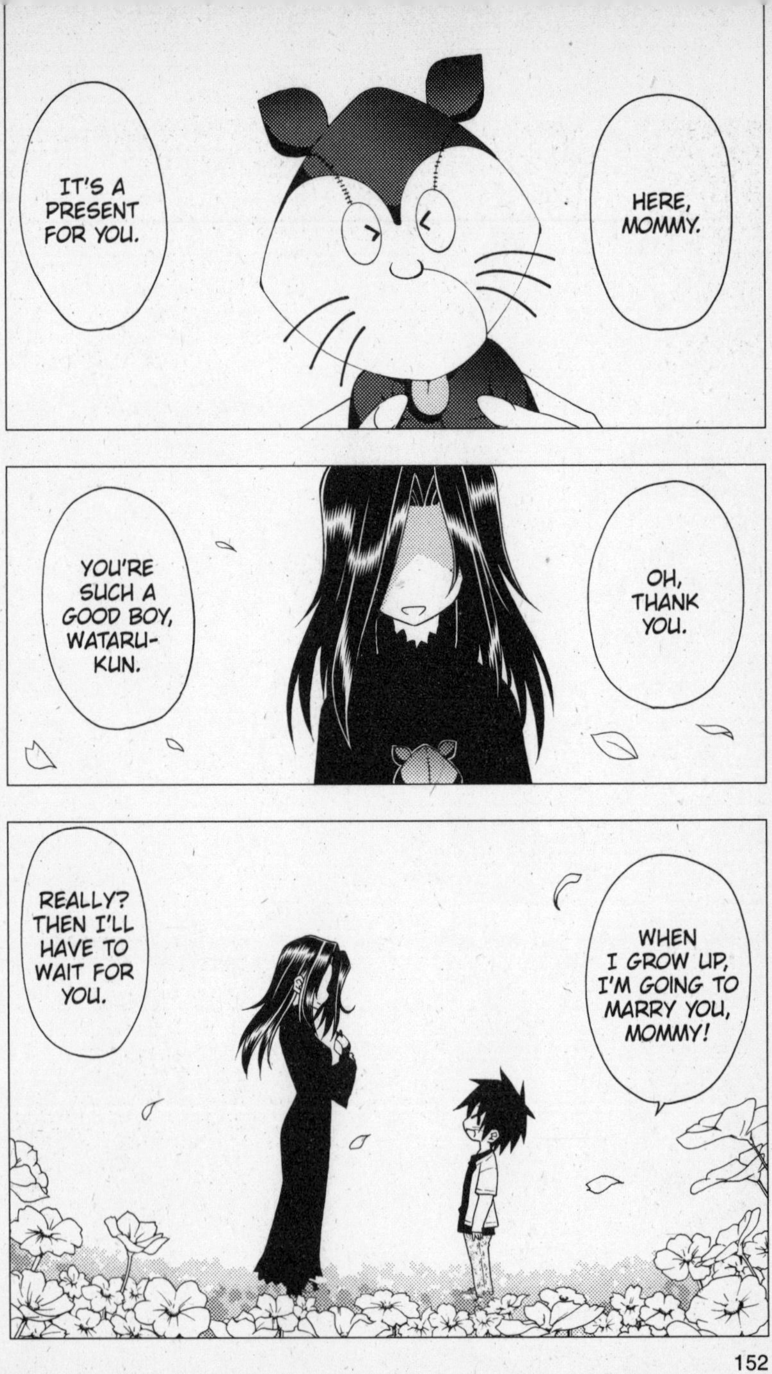
HERE, MOMMY.
IT'S A PRESENT FOR YOU.
OH, THANK YOU.
YOU'RE SUCH A GOOD BOY, WATARU-KUN.
WHEN I GROW UP, I'M GOING TO MARRY YOU, MOMMY!
REALLY? THEN I'LL HAVE TO WAIT FOR YOU.

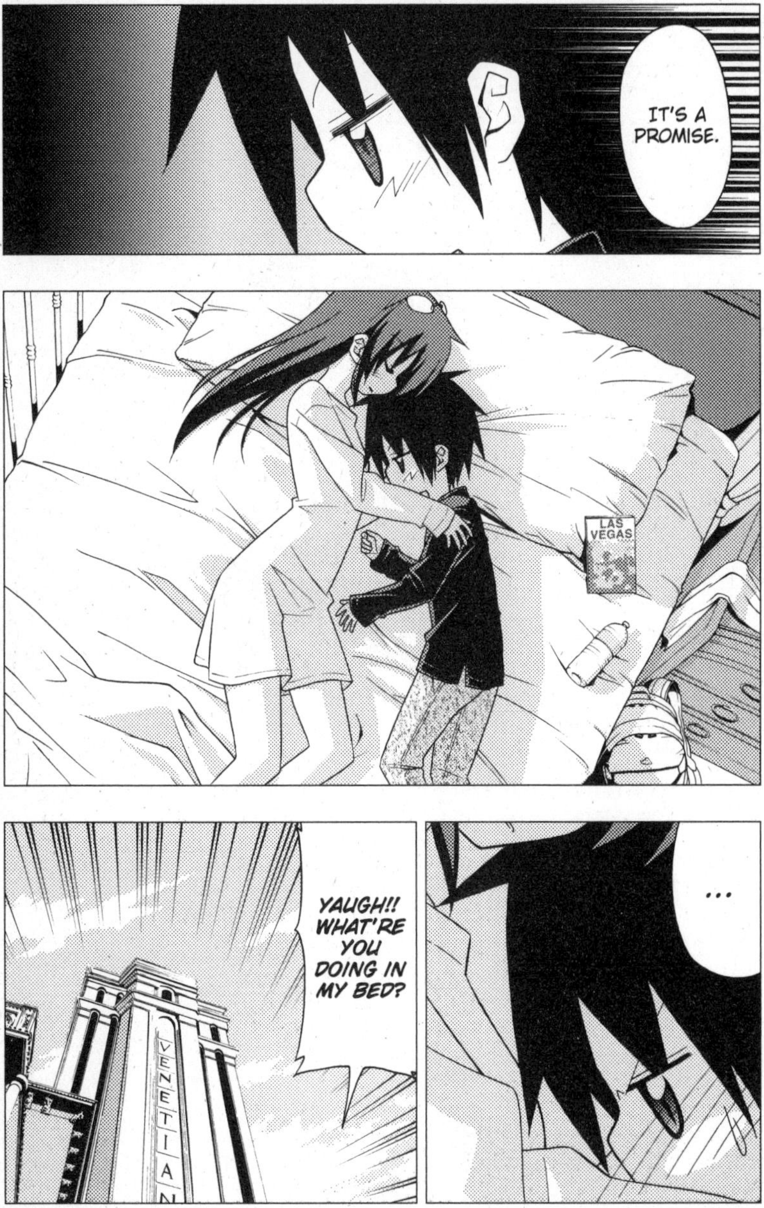
IT'S A PROMISE.
LAS VEGAS
...
YAUGH!! WHAT'RE YOU DOING IN MY BED?
VENETIAN

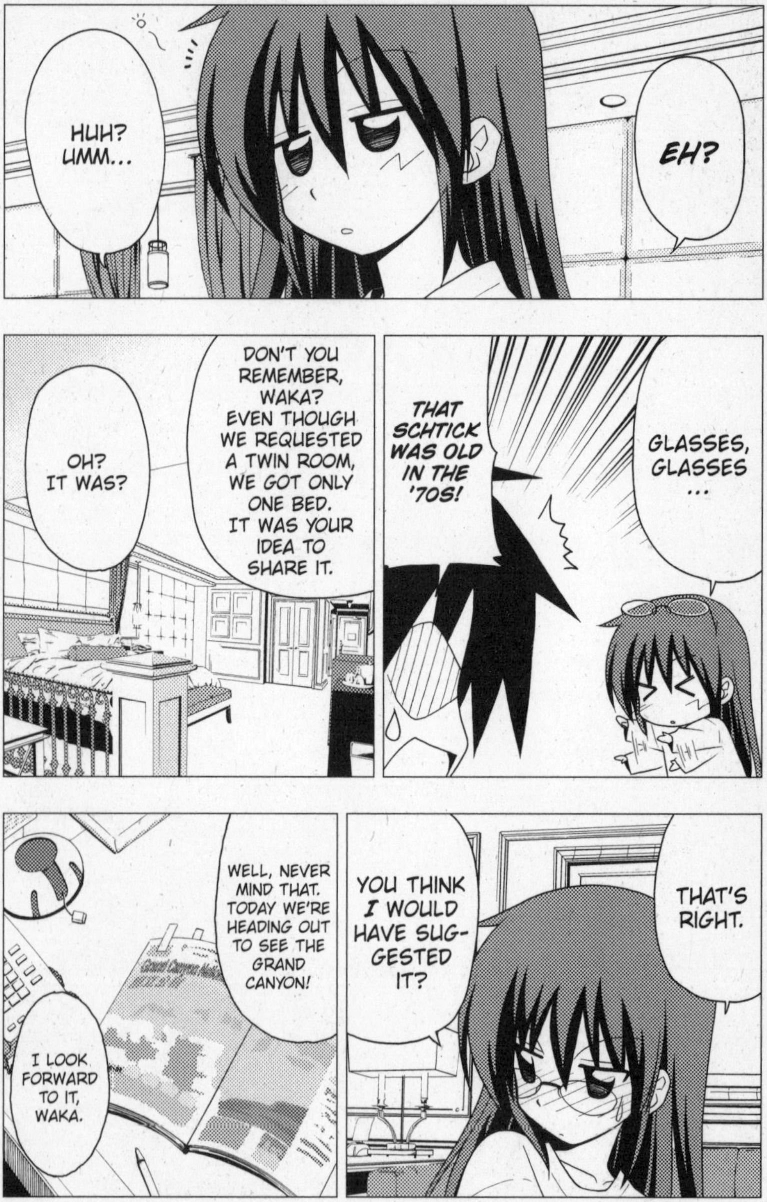
EH?
HUH? UMM...
GLASSES, GLASSES...
THAT SCHTICK WAS OLD IN THE '70S!
DON'T YOU REMEMBER, WAKA? EVEN THOUGH WE REQUESTED A TWIN ROOM, WE GOT ONLY ONE BED. IT WAS YOUR IDEA TO SHARE IT.
OH? IT WAS?
THAT'S RIGHT.
YOU THINK *I* WOULD HAVE SUG-GESTED IT?
WELL, NEVER MIND THAT. TODAY WE'RE HEADING OUT TO SEE THE GRAND CANYON!
I LOOK FORWARD TO IT, WAKA.

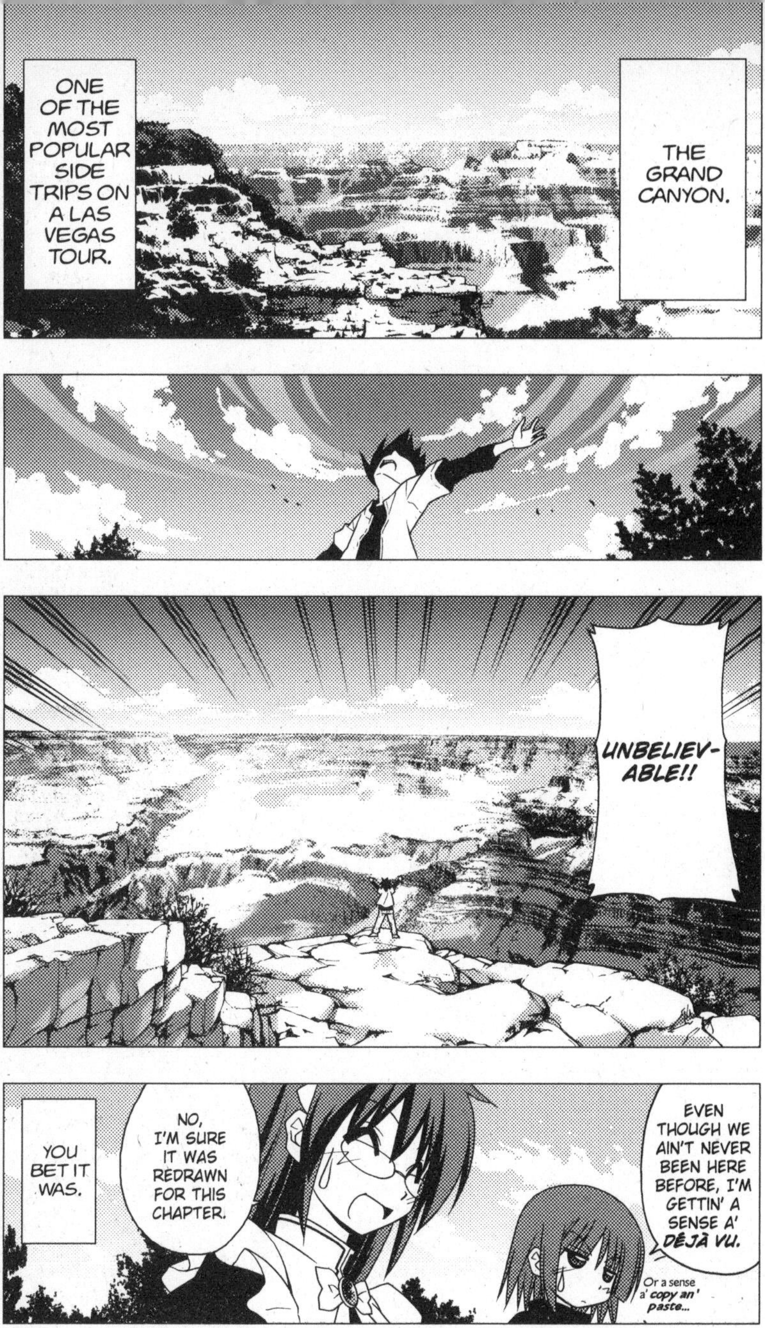
THE GRAND CANYON.
ONE OF THE MOST POPULAR SIDE TRIPS ON A LAS VEGAS TOUR.
UNBELIEV-ABLE!!
EVEN THOUGH WE AIN'T NEVER BEEN HERE BEFORE, I'M GETTIN' A SENSE A' DÉJÀ VU.
Or a sense a' copy an' paste...
NO, I'M SURE IT WAS REDRAWN FOR THIS CHAPTER.
YOU BET IT WAS.

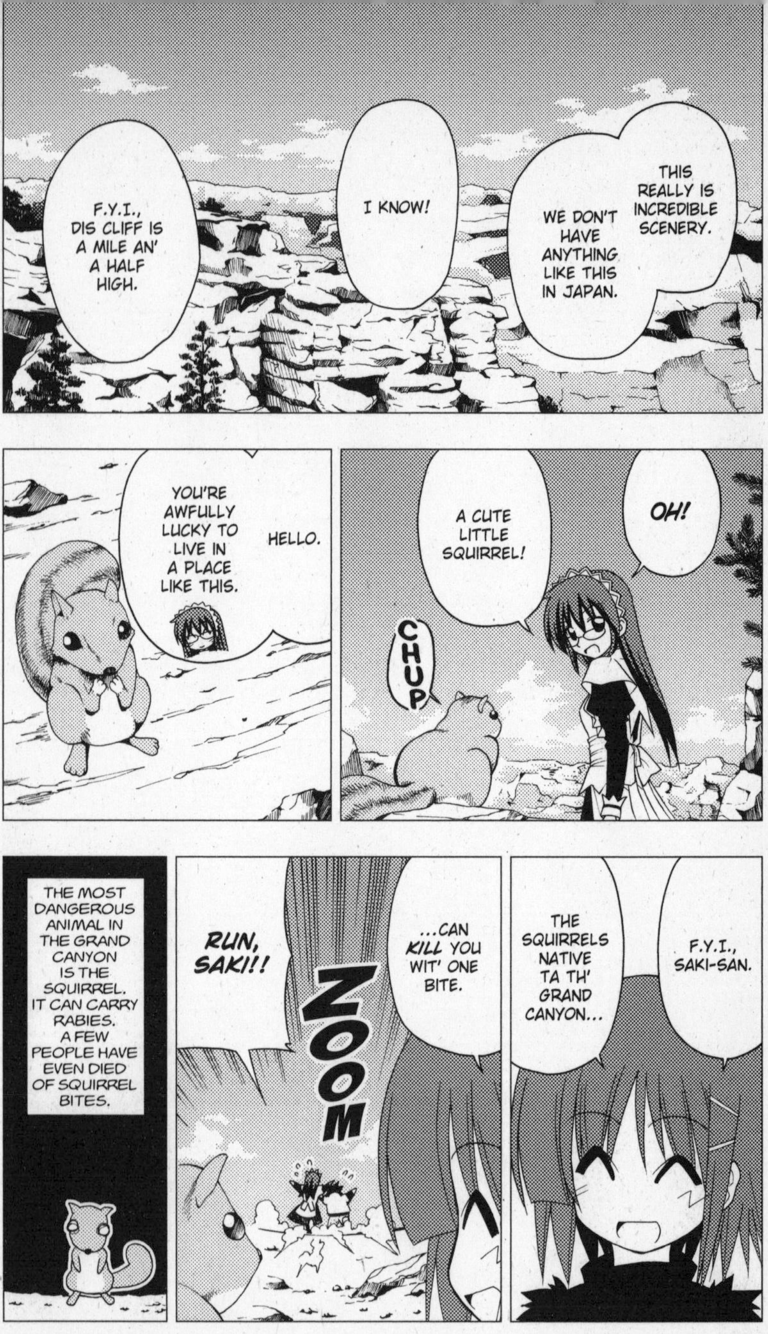
THIS REALLY IS INCREDIBLE SCENERY.
WE DON'T HAVE ANYTHING LIKE THIS IN JAPAN.
I KNOW!
F.Y.I., DIS CLIFF IS A MILE AN' A HALF HIGH.
OH!
A CUTE LITTLE SQUIRREL!
CHUP
HELLO.
YOU'RE AWFULLY LUCKY TO LIVE IN A PLACE LIKE THIS.
F.Y.I., SAKI-SAN.
THE SQUIRRELS NATIVE TA TH' GRAND CANYON...
...CAN *KILL* YOU WIT' ONE BITE.
ZOOM
RUN, SAKI!!
THE MOST DANGEROUS ANIMAL IN THE GRAND CANYON IS THE SQUIRREL. IT CAN CARRY RABIES. A FEW PEOPLE HAVE EVEN DIED OF SQUIRREL BITES.

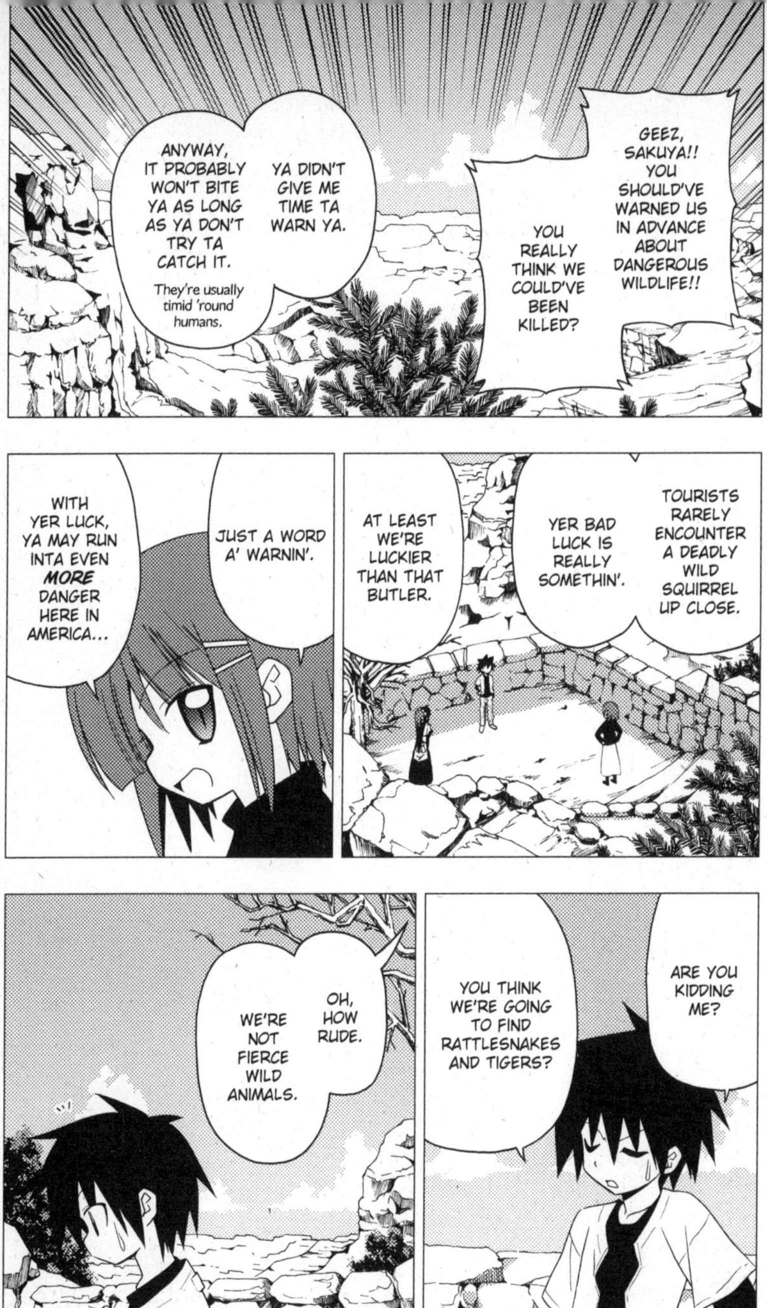
GEEZ, SAKUYA!! YOU SHOULD'VE WARNED US IN ADVANCE ABOUT DANGEROUS WILDLIFE!!
YOU REALLY THINK WE COULD'VE BEEN KILLED?
YA DIDN'T GIVE ME TIME TA WARN YA.
ANYWAY, IT PROBABLY WON'T BITE YA AS LONG AS YA DON'T TRY TA CATCH IT.
They're usually timid 'round humans.
TOURISTS RARELY ENCOUNTER A DEADLY WILD SQUIRREL UP CLOSE.
YER BAD LUCK IS REALLY SOMETHIN'.
AT LEAST WE'RE LUCKIER THAN THAT BUTLER.
JUST A WORD A' WARNIN'.
WITH YER LUCK, YA MAY RUN INTA EVEN *MORE* DANGER HERE IN AMERICA...
ARE YOU KIDDING ME?
YOU THINK WE'RE GOING TO FIND RATTLESNAKES AND TIGERS?
OH, HOW RUDE.
WE'RE NOT FIERCE WILD ANIMALS.

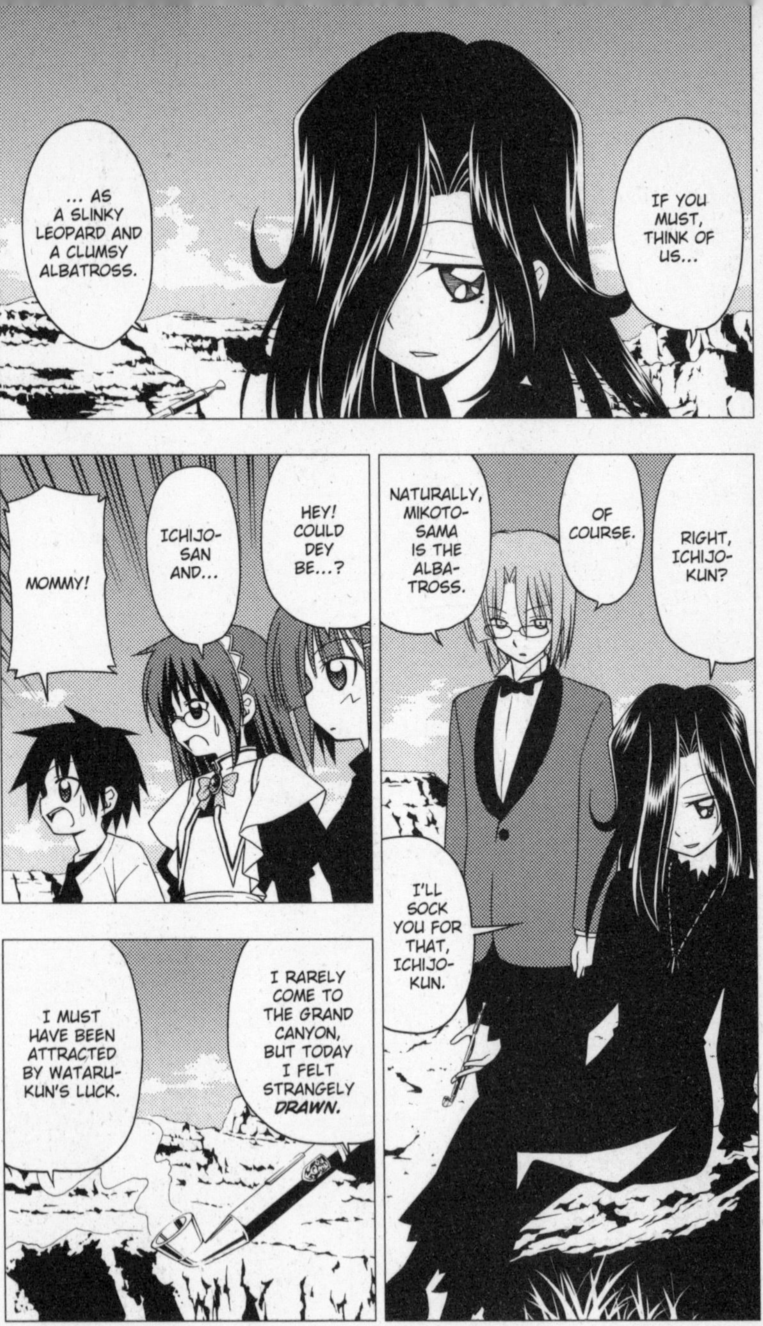
IF YOU MUST, THINK OF US...
... AS A SLINKY LEOPARD AND A CLUMSY ALBATROSS.
RIGHT, ICHIJO-KUN?
OF COURSE.
NATURALLY, MIKOTO-SAMA IS THE ALBATROSS.
I'LL SOCK YOU FOR THAT, ICHIJO-KUN.
HEY! COULD DEY BE...?
ICHIJO-SAN AND...
MOMMY!
I RARELY COME TO THE GRAND CANYON, BUT TODAY I FELT STRANGELY ***DRAWN.***
I MUST HAVE BEEN ATTRACTED BY WATARU-KUN'S LUCK.

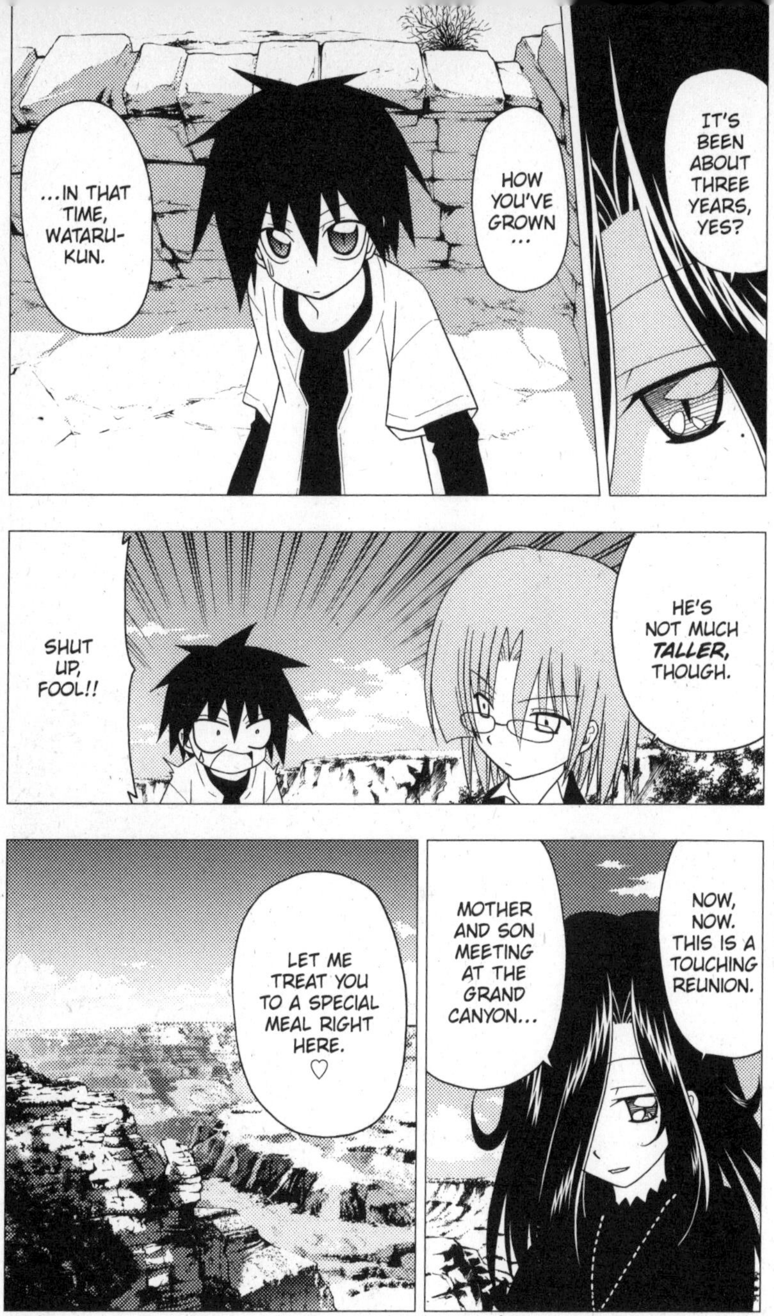
IT'S BEEN ABOUT THREE YEARS, YES?
HOW YOU'VE GROWN...
...IN THAT TIME, WATARU-KUN.
HE'S NOT MUCH **TALLER,** THOUGH.
SHUT UP, FOOL!!
NOW, NOW. THIS IS A TOUCHING REUNION.
MOTHER AND SON MEETING AT THE GRAND CANYON...
LET ME TREAT YOU TO A SPECIAL MEAL RIGHT HERE. ♡

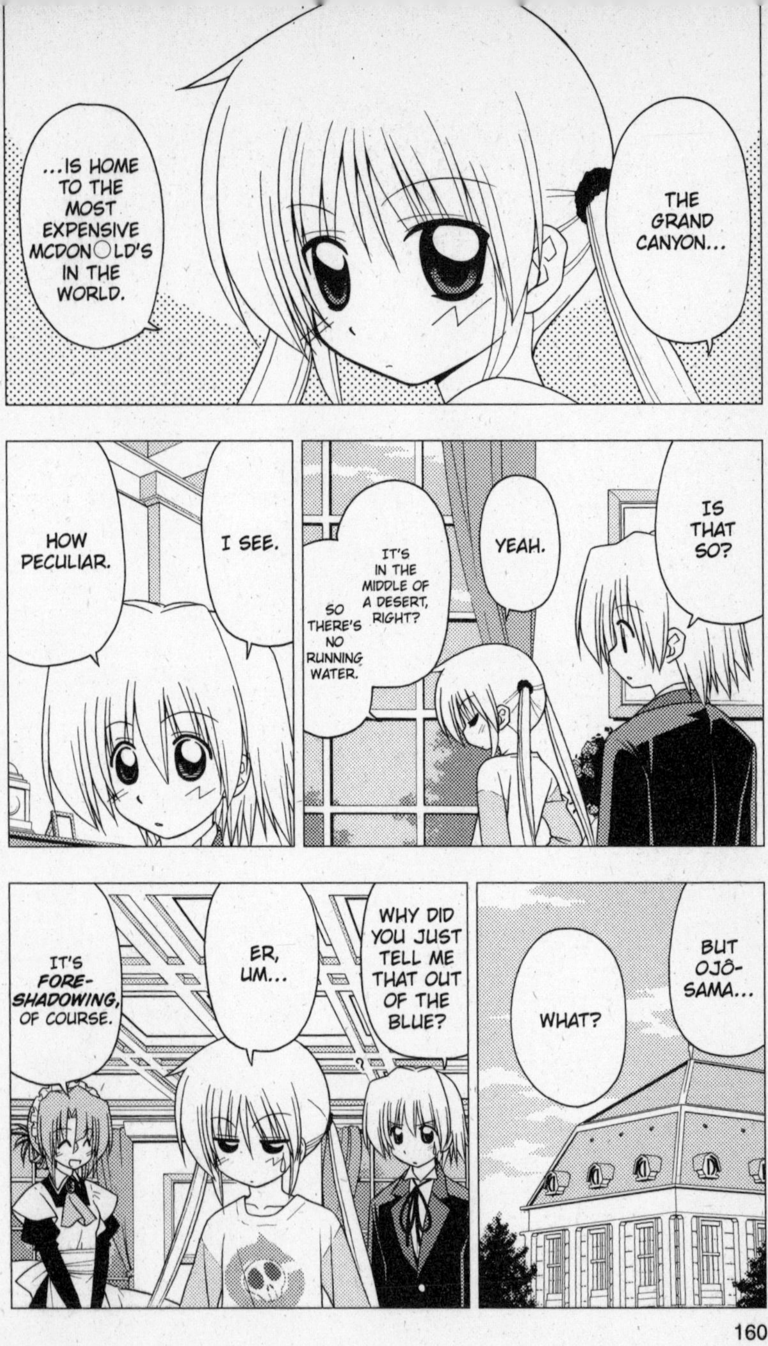
THE GRAND CANYON...
...IS HOME TO THE MOST EXPENSIVE MCDON◯LD'S IN THE WORLD.
IS THAT SO?
YEAH.
IT'S IN THE MIDDLE OF A DESERT, RIGHT?
SO THERE'S NO RUNNING WATER.
I SEE.
HOW PECULIAR.
BUT OJÔ-SAMA...
WHAT?
WHY DID YOU JUST TELL ME THAT OUT OF THE BLUE?
ER, UM...
IT'S FORE-SHADOWING, OF COURSE.

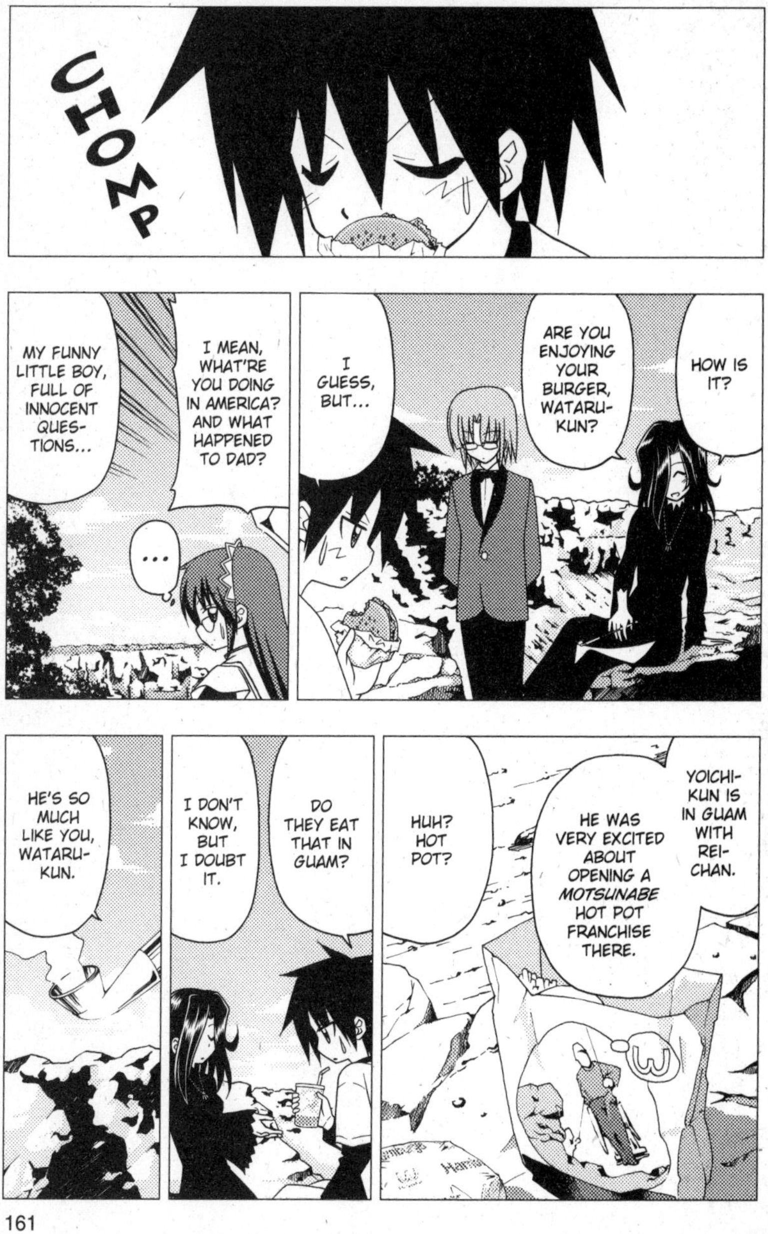
CHOMP
HOW IS IT?
ARE YOU ENJOYING YOUR BURGER, WATARU-KUN?
I GUESS, BUT...
I MEAN, WHAT'RE YOU DOING IN AMERICA? AND WHAT HAPPENED TO DAD?
MY FUNNY LITTLE BOY, FULL OF INNOCENT QUES-TIONS...
...
YOICHI-KUN IS IN GUAM WITH REI-CHAN.
HE WAS VERY EXCITED ABOUT OPENING A *MOTSUNABE* HOT POT FRANCHISE THERE.
HUH? HOT POT?
DO THEY EAT THAT IN GUAM?
I DON'T KNOW, BUT I DOUBT IT.
HE'S SO MUCH LIKE YOU, WATARU-KUN.

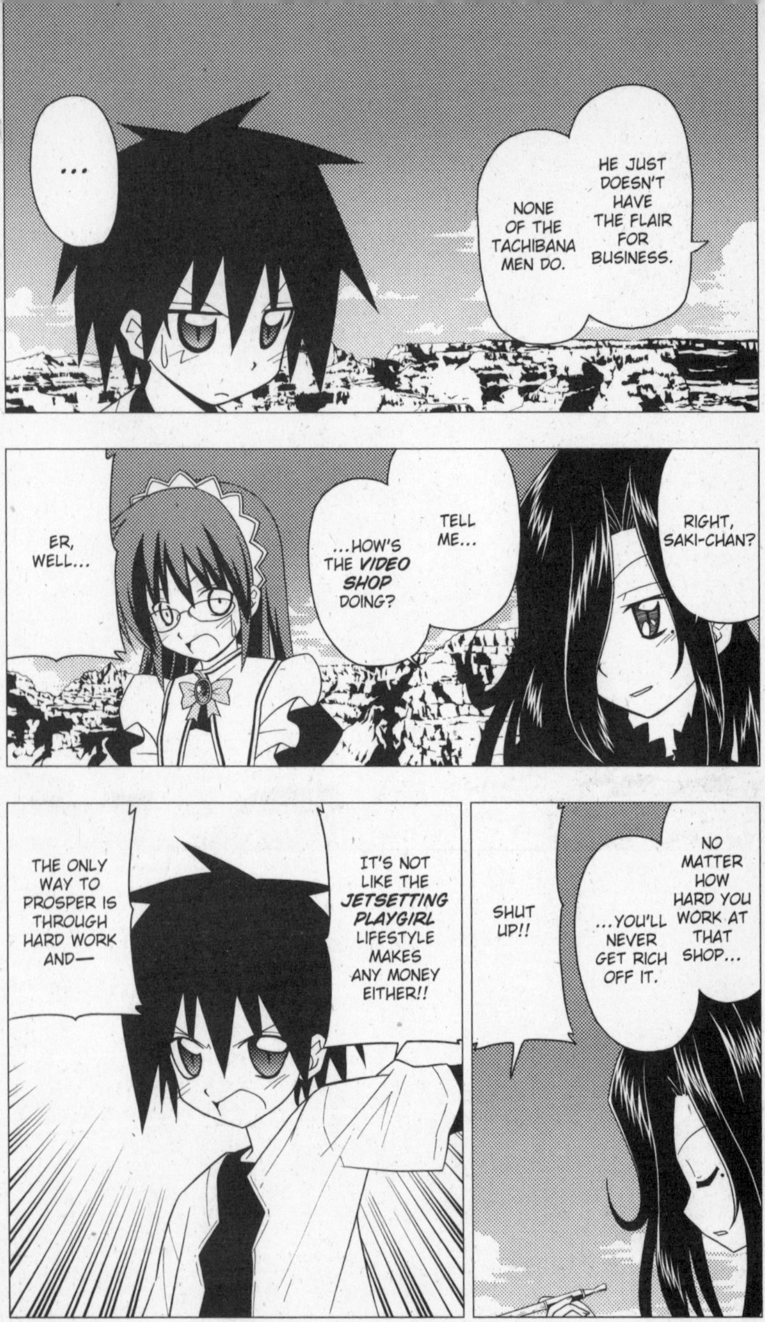

HE JUST DOESN'T HAVE THE FLAIR FOR BUSINESS.
NONE OF THE TACHIBANA MEN DO.
...
RIGHT, SAKI-CHAN?
TELL ME...
...HOW'S THE *VIDEO SHOP* DOING?
ER, WELL...
NO MATTER HOW HARD YOU WORK AT THAT SHOP...
...YOU'LL NEVER GET RICH OFF IT.
SHUT UP!!
IT'S NOT LIKE THE *JETSETTING PLAYGIRL* LIFESTYLE MAKES ANY MONEY EITHER!!
THE ONLY WAY TO PROSPER IS THROUGH HARD WORK AND—

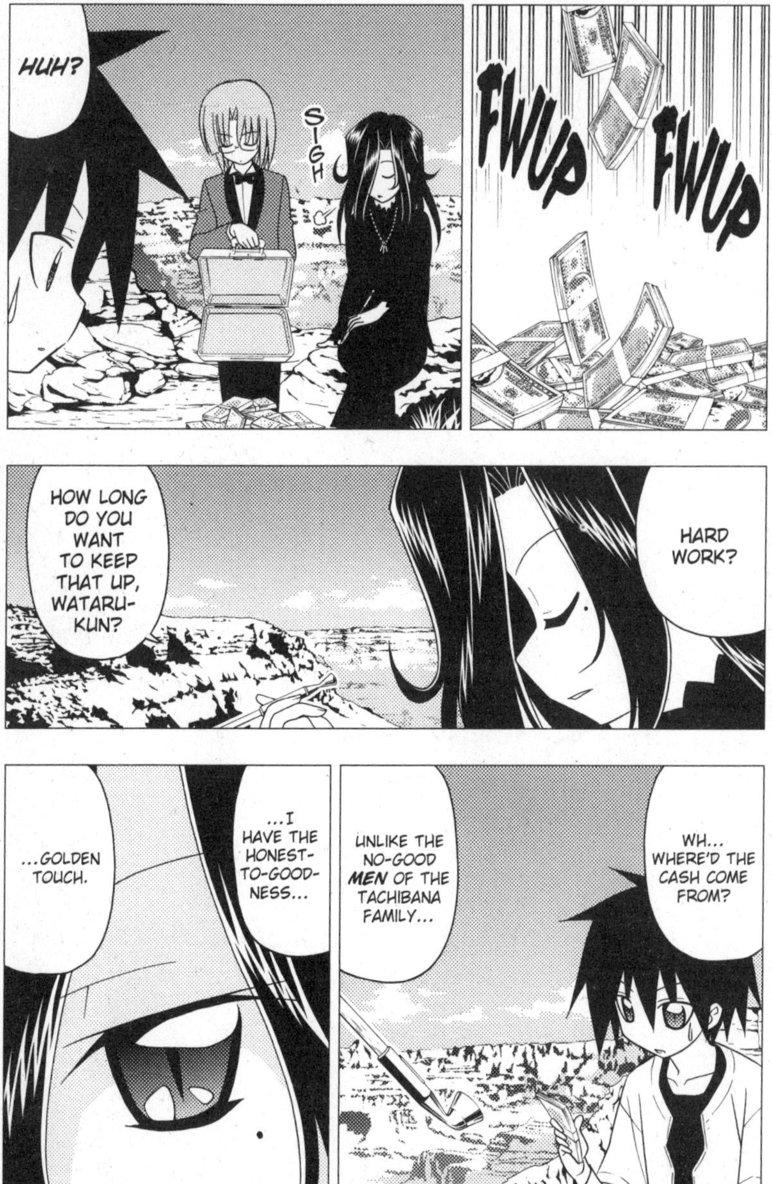
FWUP FWUP
HUH?
SIGH
HARD WORK?
HOW LONG DO YOU WANT TO KEEP THAT UP, WATARU-KUN?
WH... WHERE'D THE CASH COME FROM?
UNLIKE THE NO-GOOD MEN OF THE TACHIBANA FAMILY...
...I HAVE THE HONEST-TO-GOODNESS...
...GOLDEN TOUCH.

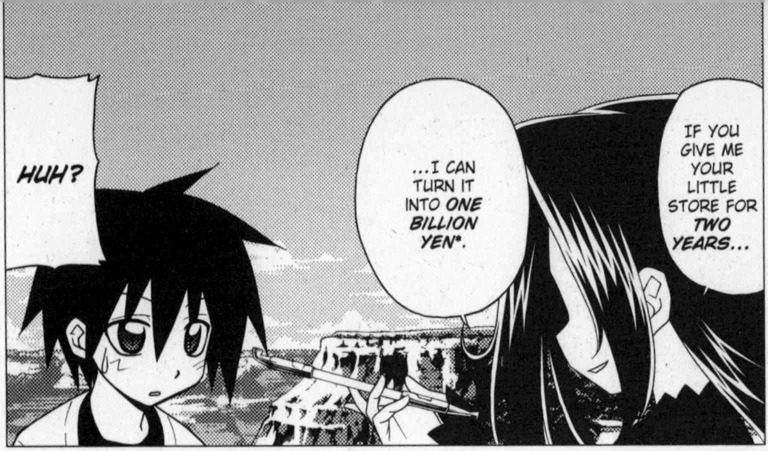
IF YOU GIVE ME YOUR LITTLE STORE FOR **TWO YEARS...**
...I CAN TURN IT INTO **ONE BILLION YEN***.
HUH?

*About $10 million.

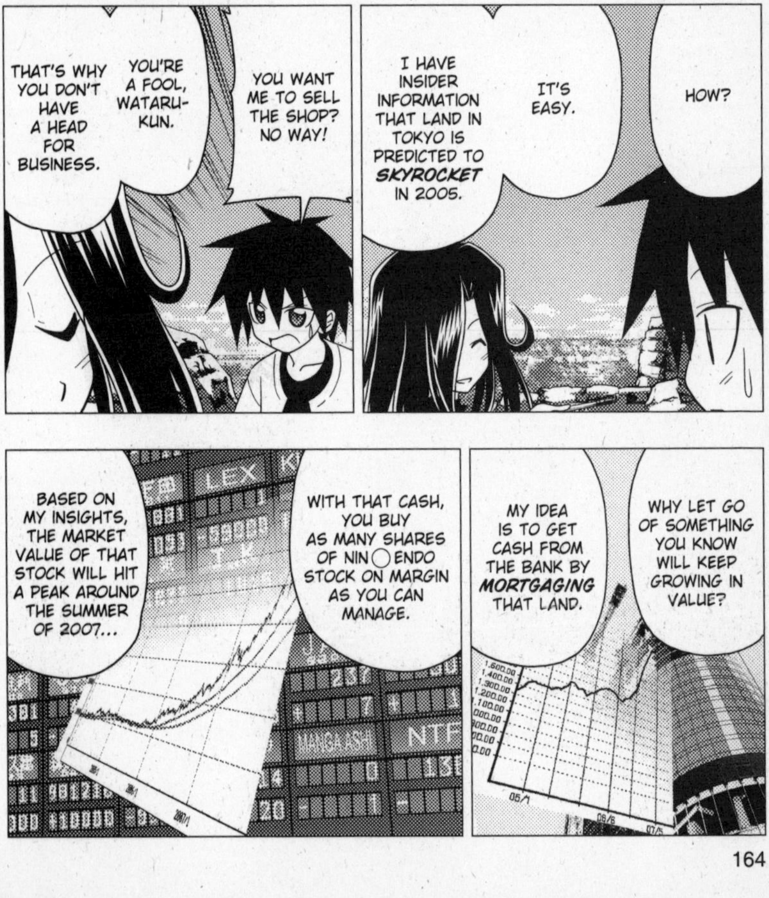
HOW?
IT'S EASY.
I HAVE INSIDER INFORMATION THAT LAND IN TOKYO IS PREDICTED TO **SKYROCKET** IN 2005.
YOU WANT ME TO SELL THE SHOP? NO WAY!
YOU'RE A FOOL, WATARU-KUN.
THAT'S WHY YOU DON'T HAVE A HEAD FOR BUSINESS.
WHY LET GO OF SOMETHING YOU KNOW WILL KEEP GROWING IN VALUE?
MY IDEA IS TO GET CASH FROM THE BANK BY **MORTGAGING** THAT LAND.
WITH THAT CASH, YOU BUY AS MANY SHARES OF NIN◯ENDO STOCK ON MARGIN AS YOU CAN MANAGE.
BASED ON MY INSIGHTS, THE MARKET VALUE OF THAT STOCK WILL HIT A PEAK AROUND THE SUMMER OF 2007...

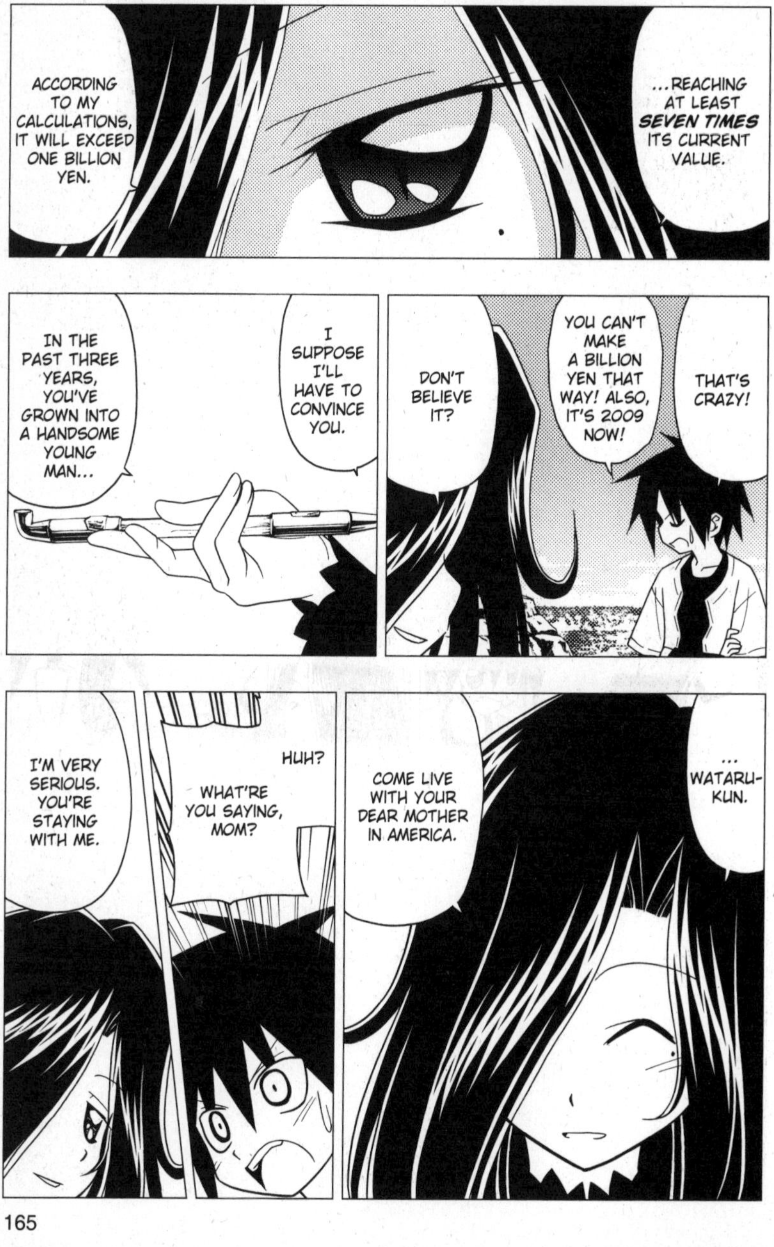
...REACHING AT LEAST ***SEVEN TIMES*** ITS CURRENT VALUE.
ACCORDING TO MY CALCULATIONS, IT WILL EXCEED ONE BILLION YEN.
THAT'S CRAZY!
YOU CAN'T MAKE A BILLION YEN THAT WAY! ALSO, IT'S 2009 NOW!
DON'T BELIEVE IT?
I SUPPOSE I'LL HAVE TO CONVINCE YOU.
IN THE PAST THREE YEARS, YOU'VE GROWN INTO A HANDSOME YOUNG MAN...
... WATARU-KUN.
COME LIVE WITH YOUR DEAR MOTHER IN AMERICA.
HUH?
WHAT'RE YOU SAYING, MOM?
I'M VERY SERIOUS. YOU'RE STAYING WITH ME.

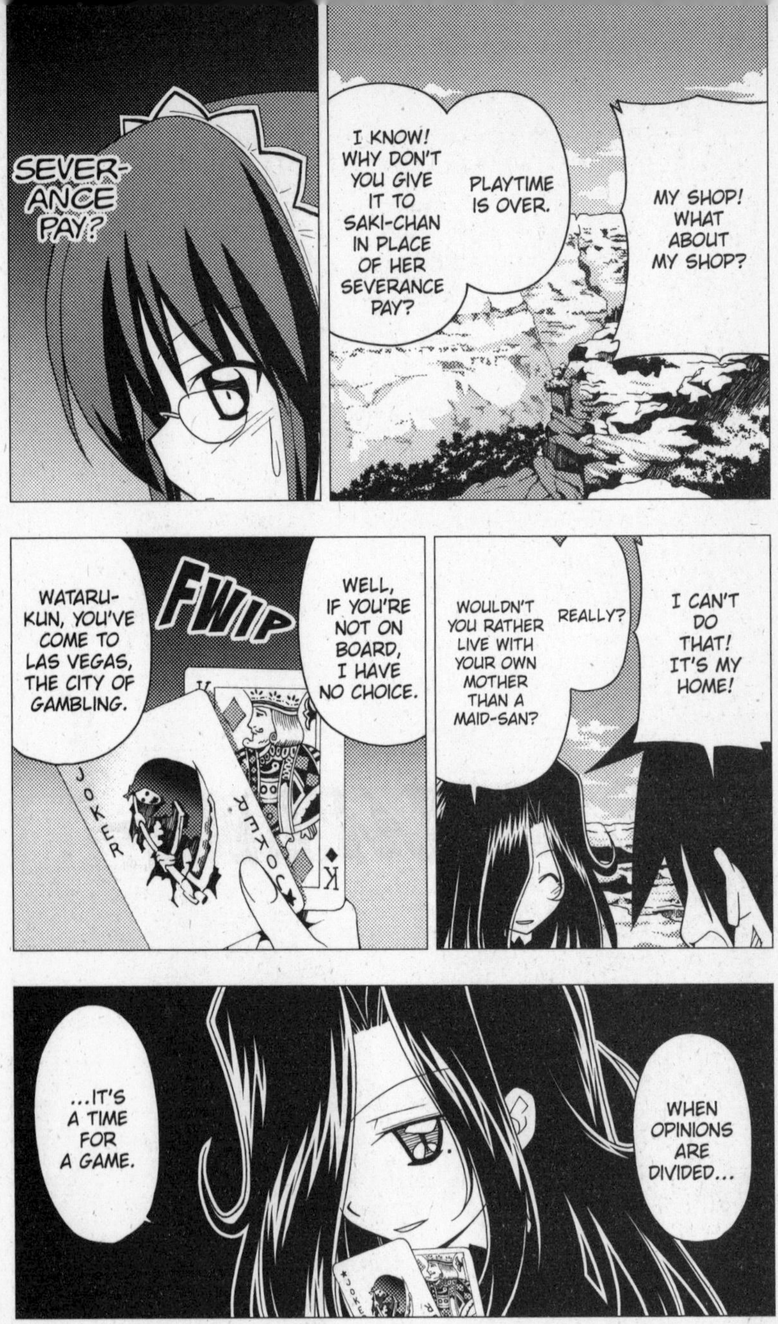
MY SHOP! WHAT ABOUT MY SHOP?
PLAYTIME IS OVER.
I KNOW! WHY DON'T YOU GIVE IT TO SAKI-CHAN IN PLACE OF HER SEVERANCE PAY?
SEVER-ANCE PAY?
I CAN'T DO THAT! IT'S MY HOME!
REALLY?
WOULDN'T YOU RATHER LIVE WITH YOUR OWN MOTHER THAN A MAID-SAN?
WELL, IF YOU'RE NOT ON BOARD, I HAVE NO CHOICE.
FWIP
WATARU-KUN, YOU'VE COME TO LAS VEGAS, THE CITY OF GAMBLING.
WHEN OPINIONS ARE DIVIDED...
...IT'S A TIME FOR A GAME.

Episode 11
"Those Who Act Boldly Are Strong. Crazy Strong."

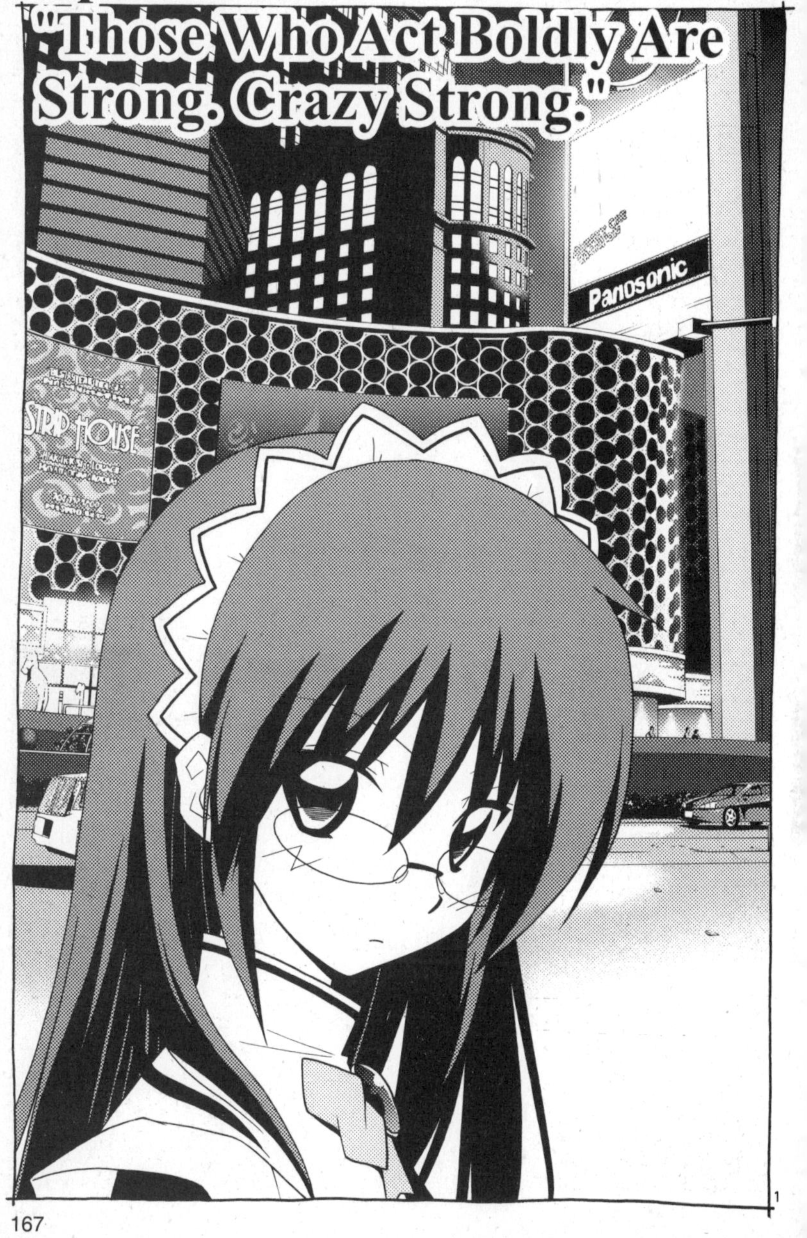
STRIP HOUSE
Panasonic

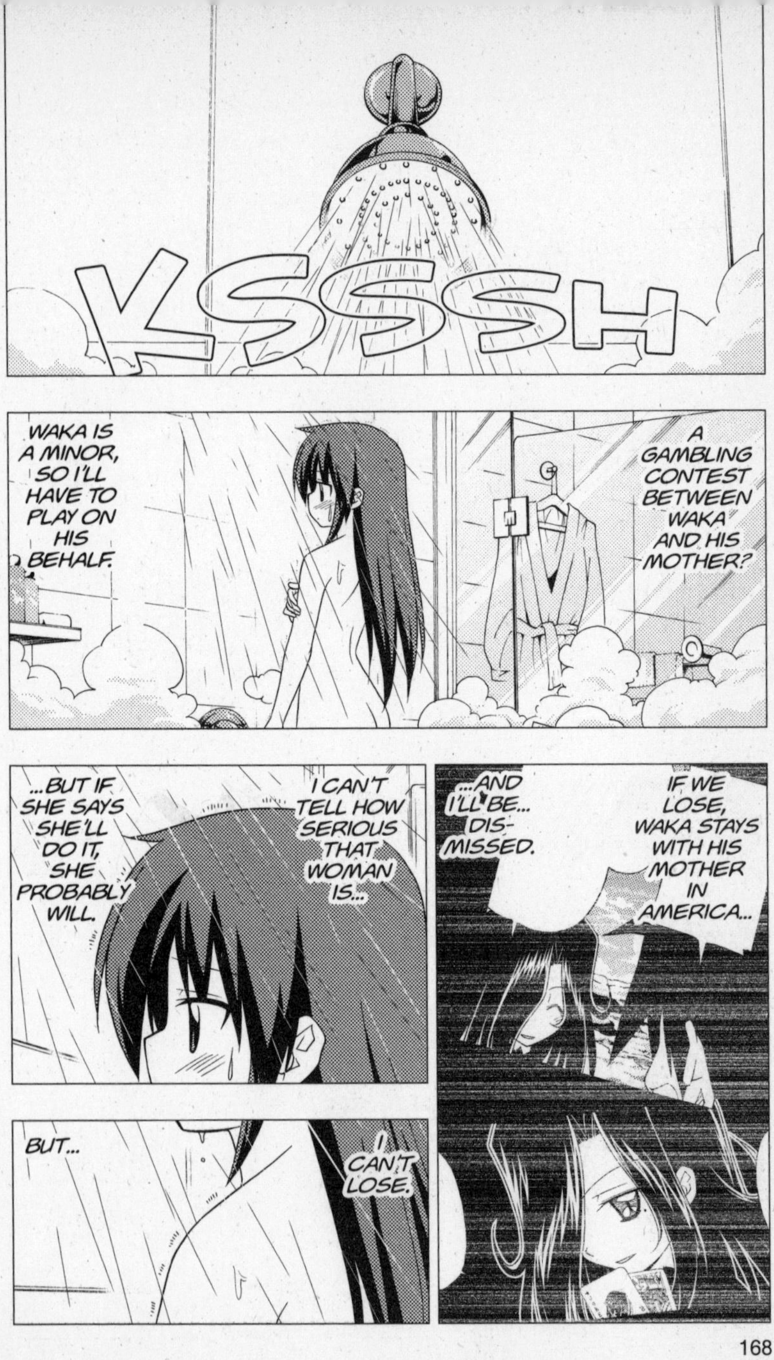
KSSSH
A GAMBLING CONTEST BETWEEN WAKA AND HIS MOTHER?
WAKA IS A MINOR, SO I'LL HAVE TO PLAY ON HIS BEHALF.
IF WE LOSE, WAKA STAYS WITH HIS MOTHER IN AMERICA...
...AND I'LL BE... DIS-MISSED.
I CAN'T TELL HOW SERIOUS THAT WOMAN IS...
...BUT IF SHE SAYS SHE'LL DO IT, SHE PROBABLY WILL.
BUT...
I CAN'T LOSE.

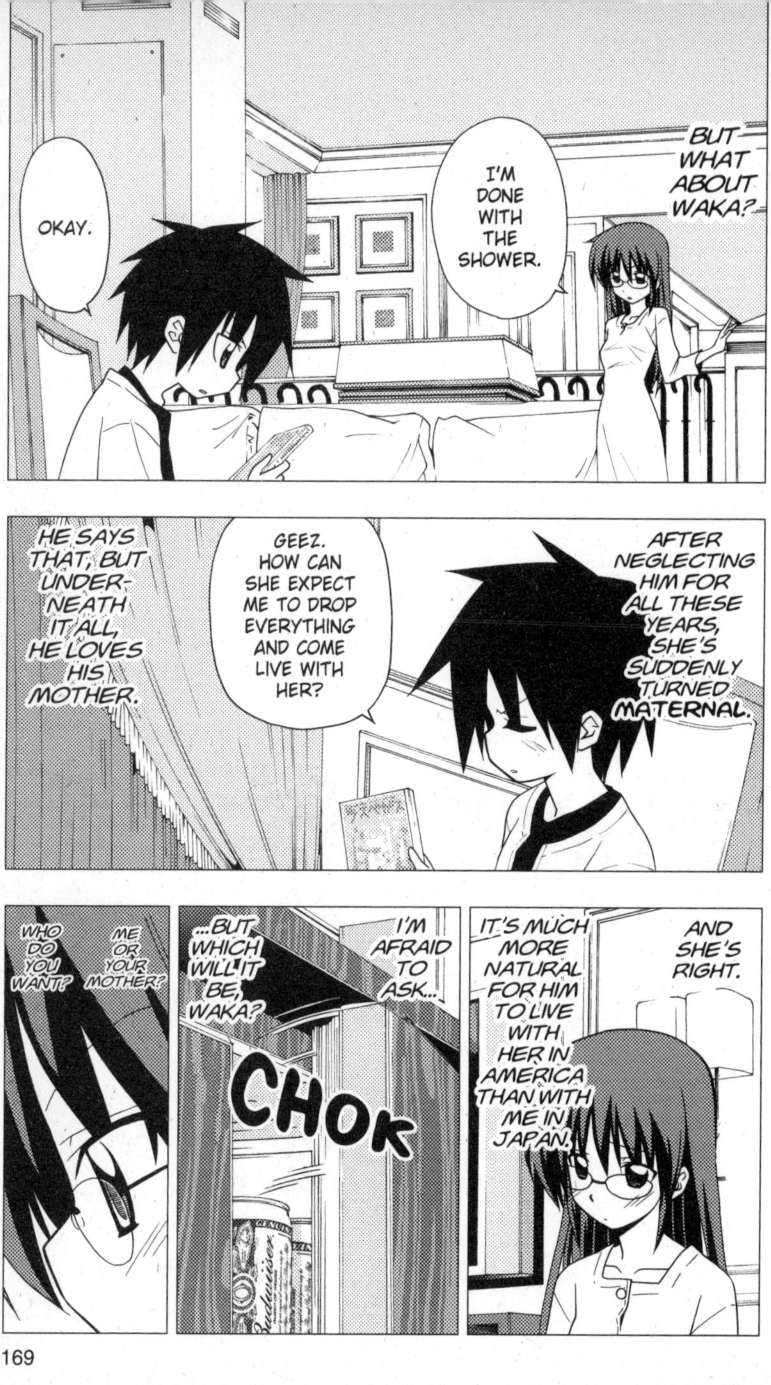
BUT WHAT ABOUT WAKA?
I'M DONE WITH THE SHOWER.
OKAY.
AFTER NEGLECTING HIM FOR ALL THESE YEARS, SHE'S SUDDENLY TURNED MATERNAL.
GEEZ. HOW CAN SHE EXPECT ME TO DROP EVERYTHING AND COME LIVE WITH HER?
HE SAYS THAT, BUT UNDER-NEATH IT ALL, HE LOVES HIS MOTHER.
AND SHE'S RIGHT.
IT'S MUCH MORE NATURAL FOR HIM TO LIVE WITH HER IN AMERICA THAN WITH ME IN JAPAN.
I'M AFRAID TO ASK...
...BUT WHICH WILL IT BE, WAKA?
CHOK
ME OR YOUR MOTHER?
WHO DO YOU WANT?

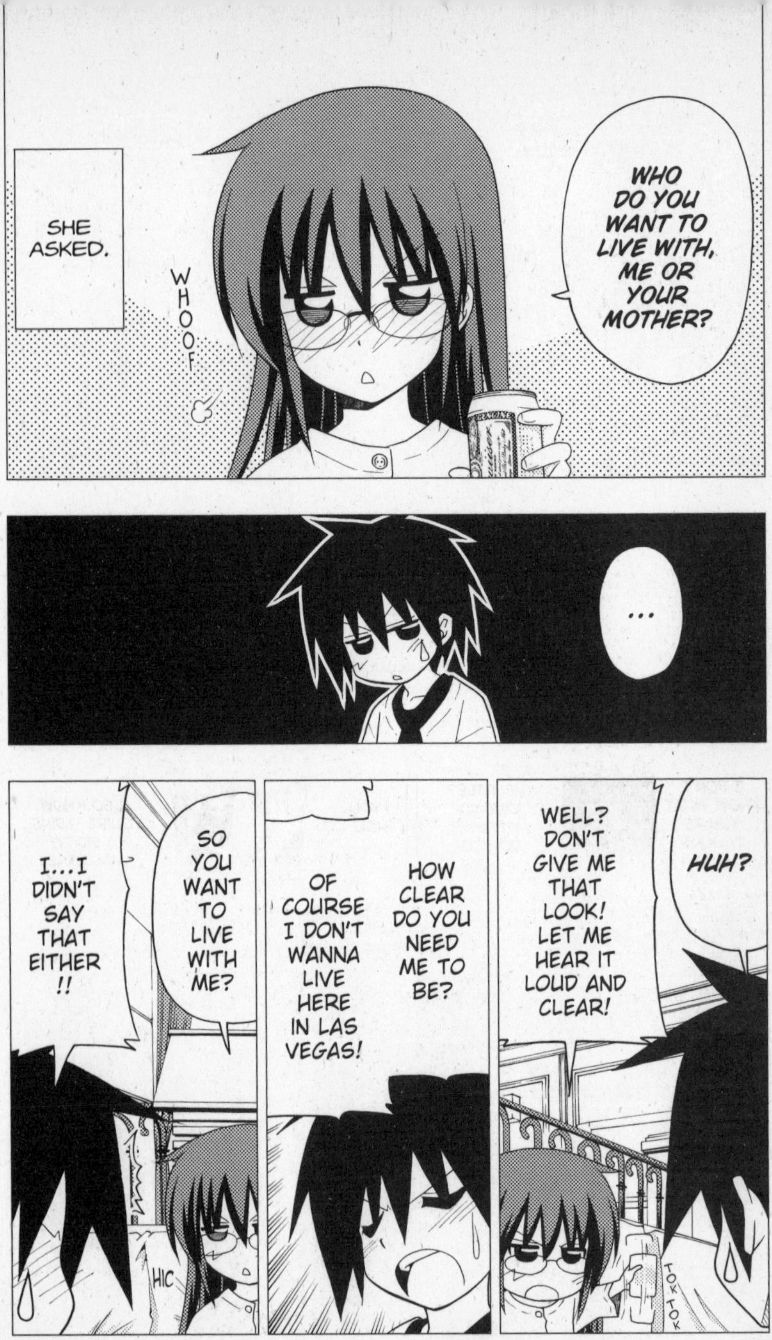
WHO DO YOU WANT TO LIVE WITH, ME OR YOUR MOTHER?
WHOOF
SHE ASKED.
...
HUH?
WELL? DON'T GIVE ME THAT LOOK! LET ME HEAR IT LOUD AND CLEAR!
TOK TOK
HOW CLEAR DO YOU NEED ME TO BE?
OF COURSE I DON'T WANNA LIVE HERE IN LAS VEGAS!
SO YOU WANT TO LIVE WITH ME?
I...I DIDN'T SAY THAT EITHER!!
HIC

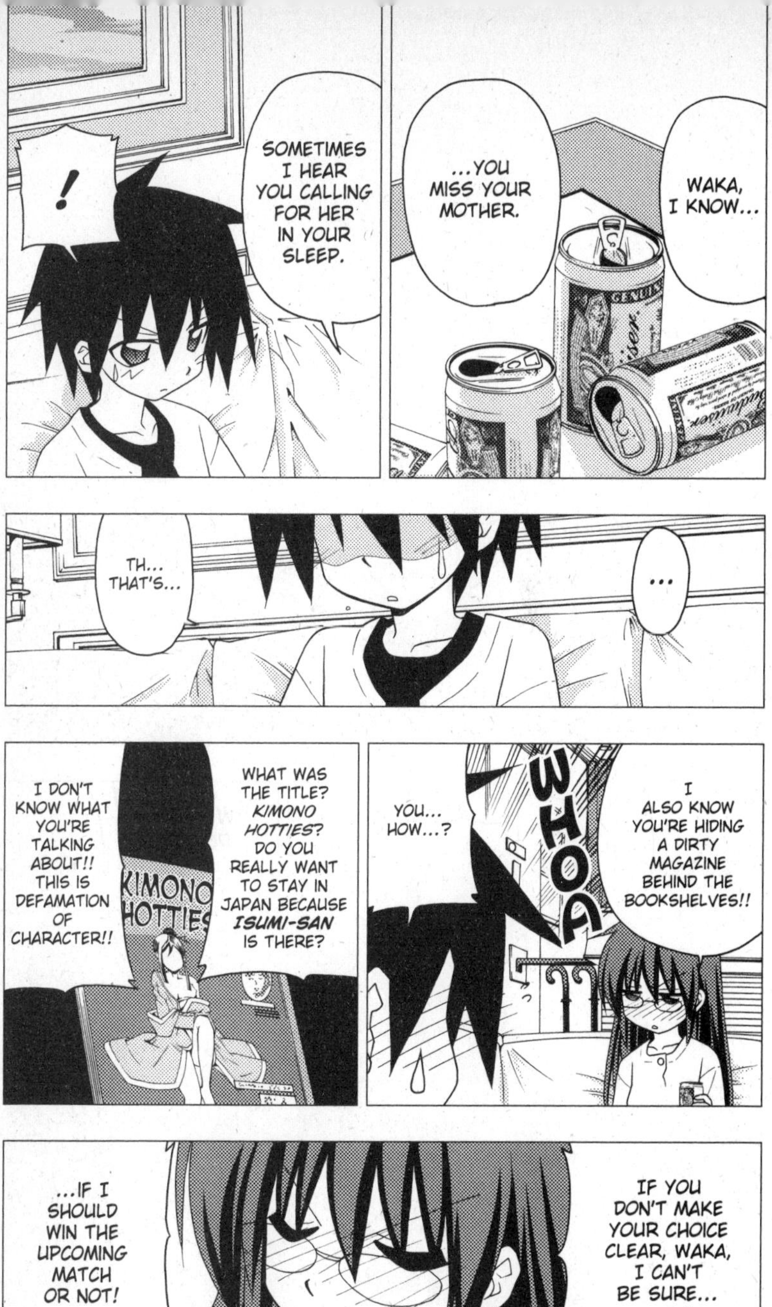

WAKA, I KNOW...
...YOU MISS YOUR MOTHER.
SOMETIMES I HEAR YOU CALLING FOR HER IN YOUR SLEEP.
!
...
TH... THAT'S...
I ALSO KNOW YOU'RE HIDING A DIRTY MAGAZINE BEHIND THE BOOKSHELVES!!
WHOA
YOU... HOW...?
WHAT WAS THE TITLE? *KIMONO HOTTIES*? DO YOU REALLY WANT TO STAY IN JAPAN BECAUSE **ISUMI-SAN** IS THERE?
KIMONO HOTTIES
I DON'T KNOW WHAT YOU'RE TALKING ABOUT!! THIS IS DEFAMATION OF CHARACTER!!
IF YOU DON'T MAKE YOUR CHOICE CLEAR, WAKA, I CAN'T BE SURE...
...IF I SHOULD WIN THE UPCOMING MATCH OR NOT!

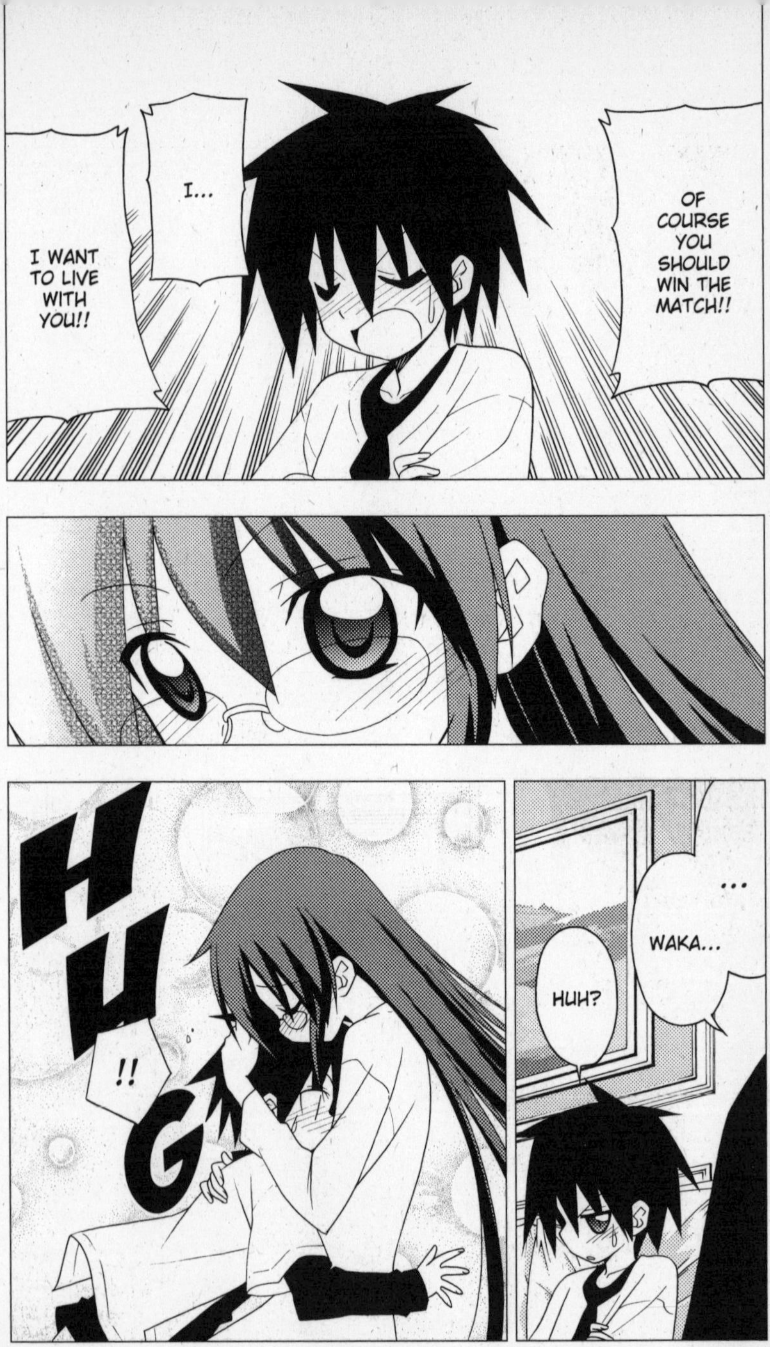
OF COURSE YOU SHOULD WIN THE MATCH!!
I...
I WANT TO LIVE WITH YOU!!
...
WAKA...
HUH?
HUG
!!

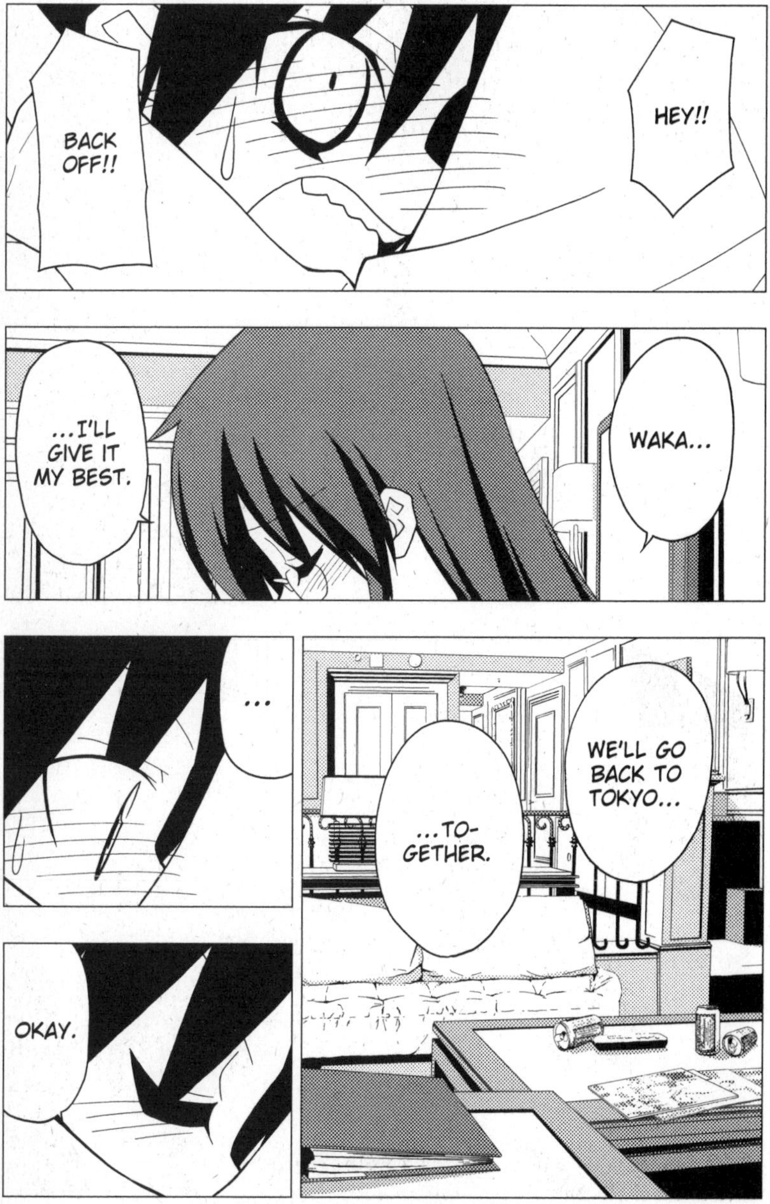
HEY!!
BACK OFF!!
WAKA...
...I'LL GIVE IT MY BEST.
WE'LL GO BACK TO TOKYO...
...TO-GETHER.
...
OKAY.

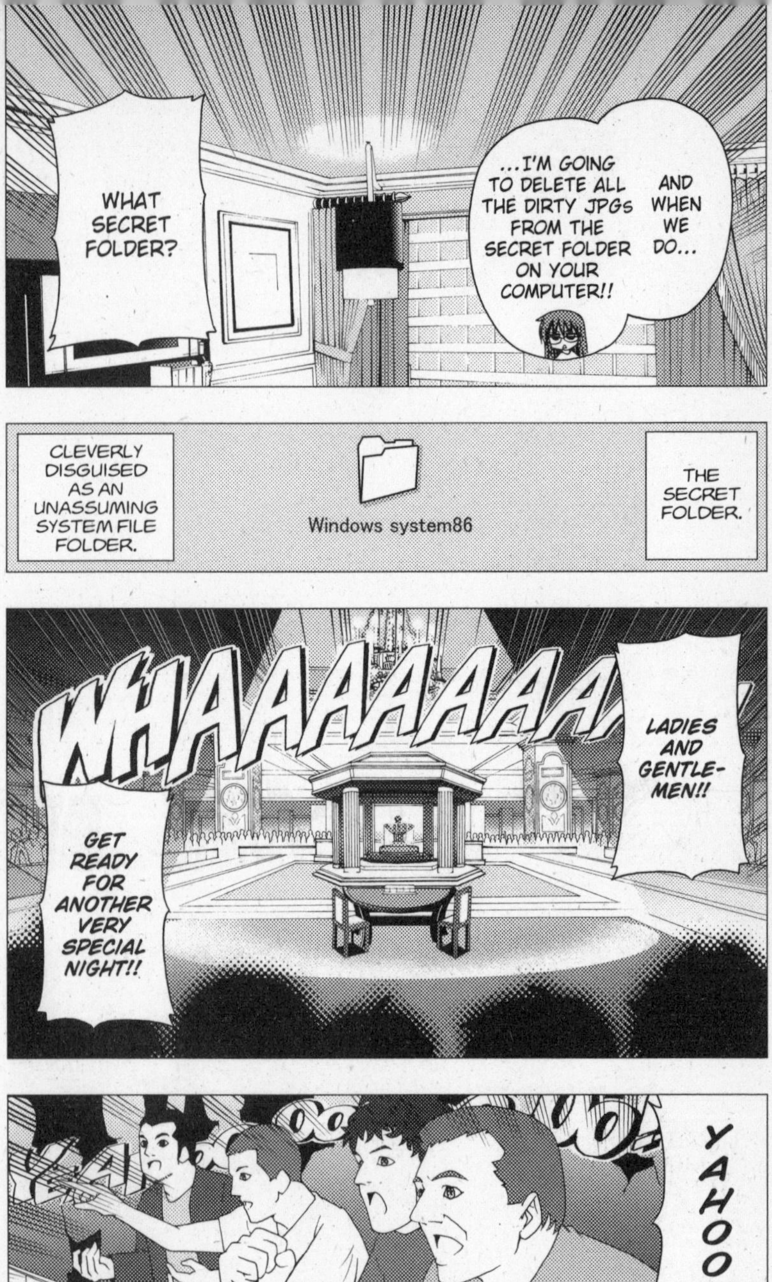
...I'M GOING TO DELETE ALL THE DIRTY JPGs FROM THE SECRET FOLDER ON YOUR COMPUTER!!
AND WHEN WE DO...
WHAT SECRET FOLDER?
THE SECRET FOLDER.
Windows system86
CLEVERLY DISGUISED AS AN UNASSUMING SYSTEM FILE FOLDER.
LADIES AND GENTLE-MEN!!
WHAAAAAAAA
GET READY FOR ANOTHER VERY SPECIAL NIGHT!!
YAHOO!!

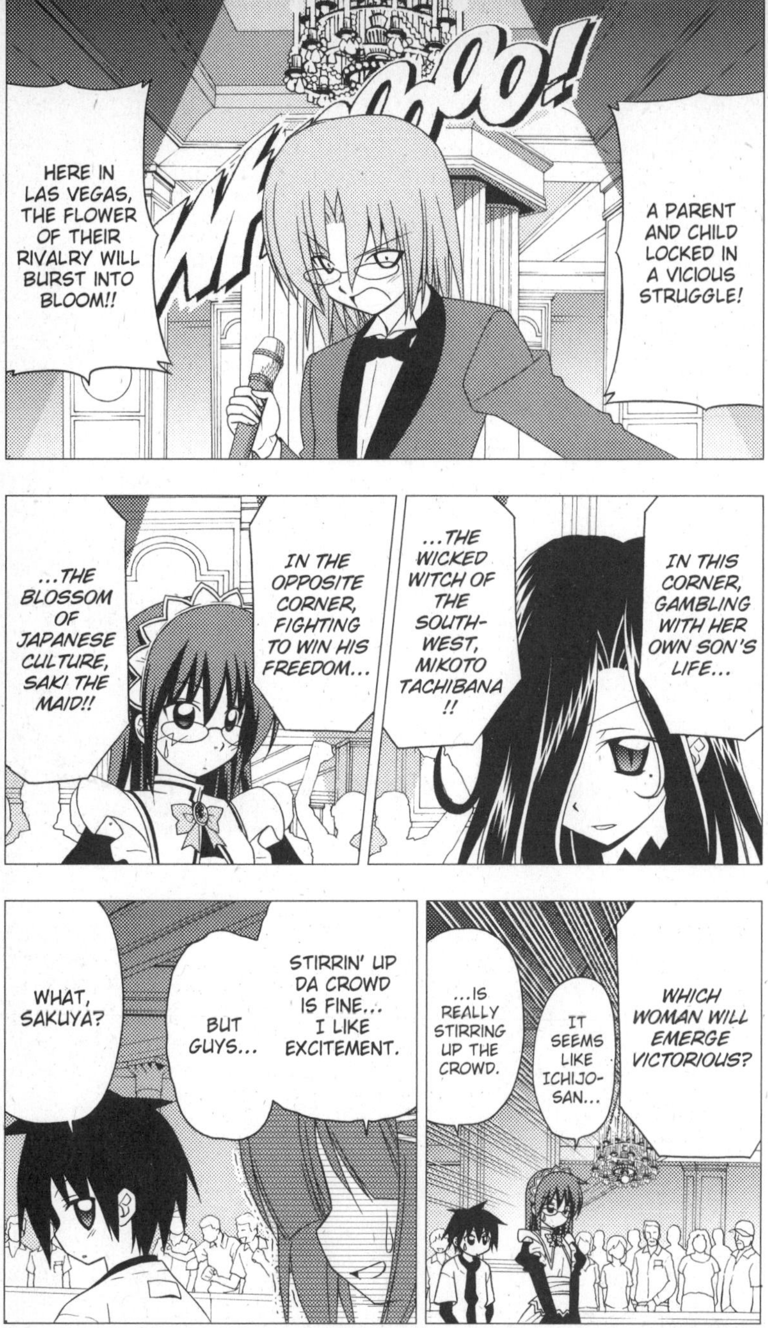
A PARENT AND CHILD LOCKED IN A VICIOUS STRUGGLE!
HERE IN LAS VEGAS, THE FLOWER OF THEIR RIVALRY WILL BURST INTO BLOOM!!
IN THIS CORNER, GAMBLING WITH HER OWN SON'S LIFE...
...THE WICKED WITCH OF THE SOUTH-WEST, MIKOTO TACHIBANA!!
IN THE OPPOSITE CORNER, FIGHTING TO WIN HIS FREEDOM...
...THE BLOSSOM OF JAPANESE CULTURE, SAKI THE MAID!!
WHICH WOMAN WILL EMERGE VICTORIOUS?
IT SEEMS LIKE ICHIJO-SAN...
...IS REALLY STIRRING UP THE CROWD.
STIRRIN' UP DA CROWD IS FINE... I LIKE EXCITEMENT.
BUT GUYS...
WHAT, SAKUYA?

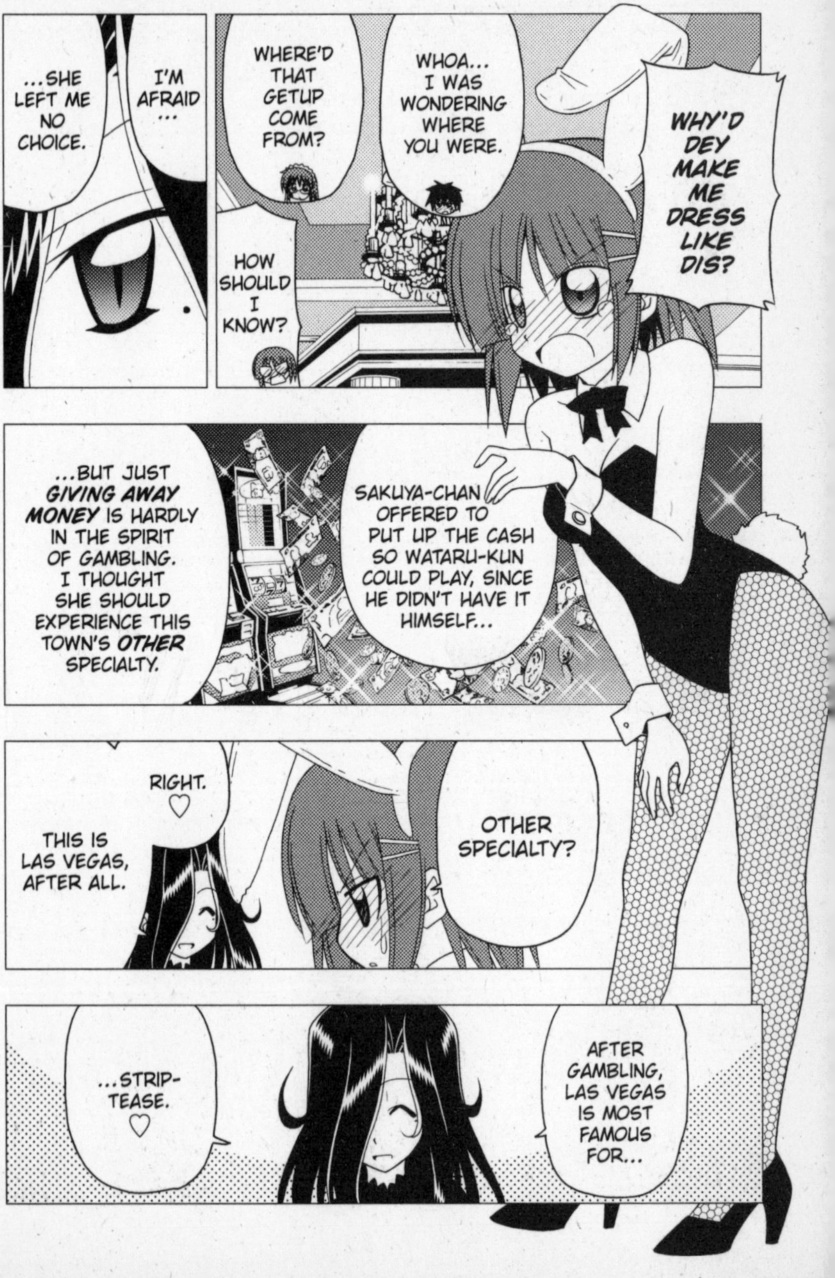
WHY'D DEY MAKE ME DRESS LIKE DIS?
WHOA... I WAS WONDERING WHERE YOU WERE.
WHERE'D THAT GETUP COME FROM?
HOW SHOULD I KNOW?
I'M AFRAID...
...SHE LEFT ME NO CHOICE.
SAKUYA-CHAN OFFERED TO PUT UP THE CASH SO WATARU-KUN COULD PLAY, SINCE HE DIDN'T HAVE IT HIMSELF...
...BUT JUST GIVING AWAY MONEY IS HARDLY IN THE SPIRIT OF GAMBLING. I THOUGHT SHE SHOULD EXPERIENCE THIS TOWN'S OTHER SPECIALTY.
OTHER SPECIALTY?
RIGHT. ♡
THIS IS LAS VEGAS, AFTER ALL.
AFTER GAMBLING, LAS VEGAS IS MOST FAMOUS FOR...
...STRIP-TEASE. ♡

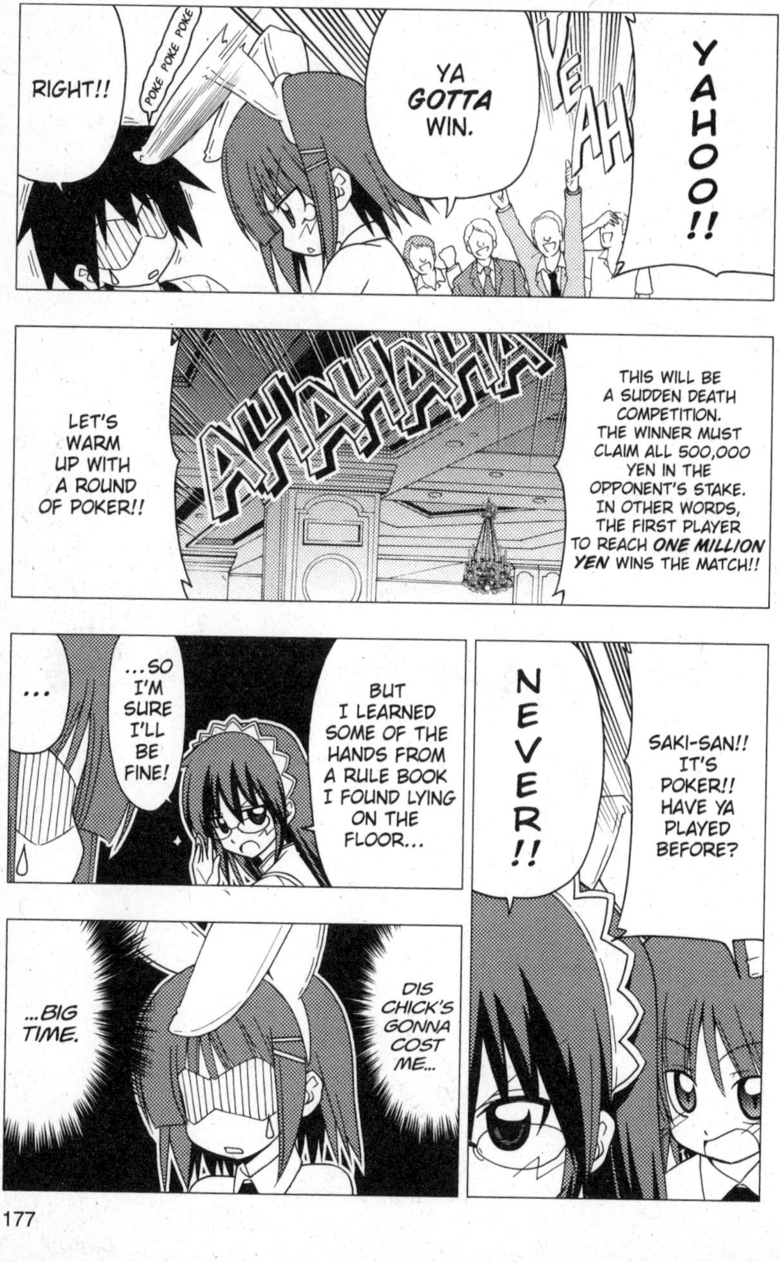
YAHOO!!
YEAH
YA GOTTA WIN.
POKE POKE POKE
RIGHT!!
THIS WILL BE A SUDDEN DEATH COMPETITION. THE WINNER MUST CLAIM ALL 500,000 YEN IN THE OPPONENT'S STAKE. IN OTHER WORDS, THE FIRST PLAYER TO REACH ONE MILLION YEN WINS THE MATCH!!
AHAHAHAHA
LET'S WARM UP WITH A ROUND OF POKER!!
SAKI-SAN!! IT'S POKER!! HAVE YA PLAYED BEFORE?
NEVER!!
BUT I LEARNED SOME OF THE HANDS FROM A RULE BOOK I FOUND LYING ON THE FLOOR...
...SO I'M SURE I'LL BE FINE!
...
DIS CHICK'S GONNA COST ME...
...BIG TIME.

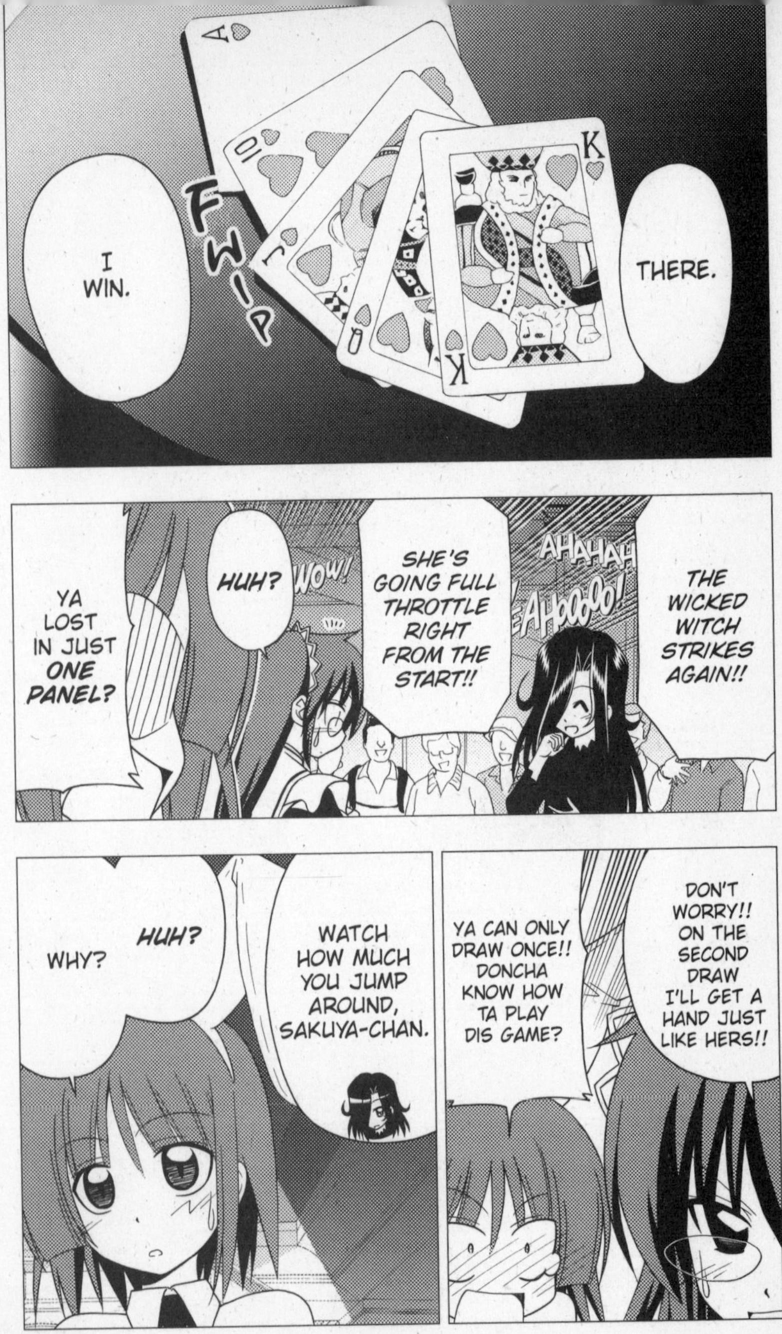
THERE.
FWIP
I WIN.
THE WICKED WITCH STRIKES AGAIN!!
AHAHAH
AHOOOOO!
SHE'S GOING FULL THROTTLE RIGHT FROM THE START!!
WOW!
HUH?
YA LOST IN JUST ONE PANEL?
DON'T WORRY!! ON THE SECOND DRAW I'LL GET A HAND JUST LIKE HERS!!
YA CAN ONLY DRAW ONCE!! DONCHA KNOW HOW TA PLAY DIS GAME?
WATCH HOW MUCH YOU JUMP AROUND, SAKUYA-CHAN.
HUH?
WHY?

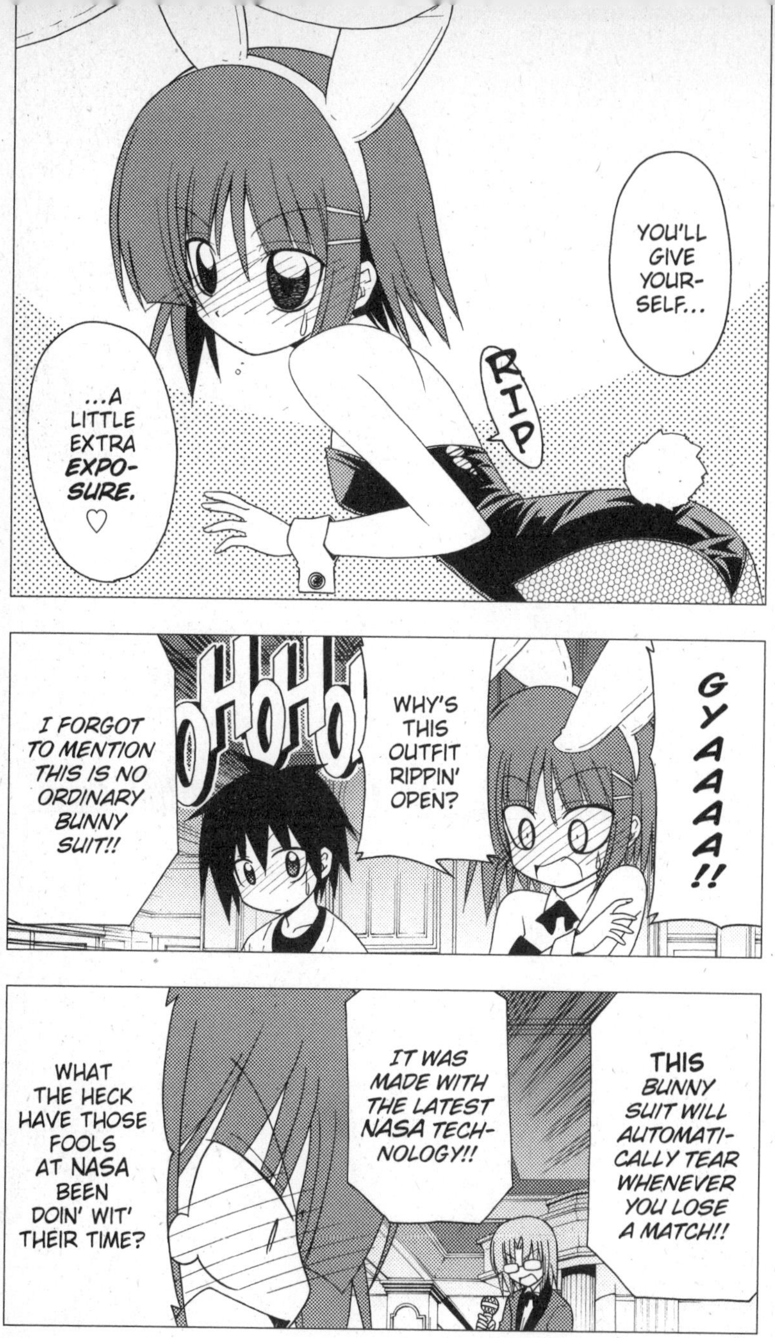
YOU'LL GIVE YOUR-SELF...
RIP
...A LITTLE EXTRA EXPO-SURE. ♡
GYAAAAA!!
WHY'S THIS OUTFIT RIPPIN' OPEN?
OHOHOHO
I FORGOT TO MENTION THIS IS NO ORDINARY BUNNY SUIT!!
THIS BUNNY SUIT WILL AUTOMATI-CALLY TEAR WHENEVER YOU LOSE A MATCH!!
IT WAS MADE WITH THE LATEST NASA TECH-NOLOGY!!
WHAT THE HECK HAVE THOSE FOOLS AT NASA BEEN DOIN' WIT' THEIR TIME?

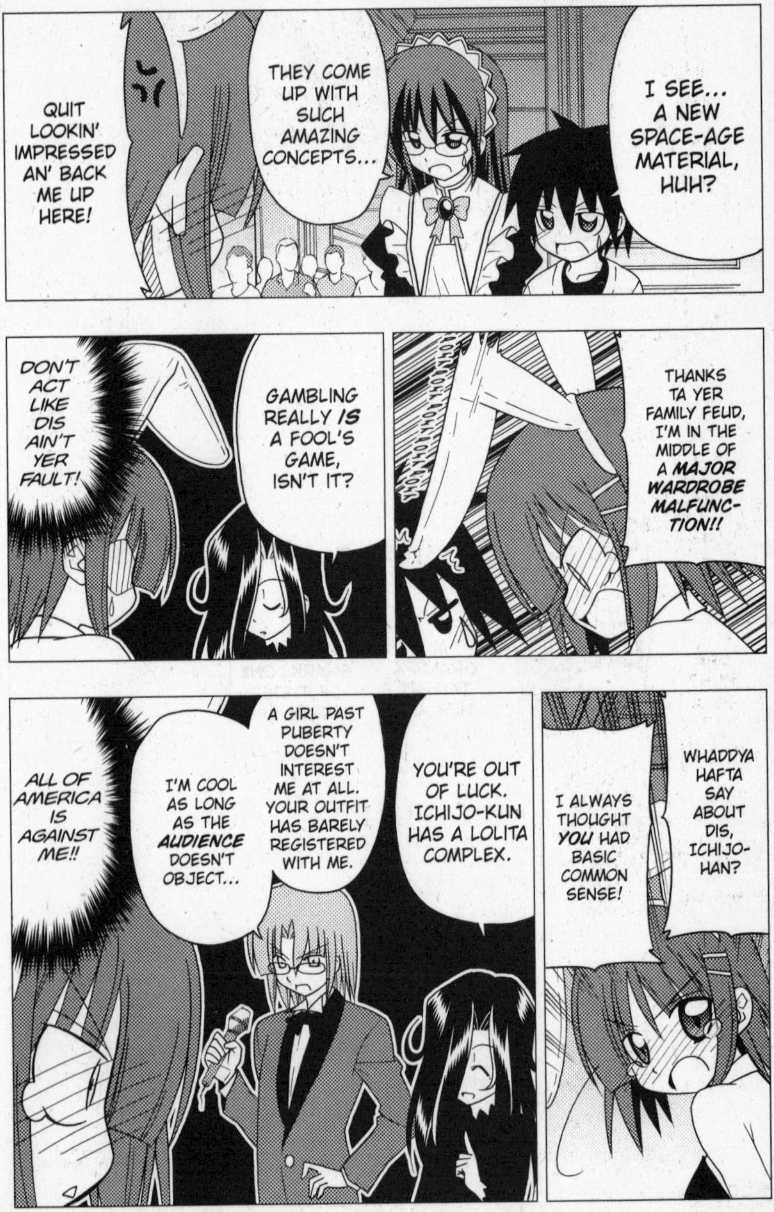
I SEE... A NEW SPACE-AGE MATERIAL, HUH?
THEY COME UP WITH SUCH AMAZING CONCEPTS...
QUIT LOOKIN' IMPRESSED AN' BACK ME UP HERE!
THANKS TA YER FAMILY FEUD, I'M IN THE MIDDLE OF A *MAJOR WARDROBE MALFUNCTION!!*
GAMBLING REALLY *IS* A FOOL'S GAME, ISN'T IT?
DON'T ACT LIKE DIS AIN'T YER FAULT!
WHADDYA HAFTA SAY ABOUT DIS, ICHIJO-HAN?
I ALWAYS THOUGHT *YOU* HAD BASIC COMMON SENSE!
YOU'RE OUT OF LUCK. ICHIJO-KUN HAS A LOLITA COMPLEX.
A GIRL PAST PUBERTY DOESN'T INTEREST ME AT ALL. YOUR OUTFIT HAS BARELY REGISTERED WITH ME.
I'M COOL AS LONG AS THE *AUDIENCE* DOESN'T OBJECT...
ALL OF AMERICA IS AGAINST ME!!

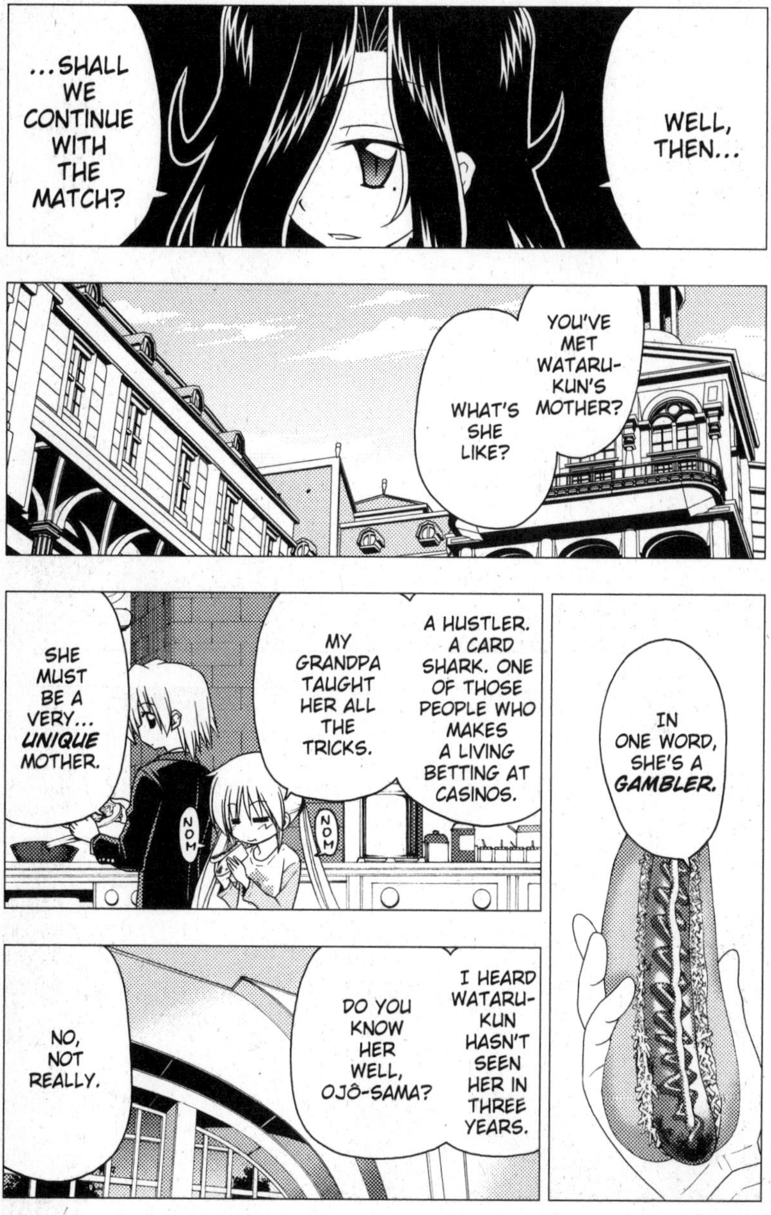
WELL, THEN...
...SHALL WE CONTINUE WITH THE MATCH?
YOU'VE MET WATARU-KUN'S MOTHER?
WHAT'S SHE LIKE?
IN ONE WORD, SHE'S A GAMBLER.
A HUSTLER. A CARD SHARK. ONE OF THOSE PEOPLE WHO MAKES A LIVING BETTING AT CASINOS.
MY GRANDPA TAUGHT HER ALL THE TRICKS.
NOM
NOM
SHE MUST BE A VERY... UNIQUE MOTHER.
I HEARD WATARU-KUN HASN'T SEEN HER IN THREE YEARS.
DO YOU KNOW HER WELL, OJÔ-SAMA?
NO, NOT REALLY.

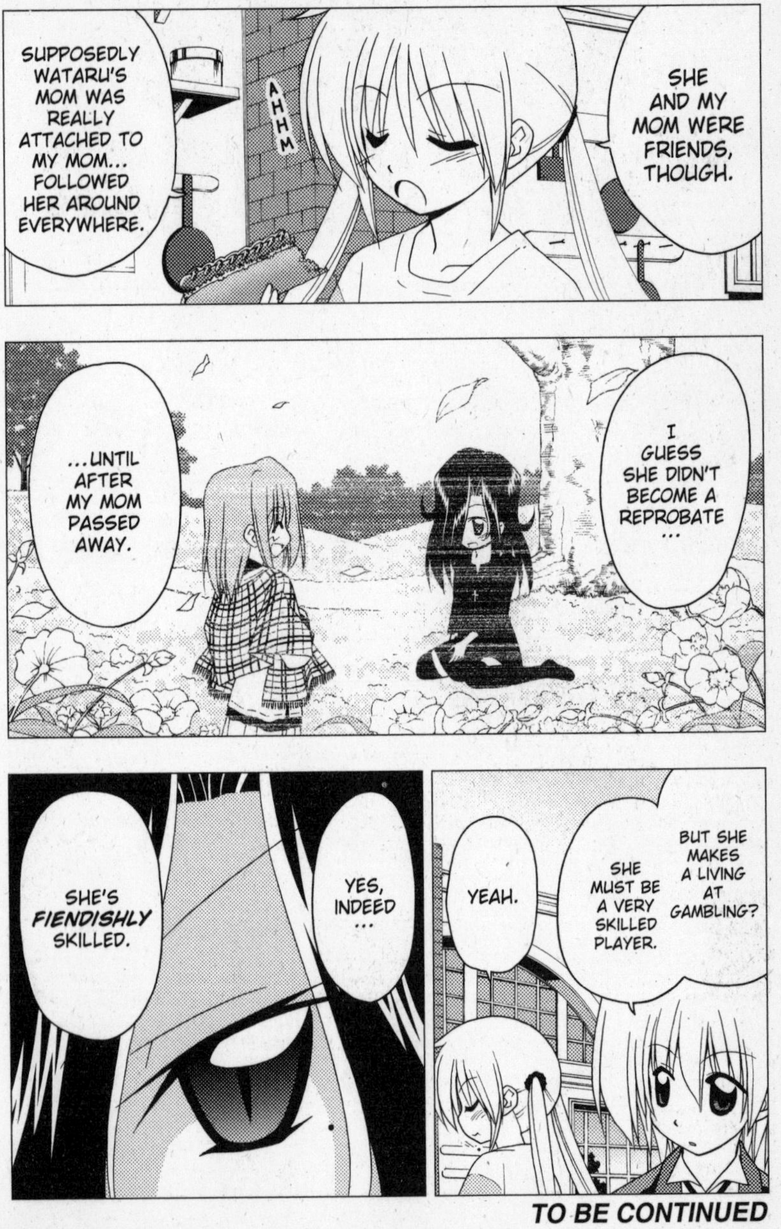
SHE AND MY MOM WERE FRIENDS, THOUGH.
AHHM
SUPPOSEDLY WATARU'S MOM WAS REALLY ATTACHED TO MY MOM... FOLLOWED HER AROUND EVERYWHERE.
I GUESS SHE DIDN'T BECOME A REPROBATE ...
...UNTIL AFTER MY MOM PASSED AWAY.
BUT SHE MAKES A LIVING AT GAMBLING?
SHE MUST BE A VERY SKILLED PLAYER.
YEAH.
YES, INDEED ...
SHE'S *FIENDISHLY* SKILLED.

TO BE CONTINUED

HAYATE THE COMBAT BUTLER

BONUS SECTION

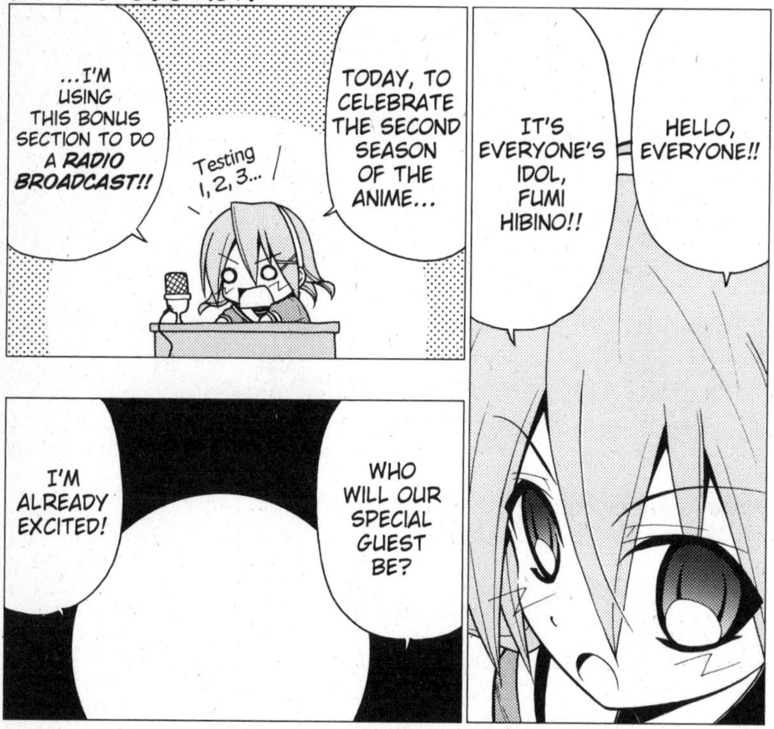

HELLO, EVERYONE!!
IT'S EVERYONE'S IDOL, FUMI HIBINO!!
TODAY, TO CELEBRATE THE SECOND SEASON OF THE ANIME...
Testing 1, 2, 3...
...I'M USING THIS BONUS SECTION TO DO A *RADIO BROADCAST!!*
WHO WILL OUR SPECIAL GUEST BE?
I'M ALREADY EXCITED!
OKAY, LET'S START!!
READY?
THIS IS FUMI HIBINO'S DISPATCH FROM RADIO STATION X365!!!

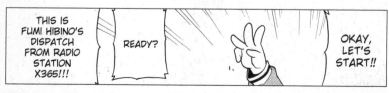

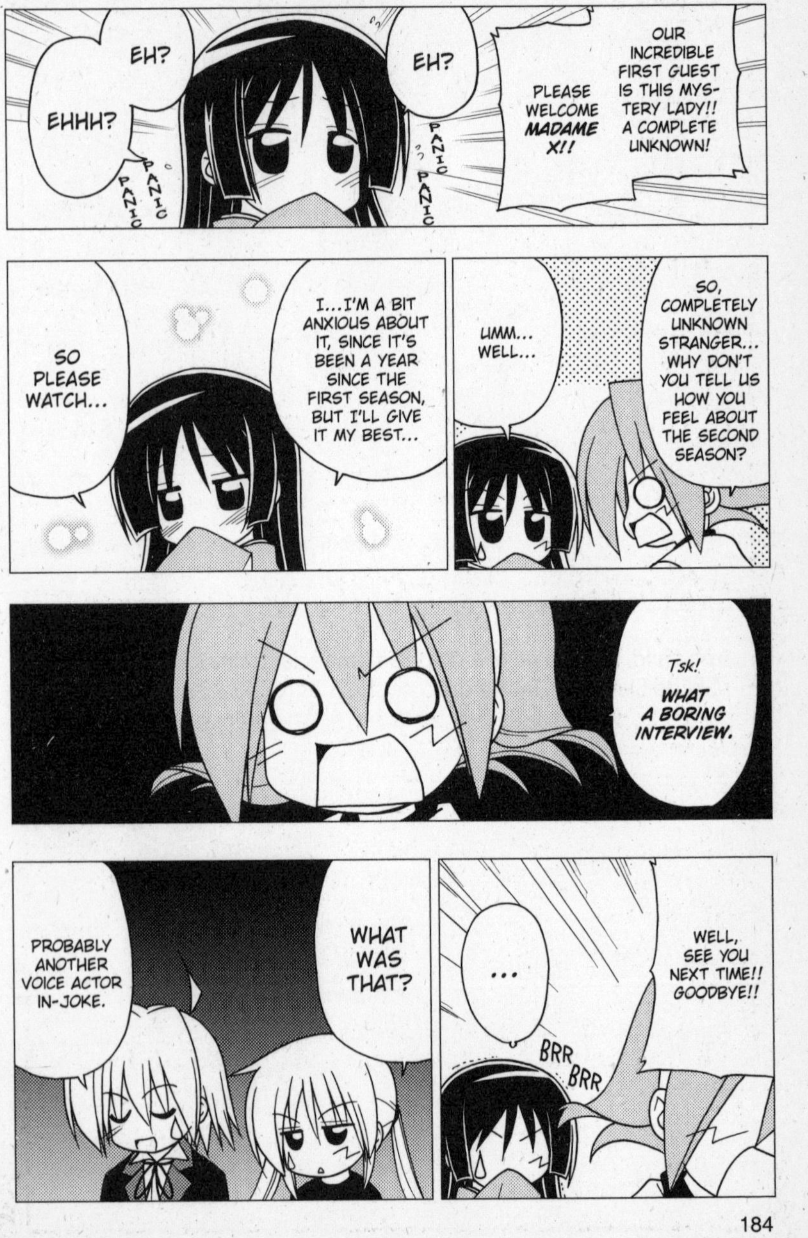
OUR INCREDIBLE FIRST GUEST IS THIS MYSTERY LADY!! A COMPLETE UNKNOWN!
PLEASE WELCOME ***MADAME X!!***
EH?
PANIC PANIC
EH?
EHHH?
PANIC PANIC
SO, COMPLETELY UNKNOWN STRANGER... WHY DON'T YOU TELL US HOW YOU FEEL ABOUT THE SECOND SEASON?
UMM... WELL...
I...I'M A BIT ANXIOUS ABOUT IT, SINCE IT'S BEEN A YEAR SINCE THE FIRST SEASON, BUT I'LL GIVE IT MY BEST...
SO PLEASE WATCH...
Tsk!
WHAT A BORING INTERVIEW.
WELL, SEE YOU NEXT TIME!! GOODBYE!!
...
BRR BRR
WHAT WAS THAT?
PROBABLY ANOTHER VOICE ACTOR IN-JOKE.

PROFILE

[Age]
30

[Birthday]
August 22nd

[Blood Type]
AB

[Family Structure]
Son (Wataru)
Husband (Youichi, who married into her family)

[Height]
150 cm
(She looks taller because she wears high heels)

[Weight]
40 kg

[Strengths/Likes]
Economics, gambling, Yukariko

[Weaknesses/Dislikes]
Children, spicy food, computers

Mikoto Tachibana

As a child, Mikoto received special financial training from Mikado Sanzenin. In the process she met Nagi's mother Yukariko and came to look up to her as an older sister, or even a goddess.

At that time she was still more or less normal, if somewhat absent-minded and slow on the uptake. But for reasons suggested in this volume, plus another key reason, she started to lose faith in life and the people around her.

Even though she has a child, she's about the same age as Yukiji.

As an artist, I find that the more I draw her, the more she grows on me. How do you feel about letting me draw her a little more?

PROFILE

[Age]
32

[Birthday]
July 10th

[Blood Type]
A

[Family Structure]
One grandmother

[Height]
173 cm

[Weight]
60 kg

[Strengths/Likes]
Wataru, young children,
his butler duties

[Weaknesses/Dislikes]
Coffee, people who address him by
his given name

Jiro-Saburo Ichijo

I delayed his first appearance for various reasons and almost lost
the chance to work him into the manga at all. But now I'm finally
able to give Ichijo-kun, the Tachibana family butler, his debut.

I gave a lot of thought to this character before *Hayate* began,
so I have deep personal feelings for him. Maybe that's why I have a
hard time writing him. He may not end up appearing that often
anyway.

My original idea was for him to have a crush on Nagi. He didn't
appear earlier in the manga because I gave that role to Ayumu
Nishizawa's little brother instead.

So that's why his character has a Lolita complex. It was cute for
Ayumu's brother to have a crush on Nagi, since they're about the
same age, but having Ichijo-kun, who's in his 30s, put the moves on
her was pretty skeevy.

He kind of looks like Ayumu's brother, but that's just a coincidence.

Even now, I find it difficult to get my mental image of Ichijo-kun
down on paper. The illustration on the back cover of this volume is
the first one that really captures Ichijo-kun as I imagine him.

HATA HERE. THE SECOND SEASON OF THE ANIME HAS BEGUN!!
HAVE YOU GUYS BEEN WATCHING IT?

BETWEEN THE MANGA AND THE ANIME I'M ALMOST DYING FROM
OVERWORK, BUT I'M HAPPY TO SEE HAYATE AND NAGI ANIMATED
AGAIN. WHETHER OR NOT YOU CAUGHT THE FIRST SEASON,
PLEASE, PLEASE WATCH AND ENJOY THE NEW EPISODES.
OH, AND IF YOU MISSED THE FIRST SEASON, THE DVDS ARE OUT
NOW, SO WHY NOT BUY THEM AND CATCH UP?

AS IF THE ANIME WASN'T ENOUGH, THERE'S A *HAYATE* VIDEO
GAME OUT AS WELL, PLUS AN OAV. IT'S BEEN A BUSY SEASON.
ANYWAY, I'LL KEEP WORKING HARD, SO WISH ME LUCK!!
FYI, *HAYATE* HAS AN OFFICIAL WEBSITE TOO...☆

HTTP://HAYATENOGOTOKU.COM

THE MANGA IS FINALLY BUILDING UP TO THE BIG GOLDEN WEEK
TRIP TO MYKONOS AND ATHENS. THIS STORY ARC INVOLVES
A LOT OF STUFF I'M NOT USED TO DRAWING, SO I'M HAVING
A TOUGH TIME.

OH, I JUST REMEMBERED THAT WHEN WE WERE DRAWING
THE LAS VEGAS CHAPTERS IN THIS VOLUME, WE WANTED
AUTHENTICITY!! SO WE WENT TO LAS VEGAS FOR RESEARCH!!
WELL, MY STAFF GOT TO GO, ANYWAY. I COULDN'T GO BECAUSE
I WAS TOO BUSY...BUT OF COURSE I PAID THEIR TRAVEL
EXPENSES. IT SEEMED LIKE THEY HAD A GOOD TIME.
WISH I COULD *GO* SOMEDAY.

WE'RE ALL WORKING HARD TO TRY TO MAKE *HAYATE THE COMBAT
BUTLER* CONTINUE TO EVOLVE, SO STICK WITH US!!

BY THE WAY, THE NEW SEASON OF THE ANIME IS ENTITLED,
HAYATE THE COMBAT BUTLER!! WITH TWO EXCLAMATION MARKS.☆

(THEY ADDED TWO EXCLAMATION MARKS TO SIGNIFY SEASON TWO.)

SEE YOU IN THE NEXT VOLUME!
AND PLEASE CHECK OUT THE WEBSITE!
THERE ARE FOUR-PANEL CARTOONS!☆

HTTP://WEBSUNDAY.NET

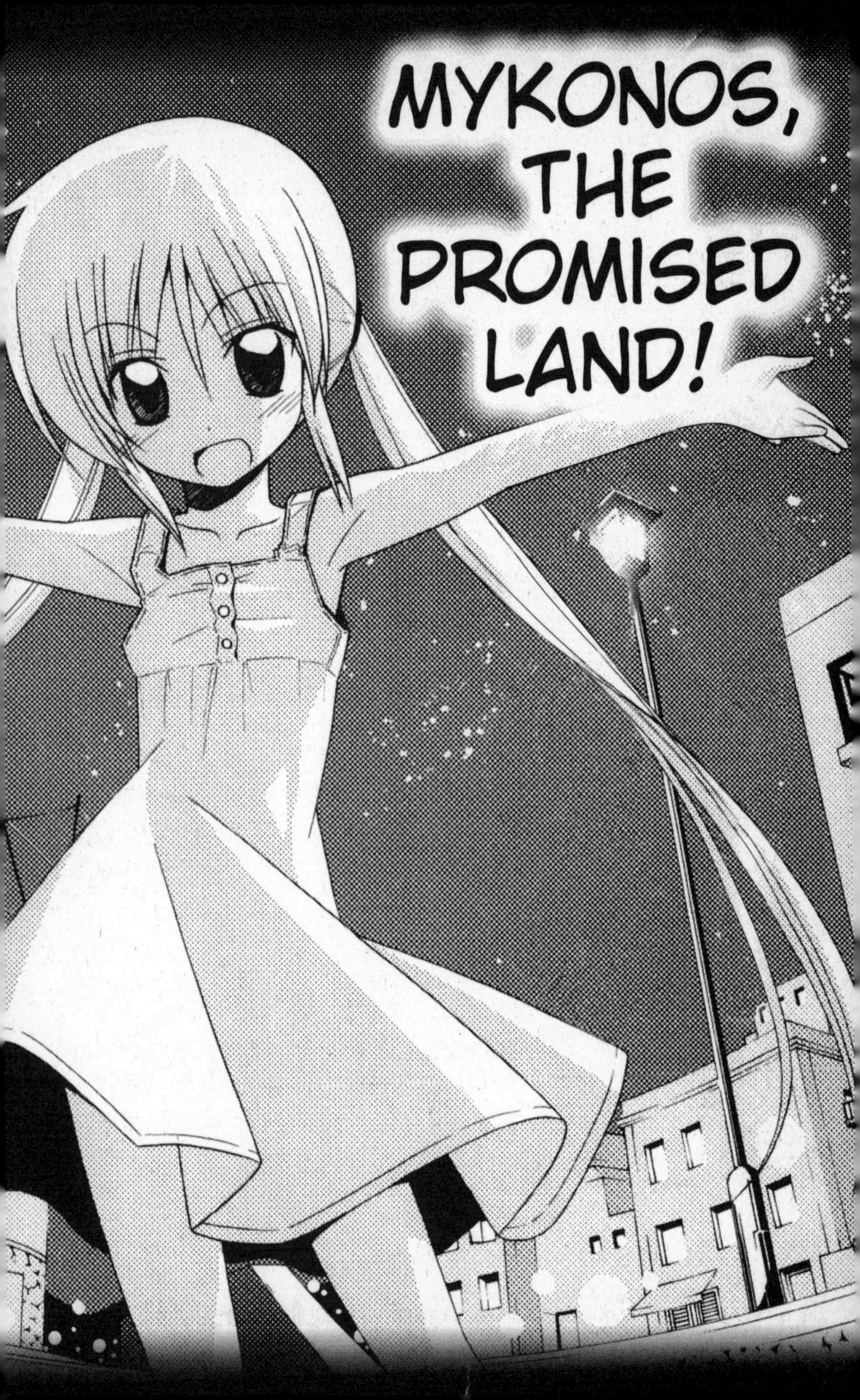
MYKONOS, THE PROMISED LAND!

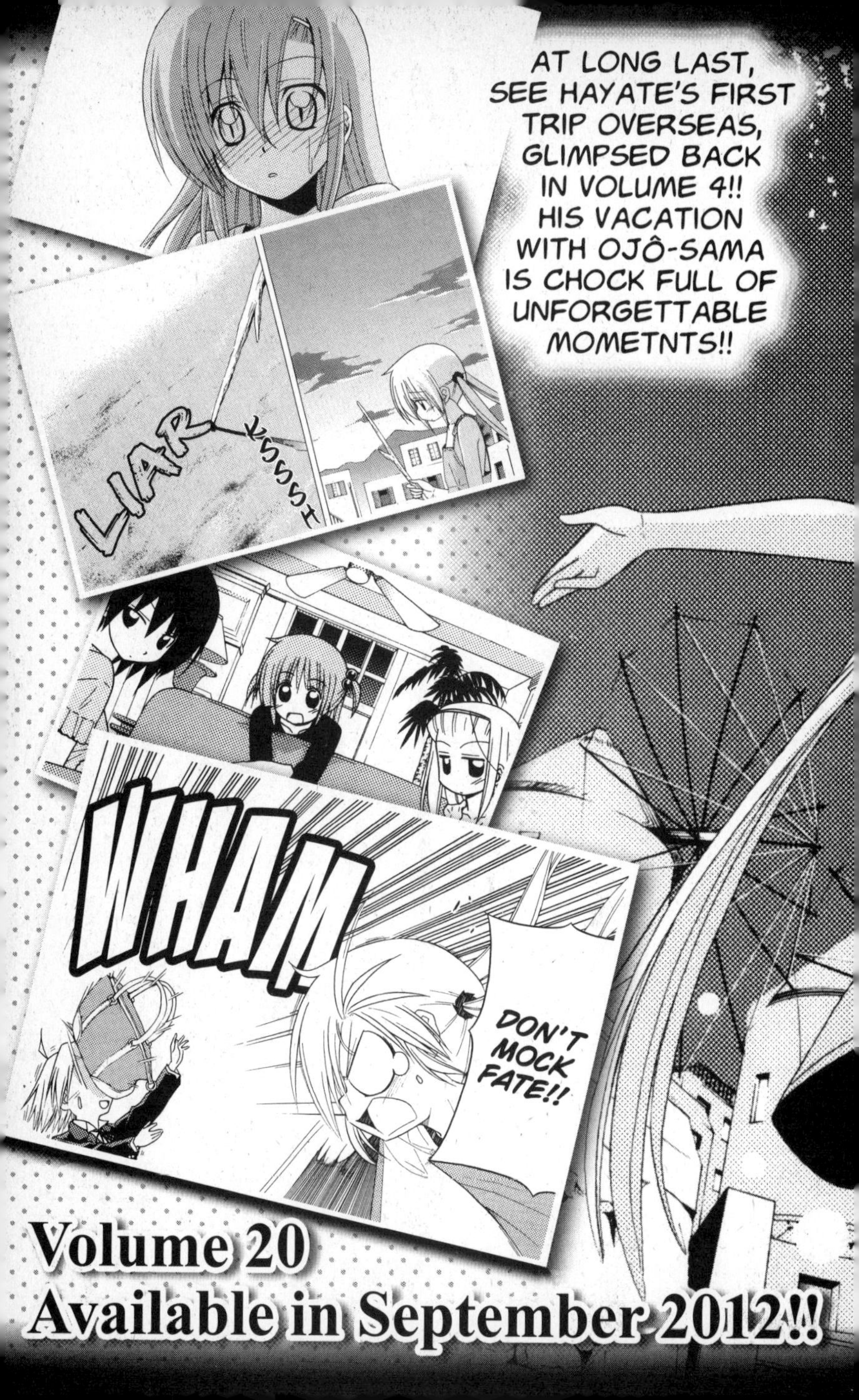
AT LONG LAST, SEE HAYATE'S FIRST TRIP OVERSEAS, GLIMPSED BACK IN VOLUME 4!! HIS VACATION WITH OJÔ-SAMA IS CHOCK FULL OF UNFORGETTABLE MOMETNTS!!
VSSST
LIAR
WHAM
DON'T MOCK FATE!!
Volume 20
Available in September 2012!!

Fumi's Introduction to Zoology

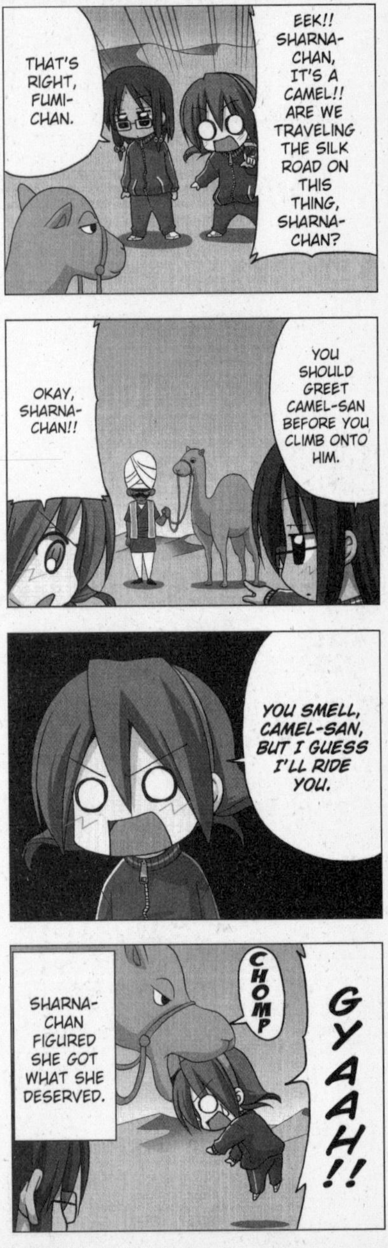
EEK!! SHARNA-CHAN, IT'S A CAMEL!! ARE WE TRAVELING THE SILK ROAD ON THIS THING, SHARNA-CHAN?
THAT'S RIGHT, FUMI-CHAN.
YOU SHOULD GREET CAMEL-SAN BEFORE YOU CLIMB ONTO HIM.
OKAY, SHARNA-CHAN!!
YOU SMELL, CAMEL-SAN, BUT I GUESS I'LL RIDE YOU.
GYAAH!!
CHOMP
SHARNA-CHAN FIGURED SHE GOT WHAT SHE DESERVED.

Sharna's Introduction to India

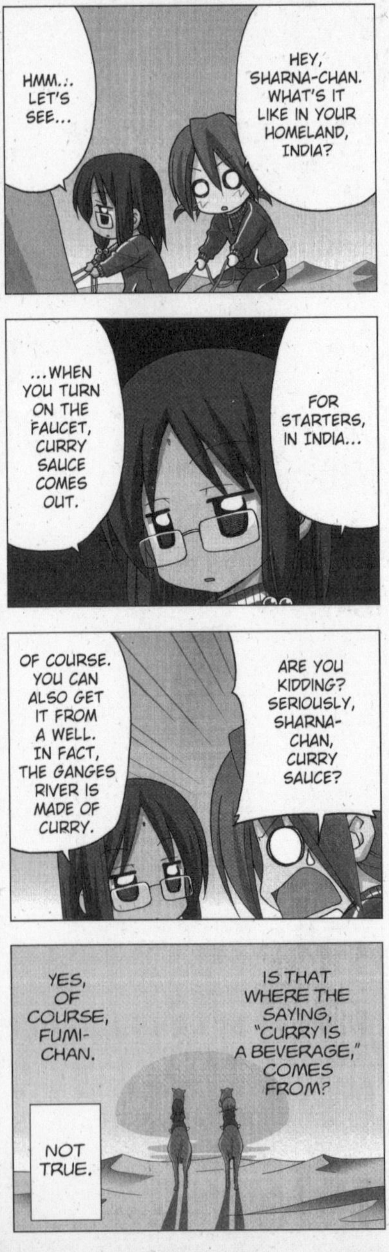
HEY, SHARNA-CHAN. WHAT'S IT LIKE IN YOUR HOMELAND, INDIA?
HMM... LET'S SEE...
FOR STARTERS, IN INDIA...
...WHEN YOU TURN ON THE FAUCET, CURRY SAUCE COMES OUT.
ARE YOU KIDDING? SERIOUSLY, SHARNA-CHAN, CURRY SAUCE?
OF COURSE. YOU CAN ALSO GET IT FROM A WELL. IN FACT, THE GANGES RIVER IS MADE OF CURRY.
IS THAT WHERE THE SAYING, "CURRY IS A BEVERAGE," COMES FROM?
YES, OF COURSE, FUMI-CHAN.
NOT TRUE.

HAYATE THE COMBAT BUTLER

(FUN DISC①)

THE BUTLER IN DEBT

ON A MISSION TO LAS VEGAS!!

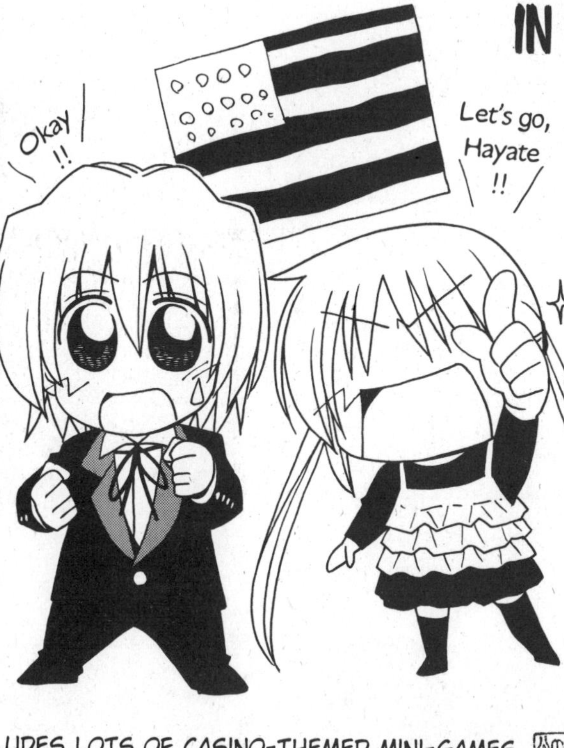
Let's go, Hayate!!
Okay!!

INCLUDES LOTS OF CASINO-THEMED MINI-GAMES.

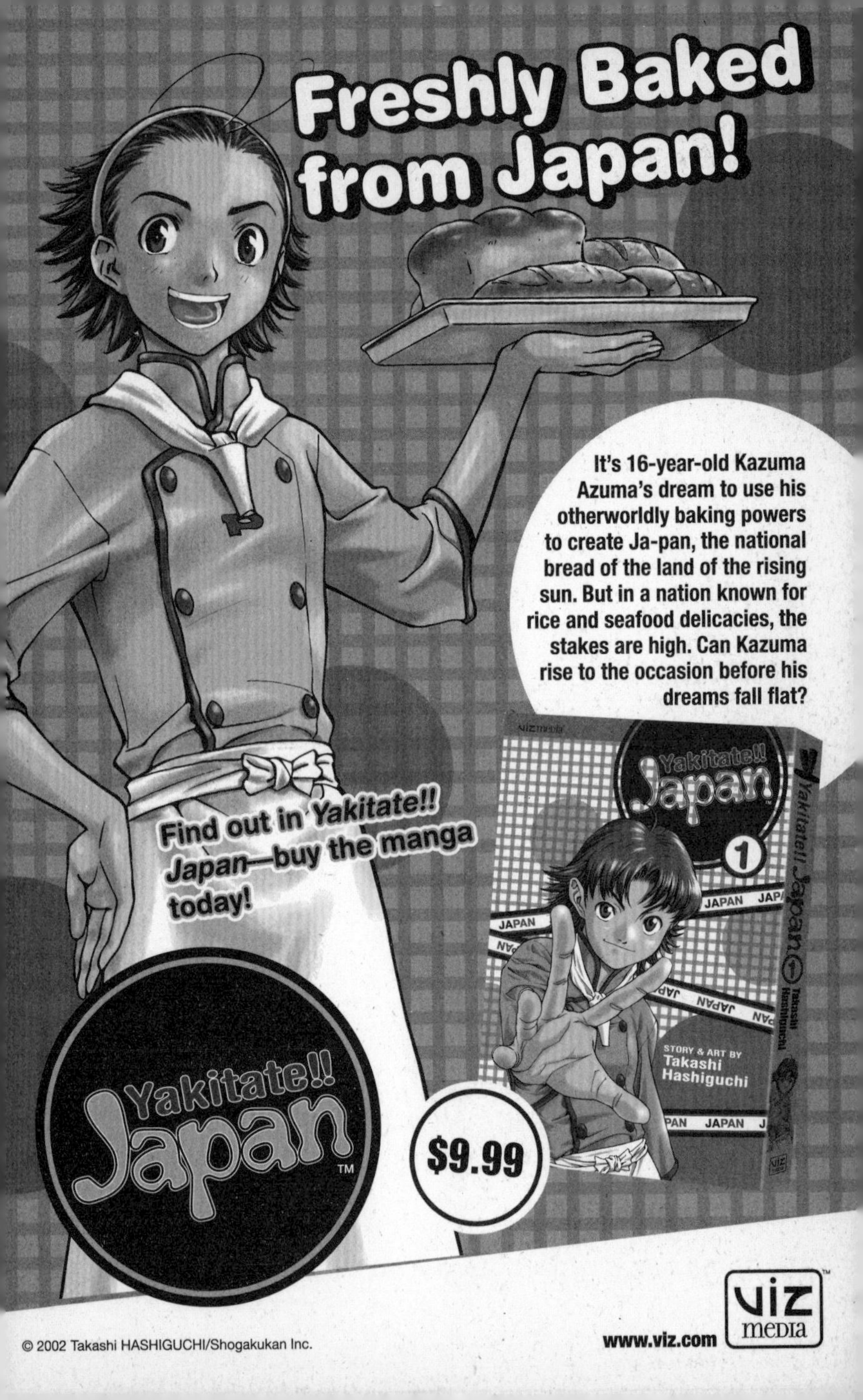
Freshly Baked from Japan!
It's 16-year-old Kazuma Azuma's dream to use his otherworldly baking powers to create Ja-pan, the national bread of the land of the rising sun. But in a nation known for rice and seafood delicacies, the stakes are high. Can Kazuma rise to the occasion before his dreams fall flat?
Find out in Yakitate!! Japan—buy the manga today!
Yakitate!! Japan™
1
STORY & ART BY Takashi Hashiguchi
$9.99
© 2002 Takashi HASHIGUCHI/Shogakukan Inc.
www.viz.com
VIZ MEDIA